Performance Evaluation of Communication Networks

For a complete listing of the *Artech House Telecommunications Library,*
turn to the back of this book.

Performance Evaluation of Communication Networks

Gary N. Higginbottom

Artech House
Boston • London

Library of Congress Cataloging-in-Publication Data
Higginbottom, Gary.
   Performance evaluation of communication networks / Gary Higginbottom
      p.   cm. — (Artech House telecommunications library)
   Includes bibliographical references and index.
   ISBN 0-89006-870-4 (alk. paper)
      1. Computer networks—Evaluation.   2. Telecommunication systems—
Evaluation.   I. Title.   II. Series.
TK5105.5.H5   1998
621.39'81—dc21   98-9286
                                                                 CIP

British Library Cataloguing in Publication Data
Higginbottom, Gary
   Performance evaluation of communication networks
   1. Computer networks   2. Computer networks—Evaluation
   I. Title
   004.6

   ISBN 0-89006-870-4

Cover design by Dutton and Sherman Design

© 1998 ARTECH HOUSE, INC.
685 Canton Street
Norwood, MA 02062

International Standard Book Number: 0-89006-870-4
Library of Congress Catalog Card Number: 98-9286

10 9 8 7 6 5 4 3 2 1

for Áine

Contents

Preface

As the title suggests, this book covers the method of communication network performance evaluation. It does so by describing the techniques of mathematical analysis and computer simulation at an introductory level. There are a great number of factors which affect the performance of a communication network. Here we are concerned with the effects of the traffic on performance, as measured by the time taken for a message to reach its destination, and the network utilisation, for example. It is intended that the text should provide an accompaniment for latter-year undergraduates and post-graduates following a course of study in networks or telecommunications with an emphasis on performance evaluation. The material is suitable for readers with an A-level mathematics equivalent background and some experience with high-level programming languages.

While most of the techniques used in performance analysis are quite well established, the areas of application are almost constantly changing. Along with the development of new functions, systems and standards are becoming more complex. Perhaps the best established area that falls in this subject category is known as teletraffic engineering, and the name is referred to often in the text. Traditionally, teletraffic engineering involves the study of voice traffic using electrical signals and automatic switching equipment.

Communication networks of all types are developing at such a rapid pace, however, and with the widespread deployment of networks that can support very high data transmission rates and a wide range of services, the task of performance evaluation is becoming increasingly complex. The task is worthwhile though, because it provides the insight required to improve operating efficiency. The amount of literature that has been produced on the subject would suggest that this rapidly developing field is emerging as an engineering discipline in its own right.

A significant portion of the material has been adapted from a selection of works, including the very popular texts by Leonard Kleinrock and Mischa Schwartz. A number of journal publications have also been reworked in various parts of the book to support particular themes. Where references are provided, and an alternative explanation may be useful, the reader may take the time required to locate this material. The referencing throughout is succinct to help in this respect. The following points should be noted, however. First, a correction in the CSMA/CD analysis by Alan Riley, a former lecturer at Manchester Metropolitan University, has been incorporated. Second, as far as the author is aware, the event graph technique has not previously been applied specifically to the task of simulating communication networks. Finally, the technique for coding the simulations was developed by William Walker, a former research colleague.

A thorough coverage of all the topics in this discipline could easily occupy a number of volumes. The selection of techniques that have been chosen for inclusion here are intended to at least provide a good overview of the subject and, in some cases, a detailed insight. The subject matter in the text may be approached in a number of ways. Readers unfamiliar with communications terminology should start from the beginning and read the chapters in order. Those who understand the context of traffic modeling within the field of voice, data, and computer communications can certainly skip Chapter 2 and may even pick chapters at will.

Finally the author wishes to acknowledge the efforts of everyone at Artech House, and Susanna Taggart in particular, for their contributions to the production of this book.

Chapter 1

Introduction

Communication networks exist in a variety of shapes and sizes and are used to share information of all kinds and for all reasons. The transfer of this information across networks create systems with traffic flows of many complexities. The purpose of traffic analysis and simulation is to understand some of the processes that affect the performance of the network. The engineer who studies the subject in depth is therefore able to assign reasoned and educated values to the parameters that constitute the design of a system. If everyone involved in the production of a network is aware of the mechanisms that affect its performance, then there is a good chance that the final product will be declared as successful.

Mathematical analysis and computer simulation are two methods for investigating network traffic performance. These modeling techniques, which are in fact used in a wide variety of engineering disciplines, provide an insight into the mechanisms that operate in complex systems. A mathematical analysis consists of one or more equations that express a measure of interest in terms of the fixed and variable parameters of the system. A trivial example of a mathematical analysis is the simple expression for the product of the number of communication channels and the data transmission rate for each channel. These two values are the parameters of the system and their product is a measure of the link capacity, or bandwidth. The method of computer simulation involves developing models in software. Typically this includes a process of writing and developing code that mimics the operation of a network. As a general rule, simulation is used when the system is complex and the mathematical analysis becomes difficult. However, it is often possible to obtain the measure of interest using both methods. The most thorough investigations include a comparison of the results using both techniques.

It is not intended that this book should deal with all the aspects of network performance analysis exhaustively. A complete reference work on the subject might easily fill a number of larger volumes. Rather, it is hoped that most of the areas for investigation are at least touched upon. While some of these areas are described in detail, others are only put in context. A selection of techniques in discrete time queueing analysis, for example, are studied in depth. Specialized simulation packages, on the other hand, are only mentioned in passing.

The remainder of this introductory chapter is presented in three sections. The first describes the performance measures that may be of interest, and each of these are dealt with in subsections. The second and third sections introduce the methods of analysis and simulation. Throughout this text, in order to avoid confusion, the process of deriving mathematical equations will be referred to as analysis. System performance evaluation, which might involve the use of both mathematical models and computer simulations, will be referred to as investigation.

1.1 PERFORMANCE MEASURES

The measures of interest depend on the system in question and are invariably used to indicate its predicted performance under certain conditions. The traffic presented to a network is often referred to as the offered load. The portion of the offered load that is successfully received at the intended destination is known as the throughput. Carried traffic is another term for throughput that is most often used in the engineering discipline, which is known as teletraffic analysis. The capacity of the system may be measured in a number of ways. One of these is the maximum possible value for the throughput, and it is therefore a measure of interest. Often some of the traffic is lost somewhere in the system and the throughput, or carried traffic, is less than the offered load. Hence the chance of losing some of the traffic is another measure that may be of interest. It takes a certain amount of time for the traffic to be conveyed from one point in a network to another, and this delay is almost certain to be of interest.

1.1.1 Capacity

The capacity of a communication network, or even just a simple link, should provide a measure for the quantity of traffic with which the system can cope. A number of different parameters can be used to measure capacity, and the most suitable normally depends on the system under scrutiny. The preceding simple example involves calculating the bandwidth of a single link, and in this case it provides an adequate measure of the capacity. However, when it is considered that devices may be connected to each end of the link and that the capacity of these devices may become important, then there are implications for the overall system capacity. The maximum amount of data that may be stored in the nodes could be a more appropriate measure in this case. Of course, this is a completely different type of measure for capacity.

The nature of the traffic may also have an effect on the true value of capacity, and this may introduce time dependency. For example, a telecommunications link may have a capacity for a particular number of simultaneous telephone calls. In certain circumstances, however, the distribution of calls in a switch can adversely affect blocking, and the number of simultaneous connections is then reduced. In general, it is probably fair to say that when the system becomes more complex the measure for capacity is less easily defined and more difficult to calculate.

Capacity is typically measured in Erlangs, bit/s and packet/s. The Erlang unit is perhaps the best established measure, having been adopted as standard in teletraffic analysis. Erlangs are introduced formally and discussed in a number of places in the text. Essentially it is a dimensionless quantity that represents the normalized intensity of traffic. While this is a suitable method for measuring the traffic on telecommunication networks, which largely consist of interconnected point-to-point links, it is not really appropriate for measuring the traffic on broadcast networks, such as Ethernet. In this case, as with most *local area networks* (LANs), packet/s is a more suitable choice of unit.

The capacities of LANs are perhaps the least straightforward to calculate. Certainly, it is never the case that the capacity of a LAN is the data transmission rate divided by the maximum packet size, or even the average packet size. The access control protocol on the LAN always introduces some overhead that reduces the useful network bandwidth. Moreover, the pattern of the traffic that is generated affects the operation of the protocol.

1.1.2 Throughput

The throughput is a measure of how much traffic is successfully received at the intended destination. Hence, the maximum throughput is equivalent to the system capacity. Ideally throughput is the same as the offered load, which is the amount of traffic actually transmitted, and this may be true in cases when the channel is error free, for example. In any case the throughput may only equal offered load up to the system capacity. In fact, the throughput is often less than the offered load when the system is operating below capacity, exacerbating the problem of choosing the exact definition of capacity itself.

A typical graph of the throughput versus offered load is depicted in Figure 1.1. The ideal characteristic shows a linear region where the two quantities are equal. Note

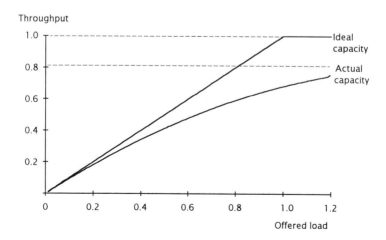

Figure 1.1 Typical throughput versus offered load characteristic.

that the units for both have been normalized so that the point where offered load and throughput equal one is that at which the system has reached the ideal capacity. This point is indicated by the uppermost dashed line. The actual characteristic is included on the graph to show that the throughput may be less than the offered load at any one point. The actual capacity of the system, indicated by the asymptote to the actual throughput, is therefore less than the ideal capacity. The extent of the departure from the ideal characteristic depends on the efficiency of the communication protocols and blocking probabilities, for example.

1.1.3 Loss Probability

The loss probability is a measure of the chance that traffic is lost. There is a number of situations that result in the loss of traffic. For example, a packet may arrive at a full buffer and it may be involved in a collision, or a call set-up request may arrive at a completely busy switch with no waiting facility. It is important to be clear about the exact definition of a performance measure. This point was made clear in the discussion on capacity, and it is particularly relevant in the case of loss probability. It can mean the probability that at least some data is lost, or it can be the probability that a certain amount of the traffic is lost. Again, the value of loss probability obtained depends on the traffic intensity and its distribution.

   The loss probability measure has traditionally been used as one of two measures in teletraffic analysis. The second measure is that of delay. In the simplest case, loss probability provides an estimate for the likelihood that a call is blocked at a switch. In a more complex situation it may be used, in conjunction with the expected delay, to estimate the performance of a blocking switch with waiting facilities. There are two

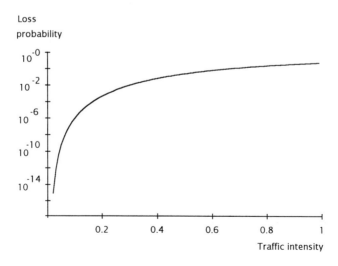

Figure 1.2 A typical loss probability characteristic.

different measures of loss probability in teletraffic analysis and these are known as time congestion and call congestion. Time congestion is the portion of time during which all trunks are busy, hence it is the probability that a call arrives to find that it will be blocked. Call congestion is the proportion of calls lost in the long run, and there is a subtle difference between the two quantities.

A typical loss probability characteristic is plotted in Figure 1.2. The curve shows that the probability of blocking increases with the intensity of traffic and that when the arrival rate is low the loss probability is less significant.

1.1.4 Delay

All communication traffic is subject to delays that are normally required to be kept to a minimum. In the simplest case the delay consists of the time required to transmit the traffic and it is not normally possible to reduce this figure. In many cases there are additional sources of delay that contribute to the overall figure. Often the transmission delay is insignificant compared with the time required to schedule the communication, or the queueing time, for example. As usual, the value obtained for the measure depends on the parameters of the system and the distribution of traffic. Often the parameters can be manipulated in such a way as to reduce the overall delay incurred by the traffic.

The mean delay, or waiting time, is one of the traditional measures in teletraffic analysis that is relevant to switches with queueing facilities. The mean delay is also plotted as a function of traffic intensity, throughput, and offered load to provide a performance characteristic that is useful in investigating the efficiency of LAN access protocols and high-speed networks. A typical mean delay versus throughput characteristic is plotted in Figure 1.3, wherein the delay is in units of time and the throughput is normalized. Often the units of delay are normalized with respect to the

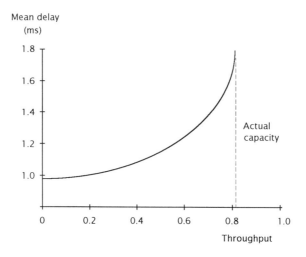

Figure 1.3 Typical mean delay versus offered load characteristic.

transmission time of a packet and, as in Figure 1.3, the throughput is normalized with respect to the ideal capacity. The throughput, and offered load for that matter, may also be given in packets/s, for example. Note that the actual capacity of the system under scrutiny is indicated by the asymptote of the curve.

1.1.5 Queue Length

When there are waiting facilities in a communication network queues will form at points of congestion. Often the length of a queue may be a parameter of interest. For example, if the mean queue length, or the average number of packets waiting to be switched at an input, can be predicted, then this may be used to estimate the required length of a buffer. Of course, it is likely that the nature of traffic in the system will result in variations from the mean that are unpredictable. Moreover, the length of a buffer has an effect on other parameters of interest, such as the loss probability. In general, the queue length is directly proportional to delay. Thus a typical queue length characteristic is similar to that presented in Figure 1.3 with delay on the vertical axis replaced by queue length in units of packets, for example.

1.2 MATHEMATICAL ANALYSIS

A complete performance investigation of all but the most simple systems will normally involve calculations of two or more performance measures. A thorough exploration into the mechanisms of the system should reveal the nature of trade-offs between various parameters of the network and its traffic. A performance investigation normally involves a qualitative comparison of so-called performance characteristics. These characteristics are obtained by drawing the graphs that show how a performance measure changes when one or more of the system parameters are varied. The illustrations in Figures 1.1, 1.2, and 1.3 are examples of such characteristics.

  Ideally, when it is the case that the analysis is straightforward, a mathematical model in the form of a simple equation can be obtained. Such an equation will express the desired performance measure in terms of the parameters of the system. These parameters include quantities such as the number of nodes and communicating devices, the packet and call generation rates, the lengths of messages, the size of buffers, and so on. The complexity of the system is normally the factor that dictates whether such an equation is obtainable.

  It is often possible to simplify the model by making assumptions about the parameters of the system. Of course, it may be the case that the investigation is to account for the effects of these parameters and we are again faced with the problem that their inclusion as a variable in the model is a factor that complicates the analysis. One of the most common assumptions required to simplify the analysis is that the system is in steady state. In this case all the performance measures obtained are average values and the effects of any variations in time on the measure are not provided. Analyses that do account for the time-varying effects, so-called transient solutions, are however sometimes possible. Another common assumption is that there are an infinite number of sources for traffic. In this case, when the arrivals are also assumed to be completely random they may be characterized by the Poisson and exponential distributions, which are often most convenient. In any case the assumptions should be clearly stated in order to preserve the ability to keep the results of an investigation in context.

In general, there are two approaches to mathematical analysis. One is to use first principles in deriving equations that are directly relevant to the system under scrutiny. The fundamental results of probability theory, for example, are often useful in this case. The other is to apply the results of queueing theory, which is a well-established branch of mathematics, and use standard techniques. Both approaches are dealt with in the text and derivations are introduced in a fashion that is suitable for beginners in traffic analysis. Some of the calculations, however, are computationally demanding and a personal computer with mathematical software is almost essential.

1.3 COMPUTER SIMULATION

The method of computer simulation is available as an alternative or supplement to mathematical analysis. Often the two methods are put to use in conjunction with each other to provide a process of validation. Comparing the results of analysis and simulation is a useful and rewarding exercise when the system under scrutiny is complex. Often it is possible to verify the correct operation of a simulation using an analysis of the equivalent system, each with the same set of assumptions. Then, provided there is a reasonable agreement between the results, the simulation may be used to investigate the operation of the system when the assumptions are relaxed. The analysis alone may not permit such a study. Given sufficient computational resources, and the time in which to utilize them, it will always be possible to produce a computer simulation for a network of any degree of complexity. Hence, the method of computer simulation may be called upon to investigate the systems that cannot be dealt with using analysis.

There are three or four options for traffic performance analysis using computer simulation. Specialized network simulation packages are available that are probably intended to be user-friendly and to reduce the model development time to a minimum. Simulation languages are also available, and these may provide more flexibility in the description of the system model. This option may be subdivided into two groups: the first representing languages that are specially developed for communication network simulation, and the second identifying those that are more generally applicable to a range of engineering disciplines. The third method, which is the one on which we concentrate in the text, is to use a high-level programming language.

The choices for simulation are therefore numerous, and the student who considers the options in some detail will probably achieve his or her aims more effectively. There is a number of obvious considerations that may be highlighted, and these are applicable to each of the preceding four options. First and foremost the resources that are accessible will provide the options that are immediately available. Next, a clear idea of the objectives for the investigation is required. After this, it is impossible to define a structured approach that is generally applicable to any investigation. There is, however, a number of characteristics that may be considered important in varying degrees. Flexibility is one of these. For example, if a model is developed, then how easy could it be modified. User-friendliness is another. If the model is developed by one person, then how easy would it be for another to use it. The amount of development time required is probably also of concern, and the tools available for analyzing the results may be another.

There is a number of specialized network simulation packages that have become popular in colleges and universities. Generally these include a graphics-based interface that is used to build a pictorial representation of the network. The results may be viewed in the form of raw data, bar charts, and graphs, for example. Often these packages include standard network components with the option for some customization. In at least one case this is provided by a module that uses the C programming language. When using standard components the user should clearly understand the model provided by the package. The current status of a protocol that is presently in use, for example, may not be the same as the final standard.

A great deal of literature has been produced for the reader who is interested in detailed discussions on packages and programming languages for communication network simulation. The *Institute of Electrical and Electronic Engineers* (IEEE) *Network* journal and *Communications Magazine* are two sources for this type of material. These also include commercial advertisements of relevant products.

In this text we approach the method of computer simulation using that which is arguably the most flexible. Developing simulations from first principles, using a high-level language, permits the user complete control over the definition and operation of the network to be simulated. The method is popularly known as that of discrete event simulation. This is due to the nature of the program in its quest to replicate a sequence of defined actions that occur at both regular and irregular points in time. The PASCAL programming language is eminently suitable for this purpose. In particular, the method of pointer variable manipulation is appropriate for the task of handling event lists. There are at least two strategies for discrete event simulation programming in a high-level languages. One of these is described in detail with a number of examples and an outline of the other is provided.

The world of computing is subject to constant enhancements and developments that may be important to students who wish to develop their skills in computer network simulation. The introduction of object-oriented techniques may bear some fruit in a number of departments, for example. Increasing processing speed is one of the factors that should enhance the lot of a computer simulator. In particular, when so-called rare-event processes are of interest the run-time for a simulation can be excessive.

1.4 SUMMARY

In this chapter the scene for the text has been set by describing various measures of performance and the methods for obtaining them. Five measures were discussed and their relationships with each other have been placed in context, regarding the process of network performance investigation. The remainder of the book is presented in seven well-defined chapters that provide a flavor of most of the disciplines involved in this expanding subject. The next chapter provides a description of the networks and protocols that may be the subject of the methods described thereafter. In some respects this chapter is intended to be an extension of the introduction, and the material will be useful for those who are unfamiliar with the subject of communications in general.

The real work begins in Chapter 3, which is concerned exclusively with mathematical analysis. It begins with some fundamental ideas that are derived from first principles. The material becomes increasingly complex and a number of standard techniques in queueing theory are presented. The results are applied to simple examples in communications to illustrate their use.

Chapter 4 is dedicated to the development of computer simulations and the methods are illustrated with examples in PASCAL. In the next chapter the event graph technique for developing simulations is introduced. This method is applied to the series of examples described in the previous chapter. A new simulation program is developed in the final section using most of the techniques for developing event graphs. The material in this chapter may be useful for those who require a more rigorous approach to developing simulation programs.

In Chapter 6 the method of discrete-time Markov analysis is presented. This is a general analytic technique that may be applied to a range of systems. The subject is dealt with in a fashion that makes it suitable for students with no previous exposure to such mathematics. It is shown, by the use of specific examples, how the methods can be effectively applied to complex slotted communication systems. In the next chapter a number of analyses that are specifically applicable to LANs are developed from first principles. The characteristics obtained using these analyses are compared with those obtained using the simulation programs developed earlier. In the final chapter a range of analytical techniques that is applicable to *wide area networks* (WANs) are presented. The focus of this material is on the analysis of switching. This is the basic mechanism of any bridging and routing network intended for telecommunications and data traffic.

A set of exercises and problems is provided for each of the chapters. The student who successfully completes these should have gained a firm grounding in the subject of communication network performance analysis and simulation. Where the interest is aroused, the text may provide one or two sources for further investigation, and many of the techniques provide a suitable platform on which a program of research may be developed.

Chapter 2

Communication Networks and Protocols

The subject of communication networks is a large and expanding one. This chapter provides an overview of the area, for completeness, and develops a framework for the study of traffic performance investigation. This is a subject that is heavily burdened with specialized terminology and a myriad of acronyms. There are many books on the subject, most of which include glossaries and extensive lists of abbreviations. A good example is Halsall's reference text, which is in its fourth edition [1].

This chapter summarizes the methods that require the development of ideas rather than being a collection of facts. The use of abbreviations and acronyms are thus avoided as far as possible. In the first section the terminology that is most commonly used is provided to avoid repeated, lengthy definitions later on.

2.1 FUNDAMENTALS

The devices that are involved in a communication are most commonly referred to as hosts and nodes. These are the terminating devices, that is, the originating and final destinations for the communication. Those devices that the communication may encounter on its journey between hosts may also be referred to as nodes and these include repeaters, bridges, routers, gateways, and switches. All types of device are connected by means of a cable or with the use of electromagnetic waves, and these are referred to as channels and links. A communication network consists of a collection of two or more nodes and one or more links. The communication itself is referred to as data and this exists in the form of bits, bytes, frames, packets, and messages.

Network protocols are the algorithms that describe a set pattern for the process of communication. A simplex communication link is one for which data may only be transferred in one direction, that is, from the transmitting host to the receiving host. In a duplex link data may flow in either direction. When the link is full duplex the data may flow in either direction at the same time. However, when a half duplex link connects two hosts, at any given time the transmission may occur in one direction only. In this case the protocol should be able to notify each of the nodes when it has the opportunity to use the channel.

A point-to-point connection for two nodes uses a single link. There may be more than one channel within the link, however. A system for which there are more than two devices on the same link and any data that is transmitted by any of the nodes is received at all the others, is known as a broadcast network. Point-to-point communication protocols are required in the set up, maintenance, and bringing down of connection-oriented and connectionless sessions; while those in broadcast networks are also required to dictate which node can access which channel and when. A typical point-to-point link is most easily illustrated using the popular method of drawing a time diagram such as that depicted in Figure 2.1. The arrow on the left-hand side of the diagram, which depicts the direction of increasing time, has been included here to aid the following description and is normally omitted.

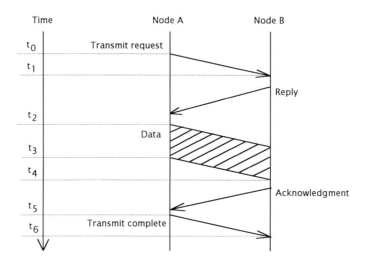

Figure 2.1 A typical time diagram for a point-to-point link.

Two nodes, A and B, are involved in a communication that consists of a total of five transmissions. Normally each transmission is identified as a particular frame or packet type; and in this case they have been named transmit request, reply, data, acknowledgement, and transmit complete. Seven critical points in time, labeled t_0 through t_6, have been noted on the diagram. The time t_0, for example, corresponds with the beginning of the session, which is the transmit request from A to B. Now the time $(t_1 - t_0)$ is that taken by the transmit request to reach B, which being the same for all transmissions, is known as the propagation delay. The time $(t_3 - t_2)$ is that required to place the data on the channel and this is known as the transmission time. Hence the total time required to send the data consists of the transmission time plus the propagation delay. Note that by drawing other four transmissions as a single, narrow line, it is assumed that their transmission times are negligible. The data transmission, on the other hand, is indicated by a shaded area. Thus a distinction is clearly made between the tranmsission time and the propagation delay.

The efficiency of this particular communication, which is given by the fraction of total time the channel is occupied by useful data, may be given by $(t_4 - t_2)/(t_6 - t_0)$. The element of doubt here is due to the fact that the total time may be taken as $(t_6 - t_0)$, as previously, or it may be taken as $(t_5 - t_0)$. Similarly the useful channel time may be taken as the total time to send the data, being $(t_4 - t_2)$ as previously, or it may be taken as the transmission time, which is $(t_3 - t_2)$. In any case the efficiency is still just one measure of performance, and the type of protocol will affect this and other measures.

Within any scientific discipline it is more or less fair to say that progress is made by the development of an agreed set of rules. At least ambiguities such as those encountered in the preceding paragraph may be avoided when a standard method is available for reference. In data communications this is manifest through the national and international bodies that exist in order to encourage the development of standards. Perhaps the best introduction of an overview of the subject of computer networks should begin with a discussion of the standards. Those that are firmly accepted, and those that are under development, will provide a framework for the description of the methods for computer networking and data communications in general.

2.2 STANDARDS

There is a number of organizations involved in the development of standards in the data communications and networking arena. The *International Organization for Standardization* (ISO), the *Institute of Electrical and Electronic Engineers* (IEEE), the *American National Standards Institute* (ANSI), and the *International Telegraph and Telephone Consultative Committee* (CCITT) are four of the most active bodies. Although the latter is no longer in existence, its recommendations have been adopted by the *International Telecommunications Union* (ITU). Briefly, these are most widely known for the OSI reference model, the 802 committees for LANs and *Metropolitan Area Networks* (MANs), FDDI, and the V and X series recommendations for public networks, in that order.

2.2.1 The OSI Model

The ISO have proposed the seven-layer *Open Systems Interconnect* (OSI) reference model for computer communications. This model, which has been described in many texts, is intended to provide a common architecture for the development of computer and data communication systems. Tanenbaums book is perhaps the most often cited reference [2]. The OSI model is based on the diagram in Figure 2.2, wherein the structure of a computer network is split into seven distinct layers. The purpose of each layer is to perform a particular set of functions and to operate independently of other layers. These functions are carried out using a specific set of algorithms, or protocols. Successful host-to-host communications on the network require that the protocols in

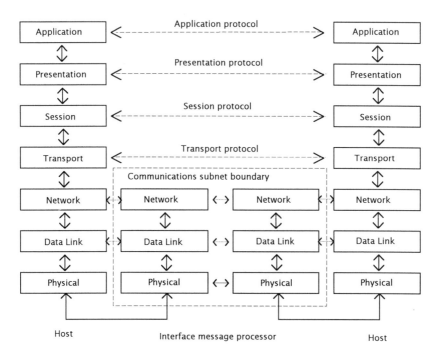

Figure 2.2 The OSI reference model.

each layer are compatible with those adjacent, above and below each other, and this is depicted on the diagram using arrows.

The hosts on the left and right sides of the diagram consist of a stack of seven sets of protocols that are depicted as boxes. The name in each box is that which has been assigned to the relevant set of protocols in the model. The host is the name that has been assigned to those devices that originate and terminate the communication, and the intermediate devices are known as interface message processors. A personal computer with a suitable network adapter, for example, is defined as a host; while a router is an example of an interface message processor. The latter therefore requires the specification of protocols up to and including layer 3, the network layer, while hosts are required to process the data using all seven layers. A very brief description of the functions of each layer are summarized in Table 2.1.

Layer 1 is the physical layer and its function is to transfer the raw bits of data over the channel. The method by which electrical or electromagnetic energy is used to transfer information from one location to another is part of the physical layer. Voltage levels and signaling schemes, for example, are specified. The second layer is the data link layer. Its function is to ensure that the bits are successfully transmitted across the physical link. The basic function of the third layer, or the network layer, is to control the flow of information through the interface message processors. This entails routing messages through the subnetwork and flow control to avoid congestion, for example.

Table 2.1
Functions of the seven OSI layers

Layer	Name	Functions
7	Application	The user interface
6	Presentation	Data code and file format conversion
5	Session	Negotiation and management of connections
4	Transport	Packetization and addressing
3	Network	Routing and flow control
2	Data link	Data framing and error checking
1	Physical	Actual transmission and signaling

Layer 4, the transport layer, deals with packetization and addressing. In order that they may be transmitted on the network the messages that enter the transport layer from above may require segmenting into smaller packets, and each packet is given addressing information to identify the source and destination for the data. Layers 5 through 7 deal with functions that are specific to the nodes at either end of the communication. The presentation layer, for example, is included to account for the possibility that different operating systems may be in use on each of the communicating hosts. In this case files and data may require some formatting.

The protocols in the first three layers are those that directly affect the traffic flow across the network. Consider the diagram in Figure 2.3 that depicts an example of data transmission in the OSI model. A message, m, is generated in the application layer of a host. It is passed down to the presentation layer, which proceeds to code the message

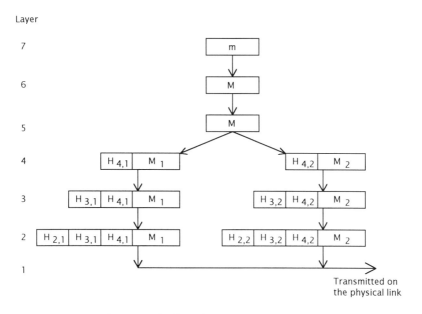

Figure 2.3 The flow of a message through a node.

into the format required by the receiving host. This produces a new message, M, which is then passed to the session layer. Since the function of the session layer is to allow different hosts to establish sessions between each other, the format of the message is not affected and it is passed on to the transport layer.

Now the transport layer must present the message to the network layer in one or more segments. The size of each segment is dictated by the allowable packet sizes in the layers below. A good example of a transport layer protocol is the *Transmission Control Protocol* (TCP), which is part of the TCP/IP protocol suite. A TCP message is broken up into pieces not exceeding 64 Kbytes. In Figure 2.3 M is split into two packets, M_1 and M_2. Each of the packets are given layer 4 headers, labeled $H_{4,1}$ and $H_{4,2}$, which normally identify the source and destination hosts. The headers also include a number that is given to each packet in order that the destination host may identify the correct sequence in which they were generated. This is used for reconstructing M in the transport layer of the destination. From this point forward each of the fragments are dealt with on an individual basis. The addresses in the transport layer header are used by the network layer to pick a suitable route through the subnetwork. Note that it is also possible for fragmentation to occur in the network layer. Additional information, such as may be required for congestion control, is tagged on to each packet in the network layer header. Finally the data link layer frames packets prior to transmission on the physical link.

A considerable amount of terminology has been developed as part of the model and the interested reader is referred to Tanenbaum [2]. This discussion of the model is closed here with the final point that the reference model is inadequate in some cases. A modified version of the data link layer is required for LANs, for example, to include the medium access control protocol that is required to co-ordinate the traffic on broadcast networks. In the following sections some of the details of the mechanisms and options available for each of the layers that have a direct effect on the network traffic are described.

2.2.2 The Physical Layer

The purpose of the physical layer is to transfer information, or data, from one place to another. A number of basic techniques for data transmission, or signaling, are possible.[1] There are two types of data and each may be transmitted using one or more of the signaling techniques. Analog data is transmitted using baseband and broadband signaling. Digital data, on the other hand, may be transmitted using either baseband and broadband signaling, or some form of modulation. Of course the process of converting analog information into digital data means that a form of modulation may be used in this case also. The terminology is often confusing to students who are new to this field. Again, there are a number of books that offer an expanded discussion of the signaling process, and Walrand provides a good introduction [3]. Those readers who prefer mathematical

---

[1] The use of the term 'signaling' to describe the electronic process here should not be confused with that normally used in descriptions of communication protocols.

treatments may find Coates [4] more interesting, while the more practically oriented may prefer Tomasi [5].

The term baseband is used to designate the band of frequencies of the signal delivered by the source or the input transducer. For example, in telephony the baseband is the audio band of 0 to 3.5 kHz. In television, the baseband is the video band occupying 0 to 4.3 MHz. For digital data or *Pulse Code Modulation* (PCM) using bipolar signaling at a rate of f_0 pulses/second, the baseband is 0 to f_0 Hz. In baseband communication, baseband signals are transmitted without modulation, that is, without any shift in frequencies of the signal. Hence, as can be seen in Figure 2.4, a sizable portion of the total signal power is found at lower frequencies centred on $f_0/2$. The method of transmission of baseband signals is known as channel or line coding.

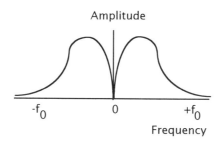

Figure 2.4 A typical baseband spectrum.

When broadband signaling is used, the result is a significant shift in the power spectrum away from $f_0/2$ because frequencies other than that of the original data are transmitted. Baseband signals are sometimes unsuitable for direct transmission over a given channel, and so they are modified using a process that is known as modulation. As an example, the process of amplitude modulation of an analogue signal is illustrated in Figure 2.5. Each of the three signals in the figure is given as a time-varying amplitude, with that in (a) representing the constant parameter signal that is to be modified, or modulated. The signal in (b) is the actual information that is required to be transmitted. In this case the information is a continuous, or analog waveform, such as may be generated by sound. The amplitude of the carrier signal is varied in sympathy with the amplitude of the information, so the actual signal transmitted is given in (c).

A great variety of modulation schemes are realizable. When the information consists of discrete signals, such as are generated by sequences of binary numbers, the pulse modulation method is often used. Pulse amplitude, pulse position, and pulse width modulation are three examples of this method. If the information is analog, then in order to utilize one of the pulse modulation techniques the signal must be quantized. Pulse code modulation is the term most often used to identify this process. Both quantized analog signals and digital data are also suitable for baseband transmission using so-called channel or line coding. A simple method for line coding, known as *non return to zero* (NRZ), is illustrated in Figure 2.6. This example depicts a sequence of nine binary digits

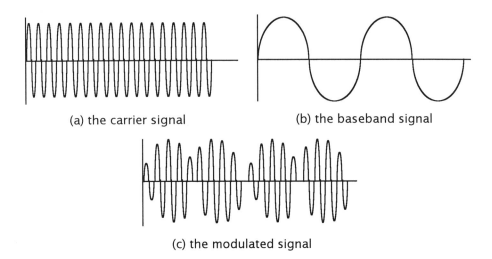

(a) the carrier signal   (b) the baseband signal

(c) the modulated signal

Figure 2.5 Amplitude modulation.

with a '1' represented by the highest amplitude and a '0' by the lowest. When return to zero signaling is used the amplitude always returns to a value of zero, usually midway along the bit, and always before the end.

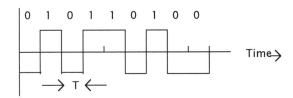

Figure 2.6 Line coding using non return to zero.

More complex line coding schemes are used to improve certain characteristics of the transmitted signal. When a return to zero code is used, for example, a timing reference is guaranteed to be supplied with every bit of information. If the signal-to-noise ratio is critical, however, then the code that provides the greatest immunity to channel noise and inter-symbol interference may be an important consideration. Error detection capabilities, efficient power spectral densities, and transparency to specific sequences of data are also factors that may be of concern.

The signaling method is generally of no consequence to the traffic analyst. As long as the amount of data and the time taken to transmit that data is known, the investigation may proceed. In fact the time taken to transmit data, or the data transmission rate, is one of the most important parameters. It has a direct impact on the efficiency with which the equipment is being utilized. All of the analytical techniques in this text account for the data transmission rate. The chapter on LANs, for example, begins with a detailed investigation of the efficiency of access control protocols; and the data transmission rate along with the end-to-end propagation delay are the two most important factors.

The method for signaling cannot be completely ignored, however. There is a number of communication protocols that are designed to deal with errors that may occur as a result of the signaling mechanism. In this case a knowledge of the expected error rates and even detailed statistical parameters of the data may be required. Moreover, there is at least one type of network that is explicitly dependent on the signaling technique as a method of providing feedback to the access control protocol. Some of the collision resolution algorithms in carrier sense multiple access networks rely on specific information about the state of the transmitted signal. An example of investigating the effects of errors and failures in the physical layer by simulation is provided in the final section of Chapter 4.

2.2.3 The Data Link Layer

The data link layer prepares the raw bits and bytes of data by framing them ready for transmission on the physical layer. Data link layer protocols are relevant in point-to-point communication links. They are also present in broadcast type systems such as LANs. In the OSI model for LANs the data link layer is replaced by the *logical link control* (LLC) and *medium access control* (MAC) layer protocols. The MAC allows the LLC to act as if a point-to-point link existed, and the LLC incoporates data link protocols. Every point-to-point link is subject to a certain number of transmission errors, limited buffer sizes, and data transmission rates. The function of the data link layer is to make the parameters of the physical link transparent to the network layers in each host. The data link protocols are therefore required to ensure that the bits of information sent over the physical link arrive in the correct order and without error. Flow control is often required in addition to explicit error detection and correction algorithms.

In order to frame the data it is necessary to delimit discrete sections of the bit stream, and there are a number of methods that can be used to achieve this. The simplest way is to insert a time gap between the frames or to delimit the start and end of frames using a special sequence of bits. Once the data has been framed, it must be correctly received in sequence, and this usually involves a process of feedback that requires the receiver to send information about the incoming frames back to the transmitter. The information feedback may also be used to implement flow control. In addition timers may be incorporated to deal with frames that disappear without trace. There are also many ways in which errors can be dealt with as an alternative to simply resending the original data. Error correcting codes, such as the Hamming code, may add a significant amount of overhead to the length of the frame, however. If the physical layer is relatively errorfree, then the overhead is largely redundant and the efficiency is significantly reduced.

Data link layer protocols for duplex communications typically include methods known as piggybacking, sliding windows, go back *n*, and selective repeat, roughly in order of increasing complexity. Piggybacking is used to describe the process whereby acknowledgments are sent along with data in order to improve efficiency. Sliding window protocols is the generic name for the more complex data link control algorithms such as go back n and selective repeat. A sliding window of size one corresponds to a simple stop-and-wait mechanism, commonly known as the *alternating bit protocol* (ABP). The timing diagrams in Figure 2.7 illustrate a typical sequence of events on the channel with and without a transmission error.

   Normally alternate packets and acknowledgments, or data and acks for short, are labeled *1* and *0*. So in (a) the frame *data 0* is acknowledged by *ack 0*, *data 1* is acknowledged by *ack 1*, and so on. In (b) the first *ack 0* was not transmitted by *B*, it was therefore not received by *A*, and *data 0* was retransmitted. Frame retransmissions are scheduled when, following the transmission of a frame, a prespecified time elapses without it being acknowledged. This is indicated in Figure 2.7(b) by the time $t_2 - t_1$, and at a minimum this must be the time taken for two propagations across the link.

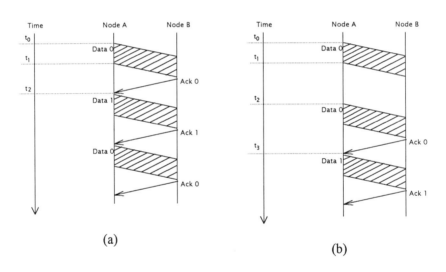

(a)

(b)

Figure 2.7 Alternating Bit Protocol: (a) without error, and (b) with error.

The size of the sliding window dictates the maximum number of unacknowledged frames. In this case it may be possible to select frames for retransmission and the algorithm is appropriately named the *Selective Repeat Protocol* (SRP). Figure 2.8 depicts the sequence of events for a four-frame window SRP channel. In this case up to four frames may be sent contiguously. Each host may have to store up to eight different frames at any one time, so three bits are required to label the frames. It is assumed that the transmitting host is constantly ready to transmit frames. In (a) it does so without error. In (b), for some reason *ack 001* is not transmitted, and so *data 001* is retranslated after a time-out.

   It is immediately obvious that SRP uses the available channel bandwidth more

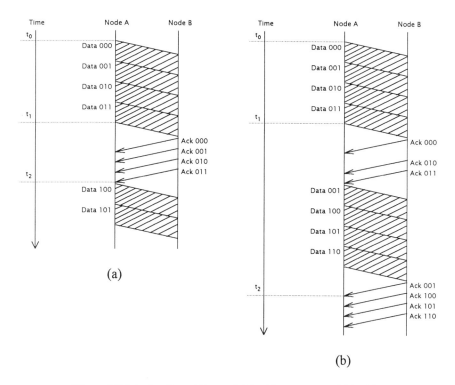

Figure 2.8 Selective Repeat Protocol: (a) without error, and (b) with error.

effectively than ABP, at the expense of an increase in the required buffer space. Walrand presents a simple analysis for the efficiency of three data link layer protocols [3], including ABP and SRP, which provide an ideal entry level technique performance analysis using first principles. This will be very briefly reviewed here.

Recall that the efficiency of a link is the fraction of time that the channel is usefully occupied. By inspecting the figures it can be seen, for example, that the efficiency, η, of ABP in the absence of errors is given by

$$\eta = \frac{t_1 - t_0}{t_2 - t_0} \tag{2.1}$$

Let the frame and acknowledgment transmission times be represented by T_f and T_a. Further let the propagation delay be T_p. Then Eq. (2.1) may be rewritten as

$$\eta = \frac{T_f}{T_f + T_a + 2T_p} \tag{2.2}$$

Now if a frame or acknowledgment transmission error occurs with probability p, then the frame is successfully transmitted with probability $(1-p)$; and if the smallest possible time-out is assumed, the efficiency reduces to

$$\eta = (1-p)\frac{T_f}{T_f + T_a + 2T_p} \tag{2.3}$$

Similarly, when SRP is errorfree, if the window size is w, we have

$$\eta = \frac{wT_f}{wT_f + wT_a + 2T_p} \tag{2.4}$$

Walrand defines efficiency in a subtly different way and obtains an expression that is slightly different to this one. This highlights a point that has been touched upon already. As long as the definition of efficiency is consistently applied to the different systems under investigation, however, the comparison of any results obtained is fair. Even though the numbers obtained here will be different to those using Walrand's equations, a qualitative evaluation should draw the same conclusions.

Deriving the efficiency of SRP in the presence of errors is not so straightforward, particularly for Walrand who considers a full-duplex channel. As was indicated in the first chapter, in order to simplify the analysis certain assumptions are made. The first is that the time-out is equivalent to wT_f. The consequence of this is that if there were no errors, then the efficiency could reach 100%. The second assumption is that the probability of error is small.

The easiest way to explain how the efficiency is derived is by considering what could happen in a cycle. A cycle consists of the transmission of four frames and the receipt of their acknowledgments. In a single complete cycle there may be a single error at the most, because of the second assumption. In the example in Figure 2.8(b) the second packet is erroneous with the consequence that the time required to clear the error, $t_2 - t_0$, consists of $8 \times T_f$, plus $4 \times T_a$, plus $4 \times T_p$. During this time, however, there are a total of seven successful frame transmissions. Hence in general, the useful time of an error cycle is $(2w-1)T_f$ and the total time of the cycle is $2wT_f + wT_a + 4T_p$. The useful time of an errorfree cycle is wT_f, and its total time is $wT_f + wT_a + 2T_p$. Such cycles occur with probabilities p and $(1-p)$, respectively; whence

$$\eta = p\frac{(2w-1)T_f}{2wT_f + wT_a + 4T_p} + (1-p)\frac{wT_f}{wT_f + wT_a + 2T_p} \tag{2.5}$$

Thus Eqs. (2.2) to (2.5) provide an analysis of the two data link layer protocols that are known as ABP and SRP. One could proceed to use these equations to compare the efficiency of the two methods. Note, however, that they provide just one quite specific type of analysis, that is, the efficiency of bandwidth utilization in terms of a number of the system parameters and assuming that the values of other system parameters are as specified. If the expected delay for the transmission of a complete packet were required, then clearly these equations are inadequate. Similarly, if the effect of different traffic arrival patterns should be accounted for, and these will certainly affect the bandwidth utilization, then again some alternative analysis is required.

2.2.4 The Network Layer

The network layer is required to take the packets of data received from the transport layer in one host and deliver them to the transport layer in another. This may require a journey that involves one or more intermediate nodes, and the essential function of the network layer protocol is one of choosing the appropriate path or route. The protocols that achieve this are commonly known as routing algorithms. Part of their job is to avoid congestion, while at the same time selecting the route that results in the most favorable performance characteristics. In addition, the network layer should be able to solve the differences in protocols between different subnetworks by converting address formats, for example.

All routing protocols rely on some form of addressing to distinguish between the possible destinations. The addressing scheme itself is usually considered to be part of the protocol. In many cases the address is split into fixed size portions that are used to decompose large networks into groups of smaller networks, often called subnets. In the same way that the error detection and correction codes affect the data link protocol, the format of an address does not have a direct impact on the performance of the network layer protocol. The routing mechanism, of which there are many, may be one of the most significant factors, however.

Perhaps the simplest routing algorithm is known as flooding. Every packet is transmitted to every node. Network management operations often require that certain information has to be broadcast, so flooding is appropriate in this case. The method is extremely inefficient, however, when the packet is only intended for receipt at one or a small number of nodes. Source routing and transparent routing are two popular methods that are used in data communications. In both of these techniques nodes choose links selectively and the overall bandwidth of the network is utilized more efficiently. Readers interested in the specific algorithms should consult another text such as Tanenbaum, for example.

The performance issues relating to routing and routing algorithms are really quite complex. In the first place one may be interested in the algorithms themselves, as distinct from their effect on the overall network performance. Issues such as speed and stability, and their trade-off, are relevant here. Even then one has to decide exactly which measure of speed and stability is appropriate. The overall network performance may be viewed as a combination of these, or another global indicator, such as total throughput, for example.

The method of analysis that is most closely related to routing networks is provided by the technique of solving networks of queues. This is one of the standard approaches in queueing theory. A simple three-node network is used as an example to illustrate the technique in Section 8.2. Essentially the performance of the system can be obtained if the probability that traffic takes a certain path is known. Routing in a traditional telecommunications network is static. Thus when a call has been established there are no further implications of the routing algorithm on the performance. In this case one is most concerned with the fact that a certain amount of the switching capability is taken up for the duration of the call. The switching process itself therefore becomes the focus of attention and its analysis has been widely addressed. A detailed discussion of switching is provided in Section 8.4.

2.2.5 The Transport Layer

The network layer provides a service to the transport layer, which is the next layer above. Essentially there are two types of service and these are known as connectionless and connection oriented. As shown in the brief list of functions assigned to each layer in Table 2.1, one of the tasks for the network layer is to break the complete message into smaller packets. Each of the packets is then passed down to the network layer, and if the service being provided is connectionless, then each of the packets are treated as individual units for transmission across the subnet. Hence the path traversed by each packet may be a different one. If the service is connection oriented, then some form of reservation process is used to hold each of the links in the complete route for the use of all the packets in a message and the path is always the same. A simple first principles analysis of the two methods, similar to that in Schwartz [6], is provided in Section 8.5.

Routing for datagram or connectionless communications is generally accomplished using routing tables at each node. When a packet arrives at the node, the destination address in the packet is inspected and compared with the addresses in the routing table. The packet is transmitted on the link that corresponds with either the destination address or the address of another node that the packet must visit on its way. It is often possible for the table to contain more than one suitable link and an algorithm must be used in this case. The algorithm will provide a method for choosing optimum path, as defined by some criteria such as that which incurs the smallest delay, for example. Other criteria that are used include the number of nodes that the packet must visit before it reaches the final destination, known as the number of hops, and costs. Moreover, the table itself may adapt to the conditions on the network to provide congestion control.

The route for connection-oriented communications may be set up in the same way as for connectionless traffic. In this case, however, the route is the same for each and every packet in the same message. The path that connection-oriented traffic follows is often referred to as a virtual circuit since the network is effectively circuit switched for a limited duration of time. The implications for traffic analysis in either case are similar to those described in the previous section, with the degree of complexity increasing.

2.3 LOCAL AREA NETWORKS

The most popular classification system for data networks is based on the geographical area covered by the network. There are three divisions with the smallest known as LANs, and these include systems that might cover the area of a small number of buildings. MANs connect devices across cities, while the largest areas are covered by *Wide Area Networks* (WANs). WANs may extend across the borders of nations and up to the orbital paths of satellites.

LANs are characterized by the protocols that make up the logical link and MAC layers. Together they constitute the equivalent data link layer of the OSI model, with the MAC residing just above the physical layer and logical link just below the network layer. The purpose for this modification is to account for the broadcast nature of LANs. They consist of a number of devices that are connected by a common transmission medium. The logical link protocol is used to set up connectionless or connection-oriented services for the network layer. The MAC protocol has two basic functions. It specifies the algorithm that is used by each of the nodes to determine when it may transmit. It also ensures that while all the packets broadcast on the LAN are received by all the nodes connected to it, only the nodes for which the packets are intended pass them up to the logical link layer. An addressing scheme is used for the latter function and any effects on the network performance are negligible, as before.

Both the logical link protocol and the part of the MAC that determines the access control can have a significant bearing on the nature of the traffic that is generated in the physical layer of the LAN. A complete access control protocol consists of a number of detailed algorithms, addressing schemes, and packet structures that combine to form a complex process. Each of the three most popular access control schemes—CSMA/CD, Token Bus, and Token Ring—have been published as books [7–9]. Fortunately, only an understanding of the basic method is required to carry out a traffic performance investigation. The electrical specifications at the physical layer, for example, have no direct impact on the flow of traffic.

2.3.1 CSMA/CD

Three access control mechanisms have reached a mature stage of standardization by the IEEE, and these are well documented and widely used protocols that will be described here and analyzed in Chapter 7. The IEEE subcommittee 802.3 have defined that which is probably the most popular. It consists of a logical bus topology that uses the carrier sense multiple access with collision detection, or CSMA/CD, access control technique. This method is incorporated in Ethernet. Physically the bus may also look like a star and it typically consists of coaxial, twisted pair, and optical fiber cables.

The CSMA/CD protocol provides a form of random access to the network. When a node is ready to transmit a packet it senses the activity on the channel. If the channel is idle, then it proceeds to transmit the packet and continues sensing the channel. If the transmission of another packet is detected before the end of the contention interval, then the two packets may have interfered with each other and they are said to have been involved in a collision. The contention interval is the maximum length of time that should elapse, following the beginning of a packet transmission and before another packet may be transmitted, in order to avoid a collision. Any node that transmits a packet and then detects a collision transmits a jamming signal that forces the other nodes on the network to refrain from attempting new packet transmissions.

The situation is depicted in the time diagram in Figure 2.9, wherein node A begins the transmission of a packet at time t_0. Before the packet has arrived at B that node begins the transmission of a new packet at t_1 and the two are destined to collide. B is the first to detect the collision and it does so at time t_2. When the beginning of the packet transmission from B reaches A, then A also becomes aware of the collision. The longest possible time taken for A to detect a collision occurs when the two nodes are situated the greatest possible distance apart and when B begins its packet transmission just before it detects the transmission from A. That is when $(t_1 - t_0)$ and $(t_2 - t_0)$ are both equal to the maximum end-to-end propagation delay for the network. The length of a contention interval is therefore twice the maximum propagation delay.

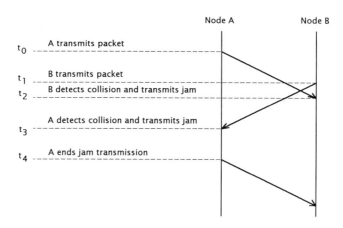

Figure 2.9 The timing diagram for a collision on a CSMA/CD network.

All the nodes that are involved in a collision reschedule packet transmissions to occur at some random time later. The method for choosing the retransmission time is known as the backoff algorithm. This algorithm should be chosen so that the possibility of further collisions are avoided and the binary exponential backoff, which is the one included in the IEEE standard, is just one example. Hence there is a number of parameters and processes that will have significant effects on the performance of a CSMA/CD network, and these are studied using a first principles analysis and simulation in Chapter 7.

2.3.2 Token Passing

The basic method of access control in token passing networks is straightforward compared to CSMA/CD. One might guess the underlying process from its name. The token passing method is used by the IEEE 802.4 and .5 committees to define the access protocol for the token bus and token ring, respectively. Quite simply a token, which is a special packet type, is passed around the network and the next node to receive it is the only one allowed to transmit a packet. Compared with CSMA/CD everything occurs in an orderly manner and, while there is still the possibility of a collision, it is extremely small, even when the traffic is heavy. The simplicity of access in token passing is enjoyed at the expense of more complex network management functions. The IEEE standard, for example, specifies that one of the nodes should make sure that the token is properly dealt with. This node is known as the monitor station, and when it is switched off the network has to choose an alternative.

There is a number of variations for the basic token passing algorithm that can have a dramatic effect on its performance. Early token release is a mechanism that allows the node to pass on the token before its packet transmission has been acknowledged. Again, each of these are dealt with using analysis and simulation in Chapter 7. The analysis for token passing systems are combinations of first principles and standard approaches.

2.4 METROPOLITAN AREA NETWORKS

There is a number of factors that become important when the size of the network is extended. There are likely to be more nodes, and it may be assumed that the amount of traffic increases in proportion. The end-to-end propagation delay is also increased, and the time required to transmit packets most certainly increases in proportion. Moreover, the fraction of cable or free space that a packet occupies is reduced, and this has implications on efficiency. These factors, coupled with the fact that traffic patterns will become less predictable, mean that a change of access control would seem appropriate if some account of the network performance is to be made.

From the performance point of view there are two general approaches for interconnecting LANs. One of these is to introduce bridges and routers that require attention in the network layer. The other is to modify the access control, or MAC layer. Bridging and routing in the network layer was addressed in the previous section. When the networks being connected are LANs, however, there is the additional dimension that there is a MAC protocol in operation. One of the analytic methods that will be studied in depth in this book is the discrete-time Markov chain. This technique is readily applied to the interconnection of CSMA/CD segments, and this is the theme of the first section in Chapter 8. Those readers who are interested in analyses that deal with interconnected token passing segments, and are prepared for some involved mathematics, may wish to consult Takine [10] as a starting point. The *Fiber Distributed Data Interface* (FDDI), and *Distributed Queue Dual Bus* (DQDB) are two MANs that include LAN type MAC protocols.

2.4.1 FDDI

The FDDI standard, which is the specification for a dual optical fiber ring operating at 100 Mbit/s, is accredited to the ANSI standards body. It is specific in its detail about the physical layer as well as the MAC and logical link control layers. In fact the standard also includes a station management protocol that is concerned with the operation of an FDDI network in all three layers. The principal reason for this is based on the physical configuration of the ring. In normal operation only one of the rings is used to transmit data. The second ring is included so that when a node fails the integrity of the path for data may be retained.

A simple schematic diagram of a four-node FDDI network is depicted in Figure 2.10. Normally the two counter-rotating rings are both operational. When one of the fibers is cut the other maintains the capability for the network to continue operating. When either both fibers are cut, or a node fails, the relays in the two adjacent nodes are activated and a smaller ring is brought into operation. The standard defines two types of station, known as A and B, with the less complex B type stations only being capable of connecting to one of the rings. Networks may be constructed using combinations of both types of station and these may be the subject of investigations that include node failures using methods that are described in Section 4.7.

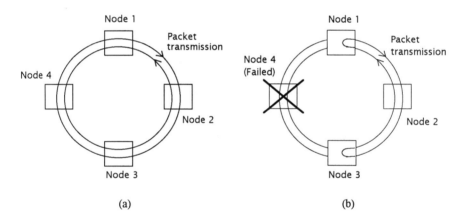

Figure 2.10 A four-node FDDI ring. In (a) both rings are operational, and in (b) node 4 has failed.

The most interesting aspect of FDDI, from a traffic analysis point of view, is the access control procedure. A certain amount of attention has been afforded to its design in considering the performance of the protocol when there is traffic that has originated from different types of source. There is specific provision for packets carrying data that are restricted to a maximum transmission delay and data that are not. These are known as synchronous and asynchronous, respectively.

Access control for FDDI is based on a token passing mechanism. In order to limit the delay for synchronous traffic each of the nodes agree on a maximum time for the token to complete a journey around the ring. This is known as the target token rotation time, or *TTRT*. The actual maximum delay for synchronous traffic is set to be $2 \times TTRT$. The allowed visit time at a node, which dictates the total amount of data it may transmit, is calculated by comparing the time elapsed since the token last visited the node, with the *TTRT*. If there is any time remaining when the node has completed the transmission of its synchronous data, then it may transmit asynchronous data. An analysis of this mechanism that follows that of Tangemann and Sauer [11] is provided in Section 7.5.

2.4.2 DQDB

A four-node DQDB network schematic is illustrated in Figure 2.11. The standard has been developed by the IEEE 802.6 committee, and it includes the definition of protocols in the same layers as for FDDI. Packet transmission takes place in the form of fixed-length frames on both buses at the same time, and in opposite directions using the same access control procedure, as is also the case for FDDI. The DQDB network, however, is split into two unconnected segments when a node fails. The access control procedure of the DQDB standard was designed to mimic the operation of a first-come first-served queue that is shared by all the nodes, hence the term distributed queue.

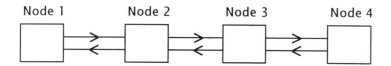

Figure 2.11 A four-node DQDB network.

All the frames are generated by the nodes at the start of each bus and they contain a header that includes two bits labeled B and R. These bits indicate whether the state of the frame is busy or not and whether the node it has just visited is making a request for data transmission, in that order. Each node keeps track of the number of requests made by the upstream nodes in its request counter. A request for transmission on one of the busses is made using the R field of a frame placed on the other bus. When a node sees an empty frame it reduces the request counter by one because it knows that a downstream node will utilize that frame. In addition, the node keeps count of all the requests made before it received any data of its own ready for transmission. To do this it sets the value of the countdown to be the same as the request counter at the same time as the data arrived. The countdown is also reduced by one when an empty frame passes through the node. When the countdown reaches zero the node knows that all the outstanding data from downstream nodes arrived after its own data. The node proceeds to transmit its data in the frame and it sets the B field appropriately. Data that are destined for a particular node must be transmitted on the bus for which that node is downstream.

The DQDB access protocol therefore achieves its goal to transmit the packets on a first-come first-served basis. Hence the average traffic delay characteristics should be favorable. Since the frames are transmitted front to back and the packet overhead is relatively small, the efficiency of the network should be high. The basic access mechanism described may be unfair, however, since the nodes closest to the end of a bus are most likely to encounter idle frames traveling downstream and busy frames traveling upstream. The network management protocol for the DQDB is supposed to deal with this anomaly, and the mechanism is popularly known as bandwidth balancing.

For a detailed discussion of the DQDB standard that, incidentally, is the IEEE 802.6 subcommittees recommendation for MANs, the reader is referred to Kessler [12]. It is generally accepted that the exact analysis of DQDB is complex. As usual simulation is readily adapted to the cause, however, and the study by Wu and Wang [13] is just one of many that have been cited in the literature.

2.5 WIDE AREA NETWORKS

The group of WANs includes larger interconnected LANs and telecommunication networks. WAN performance investigation is therefore concerned with all of the issues that are relevant to LANs, as well as the effect of protocols in the network layer, in addition to the traditional concerns in teletraffic engineering. As networking technology in general develops at pace, so too do the techniques in telecommunications, and a vast amount of documentation in the form of new proposals, standard architectures, and framing structures has been published. Fortunately, the basic methods for analysis and the techniques of simulation are generally applicable. The possible exception to this rule is the requirements for more complex traffic source models. In this section three of the most popular standards that collectively span the field of telecommunications—namely, ISDN, SDH, and ATM—are discussed.

The first communication networks consisted of mechanical switches and twisted pairs of wires that were used to transmit analog voice signals. These telecommunication networks have evolved into computer-controlled digital systems that can utilize optical fibers and satellites for the transmission of data and video signals as well as voice. There is a telecommunication network in each of the developed countries in the world and these are generally known as the *public switched telephone network* (PSTN). The heart of any telecommunication network is the device that routes and switches calls from one place to another. This device is known as an exchange. The size and functionality of exchanges vary according to their position in the hierarchy that constitutes the architecture of the PSTN.

The first generation switches were manually operated patch panels. The caller simply picked up a handset that was connected to another handset located next to the switch. A human operator responded to the request of the caller by making a suitable connection on the panel. The introduction of electro-mechanical switches and dialing handsets made human operators redundant and this resulted in the second generation of switches. Now handsets are equipped with pulse dialing and the voice signal is transmitted digitally.

2.5.1 The Digital PBX

The modern PBX, also known as a PABX (*private automatic branch exchange*) or CBX (*computerized branch exchange*), is the third generation of switching systems. These switches can provide a whole variety of services that are associated with the basic function of making telephone calls. The general structure of a PBX is illustrated in Figure 2.12.

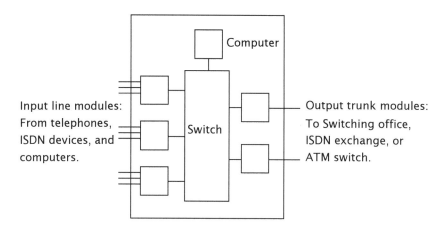

Figure 2.12 The components of an exchange.

The exchange has a modular structure that consists of a basic switch and the capability to support a variety of interfaces. Input modules present the incoming information in a suitable format and output modules transport the multiplexed signals to other switches. A module for analog telephones, for example, must digitize the incoming signal and perform the complementary function in the opposite direction. Trunk modules that connect to ISDN exchanges must output the bit stream in frames that are constructed according to a specific format. The computer unit is a general-purpose computer that runs the PBX.

Space and time division switching are the two kinds that are in common use. Space switches make connections using semiconductors. These devices enable electrical connections, just like the jumper cables in the first generation PBXs, except they may be controlled using computers and the process is performed within microseconds. Time switches, as shown in the Figure 2.13, make use of the fact that digital information can be interleaved on the same line. In this case the input lines are scanned in sequence to build up a frame with a certain number of slots. In turn, each slot may contain a fixed number of bits. In ISDN PBXs, the slots have 8 bits, and frames with 8000 slots are built and processed every second. A time division switch is also known as a time slot interchanger, which best describes the method of operation.

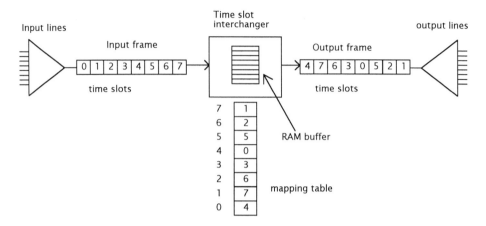

Figure 2.13 The operation of a time slot interchanger.

The interchanger depicted in the figure is a simple example, used to illustrate the basic principle, with 8 inputs and 8 outputs. When the input frame is complete and ready for processing, the mapping table, which stores the switching information, is used to reorder the slots in the buffer. The output frame is demultiplexed onto the output lines in the same order as the slots leave the interchanger and the switching has been accomplished. The role of the computer unit in a time division switch is to set up connections by adjusting the contents of the slot mapping table. The computer itself is controlled by the signaling processes that set up and maintain connections.

PBXs use various combinations of space and time division switches to take advantage of their different features. Semiconductors are limited by their size and the number of pins, or inputs and outputs, that can be supported. Time division switches, on the other hand, are required to store complete frames in a buffer. Since the number of inputs and outputs dictates the length of a frame, they also affect the length of the buffer and the processing speed required to deal with individual slots at the same rate. The analysis of switching, both space and time, is dealt with in Section 8.4.

2.5.2 The ISDN Interface

The goal of the *Integrated Services Digital Network* (ISDN) is to present users with a single interface to the PSTN that is capable of supporting data and video traffic as well as voice. The model of ISDN is layered in a similar way to the OSI protocols. Like its OSI counterpart, the ISDN physical layer deals with the mechanical, electrical, functional, and procedural aspects of the interface. The ISDN connector has eight contacts. Two are used for transmit and transmit ground and another two are used for receive and receive ground. Using a balanced transmission scheme a high level of noise immunity is achieved with ISDN cables that may be up to 1-km long. The remaining four connections are used to provide power for the terminal.

The aggregate transmission speed for ISDN is often referred to as a bit pipe. This is because it supports a number of channels that are interleaved by time division multiplexing. The speed and purpose of individual channels have been allocated letters according to the detail in Table 2.2. Various combinations of channels have been recognized as being suitable. The so-called basic rate ISDN consists of 2 B channels and a D channel while the primary rate ISDN in Europe consists of 23 B channels and a D channel.

Table 2.2
The transmission speeds for ISDN channels

Letter	Speed and Purpose
A	4-kHz analog telephone channel
B	64-kbit/s digital PCM channel for voice or data
C	8- or 16-kbit/s digital channel
D	16- or 64-kbit/s digital channel for out-of-band signaling
E	64-kbit/s digital channel for internal ISDN signaling
H	384-, 1536-, or 1920-kbit/s digital channel

The basic rate is sufficient to provide a plain old telephony service, often abbreviated as POTs, as well as 64 kbit/s of data. Each of the two B channels can handle a PCM voice channel with 8-bit samples made 8000 times a second. The signaling—that is, the transfer of information that is required to set up and manage a call—is carried out on the D channel. For data transmission the B channels may be subdivided. The physical layer frame format for basic rate traffic is shown in Figure 2.14.

48 bits in 250 microsec = 192 kbps
36 data bits (16 B1, 16 B2, 4 D) in 250 microsec = 144 kbps

F = framing bit
L = DC load balancing
E = Echo of previous D bit (for contention resolution)
D = D channel (4 bits in 4000 frames/sec = 16 kbps)
A = Activation bit
S = Spare bit

Figure 2.14 The frame format for basic rate ISDN.

The length of the frame is 48 bits, of which 36 are data. It is transmitted in 250 μs giving a data rate of 144 kbit/s but occupying 192 kbit/s of bandwidth including the overhead. The F bits contain a well-defined pattern to help keep both sides in synchronization. The L bits are there to adjust the average bit value. The E bits are used for contention resolution when several terminals on a passive bus are contending for a channel. The A bit is used for activating devices. The S bits have not yet been assigned. Finally, the B1, B2, and D bits are for user data.

There is a number of approaches that the traffic analyst can use to investigate Integrated Services networks. As with routing networks the problem must be broken down into manageable parts, the individual contribution of which may be studied independently. First, since the philosophy behind integrating services is to combine different traffic types in the same channel, a method for analyzing such combinations may be of importance. In Section 8.5 a Markov model for a simple two source system is presented. These types of model account for the mean aggregate arrival and service rates for each of the traffic types. The effects of more complicated traffic sources may also be investigated using simulation, for example, as described in Section 7.7. The effect of multiplexing different traffic sources on the same multiplexed channel may also be analyzed using the techniques described in the latter sections of Chapter 3.

ISDN uses out-of-band signaling, which is the terminology used here to describe the process of sending and receiving call processing and control information. The sequence of D bits is viewed as an independent digital channel with its own frame formats, messages, and so on.

The signaling process in ISDN is described by the CCITTs signaling system number 7, shortened to SS #7. The SS #7 protocol hierarchy is depicted in Figure 2.15. Layer 1, which corresponds to the physical layer in OSI, includes the framing formats described earlier. The principal layer 2 protocol is known as *Link Access Procedure D* (LAPD) and is concerned with delimiting frames, assigning sequence numbers to each one, and computing and verifying checksums—hence, in general, converting the potentially error prone bit stream provided by layer 1 into a reliable, sequenced frame stream for use by layer 3. As before, this layer does not have a direct impact on the traffic performance analysis.

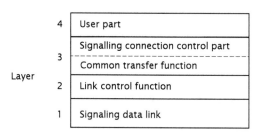

Figure 2.15 A layered model for ISDN.

Layer 3 is divided into two sublayers. One is concerned with routing calls and messages through the network of telephone exchanges. There is a wide variety of packet types for reporting the state of the system, its congestion, trunk utilization, node traffic, and so on. The other sublayer is concerned with addressing and the interface with OSI network protocols. Hence all the network layer functions, including routing, flow control, and switching, are important considerations for the traffic analyst here. In addition to this a provision is made for connectionless and connection-oriented services. The analysis of such methods is discussed in Section 8.4. In the user layer several high-level protocols have been defined. For example, the operations and maintenance application deals with managing the routing tables used to route calls on the B channels, collecting data about call set-up delays, initializing the exchange clocks, testing the network, and much more. These functions require processing time in the exchange, but they are of no direct consequence to the traffic analyst.

2.5.3 The Synchronous Digital Hierarchy

The original data transmission rates for multiplexing digital signals on telecommunication networks is known as the *plesiochronous digital hierarchy* (PDH), the word plesiochronous meaning nearly synchronous. At first digital links with different transmission speeds replaced analog links, and a number of links at different speeds were required to be multiplexed, so the individual and aggregate speeds were chosen in ad hoc fashion. More recently there has been an attempt to define a hierarchy of transmission rates that simplify the process of multiplexing digital data streams. The SDH, which is the result of this effort, is based on multiples of the 64-kbit/s transmission rate. Equivalent structures have emerged in the American telecommunications industry, and these are known as the T1 system, and SONET.

The use of multiplexing for the transmission of data and voice signals has already been described with respect to ISDN in the previous section. Again the techniques of analysis described in the later sections of Chapter 3 are relevant here. The digital transmission rates are based on the requirements of voice. Since a suitable quality is obtained when 8-bit samples are taken 8000 times per second, most standards are made up of integer multiples of 64 kbit/s. Transmission lines, or trunks, are defined in terms of the number of voice channels that can be supported. In countries that comply with the ITU recommendations, and this includes the European countries, the number voice channels is 30 and this results in an aggregate transmission rate of 2.048 Mbit/s. In North America and Japan the number of channels in a circuit is 24.

Time division multiplexed channels, such as those present in ISDN, PDH, and SDH data streams, are accessed using so-called add-drop multiplexing. A schematic diagram of an add-drop multiplexor is depicted in Figure 2.16. Transmission rates in the figure are shortened to the decimal point for convenience. The transmission rate of the circuit in this case is 140 Mbit/s and the rate accessible to the customer is 2 Mbit/s. In a networked configuration there will be at least two of these devices accessible to the customer and there will be some switching in-between.

From the customer point of view, there will always be the same amount of bandwidth available, and this may be accessed at fixed points in time. The performance of the network then concentrates on the way that this bandwidth is utilized. All the methods of analysis that have already been described in relation to switching and multiplexing are therefore relevant here. From the operator point of view, the same arguments are relevant to the supply of fixed-rate data streams. Hence the time-varying

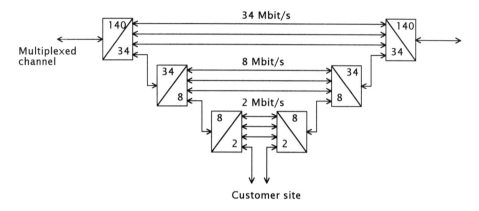

Figure 2.16 Add-drop multiplexing.

parameters of the system are different in this case. For example, when there is a rapid turnover of customers demanding varying transmission rates, the amount of plant required to satisfy this demand may be an important element. If the demand is constant, then other factors may come into play. In either case this is not the type of investigation that is covered in this text.

Telecommunication network performance analysis is therefore dependent on the dynamics of the actual traffic patterns. If a customer only requires a speed of 2 Mbit/s for short durations of time, then it is uneconomical for him or her to lease a permanent connection at this rate. Normally the requirements are for two or more services, such as may be satisfied by ISDN connections, and this complicates the situation. It is also exacerbated by the fact that different services often require different transmission rates and may tolerate less flexible framing structures. The methods for constructing traffic source models are discussed in Chapter 4. Readers who are interested in the finer details of PDH and SDH should be able to find suitable material without too much difficulty. The Institute of Electrical Engineers' Journal entitled *Electronics Communication Engineering* has published numerous readable articles. Ferguson's [14] is a good example.

2.5.4 Asynchronous Transfer Mode

Asynchronous Transfer Mode (ATM) is the proposed transfer mode for B-ISDN. It is the title that has been given to the method of transporting data on telecommunication networks and LANs alike. The proponents of ATM hail it as the universal networking technology and much has been written about such properties as its flexibility to support existing and future applications. The quality of service for ATM, regarding its efficiency in processing, switching, buffering, and management in general, seems to be an important consideration. It would appear that the network performance investigator certainly has some work to do here. Since ATM will be utilized in all networking environments, it is probably fair to say that all of the analytic and simulation modeling techniques are relevant.

ATM is based on the transport of fixed-size packets, 53-bytes long, and these are known as ATM cells. A layered model for ATM is depicted in Figure 2.17. The physical layer is the same as for the OSI model, and the so-called adaptation layer is included to present the packets from higher layers in segments of 48 bytes, ready for the ATM layer. The ATM header is 5-bytes long and includes a number of fields that are used to carry out the functions listed in the figure. One of these functions refers to *virtual path* and *virtual channel identifiers* (VPI/VCI), and these are the fields which are used to route cells across an ATM network.

	Layer	Functions
3	ATM Adaptation layer (AAL)	Segmentation and reassembly
2	ATM	Flow control, VPI/VCI translation and Multiplexing/Demultiplexing
1	Physical	Framing and Signaling

Figure 2.17 The layer model for ATM.

ATM is a connection-oriented protocol and the VCI and VPI fields identify the route that the cell should follow. The values are assigned to the VCI and VPI identifiers at the call set-up stage and remain the same throughout the duration of a connection. Hence each cell in the same communication follows the same route and its order of transmission is maintained in the correct sequence throughout its journey. Within the adaptation layer there is provision for a connectionless datagram service, however, in order to generate some compatibility with the LAN environment.

As usual, the specifics of the header formats are not important to the traffic investigator and the interested reader may consult numerous texts and articles on the subject. Onvural [15] and Jeffrey [16] are supplied as examples. Pitts and Schormans produced a book that is dedicated to the performance investigation of ATM networks [17]. Additional traffic source models have been generated in the time since ATM has surfaced and these are covered in most of these works. The *Markov Modulated Poisson Process*, often shortened to MMPP, is one such model, and it is described in the discussion of multimedia LANs in Section 7.7. Finally those readers who are interested in pursuing the aspects of network performance that are specific to ATM may be interested to know that the October 1996 edition of *Computer Networks and ISDN Systems* is a special issue on the subject.

2.6 SUMMARY

There is a vast array of protocols and standards for communication networks. Traditionally computer communications and telecommunications have been the two broad categories with which most types of network may be associated. The development of integrated service networks, however, has meant that the distinction is becoming less clear. Moreover, there is an impetus to ensure that networks that are developed independently can communicate with each other. As a consequence there has been a considerable amount of effort to provide a common framework for their evolution.

One of the most popular models for computer networks is the OSI model. Within this model there are three types of protocol that have a direct impact on the performance of the network. Data transmission rates and frame formats are defined in the physical layer. These are the most fundamental properties of communication channels as far as the performance investigation is concerned. The basic methods of analysis, using both first principles in probability theory and standard techniques queueing theory, may be used to obtain all of the performance characteristics associated with digital transmission, buffering, and multiplexing in the physical layer.

The second type of protocol that has a direct impact on the network performance resides in the data link layer. The windowing techniques that are used to achieve data link layer functions are ideal candidates for first principles analysis. Simple models for two of the basic methods were discussed in this chapter, as a taste for things to come. Finally the network layer, which includes the routing function, is perhaps the most complex process in the network, and their analysis is correspondingly difficult. Throughout the chapter references have been made to the parts of the text that deal with suitable analytical techniques. Of course the method of simulation is always available, however, and it is generally useful in any study.

In certain cases the OSI model is inadequate. LANs, for example, have MAC protocols and these were not included in the original seven-layer model. Techniques which are specific to these protocols are therefore required. The distinction between methods of analysis for MANs, WANs, and telecommunication networks becomes less well defined as there are many processes that are common to each type. In general, the performance of a communication network is more easily carried out if the system is considered to be made up of subsystems that may be analyzed on an individual basis. The ISDN, for example, is a combination of integrating traffic types, multiplexing bit streams, and switching. Each of these processes can be analyzed in great detail, as will be seen in the remainder of the text.

References

[1]   Halsall, Fred, *Data Communications, Computer Networks and Open Systems*, fourth edition, Reading, MA: Addison-Wesley Publishers Ltd., 1996.

[2]   Tanenbaum, Andrew S., *Computer Networks*, second edition, Englewood Cliffs, NJ: Prentice-Hall International, Inc., 1989.

[3]   Walrand, Jean, *Communication Networks: A First Course*, second edition, Chicago, IL: Irwin, 1997.

[4]   Coates, R. F. W., *Modern Communication Systems*, second edition, New York: MacMillan Press Ltd., 1982.

[5]   Tomasi, Wayne, *Advanced Electronic Communications Systems*, third edition, Englewood Cliffs, NJ: Prentice-Hall International, Inc., 1994.

[6]   Schwartz, Mischa, *Telecommunication Network Protocols, Modelling and Analysis*, Reading, MA: Addison-Wesley, 1987.

[7]   ANSI/IEEE Std 802.3-1985, Carrier Sense Multiple Access with Collision Detection (CSMA/CD) Access Method and Physical Layer Specification, ISBN 0-471-82749-5.

[8]   ANSI/IEEE Std 802.4-1985, Token Passing Bus Access Method and Physical Layer Specification, ISBN 0-471-82750-9.

[9]   ANSI/IEEE Std 802.5-1985, Token Ring Access Method and Physical Layer Specification, ISBN 0-471-82996-X.

[10]   Takine, T., Y. Takahashi, and T. Hasegawa, "Performance Analysis of a Polling System with Single Buffers and its Application to Interconnected Networks," *IEEE J. on Selected Areas in Communications*, Vol. SAC-4, No. 6, pp. 802–812, Sept. 1986.

[11]   Tangemann, M., and K. Sauer, "Performance Analysis of the Timed Token Protocol of FDDI and FDDI-II," *IEEE J. on Selected Areas in Communications*, Vol. 9, No. 2, pp. 271–278, Feb. 1991.

[12]   Kessler, G. C., and David A. Train, *Metropolitan Area Networks*, New York: McGraw-Hill, Inc., 1991.

[13]   Wu, J.-S., and Y.-C. Wang, "Adaptive Bandwidth Estimation and Allocation for DQDB MAN Interworking with B-ISDN," *Computer Communications*, Vol. 19, No. 5, pp. 435–444, May 1996.

[14]   Ferguson, S. P., "Implications of SONET and SDH," *IEE Electronics and Communications Engineering J.*, Vol. 6, No. 3, pp. 133–142, June 1994.

[15]   Onvural, R. O., *Asynchronous Transfer Mode Networks, Performance Issues*, second edition, Norwood, MA: Artech House Inc., 1995.

[16]   Jeffrey, M., "Asynchronous Transfer Mode: The Ultimate Broadband Solution?" *IEE Electronics and Communications Engineering J.*, Vol. 6, No. 3, pp. 1143–151, June 1994.

[17]   Pitts, J. M., and J. A. Schormans, *Introduction to ATM Design and Performance*, New York: John Wiley and Sons, 1996.

Chapter 3

Mathematical Analysis

Most of the analyses of communication network traffic involve some branch of statistical mathematics. The buffers in any communication network form queues of data waiting to be transmitted. It is reasonable to expect that the amount of data in a queue will have some effect on how long it will take before the data may be transmitted. It is also reasonable to expect that the occupancy of the queue will be determined by a number of factors such as the arrival and departure rates of the data. Queueing theory may be applied to the investigation of these factors to determine the properties of different systems. In this chapter we begin with a look at the basic principles involved in producing equations that can be used to model traffic. We find that the principles involved make up the foundations of queueing theory and we go on to describe some of the well-established techniques in this discipline. The methods are illustrated along the way with some specific examples.

The approach in the first section is not unlike Kershenbaum's introductory treatment of simple loss and delay analysis [1]. This material is the foundation for teletraffic engineering, and readers who are interested in this subject are referred to Bear [2] for a more in-depth study. Pure queueing theory is dealt with at various depths in numerous works. The one by Allen [3], which includes relevant material on probability theory, distributions, and transforms, is recommended. The later sections in this chapter focus on the solution of Markov chains, and this is largely based on the material in Kleinrock [4].

3.1 FIRST PRINCIPLES

Perhaps the simplest communication system consists of a single node that may only receive and transmit units of data at constant rates. If it receives data at a rate greater than that at which it may transmit, then some of the units will be lost. The loss probability— that is, the probability of losing at least one unit of data— is a parameter of the system that may be of interest. In this case, the loss probability is equal to one if the arrival rate exceeds the departure rate and zero otherwise. Hence the evaluation of this system is relatively straightforward. It either works or it does not. There are probably no other performance criteria of interest since the capacity of the node is simply equivalent to its data transmission rate, and there are no queueing delays. In fact this is not a queueing system at all.

If, however, the incoming data do not arrive in a constant stream and the node has some capacity for storage, then it is possible for all the data to be retained even during a time when the data arrival rate exceeds the data transmission rate. In this case we require some extra information to calculate the loss probability. Consider a node that has a data transmission rate D bit/s and arrival rate A packet/s. A packet of length L bits may be transmitted in L/D seconds and the maximum departure rate is given by the reciprocal, D/L packet/s. If a packet arrives at the node while it is busy transmitting a previous arrival, then it is stored in the buffer, possibly behind other packets that are also waiting for transmission. Otherwise, if the new packet arrives while the node is idle, then it is transmitted immediately. At this stage we will assume that once a packet has completed transmission it has been successfully dealt with. The node may then turn its attention to the next packet in the queue. Hence the maximum departure rate is the same as the output channel capacity, C, in packet/s. Now what happens to the system depends on the arrival process.

In the first instance let us assume that packets are arriving at a constant rate and constant length. When $A < C$ the channel capacity is never exceeded because the input and output rates are constant. Moreover, if the system begins with an empty buffer there will never be more than one packet at the node at any given time. Further it will always have been completely transmitted before the next arrival because the inter-arrival time, $1/A$, is always greater than L/D. Hence the queueing time is zero and the average number of packets in the system, $\overline{N}$, is less than one and equal to the utilization, which is given by

$$U = \frac{A}{C} \tag{3.1}$$

If the system somehow started with one or more packets in the nodes buffer the queue size would gradually decrease until it reached the steady-state conditions described previously.

When $A = C$ the node will always be in the process of transmitting data and the arrival rate never exceeds the departure rate. The number of packets in the system will remain constant at the initial value and hence a queueing delay may be incurred. If the system begins with an empty buffer, then it will remain empty and the queueing delay is zero. If there is one packet in the buffer at time $t = 0$, then subsequent packets will always have to wait for one packet transmission and the queuing delay will be equal to L/D seconds. In general the queueing delay is given by

$$\overline{Q} = n_{t=0} \frac{L}{D} \tag{3.2}$$

where $n_{t=0}$ is the initial number of packets in the system and $\overline{Q}$, the mean queueing delay, is the same value as the queueing delay for individual packets because the arrival and departure rates are constant. Note that in this case the utilization is one and packet loss probability is zero. Note also that Eq. (3.2) is a form of Little's result and we will see more of this equation later.

Finally if $A > C$ the node will be unable to cope with all the traffic and under steady-state conditions its buffer will be constantly full. If the buffer has a capacity for storing B packets, then the queueing delay will be $B \cdot (L/D)$ seconds. Again the utilization will be one since there will always be a packet awaiting transmission. However, the loss probability, defined as the probability that at least some data will be lost, is one. The probability that a given packet is not lost is C/A and the probability that it is lost is $1 - C/A$.

The preceding analysis provides a complete description of the performance criteria relating to a trivial case. When one or more of the assumptions are relaxed the analysis becomes more complex. Next we will consider what happens if we allow the arrival rate to vary, and there is a number of ways to do this. The packet arrivals may be random such that it is possible for any one of the three conditions $A < C$, $A = C$, and $A > C$ to occur at any time, for example.

Let the number of packets in a queue be known as the system state. Hence, if there are n packets stored in the node's buffer, then the system state is equal to n. Calculating the probability that the system may be found in a particular state at any given time is central to the analysis of any queue. The analysis of a queueing system begins with writing the balance equation that holds for the system when it is in steady state. Let P_n be the probability that the system is in state n. The balance equation may then be written as

$$AP_n = \frac{D}{L} P_{n+1} \tag{3.3}$$

This relationship follows from the fact that in steady state the number of transitions from state n to $n+1$, as given by the left-hand side, is equal to the number of transitions in the opposite direction, from $n+1$ to n, as given by the right-hand side. Rearranging Eq. (3.3) and using the fact that $U = A \cdot (L/D)$ we have

$$P_{n+1} = UP_n \tag{3.4}$$

Thus we can write the general term for P_n in terms of P_0 as

$$P_n = U^n P_0 \tag{3.5}$$

Now from the law of total probability all the P_n must sum to one such that

$$\sum_{n=0}^{\infty} P_n = 1 \tag{3.6}$$

this, of course, assuming that the system capacity is infinite. Summing the series and rearranging gives

$$P_0 = 1 - U \tag{3.7}$$

This result is perhaps intuitive. It states that the probability that the node has no packets is the same as the fraction of time that the system is idle, or one minus the utilization. Putting Eq. (3.5) into Eq. (3.7) we have

$$P_n = (1 - U)U^n \tag{3.8}$$

We now know the system state probabilities in terms of the utilization, which is in turn easily calculated from the known parameters of the system. Using the state probabilities we can obtain the performance parameters of interest. The mean queueing delay, for example, will in this case be the mean value of n multiplied by L/D, the transmission time for a packet. This is Little's result again. The expected value of n is given by

$$E[n] = \bar{n} = \sum_{n=0}^{\infty} nP_n \tag{3.9}$$

which may be rewritten using Eq. (3.8) as

$$\bar{n} = \sum_{n=0}^{\infty} n(1 - U)U^n \tag{3.10}$$

This expression may be simplified to give

$$\bar{n} = \frac{U}{1 - U} \tag{3.11}$$

It may be recognized that this is the mean of a geometric distribution with parameter U, which is what in fact we have in Eq. (3.8). Finally the mean queueing delay can be written as

$$\bar{Q} = \frac{U}{1 - U} \cdot \frac{L}{D} \tag{3.12}$$

The total delay is the queueing delay plus the packet transmission time, which gives

$$\bar{D} = \frac{1}{1 - U} \cdot \frac{L}{D} \tag{3.13}$$

Hence, the average delay is close to the packet transmission time when the system utilization is low, as expected. On the other hand, as the utilization increases, so does the delay, and as $U \to 1$ the delay becomes infinite. Moreover, when U is large small increases in utilization result in large increases in delay, as the following example illustrates.

Consider a node with a large buffer capacity that receives data in chunks of 8 bits. The node is connected to a communication line with a capacity of 96,000 bit/s. The graph in Figure 3.1 was obtained using Eq. (3.13) with $D = 96,000$ and $L = 8$ and as expected the mean delay increases with the utilization. For small values of U we expect the mean delay to be equal to L/D, in this case 0.083 ms, and the curve in the figure will intersect the vertical axis at this point. Hence the expected characteristics of the system can be predicted with relative ease, though it is a little more complex than the previous one because we allow the arrival rate to vary.

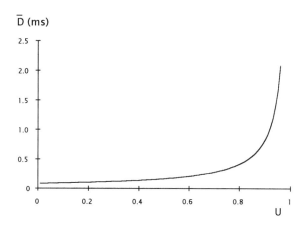

Figure 3.1 Mean delay as a function of utilization.

If we assume that the number of packets in the system is geometrically distributed, then we are also assuming that the buffer has an infinite capacity, and it is unlikely that this will ever be the case for a real system. Let the buffer capacity be limited to B packets. Now the balance equation becomes

$$P_{n+1} = \begin{cases} UP_n & \text{if } n < B \\ 0 & \text{otherwise} \end{cases} \qquad (3.14)$$

Hence continuing as before we have

$$P_n = U^n P_0 \quad \text{for } n \leq B \qquad (3.15)$$

and

$$\sum_{n=0}^{B} P_n = 1 \qquad (3.16)$$

Note that the upper limit of the summation is B in this case. Replacing the P_ns in Eq. (3.16) using Eq. (3.15) gives

$$\sum_{n=0}^{B} U^n P_0 = (1 + U + U^2 + \cdots + U^B) P_0 = 1 \tag{3.17}$$

Summing the series and rearranging for P_0 gives

$$P_0 = \frac{1 - U}{1 - U^{B+1}} \tag{3.18}$$

This expression is perhaps not intuitive as it was in the case of an infinite buffer. Note that as $B \to \infty$ the denominator of Eq. (3.18) tends to one and the previous result is obtained. The mean delay is given by the product of the mean number of packets in the node, or the system state, and the packet transmission time, as before. Using Eq. (3.9) again we have

$$\overline{n} = \sum_{n=0}^{B} n \cdot \frac{1 - U}{1 - U^{B+1}} \cdot U^n \tag{3.19}$$

The summation of this series gives

$$\overline{n} = \frac{B U^{B+2} - (B+1) U^{B+1} + U}{(1-U)(1-U^{B+1})} \tag{3.20}$$

The mean delay for $B = 5$ and $B = 10$ is plotted as a function of utilization with the same packet length and transmission rate as before in Figure 3.2. The curve obtained previously for the case when the buffer capacity is infinite is included. At small fractions

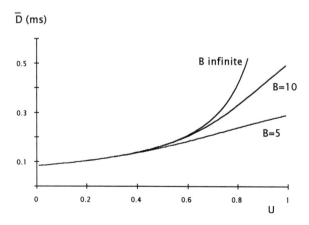

Figure 3.2 Mean delay with limited buffer space.

of utilization all three curves are superimposed and this is a result of the fact that only a small number of packets is likely to be found in the system at any time. At higher fractions of utilization the smaller buffer sizes show a reduced mean delay. This is a result of the fact that a greater proportion of the traffic is rejected. Hence the improved delay performance is at the expense of increased rejections, or loss probability.

Limiting the buffer size has therefore created the desire to investigate the loss probability, L. A simple method for calculating L is to find the probability that the system can be found in a state $s > B$ in the case when the buffer is infinite. This is given by

$$L = \sum_{n=B+1}^{\infty} P_n \tag{3.21}$$

with the P_ns calculated using Eq. (3.8). Replacing the P_ns in Eq. (3.21) we obtain

$$L = \sum_{n=B+1}^{\infty} (1-U)U^n \tag{3.22}$$

which simplifies to

$$L = U^{B+1} \tag{3.23}$$

Hence we can easily use Eq. (3.23) to find the loss probability of the system at any given utilization and buffer size. The function is illustrated in Figure 3.3 with $B = 1$, 5, and 10. The case when B is infinite will give $L = 0$ for all $U < 1$, which is the condition for stability. Our previous conclusion that for smaller buffer sizes the rejection probability increases is vindicated by the characteristics.

Next we will consider what happens if the node is connected to two communication channels. Assume that it has an infinite buffer capacity. As usual we

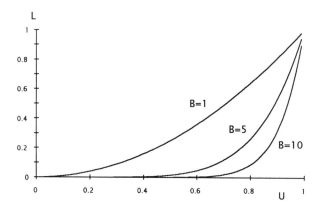

Figure 3.3 Loss probability as a function of utilization.

begin with writing the balance equations. For $n = 1$ we have the same result as before such that

$$P_1 = UP_0 \tag{3.24}$$

However for $n = 2$ there are two departures in L / D seconds and we can write

$$AP_2 = 2 \cdot \frac{D}{L} P_1 \tag{3.25}$$

Rearranging Eq. (3.25) and using the fact that $U = A \cdot (L / D)$ we have

$$P_2 = \frac{U}{2} P_1 \tag{3.26}$$

Therefore in general we can write

$$P_n = \frac{U^n}{2^{n-1}} P_0 \tag{3.27}$$

for $n > 0$. Again the law of total probabilities dictates that the sum of the P_ns must be one and therefore

$$P_0 + \sum_{n=1}^{\infty} \frac{U^n}{2^{n-1}} P_0 = \left(1 + U + \frac{U^2}{2} + \frac{U^3}{4} + \cdots \right) P_0 = 1 \tag{3.28}$$

Summing the series and rearranging we get

$$P_0 = \frac{2 + U}{2 - U} \tag{3.29}$$

The average system size can be obtained using Eq. (3.9) again and so

$$\overline{n} = \sum_{n=1}^{\infty} n \frac{U^n}{2^{n-1}} P_0 \tag{3.30}$$

Simplifying this expression and replacing P_0 using Eq. (3.29) gives

$$\overline{n} = \frac{4U}{4 - U^2} \tag{3.31}$$

and the mean queueing delay may be obtained using Little's result. We plotted mean delay as a function of utilization for $L = 8$ and with a channel speed 96,000 bit/s in

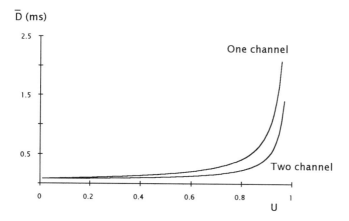

Figure 3.4 Mean delay for node with one and two channels.

Figure 3.4. As expected the delay is lower in the two-channel case.

In general a node may have m channels attached to it. We find that the balance equations become, for $n \le m$,

$$P_n = \frac{U^n}{n!} P_0 \tag{3.32}$$

and for $n \ge m$

$$P_n = \frac{U^m}{m!} \left(\frac{U}{m} \right)^{n-m} P_0 \tag{3.33}$$

And as always the sum of the P_ns must be one such that

$$\sum_{n=0}^{\infty} P_n = \sum_{n=0}^{m-1} \frac{U^n}{n!} P_0 + \sum_{n=m}^{\infty} \frac{U^m}{m!} \left(\frac{U}{m} \right)^{n-m} P_0 = 1 \tag{3.34}$$

In its most convenient form we obtain the following expression for P_0:

$$P_0 = \left\{ \sum_{n=0}^{m-1} \frac{U^n}{n!} + \frac{U^m}{m!(1-U/m)} \right\}^{-1} \tag{3.35}$$

Now the average number of packets in the node is given by

$$\bar{n} = \sum_{n=m}^{\infty} (n-m) \frac{U^m}{m!} \left(\frac{U}{m} \right)^{n-m} P_0 \tag{3.36}$$

and this simplifies to

$$\bar{n} = \frac{U^m}{m!} \frac{U/m}{(1-U/m)^2} P_0 \qquad (3.37)$$

We can confirm the result for the two-channel case. Putting $m = 2$ in Eq. (3.35) and (3.37) and replacing P_0 in the latter we obtain

$$\bar{n} = \frac{U^3}{4-U^2} \qquad (3.38)$$

Now this result gives the average number of packets in the buffer. The number of packets in the system is the sum of those in the buffer and any in service. The average number of packets in service is U, so by adding this to the right-hand side of Eq. (3.38) to obtain Eq. (3.31) the result is confirmed. A methodology for the solution of these simple systems may be recognized. In general we obtain the expression for the average number of data units in the system by solving the balance equations. More complicated systems inevitably lead to more complicated analyses, and we proceed to describe these a little more rigorously using queueing theory terminology.

3.2 THE ELEMENTS OF QUEUES

In the previous section we saw that relaxing one or two of the assumptions for even the simplest communication system makes the analysis somewhat more complex. The techniques that have been described thus far are embedded in the discipline known as queueing theory. This is a suitable point for introducing the formal guidelines of the discipline, and in the remainder of the chapter we continue to investigate some of the traditional, well-established techniques. This section introduces the short-hand queueing theory notation, attributed to Kendal, that is used to categorize the analyses. For an alternative source on this material the reader is referred to the introductory treatment by Bunday [5].

The short-hand notation for a queue most often consists of two letters and a number in the form A/B/m. The A and B represent the inter-arrival time distribution and service time distribution, respectively, and the m is an integer that indicates the number of servers for the queue. A and B most often take on one of the values D, M, or G, representing Deterministic, Markovian, and General time distributions. A number of others are also commonly used. Deterministic arrivals or services take on constant values, and in fact the most simple communications system described in the first section is a D/D/1 queue. The arrival and departure processes of queueing systems are thus modeled using stochastic processes.[1] A general arrival or service time distribution indicates that the stochastic process is arbitrary.

---

[1] Stochastic processes are defined in Appendix A.

A queue may be more completely described by the form A/B/m/K/M with the K and M values indicating the storage capacity and customer population, respectively. The absence of K and M is strictly supposed to indicate that these quantities are taken to be infinity. A less frequently used suffix can be included to tie down the service order. An M/D/2/10/1-FIFO queue, for example, may accommodate ten units originating from one customer with exponentially distributed inter-arrival times on a first-in first-out basis. It has two servers that can deal with the units at a constant rate.

3.2.1 The Arrival Process

In the last paragraph we effectively stated that a Markovian arrival process has exponentially distributed inter-arrival times. This is quite a wordy description that is perhaps worthy of one of the most widely used processes in traffic analysis. Next to deterministic arrivals it is also one of the most convenient processes with which to deal mathematically and it has been found to be relevant in many applications. Exponentially distributed inter-arrival times give rise to a completely random arrival pattern. It is governed by a strict definition, however.

3.2.1.1 Random Arrivals

Consider the short time interval $(t, t + \delta t)$ for which the probability that a single customer arrives is given by

$$P[N = 1] = \lambda \delta t + o(\delta t) \qquad (3.39)$$

where λ is the average arrival rate. Note that previously we used A for this purpose, however, from now on we will adopt the more traditional symbols. The function $o(\delta t)$ denotes a quantity that becomes negligible compared with δt as $\delta t \to 0$. The probability that no customer arrives during the same interval is

$$P[N = 0] = 1 - \lambda \delta t + o(\delta t) \qquad (3.40)$$

and the probability that more than one customer arrives is

$$P[N > 1] = o(\delta t) \qquad (3.41)$$

Then Eqs. (3.39), (3.40), and (3.41) describe a completely random arrival process that results in exponentially distributed inter-arrival times.

Alternatively the arrival pattern is random if the number of arrivals in the time interval $(t, t + \delta t)$ is independent of t as $\delta t \to 0$. Further it can be said to be completely random if the number of arrivals in this time interval is also independent of any other time interval that does not include any part of $(t, t + \delta t)$.

Most texts dealing with the properties of the exponential distribution will provide some form of derivation to support the preceding definition, and it is informative for the reader to study one or more of these. Here we begin by considering what happens in the interval $(t, t+x)$ and, in accordance with the definition, let the interval go small. What we are looking for is an expression that gives the probability that the inter-arrival time is greater than some value in terms of that value and λ. Now the probability that the inter-arrival time is greater than t is the same as the probability that there are no arrivals in the interval $(0, t)$. We can achieve this by using the previous definition to derive the probability that there are exactly n arrivals in the interval $(t, t+x)$.

Let the interval x be divided into m equal intervals of length δt. Then as $m \to \infty$ so $\delta t \to 0$ and in each interval the arrival probabilities are given by Eqs. (3.39), (3.40), and (3.41). Now the probability that there are exactly n arrivals is given by the limiting value of the binomial distribution as

$$\Pr[N=n] = \lim_{m \to \infty} \binom{m}{n} [\lambda \delta t + o(\delta t)]^n [1 - \lambda \delta t + o(\delta t)]^{m-n} \tag{3.42}$$

Using the fact that $\delta t = x/m$ and $o(\delta t) \to 0$ in the limit $\delta t \to 0$ we can rewrite Eq. (3.42) as

$$\Pr[N=n] = \lim_{m \to \infty} \binom{m}{n} \left(\frac{\lambda x}{m}\right)^n \left(1 - \frac{\lambda x}{m}\right)^{m-n} \tag{3.43}$$

After some algebra this expression may be written as

$$\Pr[N=n] = \frac{(\lambda x)^n}{n!} e^{-\lambda x} \tag{3.44}$$

and the probability that there are no arrivals in the interval $(0, t)$ is given by $n=0$ and $x = t$:

$$\Pr[\text{no arrivals in } (0, t)] = e^{-\lambda t} \tag{3.45}$$

Now the left-hand side of Eq. (3.45) is the same as one minus the probability that the inter-arrival time for the next customer, T, is greater than or equal to t, and by definition is related to the distribution function of the inter-arrival time, $F(t)$, as

$$\Pr[T > t] = 1 - F(t) \tag{3.46}$$

Therefore

$$F(t) = 1 - e^{-\lambda t} \tag{3.47}$$

Differentiating Eq. (3.47) we obtain

$$f(t) = \lambda e^{-\lambda t} \tag{3.48}$$

which is the probability density function for the exponential distribution.

Note that Eq. (3.44), which gives the probability that a certain number of customers arrive in a given interval, is the Poisson distribution with parameter λx. The derivation therefore serves to illustrate the relationship between Poisson and exponential variables.

Hence customers arriving at an average rate λ in a completely random pattern have inter-arrival times with a negative exponential distribution and probability density distribution given by Eq. (3.48). The number of customers arriving in a given time interval has a Poisson distribution. One of the properties of the completely random arrival process is that the choice of time origin is arbitrary. Therefore the time that elapses from an arbitrary moment in time, not necessarily the arrival time of the last customer, to the arrival of the next customer, is a random variable T with negative exponential distribution. This is known as the memoryless property and points to the reason why the letter M, for Markovian, is used to represent the exponentially distributed arrival process. A Markovian stochastic process exhibits the memoryless property.

A convenient method for describing the arrival process is in terms of the distribution function of the inter-arrival time. If the arrival times for successive customers are independent and have a general distribution function $G(t)$, then we have general independent arrivals. In the preceding case above we have completely random arrivals and $G(t)$ takes the form

$$G(t) = 1 - e^{-\lambda t} \tag{3.49}$$

In the deterministic arrival process $G(t)$ takes the form

$$G(t) = \begin{cases} 0 & \text{for } t < c \\ 1 & \text{for } t \geq c \end{cases} \tag{3.50}$$

and the arrivals occur at a constant rate with inter-arrival time c. Some justification should be made for choosing a particular arrival pattern and this is not a trivial task, particularly in view of the more complex arrival processes that are now introduced.

3.2.1.2 Batch Arrivals and Burstiness

The inter-arrival time distributions provide a mechanism for modeling the arrival of an entity that is to be transferred from one location to another. What that entity actually consists of is also of concern because it affects the way we dealt with it. This point is illustrated by the example in the previous section for which the network utilization depends on the length of a packet. We may then refer to the arrival process as describing the pattern of arrival for packets. However, this appears to restrict us to arrivals of a fixed length. If we only use one probability distribution to describe the arrival process, then this is indeed the case. That is, we allow the spacing of arrival instants to vary, but not the arrival duration, which translates directly into the packet length. Thus, in general, we may be interested in the effects that are brought about by allowing the length of arrivals as well as the time in-between arrivals to vary.

We may refer instead to the arrival of batches of data units in the form of messages. In general, a data unit may be any fixed number of bits: an 8-bit byte or a 1,000-bit packet, for example, or even just one bit. In other words the message is the subject of a single arrival and it consists of a number of bits, bytes, or packets. Hence, in more general terms than before we have batch arrivals. The size of a batch may be modeled in a number of ways. The simplest batch arrival process is one for which the number of data units in each message is always the same, or constant, in which case the system analysis is probably most straightforward. These types of arrival pattern are relevant in systems that involve deterministic amounts of data such as large file transfer and raw video transmission. More interesting arrival processes occur in the less deterministic patterns resulting from voice and data communications that are characterized by random batch sizes. As usual, we can model random batch sizes using a variety of probability distributions.

Discrete random variables derived from any probability distribution are candidates for use in modeling batch arrival processes. A number of the discrete probability distributions have some interesting properties that are relevant to the application of network traffic, and it is informative to investigate these here. We will begin by using the geometric distribution with parameter q, for which the probability that there are k data units in a batch is given by

$$\Pr[X = k] = q^k (1-q) \tag{3.51}$$

where X is the random number representing the message or batch size. This expression is derived intuitively by considering that the message is constructed as a sequence of trials for which the outcome may be considered as a success or a failure. Specifically we will allow the length of the batch to increase by one data unit with probability q. The probability that we will obtain k successive successes followed by a failure is the same as the probability that the message will contain k data units, and this is given by Eq. (3.51). The properties of an arrival process with batch sizes using this model will thus have the same properties as the geometric distribution.

In a more general sense we could choose the batch size from any sequence of Bernoulli trials. If we take the message length as given by the number of successes in n trials— that is k successes followed by $n-k$ failures— then we have

$$\Pr[X = k] = q^k (1-q)^{n-k} \tag{3.52}$$

In fact there may be no reason why the successes should occur in that specific order and we may write

$$\Pr[X = k] = \binom{n}{k} q^k (1-q)^{n-k} \tag{3.53}$$

where the additional factor accounts for the number of possible combinations of k successes from n independent trials in any order. For example, consider a multiplexor that is connected to n data sources. At any given time each source generates a packet with probability q. The event that k packets are generated is given by Eq. (3.53) and the length of a message constructed by placing each of the packets in a contiguous chain is then X.

We can recognize Eq. (3.53) as the binomial distribution. The mean value of the batch length generated using this distribution is given by nq. Consider what happens if we allow n to increase without limit and we require the mean batch length to remain a constant nq. In this case the success probability must tend to zero. Now

$$\lim_{\substack{n \to \infty \\ q \to 0}} \frac{n!}{k!(n-k)!} q^k = \frac{(nq)^k}{k!} \tag{3.54}$$

and

$$\lim_{\substack{n \to \infty \\ q \to 0}} (1-q)^{n-k} = e^{-nq} \tag{3.55}$$

So from Eqs. (3.53) to (3.55) we have

$$\Pr[X = k] = \frac{(nq)^k}{k!} e^{-nq} \tag{3.56}$$

This is the Poisson distribution with parameter nq, and we have shown that it may be used to generate random batch sizes from an infinite number of sources. Obviously this is not illustrated well by our multiplexor example. However, it may be useful for modeling single sources for which there is no known limit to the message size.

The arrival process determines a property of network traffic known as burstiness. Burstiness is not a term that has been used in established methods in queueing theory. It has been applied more recently to help in the study of communication network traffic. Essentially it provides another parameter that may be of interest in the system performance analysis. One measure of the traffic burstiness, B, is obtained numerically using the ratio of the mean and peak arrival rates.

Consider a node that is collecting single data units from a number of sources and grouping them into batches for output onto a single communications channel. For geometrically distributed batch sizes with a mean $q/1-q$ the burstiness of the traffic on the channel is given by

$$B_{\text{geo}} = 1 - U\frac{q}{(1-q)} \tag{3.57}$$

where U is the utilization, such that the second term on the right-hand side represents the normalized mean arrival rate divided by the peak rate. Since a measure of burstiness will be expected to be small when the peak rate is close to the mean rate, we subtract the normalized ratio from one to get Eq. (3.57). Similarly for the binomially distributed batches we obtain

$$B_{\text{bin}} = 1 - Uq \tag{3.58}$$

and for Poisson batches, which we must assume have originated from an infinite number of sources, we have

$$B_{\text{poi}} = 1 - U \tag{3.59}$$

Burstiness is plotted as a function of utilization for each of the distributions in Figures 3.5 and 3.6. Note that $B_{\text{poi}} = B_{\text{bin}}$ when $q = 1$.

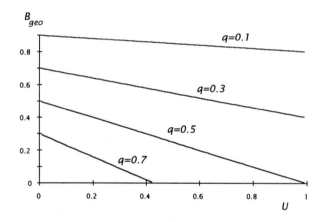

Figure 3.5 Burstiness as a function of utilization for geometric batches.

3.2.2 The Service Mechanism

The service discipline, the number of servers, and the server availability are all part of the service mechanism; and its operation is highly dependent upon them. In the remainder of this chapter we will assume that the service discipline is first come first served. In a real communication system that operates a system of priorities this may not be the case however. The number of servers and server availability are two aspects of the service mechanism that we will investigate in some detail. The server in a single-server queue is

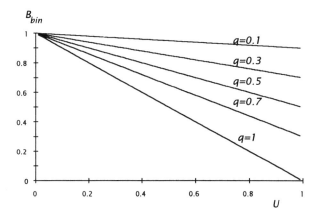

Figure 3.6 Burstiness as a function of utilization for binomial batches.

not always available, since at any given time a customer may be utilizing that service and subsequent arrivals are required to wait. Hence the time dependency of the service mechanism may be modeled using probability distributions in the same way as the arrival process.

In real communication networks it is perhaps easier to specify the service time distribution than it is to justify the choice of arrival time distribution. For example, consider what happens when a node has the exclusive use of a channel whose capacity is never exceeded. Service begins at the same instant as an arrival occurs, and the service time is dictated by the arrival pattern, which is directly proportional to the packet or message size. Thus having specified the arrival process we have also determined the service time. In more complex networks, however, the service time distribution depends on the activity of more than one queue and their interaction with the access mechanism.

We will illustrate one type of service mechanism that results in a distribution well known for its applications in telecommunications. Consider a service facility, such as a telephone exchange, that is able to handle calls at a particular average rate, μ. Further let us assume, as is generally accepted to be reasonable, that the service time for calls is completely random. Then the service time distribution, $b(x)$, is given by the negative exponential distribution

$$b(x) = \mu e^{-\mu x} \tag{3.60}$$

and the mean duration of a call is $1/\mu$. Now let the service facility be divided into two stages, as depicted in Figure 3.7, such that each call must enter the second stage when it has left the first. Note that only one customer is allowed in either stage at any one time.

Let the service time in each stage be exponentially distributed with mean $1/2\mu$ such that the mean duration of the overall service, which is simply the sum of the individual means, remains $1/\mu$. Now the distribution function for the service time in each stage, $b_{1,2}(x)$, is given by

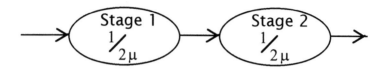

Figure 3.7 The two-stage service facility.

$$b_{1,2}(x) = 2\mu e^{-2\mu x} \tag{3.61}$$

The distribution of a random variable, which is given by the sum of two independent random variables, is given by the convolution of each distribution. Hence the distribution of the overall service time, $b(x)$, is the convolution of $b_1(x)$ and $b_2(x)$, and it may be obtained using Laplace transforms. If we denote $\mathcal{B}(s)$ and $\mathcal{B}_{1,2}(s)$ to be the transforms of $b(x)$ and $b_{1,2}(x)$, respectively, then we can make use of the fact that

$$\mathcal{B}(s) = \mathcal{B}_1(s)\,\mathcal{B}_2(s) = [\mathcal{B}_{1,2}(s)]^2 \tag{3.62}$$

The transform of the exponential distributions in $b_{1,2}(x)$ are given by

$$\mathcal{B}_{1,2}(s) = \int_0^\infty 2\mu e^{-2\mu x} e^{-sx}\,dx \tag{3.63}$$

whence

$$\mathcal{B}_{1,2}(s) = \frac{2\mu}{s+2\mu} \tag{3.64}$$

So from Eqs. (3.62) and (3.64) we obtain

$$\mathcal{B}(s) = \left(\frac{2\mu}{s+2\mu}\right)^2 \tag{3.65}$$

which is easily inverted to give

$$b(x) = 2\mu(2\mu x)e^{-2\mu x} \tag{3.66}$$

It is easily seen that if we generalize the service facility as a sequence of r stages and the duration of the overall service remains $1/\mu$, then each stage will incur a mean duration of $1/r\mu$. The transforms of the distributions of the time spent in each stage are given by

$$\mathcal{B}_{1,2...r}(s) = \frac{r\mu}{s+r\mu} \tag{3.67}$$

and the overall service time is given by

$$B(s) = \left(\frac{r\mu}{s+r\mu}\right)^r \tag{3.68}$$

When this transform is inverted we obtain

$$b(x) = \frac{r\mu(r\mu x)^{r-1}e^{-r\mu x}}{(r-1)!} \tag{3.69}$$

The family of distributions given by this last expression is known as the r-stage Erlang distribution, normally denoted by the symbol E_r. Along with the completely random nature of the exponential distribution, it has the useful property that for any integer $r > 0$, its mean value is $1/\mu$. We will look at some applications for the Erlang distributions later. For now, this is a suitable point for discussing one of the fundamental laws in queueing theory.

3.2.3 Little's Result

The formula that is Little's result is to queueing theory what Ohm's law is to electronics. This fundamental expression for delay has been mentioned in a number of places already. While the result is probably intuitive, it is worth spending a moment or two considering how it might be derived a "little" more rigorously. Little's law states that *the average number of customers in a queueing system is equal to the average arrival rate of customers to that system, times the average time spent in that system.*[2] This may be written as

$$\overline{N} = \lambda\overline{Q} \tag{3.70}$$

where $\overline{Q}$ is the same quantity used in the first section.

This general result, which is independent of the arrival and service time distributions and the queueing discipline, may be derived as follows. Consider the graph in Figure 3.8 that depicts an arbitrary distribution of the number of customers in a queueing system, n, as a function of time, t. The shaded area is the total time spent by all the customers in the system. Let this time be represented by the function $A(\tau)$, where the interval of time under consideration is $(0, \tau)$. Thus

$$A(\tau) = \int_0^\tau n(t)dt \tag{3.71}$$

---

[2] This is the definition given by Kleinrock in [2].

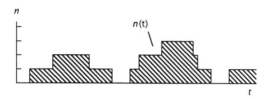

Figure 3.8 The number of customers in a queueing system as a function of time.

The average number of customers in the system in the same interval, N_τ, is therefore given by

$$\overline{N_\tau} = \frac{A(\tau)}{\tau} \qquad (3.72)$$

and the average time spent by a customer in the system is

$$\overline{T_\tau} = \frac{A(\tau)}{a(\tau)} \qquad (3.73)$$

where $a(\tau)$ is the total number of arrivals in the interval. Now, if the arrival rate averaged over the interval is λ_τ, then $a(\tau) = \tau \lambda_\tau$. Using this fact, and eliminating $A(\tau)$ from Eqs. (3.72) and (3.73), gives

$$\overline{N_\tau} = \lambda_\tau \overline{T_\tau} \qquad (3.74)$$

Imagine that the interval is extended to infinity. The values of $\overline{N_\tau}$ and $\overline{T_\tau}$ remain finite if the number of arrivals does not exceed the number of departures without limit. In this case Eq. (3.74) is the same as Eq. (3.70), with the only assumption being that there is some limit to the number of arrivals and the times spent in the system by each customer. Hence Little's result applies to all the queueing systems with finite arrival rates and service times.

The one subtle difference between the limiting case of Eq. (3.74) and Eq. (3.70) is in the definition of the average time. In the former we have defined this variable to be $\overline{T}$, the average time in the system; whereas the latter considers $\overline{Q}$, which is the average time in the queue. Strictly speaking, therefore, $\overline{N}$ in the limiting case of Eq. (3.74) is the average number of customers in the system while in Eq. (3.70) it is the average number of customers in a queue. Of course the two cases are equivalent when the queue is actually defined as the system. If the system includes the server as well as the queue, however, then the total number of customers includes the number of customers in service as well as those in the queue, and the mean time in the system is the sum of the mean service time and the mean queueing time.

3.3 BIRTH-DEATH PROCESSES

Methods in the study of birth-death processes, which are appropriate for modeling changes in the size of a population, are extremely useful in the analysis of communication networks that may be described by the number of messages present. A birth-death process is one in which the value of the system state may only change by one and is a special case of the more general Markov processes. A Markov process results if the next state of a system depends only on the present state and not on any previous states. Hence a birth-death process, in which state transitions may only occur between neighboring states, may describe a communication system in which packets arrive and depart in an orderly fashion. In what follows we will derive some of the theory for birth-death models beginning with the general, or transient, solution, continuing with the steady-state solution, and ending with some more specific models.

3.3.1 The Transient Solution

The transient solution of the general birth-death model provides analytic expressions for the system parameters in terms of the number of customers and the arrival and departure rates at any time. Let the system state be n, the number of customers present. Single-step transitions are only permitted from n to $n-1$ or $n+1$. Further, let the arrival and departure rates when the system is in state n be denoted by λ_n and μ_n, respectively. Also let the probability that the state of the system at time t is n be $p_n(t)$.

Consider the time interval $(t, t+\delta t)$. There are three possibilities that at time $t+\delta t$ the state of the system is n: first, that there were n customers in the system at time t and no arrivals occurred during the interval; second, there were $n-1$ customers at t and one arrival occurred in the interval; and third, there were $n+1$ customers and one departure. The probability that the state of the system is n at the end of the interval is therefore given by

$$
\begin{aligned}
p_n(t+\delta t) = \ &p_n(t)p_{n,n}(t,t+\delta t) \\
&+p_{n-1}(t)p_{n-1,n}(t,t+\delta t) \\
&+p_{n+1}(t)p_{n+1,n}(t,t+\delta t)
\end{aligned}
\tag{3.75}
$$

where each of the first three terms on the right-hand side correspond with the three possibilities described and $p_{i,j}(t,t+\delta t)$ is the probability that the system ends up in state i at a time $t+\delta t$, given that it was in state j at time t. Since it is impossible to have a negative number of customers, we must add the condition $n>0$ so that the subscript in the second term on the right-hand side remains positive. For $n=0$ we have

$$
p_0(t+\delta t) = p_0(t)p_{0,0}(t,t+\delta t) + p_1(t)p_{1,0}(t,t+\delta t)
\tag{3.76}
$$

Now the probabilities $p_{i,j}(t,t+\delta t)$ are given by

$$p_{i,j}(t,t+\delta t) = \begin{cases} 0 & \text{for } j+1 < i < j-1 \\ \lambda_j \delta t + o(\delta t) & \text{for } i = j+1 \\ \mu_j \delta t + o(\delta t) & \text{for } i = j-1 \\ [1-\lambda_j \delta t + o(\delta t)][1-\mu_j \delta t + o(\delta t)] & \text{for } i = j \end{cases} \tag{3.77}$$

where the first condition results from the fact that the system is described by a birth-death process, the second condition is the probability that a birth occurs, the third is the probability of a death, and the fourth is the case when the population remains the same. As before $o(\delta t)$ becomes negligible compared with δt as $\delta t \to 0$.

Using Eq. (3.77) in Eqs. (3.75) and (3.76) and simplifying we obtain

$$\begin{aligned} p_n(t+\delta t) &= p_n(t)[1-(\lambda_n + \mu_n)\delta t] \\ &\quad + p_{n-1}(t)\lambda_{n-1}\delta t \\ &\quad + p_{n+1}(t)\mu_{n+1}\delta t + o(\delta t) \end{aligned} \tag{3.78}$$

for $n > 0$ and

$$\begin{aligned} p_0(t+\delta t) &= p_0(t)(1-\lambda_0 \delta t) \\ &\quad + p_1(t)\mu_1 \delta t + o(\delta t) \end{aligned} \tag{3.79}$$

for $n = 0$. By subtracting $p_n(t)$ and dividing by δt Eqs. (3.78) and (3.79) can be expressed as two differential equations that describe the transient behavior of the system as follows

$$\begin{aligned} \frac{dp_n(t)}{dt} &= \lambda_{n-1}p_{n-1}(t) - (\lambda_n + \mu_n)p_n(t) + \mu_{n+1}p_{n+1}(t) \\ \frac{dp_0(t)}{dt} &= -\lambda_0 p_0(t) + \mu_1 p_1(t) \end{aligned} \tag{3.80}$$

These equations are known as the birth-death equations and they are used in a great number of applications from a variety of disciplines in science and engineering. The time-dependent behavior of the system state is thus obtained from the solution of Eqs. (3.80) along with the law of total probability and some initial conditions.

It is informative to look at a more intuitive method for deriving the birth-death equations by inspecting the state transition diagram. This is a method that will be used frequently in this text. The state transition diagram for the birth-death model is depicted in Figure 3.9.

Each of the ellipses in the figure represents a system state and the arrows to and from each state represent a state transition. The labels on each arrow correspond to the previous definitions of the arrival and departure rates. The rate of change of the probability that the system can be found in state 0 is the difference between the flow into state 0, given by $\mu_1 p_1(t)$, and the flow out $\lambda_0 p_0(t)$. The flow to and from state n is

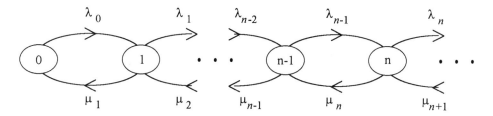

Figure 3.9 State transition diagram for the birth-death process.

given by

flow rate into $n = \lambda_{n-1}p_{n-1}(t) + \mu_{n+1}p_{n+1}(t)$ (3.81)

flow rate out of $n = (\lambda_n + \mu_n)p_n(t)$ (3.82)

and the birth-death equations follow.

To illustrate a simple application of the birth-death equations consider a source of communication traffic. We will model the source as a pure birth process for which all the μ_n are zero. Further we will assume that the traffic is generated at a constant rate such that $\lambda_n = \lambda$ for all n. In this case Eqs. (3.80) become

$$\frac{dp_n(t)}{dt} = \lambda p_{n-1}(t) - \lambda p_n(t)$$
$$\frac{dp_0(t)}{dt} = -\lambda p_0(t)$$ (3.83)

Assume that at $t = 0$ the source has generated no traffic and the initial condition is given by $p_0(0) = 1$. We can solve for $p_0(t)$ from the second differential equation in (3.83) and the initial condition to obtain

$$p_0(t) = e^{-\lambda t}$$ (3.84)

Using standard methods to solve the first equation in (3.83) we obtain, by induction,

$$p_n(t) = \frac{(\lambda t)^n}{n!} e^{-\lambda t}$$ (3.85)

Now Eq. (3.84) tells us that the inter-generation time for traffic is exponentially distributed and Eq. (3.85) dictates that the amount of traffic is generated according to the Poisson distribution. Hence a traffic source that is modeled as a pure birth process with a homogeneous generation rate is Markovian and the intimate relationship between Poisson and exponential variables is demonstrated again.

3.3.2 The Steady-State Solution

The solution of the birth-death equations becomes more complex when the assumptions about arrival and departure rates are relaxed. Further, the amount of information that is provided by their solution may be surplus to the requirements of a system analysis. For example, in order to assess the efficiency of two systems it may be sufficient to qualitatively compare their expected states over a long period of time. If we assume that steady-state conditions exist, the solution of the birth-death equations is straightforward and this can provide more succinct information regarding the performance of communication systems.

In steady state, the rate of change of the probability that the system exists with a particular value of n is zero or

$$\lim_{t \to \infty} \frac{dp_n(t)}{dt} = 0 \qquad (3.86)$$

Intuitively this means that, over a long period of time, the flow into a particular state is equal to the flow out of that state. It follows from this argument that if the flow rates were not equal, a steady-state solution does not exist and the system is said to be unstable.

Using Eq. (3.86) in the birth-death equations we obtain the result

$$0 = \lambda_{n-1} p_{n-1} - (\lambda_n + \mu_n) p_n + \mu_{n+1} p_{n+1}$$
$$0 = -\lambda_0 p_0 + \mu_1 p_1 \qquad (3.87)$$

where the dependency on t has been dropped from the $p_n(t)$s. From the second of these equations we obtain

$$p_1 = \frac{\lambda_0}{\mu_1} p_0 \qquad (3.88)$$

From Eq. (3.85) we obtain, by induction,

$$p_n = \frac{\lambda_0 \lambda_1 \lambda_2 \cdots \lambda_{n-1}}{\mu_1 \mu_2 \cdots \mu_n} p_0 \qquad (3.89)$$

Now from the law of total probability we have

$$\sum_{n=0}^{\infty} p_n = 1 \qquad (3.90)$$

and we can solve for all the p_n using this result with Eq (3.89). It may be easily shown that p_0 is given by rearranging Eq (3.89), expressed in terms of a product, and using Eq (3.90), as

$$p_0 = \frac{1}{1 + \sum\limits_{n=0}^{\infty} \prod\limits_{i=0}^{n-1} \frac{\lambda_i}{\mu_{i+1}}}$$

(3.91)

We have already stated that in order for the steady-state solution to exist the flow of the system into a particular state must equal the flow out as $t \to \infty$. Perhaps less precisely, though more accessible, the condition for stability may be expressed as follows. First, the probability that there are no customers in the system has to be greater than zero; in other words, it must be empty for at least some of the time, and so $p_0 > 0$. Naturally we also require that $p_0 \leq 1$. Then, from Eq. (3.91)

$$0 < \frac{1}{S} \leq 1$$

(3.92)

where

$$S = 1 + \sum_{n=0}^{\infty} \prod_{i=0}^{n-1} \frac{\lambda_i}{\mu_{i+1}}$$

(3.93)

which requires that the series converges.

A number of simple examples will illustrate the usefulness of the steady-state, or equilibrium, solution to the birth-death equations. Consider what happens when the system state cannot exceed a given value. Such is the case for a buffered network node that is being modeled using the number of packets in the buffer for the state variable. Let the buffer size be m and assume a homogeneous system for which the arrival and departure rates are the same, irrespective of the system state, and equal to λ and μ, respectively. In this case we have

$$\lambda_n = \begin{cases} \lambda & \text{for } n < m \\ 0 & \text{otherwise} \end{cases}$$

(3.94)

in order that no packets are generated when the buffer is full, and

$$\mu_n = \mu \quad \text{for } n = 1, 2, 3, \ldots, m$$

(3.95)

Note that in Eq. (3.94) $\lambda_n = 0$ for $n \geq m$ because the state variable has a maximum value of m and not because the arrival rate actually changes. Putting Eqs. (3.94) and (3.95) in Eq. (3.89) gives

$$p_n = \frac{\lambda^n}{\mu^n} p_0 \quad \text{for } n < m$$

(3.96)

and obviously $p_n = 0$ otherwise. Now, often the ratio λ/μ is known as the traffic intensity and it is represented by the symbol ρ. Hence from Eq. (3.93) we obtain

$$S = 1 + \sum_{n=0}^{m} \rho^n \qquad (3.97)$$

which is finite and so satisfies the condition for stability. Incidentally, when the state space for the homogeneous system is infinite and $\rho > 1$ the series is divergent and the queue is unstable. This result is intuitive since in order for the traffic intensity to exceed unity we must have $\lambda > \mu$, whence the arrival rate exceeds the departure rate and the system state grows without limit.

Returning to the finite state space example there is a poignant result that is worth noting. It is the result for p_n, which is obtained as follows. Using Eqs. (3.91), (3.93), and (3.97) we have

$$p_0 = \frac{1-\rho}{1-\rho^{m+1}} \qquad (3.98)$$

Also, from Eq. (3.96)

$$p_n = \rho^n p_0 \quad \text{for } n < m \qquad (3.99)$$

So combining the last two equations we have

$$p_n = \frac{(1-\rho)\rho^n}{1-\rho^{m+1}} \qquad (3.100)$$

Putting $n = m$ in this equation gives the probability that the system is full, which is directly proportional to the amount of time that the system spends in this state and the number of customers that are rejected. As was stated previously, even though the buffer is full, there are still new arrivals and, because there is no room for them to be stored, they are rejected. Hence the packet loss probability for a buffered communication node that is modeled using the homogeneous birth-death process is easily calculated.

A system designer may decide that the loss probability is too high and build in some defense mechanism. One method for reducing the loss probability is to discourage the packet arrivals. A flow control procedure would have to be implemented by the engineer. This system can be modeled using a non-homogeneous birth-death process with the λ_n chosen to be a reducing function of n using

$$\lambda_n = \lambda f(n) \qquad (3.101)$$

For example, if we look at the special case where the generation rate is discouraged by a factor $1/n + 1$ when there are currently n packets in the buffer we have

$$\lambda_n = \frac{\lambda}{n+1} \tag{3.102}$$

In this case it is assumed that the buffer is infinitely large. This will never be the case, however, in many cases such an assumption may be acceptable. Here we are surmising that the buffer is large enough so that the rejection probability is negligible. Equation (3.89) becomes

$$p_n = \frac{\lambda^n}{n!\,\mu^n}\, p_0 \tag{3.103}$$

Using the law of total probability and replacing λ/μ with ρ it is easy to show that for the probability of the system being empty we obtain

$$p_0 = e^{-\rho} \tag{3.104}$$

Replacing p_0 in Eq. (3.103) with the expression in Eq. (3.104) we obtain

$$p_n = \frac{\rho^n}{n!}\, e^{-\rho} \tag{3.105}$$

which, yet again, is the Poisson distribution with parameter ρ. Interestingly the same result is obtained for the system that is modeled using $\lambda_n = \lambda$ and $\mu_n = n\mu$. As we have already seen, once the probability distribution for the system states are known, a number of performance parameters may be calculated. These two examples have served to illustrate the use of birth-death equations for modeling the traffic in a communications system. The next section systematically deals with the queues that are modeled as birth-death processes.

3.4 ELEMENTARY QUEUEING THEORY

3.4.1 The *M/M/1* Queue

The $M/M/1$ queue is a birth-death process with $\lambda_n = \lambda$ for all n, $\mu_n = \mu$ for $n = 1, 2, 3, \ldots$, and $\mu_0 = 0$. The condition $\mu_0 = 0$ corresponds with the situation where the death rate in a system with no population is zero. The transient behavior of the $M/M/1$ queue can therefore be obtained from the time-dependent birth-death equations. In the previous section we looked at the special case when the death rates are zero, however, in this case the solution is quite complex and is beyond the scope of this text. The equilibrium solution is more tractable and we will find that a number of points that were addressed in the previous section are relevant here.

Applying the conditions for the $M/M/1$ queue to the steady-state solution in Eqs. (3.89) and (3.91) we obtain

$$p_n = \left(\frac{\lambda}{\mu}\right)^n p_0 \qquad (3.106)$$

and

$$p_0 = \frac{1}{1 + \sum_{n=1}^{\infty}\left(\frac{\lambda}{\mu}\right)^n} \qquad (3.107)$$

Summing the series and rearranging we can write the following expression for p_0

$$p_0 = 1 - \frac{\lambda}{\mu} \qquad (3.108)$$

Now consider our model for a communication node in which λ and μ represent the arrival and departure rates for packets. In this case $\rho = \lambda/\mu$, being the traffic intensity, may be interpreted as the utilization of the communications channel, U. Thus Eq. (3.108) is exactly the same as Eq. (3.7), which was obtained in the first section, so the simple model we developed there is in fact the same as for the $M/M/1$ queue.

The model can be developed in a more formal manner using queueing theory terminology. The mean number of customers in the system, as before, is given by Eq. (3.9) and the result obtained in Eq. (3.11) may be rewritten, by replacing U with λ/μ, as

$$\overline{n} = \frac{\lambda}{\mu - \lambda} \qquad (3.109)$$

Now the number of customers in the system consists of customers waiting in the queue, or the occupancy, L, and customers that are being served. The value of L is obtained by realizing that when the system is in state $n \geq 1$ there will be one customer being served and we have

$$L = \sum_{n=1}^{\infty}(n-1)p_n \qquad (3.110)$$

Thus

$$L = \sum_{n=1}^{\infty}np_n - \sum_{n=1}^{\infty}p_n \qquad (3.111)$$

Noting that the first summation on the right-hand side of Eq. (3.111) is the same as the mean number of customers in the system, and using the fact that all the probabilities in the second summation plus p_0 must sum to one, we obtain

$$L = \bar{n} - (1 - p_0) = \frac{\rho}{1 - \rho} - \rho \qquad (3.112)$$

which may be rewritten in terms of the arrival and departure rates as

$$L = \frac{\lambda^2}{\mu(\mu - \lambda)} \qquad (3.113)$$

This expression may be derived intuitively if we realize the fact that the mean number of customers being served is the same as the utilization or traffic intensity ρ such that $\bar{n} = L + \rho$.

We turn our attention now to the total time a customer spends in the system. This is the waiting time, or queueing delay, plus the service time. The queueing delay is calculated by considering that upon arrival the system is in the state such that there are n customers already present in the queue. The distribution function for the queueing delay, $Q(t)$, being the probability that the queueing delay is less than or equal to t, may be derived as follows. We have

$$Q(t) = p_0 + \sum_{n=1}^{\infty} p_n \cdot P[n \text{ customers served in } (0,t) \; / \; n \text{ customers exist}] \qquad (3.114)$$

We already have expressions for p_0 and p_n in Eqs. (3.108) and (3.106), respectively. Now the probability distribution function for n customers being served in the interval $(0, x)$ was derived in Section 3.2.2. Thus using Eq. (3.69) with a mean service time $1/\mu$ this is given by

$$P[n \text{ customers served in } (0,t)] = \frac{\mu(\mu x)^n}{(n-1)!} e^{-\mu x} \qquad (3.115)$$

and the unknown probability in Eq. (3.114) is thus given by

$$P[n \text{ customers served in } (0,t)/ n \text{ customers exist}] = \int_0^t \frac{\mu(\mu x)^n}{(n-1)!} e^{-\mu x} dx \qquad (3.116)$$

Hence Eq. (3.114) becomes

$$Q(t) = (1 - \rho) + \sum_{n=1}^{\infty} \rho^n (1 - \rho) \int_0^t \frac{\mu(\mu x)^n}{(n-1)!} e^{-\mu x} dx \qquad (3.117)$$

which it may be shown simplifies to

$$Q(t) = 1 - \rho e^{-\mu t (1 - \rho)} \qquad (3.118)$$

We can now derive an expression for the density distribution of the total delay, $d(t)$, which is the convolution of the density distributions for the queueing and service times. The density distribution for the queueing time is the derivative of Eq. (3.118) given by

$$q(t) = \delta(t)(1-\rho) + \lambda(1-\rho)e^{-\mu t(1-\rho)} \tag{3.119}$$

where $\delta(t)$ is the dirac-delta function, which has the property

$$\int_{t=0}^{\infty} \delta(t)dt = 1$$

and we have accounted for the fact that the probability that the queueing time is zero is equal to $(1-\rho)$. The service times for the $M/M/1$ queueing system are by definition exponentially distributed, and we can therefore write the following equation for the density of the total delay

$$d(t) = (1-\rho)\mu e^{-\mu t} + \int_{0}^{t} \lambda(1-\rho)e^{-\mu(t-\tau)(1-\rho)}\mu e^{-\mu\tau}d\tau \tag{3.120}$$

The right-hand side is easily simplified to give

$$d(t) = (\mu-\lambda)e^{-(\mu-\lambda)t} \tag{3.121}$$

Hence the total delay has an exponential distribution function with parameter $(\mu-\lambda)$. Since the algebraic sums of exponentially distributed random variables are themselves exponentially distributed, this result is reasonable. The mean value is thus given by

$$\overline{d} = \frac{1}{\mu-\lambda} \tag{3.122}$$

and replacing one of the terms in the denominator with ρ it is easily shown that

$$\overline{d} = \frac{\overline{n}}{\lambda} \tag{3.123}$$

and we have verified Little's result for this particular queueing system. So with hindsight we could have obtained Eq. (3.122) using Little's result in Eq. (3.109), as in fact we did in the first section.

In summary then the parameters of the $M/M/1$ queue queueing system in equilibrium—namely, total delay and queueing delay—may be easily calculated provided the condition for stability is satisfied for any given values of mean arrival and departure rates. In some applications it is more realistic to consider what happens when the queueing system may only store a certain number of customers. This queue is denoted by $M/M/1/k$ queue. This is known as a loss system because customers arriving at a full facility are lost.

3.4.2 The $M/M/m/k$ Queue

More generally there may be m servers so that up to m customers may be in service at any one time. In this case the birth and death rates are given by

$$\lambda_n = \begin{cases} \lambda & \text{for } n < k \\ 0 & \text{otherwise} \end{cases} \tag{3.124}$$

and

$$\mu_n = \begin{cases} n\mu & \text{for } 0 < n < m \\ m\mu & \text{for } m \le n < k \end{cases} \tag{3.125}$$

where we are reasonably assuming that the number of servers is less than the total system capacity, $m < k$. Utilizing Eq. (3.89) we obtain

$$p_n = \begin{cases} \dfrac{\lambda^n}{\mu^n} \dfrac{1}{m!(k-m)m} p_0 & \text{for } n \le k \\ 0 & \text{for } n > k \end{cases} \tag{3.126}$$

As usual the p_ns must sum to one and we can write

$$p_0 = \frac{1}{1 + \displaystyle\sum_{n=1}^{k} \dfrac{\lambda^n}{\mu^n} \dfrac{1}{m!(k-m)m}} \tag{3.127}$$

As we stated earlier one of the characteristics of systems with a finite waiting room is the finite possibility that customers are lost. The probability that a customer arrives to find a full system is given by Eq. (3.126) with $n = k$. We have plotted the loss probability as a function of utilization for the $M/M/1/k$ queue in Figure 3.10. Note that the abscissa has a logarithmic scale and under low load conditions the loss probability is very small. The loss probability increases with smaller values of system capacity as expected.

The $M/M/m/m$ queue is a special case of the previous system for which the number of servers is equal to the capacity of the facility. This is another piece of queueing theory that is attributed to Erlang. Unfortunately we cannot simply put $k = m$ into the preceding analysis since the condition $k > m$ was imposed on the birth-death coefficients. Instead we begin with

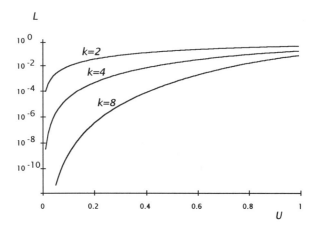

Figure 3.10 Loss probability as a function of utilization for the $M/M/1/k$ queue.

$$\lambda_n = \begin{cases} \lambda & \text{for } n < m \\ 0 & \text{otherwise} \end{cases} \qquad (3.128)$$

and

$$\mu_n = n\mu \quad \text{for } n = 1, 2, \ldots, m \qquad (3.129)$$

The reader is encouraged to verify (see Exercise 3.10) that

$$p_n = \begin{cases} \dfrac{\lambda^n}{\mu^n} \dfrac{1}{n!} p_0 & \text{for } n \le m \\ 0 & \text{for } n > m \end{cases} \qquad (3.130)$$

and the fact that the p_ns must sum to one give

$$p_0 = \dfrac{1}{\displaystyle\sum_{n=0}^{k} \dfrac{\lambda^n}{\mu^n} \dfrac{1}{n!}} \qquad (3.131)$$

Now the probability that the facility is full is given by Eq. (3.130) with $n = m$, and this is known as Erlangs B formula.[3] The loss probabilities are plotted in Figure 3.11.

We will illustrate the use of some of the results of the $M/M/m/k$ queue here with an example involving some kind of multiplexor that is connected to a communications line. Consider the possibility that the line may be utilized in time division multiplexing fashion with an overall capacity, or data transmission rate, of D bit/s. Let the number of channels be m, corresponding to the number of servers in the queueing model, such that the capacity of each channel is D/m bit/s. Assume

---

[3] Erlang's C formula is the result obtained for the $M/M/m/\infty$ queue.

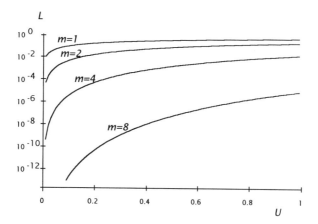

Figure 3.11 Erlangs B formula with $m = 1, 2, 4$ and 8.

exponentially distributed arrival times and message lengths so that we are justified in using the $M/M/m/k$ queue as a model. The source of the messages is an infinite population of terminals that are connected to the input side of the multiplexor. A schematic diagram of the system is illustrated in Figure 3.12.

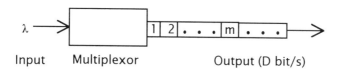

Figure 3.12 A multiplexor with m output channels.

The probability that the system is in state n is thus given by Eq. (3.126) and the average number of customers, or the expected state of the system, can be found using

$$E[n] = \sum_{n=0}^{\infty} n p_n \tag{3.132}$$

Replacing the p_ns we obtain

$$E[n] = \sum_{n=0}^{\infty} n \frac{\lambda^n}{\mu^n} \frac{1}{m!(k-m)m} p_0 \tag{3.133}$$

and the mean queueing delay is easily calculated using this equation and Little's result. In Figure 3.13 we plotted the mean delay as a function of utilization for one-, two-, three-, and five-channel TDM. The service time is calculated assuming an average message length of 1,000 bits and a data transmission rate of 10 Mbit/s. Characteristics in Figures 3.13(a) and 3.13(b) correspond to the cases for which the capacity of the buffer is 5 and 10 packets, respectively.

There is a larger mean delay when there are more channels because there is a greater amount of traffic accepted and the service time is proportionately longer. Similarly, the mean delays are greater when there is more storage capacity in the system. There is a reduction in the mean delay when the system is close to saturation because most of the traffic is rejected. The small portion of messages that are accepted are therefore likely to enter into service more quickly.

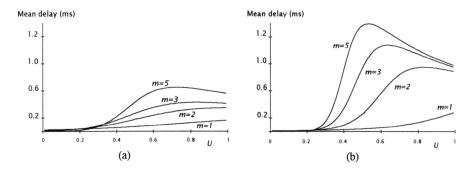

Figure 3.13 Mean delay for TDM with (a) capacity = 5 and (b) capacity = 10.

In Figure 3.14 we plotted the probability that the system is full, that is, when all servers (slots in the TDM stream) and the waiting room (buffers in the multiplexor) are occupied, for the 2- and 5-channel cases with capacities of 5 and 10. These characteristics relate directly to the probability that traffic is lost. Close to saturation, there is a greater chance that the system is fully occupied when most of the traffic is being accepted, and as expected this probability increases with the capacity and number of channels.

Consider what happens if the capacity is assumed to be infinite ($M/M/m$ queue). Deriving the probability distribution for the system state is left as an exercise for the reader. *Hint:* Calculating the mean system state may be simplified using the fact that

$$\sum_{n=m+1}^{\infty} n \left(\frac{\lambda}{\mu}\right)^n \frac{1}{m!m^{n-m}} = \frac{\lambda^{m+1}(\mu-\lambda+\mu m)m}{\mu^m(\mu m-\lambda)^2 m!} \tag{3.134}$$

An example of the results for the $M/M/m$ queue are given in Figure 3.15 where we compare the total mean delay, queueing plus service, versus throughput characteristics for a 50-kbit/s output line. The line is either utilized as a single channel at the full transmission rate or five channels operating at 10 kbit/s. The results for exponentially distributed message lengths with means of 1000 and 2000 bits are plotted in each case.

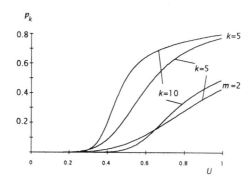

Figure 3.14 Occupancy probability for TDM.

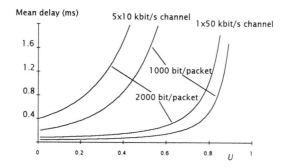

Figure 3.15 Mean delay for 5-channel TDM compared with single channel.

3.4.3 Finite Population $M/M/m/k/s$

A real system can have neither infinite capacity or infinite population source. As a final example of applications for the birth-death queueing systems we will derive the state probability distribution for the $M/M/m/k/s$ facility. Here we have s population sources and in order to simplify the analysis we will assume that $m \leq k \leq s$. Hence again we have the possibility that there may be more customers in the system than there are being served at any one time and customers arriving at the facility when it is in state k are lost. In this case we have

$$\lambda_n = \begin{cases} \lambda(s-n) & \text{for } 0 \leq n < s-1 \\ 0 & \text{otherwise} \end{cases} \tag{3.135}$$

because the sources act independently and when there are n customers in the system, either queueing or receiving service, there are $(s-n)$ sources generating packets at an average rate λ. Also

$$\mu_n = \begin{cases} n\mu & \text{for } 0 < n < m \\ m\mu & \text{for } m \leq n \end{cases} \qquad (3.136)$$

Using Eq. (3.89) we obtain, after some algebra,

$$P_n = \begin{cases} \left[\left(\dfrac{\lambda}{\mu}\right)^n \binom{s}{n} \right] p_0 & \text{for } 0 \leq n \leq m-1 \\ \left(\dfrac{\lambda}{\mu}\right)^n \binom{s}{n} \dfrac{n!}{m!} m^{m-n} p_0 & \text{for } m \leq n \leq k \end{cases} \qquad (3.137)$$

Using the fact that the p_ns must sum to one we obtain the following expression for p_0

$$p_0 = \left\{ \sum_{n=0}^{m-1} \left(\frac{\lambda}{\mu}\right)^n \binom{s}{n} + \sum_{n=m}^{k} \left(\frac{\lambda}{\mu}\right)^n \binom{s}{n} \frac{n!}{m!} m^{m-n} \right\}^{-1} \qquad (3.138)$$

and the probability that a customer arrives to find the system full is given by calculating p_k.

In Figure 3.16 we plotted the loss probability as a function of traffic intensity for (i) $M/M/1/1/1$, (ii) $M/M/1/1/2$, and (iii) $M/M/1/2/2$. The curves show that as the waiting room increases, the blocking probability is reduced over the whole range of traffic intensity, while if the number of servers is increased, then the blocking probability is only significantly reduced at low loads. In a similar fashion as before this analysis can be used to model a simple communications node with s incoming lines, buffer size k, and one outgoing line with m TDM channels.

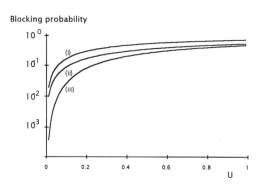

Figure 3.16 Blocking probability as a function of utilization for the $M/M/m/k/s$ queue.

3.5 MARKOV CHAINS

The queueing systems in the previous section were restricted to state transitions between nearest neighbors only. A Markov chain is a more general memoryless stochastic process that allows state transitions beyond the nearest neighbor. One application of this possibility in communications traffic analysis is the modeling of systems with batch arrival and departure processes. That is, where the system sate represents the number of packets in the system, then a batch arrival will result in a jump from one state to another, which is advanced from the previous by the size of the batch. Similarly for a system that may service more than one packet at a time, such as in frequency or wavelength division multiplexing, the state may be reduced by the number of frequency channels in one transition. In this section we begin with developing the $M/E_r/1$ queue, following the methods in Kleinrock [4], which provides the most simple model for constant size batch arrivals. The symbol E_r represents Erlangian service times, as given by Eq. (3.69). This is the complete service time for the r individual, exponentially distributed service times, as required for a message with r packets.

3.5.1 Fixed-Size Batch Arrivals

The quantity that represents the system state must now account for the number of service stages left to be completed by the customer that is currently being serviced. A convenient way of doing this is to consider the total number of stages yet to be completed by all of the customers in the system. If we denote this value by the symbol j, then the system state is given by

$$j = (n-1)r + (r-i+1) \tag{3.139}$$

where, as before, n is the number of customers in the system and the one in service has reached stage i. Hence the first term on the right-hand side of Eq. (3.139) is the total number of stages to be completed by the queueing customers and the second term is the number of stages remaining for the customer in service.

The probability flow balance equations may be deduced by inspecting the state transition diagram in Figure 3.17. Customers arrive at a rate λ in batches of size r. The mean departure rate from each state is $r\mu$, so the overall service time for a customer, being r-stage Erlangian, is $1/\mu$.

If the system is in equilibrium, from the flow into and out of state 0, we have

$$r\mu p_1 = \lambda p_0 \tag{3.140}$$

and the flow into and out of state j is described by

$$\lambda p_{j-r} + r\mu p_{j+1} = (\lambda + r\mu)p_j \tag{3.141}$$

We will use the method of z-transforms, as described in the appendix, to solve for the

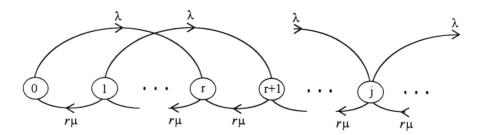

Figure 3.17 State transition diagram for fixed-size batch arrivals of size r.

p_j s. Multiplying both sides of Eq. (3.141) by z^j and summing over all j we obtain

$$\sum_{j=1}^{\infty} \lambda p_{j-r} z^j + \sum_{j=1}^{\infty} r\mu p_{j+1} z^j = \sum_{j=1}^{\infty} (\lambda + r\mu) p_j z^j \qquad (3.142)$$

With the intention of extracting terms for $P(z)$, Eq. (3.142) may be written as

$$\lambda z^r \sum_{j=1}^{\infty} p_{j-r} z^{j-r} + \frac{r\mu}{z} \sum_{j=1}^{\infty} p_{j+1} z^{j+1} = (\lambda + r\mu) \left\{ \sum_{j=0}^{\infty} p_j z^j - p_0 z^0 \right\} \qquad (3.143)$$

The first term on the left-hand side of Eq. (3.142) is equivalent to $\lambda z^r P(z)$ because we can add the term for $j = 0$ to the summation without affecting its value. In the second term, however, we must compensate for the first two terms of $P(z)$ and we thus obtain

$$\lambda z^r P(z) + \frac{r\mu}{z}[P(z) - p_0 z^0 - p_1 z^1] = (\lambda + r\mu)[P(z) - p_0] \qquad (3.144)$$

Rearranging Eq. (3.144) and replacing p_1 using Eq. (3.140), we obtain the equation

$$P(z) = \frac{r\mu p_0(1-z)}{r\mu + \lambda z^{r+1} - z(\lambda + r\mu)} \qquad (3.145)$$

From one of the properties of z-transforms, simply stated that the sum of the steady-state probabilities is one, we know that $P(1) = 1$. Hence using L'Hospital's rule,[4] Eq. (3.145) gives

---

[4] L'Hospital's rule states that if two functions, $f(x)$ and $g(x)$, are zero at the same point, x_0, and the quotient of their values after differentiating are nonzero at that point, then
$$\lim_{x \to x_0} \frac{f(x)}{g(x)} = \lim_{x \to x_0} \frac{f'(x)}{g'(x)} = \chi.$$

$$\frac{r\mu p_0}{(r+1)\lambda - \lambda - r\mu} = 1 \qquad (3.146)$$

Substituting the expression for p_0 obtained using Eq. (3.146) into Eq. (3.145) gives

$$P(z) = \frac{r\mu(1-\lambda/\mu)(1-z)}{r\mu + \lambda z^{r+1} - z(\lambda + r\mu)} \qquad (3.147)$$

We now need to invert the transform which may be carried out using partial fractions. First, by the last factor in the numerator, we can see that one of the roots is given by $z = 1$. Dividing the denominator by $(1-z)$ leaves the expression $r\mu - \lambda(z - z^{r+1})/(1-z)$. Let the remaining r roots be denoted by $z_1, z_2, ..., z_r$. Then Eq. (3.147) may be rewritten, dividing through by $r\mu(1-z)$, as

$$P(z) = \frac{(1-\lambda/\mu)}{(1-z/z_1)(1-z/z_2)\cdots(1-z/z_r)} \qquad (3.148)$$

where $z_1, z_2, ..., z_r$ are the roots of

$$1 - \lambda(z - z^{r+1})/r\mu(1-z) = 0 \qquad (3.149)$$

Equation (3.148) may now be expanded using partial fractions as

$$P(z) = (1-\lambda/\mu)\sum_{i=1}^{r}\frac{A_i}{(1-z/z_i)} \qquad (3.150)$$

where $A_i = \prod_{\substack{j=1 \\ j\neq i}}^{r}\frac{1}{(1-z_i/z_j)} \qquad (3.151)$

is a constant. Using the fact that the z-transform of $A\alpha^j$ is $A/(1-\alpha z)$, inverting Eq. (3.150) gives

$$p_j = (1-\lambda/\mu)\sum_{i=1}^{r}\frac{A_i}{z_i^{\,j}} \qquad (3.152)$$

Thus we have obtained the solution for the steady-state distribution of the number of stages left in the system. We are more likely to be interested in the probabilities of the number of customers, n, which is easily calculated using

$$p_n = \sum_{j=(n-1)r+1}^{nr} p_j \qquad (3.153)$$

This is simply the sum of the probabilities that the nth customer is somewhere in the system. Using this value we can go on to calculate the performance metrics of interest. A simple example will provide a useful illustration at this point.

For $r = 1$, from Eq. (3.147), we obtain

$$P(z) = \frac{\mu(1-\lambda/\mu)(1-z)}{\mu + \lambda z^2 - \lambda z - \mu z} \tag{3.154}$$

which is easily simplified and inverted to give

$$P_j = \left(1 - \frac{\lambda}{\mu}\right)\left(\frac{\lambda}{\mu}\right)^j \tag{3.155}$$

Clearly in this case, and as may be verified by inspecting Eq. (3.139), the number of stages remaining in the system is equivalent to the number of customers in the system. Hence, $n = j$ and, as should have been expected, we obtain the same result as for the $M/M/1$ queue. If r is greater than one we have to find the roots $z_1, z_2, \ldots, z_r$ of Eq. (3.149), which may be written

$$\left(z + z^2 + \cdots + z^r\right) - \frac{2\mu}{\lambda} = 0 \tag{3.156}$$

For $r = 2$ values of z_1 and z_2 are easily found as the roots of a quadratic equation. When $r = 3$ the roots are given by

$$z_1 = s_1 + s_2 - \frac{1}{3} \tag{3.157}$$

and

$$z_{2,3} = -\frac{1}{2}(s_1 + s_2) - \frac{1}{3} \pm i \frac{\sqrt{3}}{2}(s_1 - s_2) \tag{3.158}$$

where

$$s_{1,2} = \left[q \pm \left(p^3 + q^2\right)^{\frac{1}{2}}\right]^{\frac{1}{3}} \tag{3.159}$$

Here we have $p = 2/9$ and $q = (1 + 9\mu/\lambda)/6 - 1/27$.

This model is suitable for representing a buffer that accepts data as messages consisting of r variable-length packets arriving at random and releases them at a fixed transmission rate. In Figure 3.18 we plotted the mean delay, calculated using the mean number of messages in the system, from the distribution obtained using Eq. (3.153) and

Little's result, as a function of traffic intensity. The service time was calculated assuming a data transmission rate of 10 Mbit/s. As we saw in Section 3.2.2 the sum of independent, exponentially distributed variables is Erlang distributed, and it is correct to say that the message lengths are Erlang distributed. After all, the model is that of a queue with Erlang-distributed service times. Hence if the mean packet length is l, then the mean message length is rl.

The characteristics for message lengths of 1, 2, and 3 packets show that, as expected, the delay steadily increases. An infinite buffer is assumed in this model and, since there are no rejections or losses, as the system saturates the delay will increase to infinity in sympathy with the queue occupancy. As the traffic intensity increases the mean delay for larger messages is reduced because the individual packets arrive in a more orderly fashion. It should not be expected that the improvement will be significant, however, and this is shown in the results obtained.

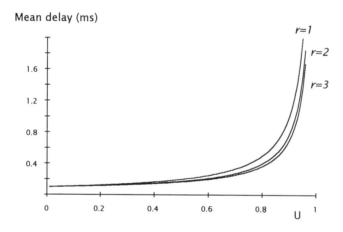

Figure 3.18 Mean delay as a function of load for fixed-length messages.

When applying the results of queueing theory to real applications it is important to understand exactly what is being modeled. In the analysis of the $M/E_r/1$ queue above the arrival rate, λ, is the number of batches of size r arriving in unit time. Hence in the example this equates to messages per second. Similarly, the departure rate, μ, equates to the number of messages served per second. In the example we calculated λ and μ such that the mean message length was 1,000 bits, irrespective of the batch size. Hence the mean packet length for the case $r = 3$ in this example is $1,000/3$ bits.

Note that the mean delay in Figure 3.18 is that of messages and not individual packets. At low traffic loads the most significant contribution to delay is the service time. Hence the service time is that required to transmit a message, which is 0.1 ms in this example.

The characteristics in Figure 3.19 were obtained using the same analysis as previously. Again the results are based on a data transmission rate of 10 Mbit/s. This time the arrival and departure rates were calculated such that the mean packet length was 1,000 bits. Hence the mean message lengths in this case are 1,000, 2,000, and 3,000 bits corresponding to the cases for which $r = 1, 2$, and 3, respectively. The mean message service times are therefore 0.1, 0.2, and 0.3 ms and the low load delays obtained confirm this.

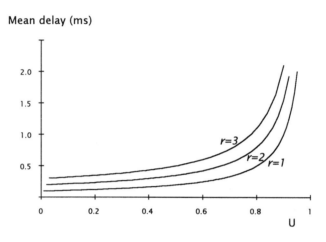

Figure 3.19 Mean delay as a function of load for fixed-length packets.

3.5.2 Fixed-Size Batch Service

This kind of model may be suitable for analyzing systems that wait until a certain message size is reached before releasing the data for transmission. The $E_r / M / 1$ queue provides a model for such analysis. In this case the Erlangian-distributed arrival process describes a message source with fixed-length batch sizes being generated in a completely random fashion. The service of a particular message cannot begin until all of its constituent parts have been generated, or arrived, and only one complete message may be served at any one time.

As before we take the state of the system to be the number of stages left to be completed. In this case we mean this to be the number of stages at arrival and this is given by

$$j = rn + i - 1 \qquad (3.160)$$

where r is the batch size, as defined previously, n is the number of customers that have already arrived, and i is the number of arrival stages already completed by the customer that is currently arriving.

From the state transition diagram, which is depicted in Figure 3.20, the balance of probability flow to and from state 0 when the system is in equilibrium gives

$$\mu p_r = r\lambda p_0 \tag{3.161}$$

When the system is in states $0 < j < r$ we have

$$\mu p_{j+r} + r\lambda p_{j-1} = r\lambda p_j \tag{3.162}$$

and for $j \geq r$

$$\mu p_{j+r} + r\lambda p_{j-1} = r\lambda p_j + \mu p_j \tag{3.163}$$

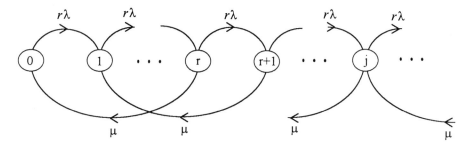

Figure 3.20 State transition diagram for fixed-size batch service.

So we begin the process of obtaining the steady-state solution by deducing the z-transform. Multiplying Eqs. (3.162) and (3.163) by z^j and summing over corresponding ranges of j we obtain

$$\sum_{j=1}^{\infty} \mu p_{j+r} z^j + \sum_{j=1}^{\infty} r\lambda p_{j-1} z^j = \sum_{j=1}^{\infty} (\mu + r\lambda) p_j z^j - \sum_{j=1}^{r-1} \mu p_j z^j \tag{3.164}$$

The second summation on the right-hand side of Eq. (3.164) compensates for the terms added to the first summation on the same side. Collecting terms we obtain

$$\frac{\mu}{z^r}\left[P(z) - \sum_{j=0}^{r} p_j z^j \right] + r\lambda z P(z) = (\mu + r\lambda)[P(z) - p_0] \tag{3.165}$$

Rearranging Eq. (3.165), substituting for p_0 using Eqs. (3.161), and substituting λ/μ with ρ, we obtain

$$P(z)\{r\rho z^{r+1} - (1+r\rho)z^r + 1\} = \sum_{j=0}^{r-1} p_j z^j - z^r \sum_{j=0}^{r-1} p_j z^j \tag{3.166}$$

Hence the z-transform of the steady-state distribution is given by

$$P(z) = \frac{\left(1 - z^r\right)\sum\limits_{j=0}^{r-1} p_j z^j}{\left(r\rho z^{r+1} - (1 + r\rho) z^r + 1\right)} \tag{3.167}$$

As before, in the next step of the solution, we look to invert the transform by expanding into partial fractions. First we can eliminate the summation of $(r-1)$ unknown probabilities in the numerator of Eq. (3.167) as follows. The denominator has $r+1$ roots, one of which is obviously $z = 1$. Using Rouche's theorem it can be shown that one of the other roots, say z_0, is such that $|z_0| > 1$ and the remaining $(r-1)$ zeroes lie in the region $|z| < 1$.[5] Now the z-transform of a probability distribution must be analytic in the range $|z| < 1$ so that anywhere the denominator is zero, so must the numerator. Only the second factor in the numerator can possibly equal zero at any place other than $z = 1$. Hence Eq. (3.167) may be written as

$$P(z) = \frac{\left(1 - z^r\right) k}{(1 - z)(1 - z/z_0)} \tag{3.168}$$

where k is the constant that remains behind as a result of canceling the summation with the $(r-1)$ factors representing the zeros of the denominator and is given by

$$k = \frac{\sum\limits_{j=0}^{r-1} p_j z^j}{(1 - z/z_1)(1 - z/z_2)\cdots(1 - z/z_{r-1})} \tag{3.169}$$

The value of k may be obtained using the fact that $P(1) = 1$. Using L'Hospital's rule, Eq. (3.168) gives

$$k = \frac{1}{r}(1 - 1/z_0) \tag{3.170}$$

and we obtain $P(z)$ in a form suitable for applying partial fractions as

$$P(z) = \frac{(1 - z^r)(1 - 1/z_0)}{r(1 - z)(1 - z/z_0)} \tag{3.171}$$

Hence using partial fractions, after factoring the rth-degree polynomial we obtain

---

[5] Rouche's theorem states that if two functions, $f(x)$ and $g(x)$, are both analytic on and within a closed contour, C, and also if $|f(x)| < |g(x)|$ on C, then $f(x)$ and $f(x) + g(x)$ have the same number of zeros inside C.

$$P(z) = \frac{(1-z^r)}{r} \left\{ \frac{1}{(1-z)} - \frac{1/z_0}{(1-z/z_0)} \right\} \tag{3.172}$$

This expression can be inverted using the fact that if $F(z)$ is the z-transform of the series f_n, then $z^r F(z)$ is the transform of f_{n-r}. It can be shown that for $j \geq r$

$$P_j = \frac{1}{r} z_0^{r-j-1} (1-z_0^{-r}) \tag{3.173}$$

while for $0 \leq j < r$ we have that $z^r P(z) = 0$ and we obtain

$$P_j = \frac{1}{r} (1 - z_0^{-j-1}) \tag{3.174}$$

Now the probability that there are n customers in the system is equivalent to the sum of the probabilities that there are between rn and $r(n+1)-1$ arrival states, inclusive, remaining in the facility. Thus we have

$$P_n = \sum_{j=rn}^{r(n+1)-1} P_j \tag{3.175}$$

Substituting Eqs. (3.173) and (3.174) into Eq. (3.175) we obtain

$$P_n = \begin{cases} \displaystyle\sum_{j=rn}^{r(n+1)-1} \frac{1}{r} z_0^{r-j-1} (1-z_0^{-r}) & \text{for } n > 0 \\ \displaystyle\sum_{j=0}^{r-1} \frac{1}{r} (1-z_0^{-j-1}) & \text{for } n = 0 \end{cases} \tag{3.176}$$

Using the fact that the denominator of Eq. (3.167) is zero when $z = z_0$ we get $1 - z_0^{-r} = r\rho(z_0 - 1)$ and the summations in Eq. (3.176) may be simplified to give

$$P_n = \begin{cases} \rho z_0^{-rn} (z_0^r - 1) & \text{for } n > 0 \\ 1 - \rho & \text{for } n = 0 \end{cases} \tag{3.177}$$

We are now in a position to illustrate the use of the $E_r / M / 1$ queueing system in an example. Note that, as was the case for the $M / E_r / 1$ queue, with $r = 1$ the system is the same as for $M / M / 1$ and these results are already at hand. For $r = 2$ the root z_0 is the one found to be in the region $|z| > 1$, obtained from the solution of the quadratic given by equating the denominator of Eq. (3.167) with zero, after factoring the term $(1-z)$. Similarly for $r = 3$ we take the simple root of the cubic equation obtained from the denominator.

Whereas the $M / E_r / 1$ queue is suitable for modeling traffic sources, or buffers, with batch arrivals, the $E_r / M / 1$ queue is suitable for modeling a buffer with batch service. In the example of the previous section, the arrival and departure rates for Figure 3.18 were chosen such that the mean message length was 1000 bits for each of the message sizes of 1, 2, and 3 packets. The equivalent characteristics for a source that generates packets and releases them in batches of 1, 2, and 3 packets is presented in Figure 3.21. It may be observed that the results for each of the models are similar. In fact, when they are superimposed there is very little difference. This outcome is reasonable since there may be little difference between the delay incurred by messages that are constructed as packets arriving in a queue, which is effectively what happens in the $M / E_r / 1$ model, or in service, which is what happens in the $E_r / M / 1$ case.

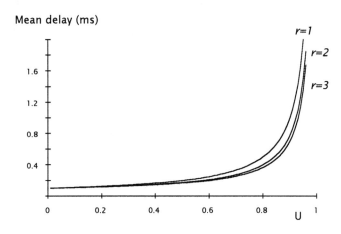

Figure 3.21 Mean delay as a function of load with batch service.

In Figure 3.22 we compare the mean delay characteristics of the two models for batches of 2 and 3 packets when the message lengths are 2000 and 3000 bits. Again, at low loads, the mean message delay is dominated by the service time and this is the same for each of the two cases. With a data transmission rate of 10 Mbit/s the service time for 2000- and 3000-bit messages is 0.2 and 0.3 ms. The characteristics are quite similar, and as before there is no apparent reason to expect that this situation is unreasonable.

3.5.3 General-Sized Batch Arrivals

In some communications the size of batches will not be a constant. Speech, for example, consists of so-called talk-spurts and quiet periods that have random time durations. Hence a period of digitized speech consists of a variable number of bits. In recent years there has been some effort dedicated to the task of utilizing the quiet periods in the voice channels of integrated service networks. Even the least adventurous data communications systems in use, however, require the transmission of unpredictable

Mean delay (ms)

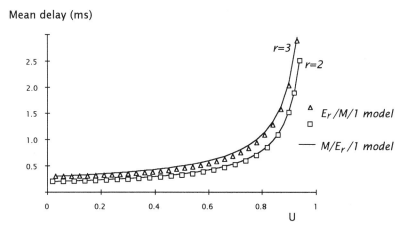

Figure 3.22 Comparison of delays for batch arrivals and service.

message lengths. Thus, in general, batch arrival and departure sizes may vary and the analysis of such systems is of interest.

Consider the arrival process, which may be described as follows. Customers arrive in batches at instants in time that are exponentially distributed. The size of a batch is governed by the probabilities

$$g_i = \Pr[\text{ batch size } = i \,] \tag{3.178}$$

The shorthand notation for the service times of a queue with geometrically distributed batch sizes may be taken as M^{geom}. Again, let the system state, n, represent the number of customers present in the facility at any given time. The state transition diagram for the system is depicted in Figure 3.23.

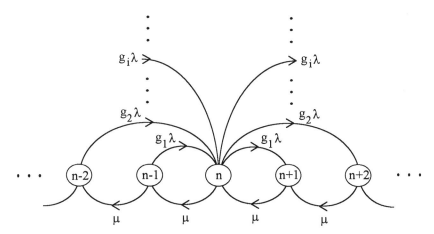

Figure 3.23 State transition diagram for the general-sized batch arrival system.

The analysis may be carried out in the same fashion as for the $M/E_r/1$ queue, beginning with writing the probability flow balance equations. By inspecting Figure 3.23 we can write these as follows. First, at the state $n = 0$, the total departure rate is given by the sum of all the $g_i \lambda$, which, due to the fact that all the g_i sum to one, is simply λ. Thus we have

$$\lambda p_0 = \mu p_1 \tag{3.179}$$

Similarly the departure and arrival rates due to the arrival process for any state n is also λ and therefore we have

$$(\lambda + \mu) p_n = \mu p_{n+1} + \lambda \sum_{i=0}^{n-1} g_{n-i} p_i \tag{3.180}$$

In order to solve these equations using z-transforms we multiply by z^n and sum over all n. Thus from Eq. (3.180) we obtain

$$\sum_{n=1}^{\infty} (\lambda + \mu) p_n z^n = \sum_{n=1}^{\infty} \mu p_{n+1} z^n + \lambda \sum_{n=1}^{\infty} \sum_{i=0}^{n-1} g_{n-i} p_i z^n \tag{3.181}$$

Now in order to extract $P(z)$ from the double summation we must change the order of execution. The region of summation is the shaded area of the sketch in Figure 3.24. From the figure we can see that

$$\sum_{n=1}^{\infty} \sum_{i=0}^{n-1} \equiv \sum_{i=0}^{\infty} \sum_{n=i+1}^{\infty} \tag{3.182}$$

and Eq. (3.181) may be rewritten, putting $j = n - i$, as

$$\sum_{n=1}^{\infty} (\lambda + \mu) p_n z^n = \sum_{n=1}^{\infty} \mu p_{n+1} z^n + \lambda \sum_{i=0}^{\infty} p_i z^i \sum_{j=0}^{\infty} g_j z^j \tag{3.183}$$

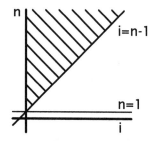

Figure 3.24 The region of summation.

Note that in allowing the lower limit of the final summation of the terms in g_i to be zero we have assumed that no arrivals are permitted when the system is in transit to state zero. Hence writing the z-transform of the probability distribution for the batch size as

$$G(z) = \sum_{j=0}^{\infty} g_j z^j \tag{3.184}$$

and collecting the terms in p_n we obtain

$$(\lambda + \mu)\{P(z) - p_0\} = \frac{\mu}{z}\{P(z) - p_0 - zp_1\} + \lambda P(z)G(z) \tag{3.185}$$

which may be rearranged as

$$P(z) = \frac{\mu(1-z)p_0}{\mu(1-z) - \lambda z[1 - G(z)]} \tag{3.186}$$

As before we can use L'Hospital's rule to find p_0 and we obtain $(1 - \lambda/\mu)$ for this.

At this stage we are now looking to arrange the expression for $P(z)$ into a form that may be inverted. In order to carry out this step we require a specification of $G(z)$. In order to continue with the development we will assume that the batch sizes follow a geometric distribution with parameter q. In this case we have

$$g_i = q^i(1-q) \tag{3.187}$$

so that

$$G(z) = \sum_{i=0}^{\infty} q^i(1-q)z^i \tag{3.188}$$

and summing the series we obtain

$$G(z) = \frac{(1-q)}{(1-qz)} \tag{3.189}$$

Substituting this expression for $G(z)$ into Eq. (3.186) and using the fact that $p_0 = (1 - \lambda/\mu)$, we obtain

$$P(z) = \frac{\mu(1 - \lambda/\mu)(1 - qz)}{\mu(1 - qz) - \lambda qz} \tag{3.190}$$

Now we are looking to rewrite this equation in a form that may be inverted. Separating the factors of z in the numerator we obtain

$$P(z) = \frac{\mu(1-\lambda/\mu)}{\mu(1-qz)-\lambda qz} - \frac{\mu(1-\lambda/\mu)qz}{\mu(1-qz)-\lambda qz} \tag{3.191}$$

The first expression on the right-hand side is easily inverted by making use of the transform pair $A\alpha^n \Leftrightarrow A/(1-\alpha z)$. The second term may also be inverted using this relationship along with the property that the series resulting from the inverse transform of $zF(z)$ is f_{n-1}. The inverse of Eq. (3.191) is thus given by

$$p_n = \left(1-\frac{\lambda}{\mu}\right)\left[q\left(1+\frac{\lambda}{\mu}\right)\right]^n - q\left(1-\frac{\lambda}{\mu}\right)\left[q\left(1+\frac{\lambda}{\mu}\right)\right]^{n-1} \tag{3.192}$$

Note that here we cannot simply replace the ratio of the arrival and departure rates with the traffic intensity ρ because in this case it is modified by the batch size. This equation may be simplified to give

$$p_n = q^n \frac{\lambda}{\mu}\left(1-\frac{\lambda}{\mu}\right)\left(1+\frac{\lambda}{\mu}\right)^{n-1} \tag{3.193}$$

As usual the average number of customers may be obtained from the sum of the products np_n over all possible n from which

$$E[n] = \sum_{n=0}^{\infty} nq^n \frac{\lambda}{\mu}\left(1-\frac{\lambda}{\mu}\right)\left(1+\frac{\lambda}{\mu}\right)^{n-1} \tag{3.194}$$

The summation may be simplified and we obtain

$$E[n] = \frac{q\dfrac{\lambda}{\mu}\left(1-\dfrac{\lambda}{\mu}\right)}{\left(1-q-q\dfrac{\lambda}{\mu}\right)^2} \tag{3.195}$$

Consider a communications node that is being modeled using the $M/M^{\text{geom}}/1$ queue such that the average number of packets in the system, including the node buffer and the communication line, is given by Eq. (3.195). The output line operates at 10 Mbit/s and geometrically distributed messages consist of a random number of 1000-bit packets. In Figure 3.25 we plotted the mean delay as a function of traffic intensity for $q = 0.5$, 0.6, and 0.7. If the message arrival rate remains constant we would reasonably expect the capacity of the line to be reduced by the factor $q/1-q$, being the mean message length, and this is indeed the case. At $q = 0.7$, for example, the average message length is $0.7/0.3 \approx 2.3$ packets. Hence the capacity in this case will be around $1/2.3 \approx 0.4$ as a fraction of the case for which the message length is on average one packet long, that is, when $q = 0.5$.

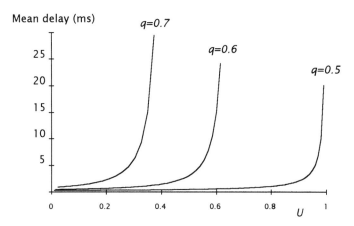

Figure 3.25 Mean delay versus traffic intensity for geometrically distributed batch arrivals.

3.6 CONCLUDING REMARKS

In this chapter we dealt exclusively with some of the techniques in mathematical analysis. The buffers in communication systems very closely resemble queueing systems, and there is a great deal of well-established theory on their analysis. A range of these analyses was presented. In each case an example was provided to illustrate the application of the techniques. All of the queueing systems discussed in this chapter are relevant for the analysis of individual nodes, such as TDM multiplexors, for example. When nodes are interconnected they form networks of queues. These systems are the subject of another branch of queueing theory, and this will be touched on in the final chapter.

The exercises that follow are intended as a guide to the type of problems that the reader should now be able to tackle. Problems that are numerically intensive have been avoided, however, the act of reproducing the results presented in the text should be informative. In the next chapter we will deal exclusively with the simulation of networks and nodes. The bulk of the material is based on using a high-level language, and PASCAL-coded listings are provided.

Exercises

3.1 A simple node with an infinite buffer transmits data at 96,000 bit/s in 1000-bit packets. The node effectively introduces a delay that consists of the queueing delay and the retransmission delay. What values of utilization cause delays in excess of 25 and 50 ms?

3.2 A multiplexor, which is being modeled as a queueing system, has 32 output channels, each of which may transmit data at 2 Mbit/s. Assume that the outputs are evenly utilized and calculate the average number of bytes in the buffer of the multiplexor when it is accepting a total of 2.4 Mbyte/s at the input. The processing time is negligible and the service time is equal to the transmission time for a byte of data on one channel.

3.3 A node receives data from each of n inputs at a rate of 64 kbit/s and transmits on a single output at a rate of 2 Mbit/s. The data arrives in bytes and the node has a buffer that can store just 10 bytes of data. It takes 1 μs to process each byte. If each of the inputs are constantly active and the loss of data cannot be tolerated, calculate the maximum value for n. If n is fixed at 100, what is the probability that some data is lost when the packets arrive in a completely random fashion at an average rate of 1000 per second on each channel? The transmission time is not included in the processing time.

3.4 In words, what is on the opposite side of the equation to the mean arrival rate when Little's law is rearranged?

3.5 Write down the expression for the mean queueing delay of packets that arrive at a node with m output channels in terms of the utilization, m, packet length, and transmission rate. Assume that the packets are all the same length and that the output channels are all operating at the same transmission rate. Next derive an expression for the total delay.

3.6 Packets arrive in a completely random fashion, following a negative exponential distribution, at an average rate of 100 every second. What is the probability that at least one packet arrives within a millisecond? What is the probability that just one arrives?

3.7 A server consists of two stages, each with a mean departure rate of μ customers per second. As soon as the customer leaves the first stage it enters the second stage, and only one customer may be present in the server at any one time. Derive the probability distribution function for the overall service time if the service times in each stage are independent random variables with a negative exponential distribution. What is the distribution function of the total service time if the individual service times are different? *Hint:* The first part is the sum of two independent random variables. The second part may be obtained as the product of the individual Laplace transforms of the distributions. The inverse transform is obtained using the Laplace transform pair $e^{-at}\sin \omega t \Leftrightarrow \omega/[(S+a)^2 + \omega^2]$.

3.8 Derive Eqs. (3.104) and (3.105).

3.9 The probability density for the total delay in an $M/M/1$ queue was derived in Section 3.4.1. Why is it not possible to use the product of Laplace transforms to convolute the individual distributions for the arrival and service times ?

3.10 Derive expressions for the state probability distribution of the $M/M/m/m$ queue for which $\lambda_n = \lambda$ for $n < m$ and zero otherwise and $\mu_n = n\mu$ for $n = 1, 2, ..., m$. Hence derive Eqs. (3.130) and (3.131).

3.11 Starting with the birth-death coefficients for the $M/M/m$ queue, derive Erlang's C formula.

3.12 The $M/E_r/1$ queue is to be used to model the arrival and departure of messages to and from a buffer. Assume that messages arrive as batches of exponentially distributed packets. Write down the expression for the distribution of the number of packets in the system and derive an expression for the mean packet delay.

3.13 Draw the state transition diagram for the $M/E_r/2$ queue and write down the flow balance equations.

3.14 Write down the discrete probability distribution representing batch size when this parameter is a constant value. Hence derive the z-transform of the probability distribution for batches of size r. Using Eq. (3.186), by substituting for $G(z)$, verify that the state distribution obtained using the analysis for general size batches is the same as for the $M/E_r/1$ queue.

References

[1]   Kershenbaum, Aaron, *Telecommunications Network Design Algorithms*, New York: McGraw Hill, Inc., 1993.
[2]   Bear, D., *Principles of Telecommunication Traffic Engineering*, third edition, London: Peter Peregrinus, Ltd., 1988.
[3]   Allen, A. O., *Probability, Statistics and Queueing Theory*, New York: Academic Press, 1978.
[4]   Kleinrock, L., *Queueing Sytems, Volume 1: Theory*, New York: John Wiley & Sons, 1975.
[5]   Bunday, Brian D., *Basic Queueing Theory*, London: Edward Arnold, Ltd., 1986.

Chapter 4

Computer Simulation

Computer simulation is one of two methods used to analyze communication network traffic. This is a discipline that has received much attention, and there is a great deal of material available for study. It is not intended to provide a definitive text on this subject here, as such a document might easily occupy a number of volumes.

We will concentrate on the use of a high-level programming language for producing customized simulations. The examples are illustrated with PASCAL code. The language syntax in this case is quite readable, and the code may easily be translated into 'C', for example. On completing the material in this chapter, the reader should be able to use the techniques to produce simulations of the systems in which she or he is specifically interested. The technique adopted is known widely as the method of discrete event simulation for reasons that will become apparent.

There are a number of books dedicated to the methods that are generally applicable to simulation. The text by Law and Kelton is regularly cited [1], and that of Pooch and Wall is one of the more recent contributions [2]. Following a brief digest of the general techniques that are explained in detail in these books, simulation programs for token-passing LANs and WANs and slotted systems are developed. The majority of the material in this chapter is therefore devoted to specific examples.

4.1 SIMULATION METHODOLOGY

A number of alternatives is available to those interested in simulating communication networks. The choice of using a high-level language to develop simulations from first principles is exercized in this text. In addition there have been languages such as Simscript and Simula developed specifically for the purpose. Packages such as BONeS and Netsim, which model specific systems and take away much of the development time from the user, have also been produced. A discussion of the choice of simulation platforms that are available is given by Law in [4], and some of these are described in more technical detail in [5].

In the first section of this chapter some of the methods that are used to develop and validate simulations will be described. All simulations require input and produce output. Normally the input required follows from the nature and purpose for simulation of the system under scrutiny. Output data analysis is also a major consideration for any simulation experiment, and this will be dealt with here.

4.1.1 Coding Methods

As was briefly mentioned in Chapter 1, there are three or four options for traffic performance analysis using computer simulation: packages, specialized and general simulation languages, and high-level languages. Fortran, 'C', and PASCAL are popular high-level languages for simulation. There are a number of features that the programming language requires. A set of minimum features are necessary for all simulation programs, and there are additional ones that are useful in some cases. Of course there is always the option of coding in assembler, which would provide complete flexibility. For all except for the most accomplished programmer, however, this method could be excessively time consuming.

Simulations are models for stochastic processes. Hence one of the functions required is the capability to generate random variables. Most high-level languages provide a function that returns a uniform random variable. One or two additional lines of code are required to transform the value returned into a random variable that has a distribution that may be chosen by the programmer. Normally this procedure will be adequate. There are, however, alternative methods for developing customized algorithms. Various tests can be applied to the series of numbers generated by any method to verify the quality of the algorithm, and these will be discussed later. Apart from a random number generator, only the capability for manipulating real numbered variables is required to implement the simplest simulations.

Let us illustrate the discussion in these first few sections using a simple model, and exponentially distributed arrivals will provide a good example for this. The simulation program, implemented in PASCAL code, is given in Figure 4.1. This program could easily have been implemented in another language, such as Fortran, 'C', or even BASIC, for example. Two variables are used. One of these has been labeled *time*, and its purpose is to provide a clock for the system. The other is used to keep count of the number of arrivals that have occurred. The simulation begins with the initialization of these two variables and then enters a *repeat* statement that consists of two lines. The first line within the repeat statement increments *time*, or the system clock, by an amount that is calculated using the expression $-(1/\lambda)\ln(random)$. Here λ is the mean arrival rate and *random* is the parameter used to instruct the compiler to return a random uniform variable that lies in the interval $(0,1)$. A random variable that is calculated using this expression is exponentially distributed, hence the system clock is forwarded by a random time that is exponentially distributed with a mean of $(1/\lambda)$. The second line within the *repeat* statement simply increments the arrival count. Hence at each iteration, or every time the *repeat* statement is executed, the program simulates an arrival. The constant *maximum_arrivals* is used in the condition to terminate the *repeat*, and in this case 1000 arrivals are permitted. The *writeln* statement outputs the average arrival time, which we expect to be 2 when the constant *lambda* is set to be 0.5. The actual value

```
program exponential_arrivals;
const
  lambda = 0.5;
  maximum_arrivals = 1000;
var
  time: real;
  arrival_count: longint;
begin
  time := 0;
  arrival_count := 0;
  repeat
    time := time + (-1/lambda)*ln(random);
    inc(arrival_count);
  until arrival_count = maximum_arrivals;
  writeln('Average inter-arrival time = ', time/arrival_count);
end.
```

Figure 4.1 PASCAL code to simulate arrivals with exponentially distributed inter-arrival times.

output by the program was 2.075, and we shall say something about the apparent discrepancy later.

Two methods for coding simulations in high-level languages are used, and these are known as time-driven and event-driven simulations. The previous example is event-driven because the focus of the code is on what happens when the event of arrival occurs. Specifically, when an arrival occurs the system clock and the arrival count are updated. An equivalent time-driven simulation, in which the system clock is incremented in fixed time intervals, is listed in Figure 4.2.

In this case the *repeat* statement is executed every time the system clock is advanced by a fixed time interval. This is set by the constant labeled *time_interval*. An initial arrival time has been assigned to the new variable *arrival_time* before entering the *repeat* statement. An *if* statement is used to check whether the arrival has occurred by comparing *arrival_time* with the system clock. If *time* is greater than or equal to the *arrival_time*, then the arrival count is incremented and a new *arrival_time* is generated. Otherwise the system clock is incremented and the process is repeated.

The same result as before was obtained using this program. Note, however, that the repeat statement has to be executed a significant number of times greater using the time-driven simulation than when using the event-driven simulation. In our case the program run times were 40 seconds and less than 1 second, respectively. The run time for the time-driven simulation can be reduced by increasing the value of *time_interval*. This is at the expense of the resolution, however, since the simulated arrival effectively occurs at the end of the interval. Running the simulation with a time interval of 1 second reduced the run time to less than 1 second, and the mean arrival time obtained in this case was 2.6. Clearly the reduction in run time has been obtained at the expense of accuracy.

```
program exponential_arrivals; {time_driven}
const
  lambda = 0.5;
  maximum_arrivals = 1000;
  time_interval = 0.0005;
var
  time: real;
  arrival_time: real;
  arrival_count: longint;
begin
  time := 0;
  arrival_count := 0;
  arrival_time := time + (-1/lambda)*ln(random);
  repeat
    time := time + time_interval;
    if time >= arrival_time then
    begin
      inc(arrival_count);
      arrival_time := time + (-1/lambda)*ln(random);
    end;
  until arrival_count = maximum_arrivals;
  writeln('Average inter-arrival time = ', time/arrival_count);
end.
```

Figure 4.2 Time-driven simulation of arrivals with exponentially distributed inter-arrival times.

It is always possible to implement simulations by coding either of the time- or event-driven methods. The use of one or the other may be more convenient in different circumstances. In the previous examples it would appear that there are no advantages to be gained using the time-driven technique. It requires both the use of more constants and variables as well as incurring a greater run time.

In either case, more complex simulation models generally require lengthier programs and larger numbers of variables and constants. Again, these may normally be dealt with using any of the high-level languages that have been mentioned. With certain types of complexity, however, there are advantages to be gained when particular data types can be utilized, for example. At this point it becomes difficult to discuss the methods in general terms and it is probably more suitable that specific models be discussed individually. However, it is appropriate that list processing techniques should at least be mentioned.

When there is more than one type of event, and indeed more than one instance of the same event, then some form of list has to be set up and maintained. A list of events is usually required for all but the simplest simulations, and again this is true for both event-driven and time-driven solutions. The most basic method for storing a list is to use an array. Fortran is widely used for coding simulations and the list processing function for it is limited to this method. There are basic inefficiencies with the use of arrays for list processing, however. One of the often performed jobs in a simulation program is the addition and deletion of entries in the list. Since it is logical, and most convenient, that the list be maintained in a chronological order, this could require shifting all or most of the elements in an array. A more efficient method for storing lists of events is to use the pointer type variables that are available in the 'C' and PASCAL languages.

Of course there are the usual concerns that a programmer must address when he or she is involved in the production of software. The choice of language is one of these, and availability and familiarity are just two of the factors that come into play. In general, the 'C' and PASCAL compilers are perhaps the two most popular programming languages used in the engineering disciplines. These two languages, for the reasons outlined previously, are particularly suitable in this case. The reader may choose either without loosing any advantages that are specific to implementing simulations. All the examples presented later in this chapter are illustrated with PASCAL code and assuming the event-driven methodology. List processing is achieved using the pointer, or linked-list approach, and this will be described in detail shortly.

There are alternative approaches for simulating communication networks, as we have stated already. There are general simulation languages, specialized simulation languages, and very specific network simulation packages. The absence of any great detail in these topics is not intended to discourage the reader's interest.

4.1.2 Validation

The process of validating simulation programs is carried out to confirm that the system to be modeled is accurately represented; in other words, to make sure that the program simulates the intended system. Although this may seem an obvious requirement, and indeed some degree of validation should naturally occur during the development stage, it is an activity that should benefit the overall outcome of an investigation if it is considered as a unique entity. This is probably more true when it is applied to simulations that are developed using a high-level language. The flexibility that is afforded the developer in this case may not work in her or his favor.

Again, as seems to be a recurring theme in software development, there are no specific rules that may be applied to the process of validation. There are, however, some reasonable approaches for increasing one's confidence that the task has been completed successfully. Individual chunks of code, functions, and procedures, for example, may be scrutinized to ensure that they operate as expected. Also, the overall flow of execution can be interrogated by selecting suitable output for run-time. It is always possible to print the events as they occur, along with the time of occurrence, for example. If the resulting output is as expected and all the possible sequences have been explored, then a firm basis for assuming that the simulation is valid has been established. Normally these tasks are referred to using a formal terminology such as *checking* for the scrutiny of code, and *test coverage* to indicate that portions of code work as expected.

Perhaps the most convincing method for validating the results of any experiment is to repeat it using a different set of apparatus. In the case of simulating communication networks this may be achieved by developing the code in a different language, using an alternative simulation platform, or even by tasking another person. The most popularly reported method of validation is through the derivation of an equivalent analysis, however. If a mathematical expression for the outcome of a process can be derived and the same result as the simulation is obtained when similar parameters are input, then at least it is certain that the model is valid in one particular case. If the results agree over a whole range of input parameters, then in fact both of the models are validated over this range. This method is illustrated in a number of sections throughout the text.

The ultimate validation, of course, will be performed when the real system is implemented and the experimental data compared with actual results.

4.1.3 Run Time

Once a simulation is prepared and validated one or more experiments have to be carried out to obtain the output data. An experiment is performed when the simulation program is executed. An important consideration when running any simulation program is the number of iterations that the code is allowed to execute. Ideally the number of iterations would be infinite. However, this would require an infinite run time. Instead a suitable point for terminating execution has to be set. This is the point at which acceptable results are obtained. The acceptability of results is not an easy thing to determine because one does not know what is acceptable a priori. After all, this is the reason for developing a simulation in the first place. There are really two phases in studying the output data of simulation runs. The objective of the first phase is to make sure that the simulation has been run in a manner that is known to produce reliable results. The second is the analysis of the data to determine system performance.

In the example of the arrivals in Section 4.1.1, the output was the mean inter-arrival time and the accuracy was really quite poor. A simulated value of 2.075 was obtained, compared with the expected value of 2.000, when the mean arrival rate is 0.5. It would appear that the investigator should expect errors up to the first decimal place. In fact, when the program was run with *maximum_arrivals* of 2000 and 5000, the mean inter-arrival times of 2.024 and 2.013 were obtained, respectively. Hence when the simulation is allowed to run for a longer period of time, it appears that the accuracy of the results are improved. Note, incidentally, we are implementing that method of validation which is to compare the results of simulation with that predicted by theory, albeit with a trivial example.

The apparent dependence of the results of simulation on the number of iterations is generally applicable to the simulation of any stochastic process. By allowing the simulation to collect data over a longer time interval, statistical anomalies are smoothed out and the average values are closer to the theoretical expectation. In fact it is possible to identify different stages for the progress of more complex simulations. These stages are recognized by their effect on the output data. Following start-up, at some point the system is said to have reached its steady state. Then one may be confident that the average values are accurate to some known degree. The time before steady state has been reached consists of what is known informally as the "warm-up" period and the transient period. The warm-up period is included to indicate that it may be favorable to delay the commencement of data collection, and the transient period produces unreliable data. Hence the simulation has reached steady state when the effects of perhaps unrealistic initial conditions have become insignificant. The steady-state condition may be tested using statistical confidence intervals.

There are a number of techniques for quantifying the range, or bounds, of statistical data. The Markov bound is one of these, however, it is less tight than the limits provided by Chebycheff's inequality. An even tighter bound is obtained if it is assumed that the data is normally distributed. First consider the interval provided by Chebycheff's inequality, which may be expressed as

$$\Pr\left[|X - \mu| \geq \gamma\right] \leq \frac{\sigma^2}{\gamma^2} \tag{4.1}$$

Here X is a sample taken from an arbitrary distribution that has a mean μ and variance σ^2. The inequality in Eq. (4.1) may be rewritten in a form that provides a bound for the probability that the sample is located somewhere in the region $\mu - \gamma < X < \mu + \gamma$ as

$$\Pr\left[|X - \mu| < \gamma\right] > 1 - \frac{\sigma^2}{\gamma^2} \tag{4.2}$$

The true mean and variance for the output data of a simulation run are not known. However, the sample mean and variance may be incorporated in the following manner. The sample mean is given by

$$\mu(J) = \frac{1}{J}\sum_{j=1}^{J}\mu_j \tag{4.3}$$

where the μ_j are the simulation output means obtained after J iterations. The fact that each sample is itself an average may be confusing. The sample variance is given by

$$\sigma^2(J) = \frac{1}{J-1}\sum_{j=1}^{J}[\mu_j - \mu(J)]^2 \tag{4.4}$$

and this is related to the true variance through the expression

$$\sigma^2 = \frac{\sigma^2(J)}{J} \tag{4.5}$$

Hence, replacing σ^2 with $\sigma^2(J)/J$ in Chebycheff's inequality, the probability that an arbitrary sample is bounded above and below the true mean by γ is better than $\left(1 - \sigma^2(J)/J\gamma^2\right)$. Thus if J is large, then the confidence is improved, as should be expected.

If it can be assumed that the samples are taken from a normal distribution, then an alternative bound is available. The 95% confidence interval for the normal distribution is given by ± 1.96 standard deviations from the true mean. In fact if J is large enough, then this assumption is fair. Hence it may be stated that the true mean is $\mu(J) \pm 1.96\sigma(J)/\sqrt{J}$ with 95% certainty. The factor $\sigma(J)/\sqrt{J}$ is the sampled standard deviation.

The data in Table 4.1 was obtained using the arrivals program of the first section. Additional lines of code were used to output the variance and confidence intervals. In each case the mean arrival rate input was 10, so the true mean of the data should be 0.1. As expected the mean is predicted more accurately when the number of iterations is large. After 1000 iterations Chebycheff's inequality indicates that the value of 0.104 is within 0.05 of the true mean with a 99.5% certainty. Of course the accuracy is actually greater by a factor of 10. The 95% confidence interval of 0.007, obtained by assuming that the samples are normally distributed, is much closer to the true accuracy.

Table 4.1
Confidence intervals for the mean inter-arrival time

Iterations	Mean	Variance	Confidence $(\gamma = 0.05)$	95% confidence interval
100	0.124	0.040	84.1	0.040
200	0.112	0.024	95.2	0.021
300	0.114	0.021	97.2	0.016
400	0.110	0.019	98.1	0.013
500	0.108	0.017	98.7	0.011
1000	0.104	0.013	99.5	0.007

The acknowledgment of the existence of a warm-up period has implications for the methods of collecting data in a simulation program. The arrivals program is a relatively simple simulation and there will be no effect of a warm-up time on the output. This assumption is corroborated by delaying the collection of data for a certain number of iterations and comparing the results with the data in Table 4.1. A minor difference is noticeable, due to the effect of the random number generator, and again as the number of contributing iterations is increased this difference becomes negligible. For more complex simulations, however, it is good practice to ensure that steady-state data are not collected until steady-state conditions are prevalent.

4.1.4 Output Analysis

As we have stated there are two phases in studying the output data of simulation runs. The previous subsection describes how the objective of the first phase is to make sure that a simulation is run in a manner that is known to produce reliable results. During the discussion of the example frequent references to the accuracy of the output data were made. Specifically, the mean and its statistical confidence intervals were obtained. In the second phase of output analysis the data that are used to determine the system performance are analyzed. Hence the same calculations are appropriate in both phases. Moreover, any relevant methods of validation are also useful in either case. Apparently there is no clear boundary between the processes for obtaining steady-state conditions and output analysis. This lack of clarity is exacerbated when one considers that a degree of output analysis is required in order to determine the prevalence of steady-state conditions. There is a distinct purpose in each phase, however, and different techniques for presenting the results of analysis may be suitable.

The purpose of a simulation program is to determine how a system will react when certain conditions prevail. The simulation that models the system is therefore given the input parameters that mimic these conditions, and the output of the simulation run is supposed to provide an indication of what the reaction will be. Output analysis is required to interpret the data and quantify the reactions or measures of interest.

A graph of the data in Table 4.1 is depicted in Figure 4.3. This is an alternative method for presenting the output. The mean inter-arrival times are plotted as data points, and the values of the 95% confidence intervals are included as error bars. The graph clearly shows, by comparison of the data obtained with the real mean, that all of the results are correct, to varying degrees of accuracy. We therefore conclude that the concept of warm-up is not relevant in this case. The purpose of the simulation was to generate traffic with exponentially distributed inter-arrival times at a specific mean value, and this was achieved in a predictable fashion.

In another situation there may be a requirement for traffic to be generated within certain limits, however, then a new criteria for output analysis must be established. For example, if our generator is to be used in a simulation that requires the 95% confidence interval for the mean inter-arrival time be less than 0.2, then the warm-up time is at least 300 iterations. Of course, the investigator may be interested in the values associated with

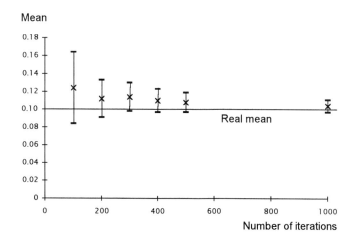

Figure 4.3 Output analysis of inter-arrival times.

transient conditions or any problems that may arise in the initial stages following system start-up. For example, the maximum value of a parameter may be important. In this case data should be collected throughout the period of a simulation. A thorough treatment of output data analysis is beyond the scope of this section. The interested reader should consult a text such as Law and Kelton [1].

4.2 DISCRETE EVENTS

Like many real-life processes the operation of a communication network can be described by a sequence of events that take place at certain points in time. In order to simulate this sequence of events on a computer and produce some statistics that reflect the patterns of activity, it is required that the process is replicated within a program. The system is realized by describing it in terms of constants, types, and variables. In order to demonstrate the techniques of implementing code for simulation the following material becomes quite specific. The PASCAL programming language is exclusively adopted for this particular technique because its pointer variables are ideally suited. On first reading the description of the technique may not appear to have any ordered construction. There is a logical progression to the development of ideas, however, and the reader is encouraged to persevere.

One particular variable type, conveniently known as an event, is required, and variables of this type are set up in a list. During run time each entry in the list is inspected and action is taken depending on the values of certain variables or fields within the event type. This action may cause new events to be inserted in the list, and the fields in other types may also be modified. One of the fields in the event type is used to store the time associated with that event, and the list is maintained in chronological order. Each entry in the list uses a pointer to identify the preceding and proceeding entries. Such a linked list is depicted in Figure 4.4. As described it has a dynamic structure in that it can be modified during run time.

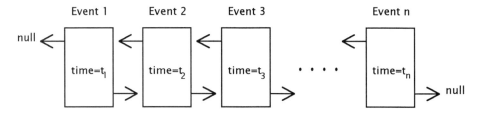

Figure 4.4 Linked-list of events.

There is a number of essential components for a typical communication network simulation program, and these can be described as follows. The network itself is composed of a number of variables of a type that is conveniently labeled as *node*. Typically the *node* will contain fields that are used to describe the state of its buffer and various times relating to the generation and transmission of traffic. Different parameters of the network, such as the number of nodes, data transmission rate, and propagation delay, are stored in globally declared constants and variables. These parameters may be assigned values or initialized at the start of the program execution.

The linked list is used to keep a chronologically ordered list of records that represent the complete sequence of events, at any given time, on the network. The list will be altered through the course of a simulation according to the arrival and transmission of messages. One of the principle functions of the program is the code used to simulate the transmission of the messages. Its structure will be dictated by the algorithms for the communication protocol. This is required to ensure that the simulation follows a strict set of rules so that the transmission of packets on the network exactly follows the pattern dictated by the chosen protocol. Statistics are collected in the *node* types and in global variables through the course of the simulation, and these are suitably manipulated for output.

At the start of program execution storage space is allocated for each *node*, a new event list is created, and the input parameters are initialized. Next, a *case* statement is repeated until predetermined criterion has been met. As an example of this statement, for a simple token passing protocol, the following code will suffice:

```
repeat
  next_event := front_of_eventque^
  case next_event of
    tokenpass: tx_token;
    transmit_data: tx_packet;
    generate_data: generate_message;
  end;
until packets_transmitted = limit
```

The implications of the detail of this code should become clear later.

Finally the data is compiled and output to file and or screen for analysis. This is essentially the method of implementing a discrete event simulation program. In the next section the theme of token passing will be used as an example to develop the minimum code required for a complete simulation program.

4.2.1 Simple Token Passing

A complete simulation program for a simple token passing algorithm, which operates as follows, may be constructed from an amalgamation of the procedures and chunks of code listed in this subsection. To begin with a description of the system is in order. A network of nodes share a common transmission medium. A special data packet, known as the token, is passed to each node in an orderly fashion. When a busy node receives the token it is allowed to transmit a single packet that contains the regular data. Following the packet transmission it passes the token on to the next node. An idle node simply passes the token on as soon as it is received. A flow chart of the program that will simulate this system is presented in Figure 4.5.

After the program begins the global constants, including data transmission rate, bit transmission time unit, propagation delay, and node population, are defined. The bit transmission time unit, or *btu*, is the unit of time that the program uses, and it is simply the reciprocal of the data transmission rate. Hence the transmission time for a packet is given by its length in bits. The packet length and token length are also defined as global constants.

Two types of record are used in the program, one each for the event and node labels. The event record has an associated pointer and the resulting two types for events are thus declared as follows:

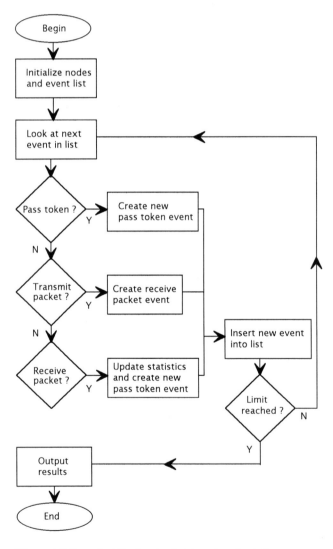

Figure 4.5 Flow chart for the simple token ring simulation program.

event_ptr = ^*event*;
event = **record**
  event_time: real;
  que_back, que_front: event_ptr;
  control_procedure: event_type;
  node_id: integer;
end;

The labels for the fields in *event* are intended to identify their purpose. The first, *event_time*, is defined as a ***real*** and is used to store the time, in *btu* units, at which the event is to occur. The fields *que_back* and *que_front* are *event_ptr* types and so may used to point to variables of a similar type. Readers familiar with the technique of linked lists will have guessed the purpose of these fields. *control_procedure* is used to identify the type of event for use in the ***case*** statement, as mentioned earlier. It is an *event_type* that has been defined in the ***type*** statement declared before the event as

event_type = (*pass_token, tx_packet, rx_packet, gen_packet*);

The final integer field in *event* is used to store the identity of the node that is associated with the event.
    The three types declared as follows are used for *node* variables. Namely, these are the *node* type itself, a pointer labeled *node_ptr*, and a ***record*** labeled *buffer* that is used to define one of the *node* field variables.

buffer = **record**
  que_length: integer;
  arrival_time: array[1..buffer_size] of real;
end;

node_ptr = ^*node*;
node = **record**
  index, packet_count: integer;
  tx_que: buffer;
  lambda: real;
  av_que_time: real;
end;

The integers *index* and *packet_count* are used to store the identity of the node and the number of packets it has transmitted, respectively. The field *tx_que* is the *buffer* type that contains space for a count of the number of packets awaiting transmission and the arrival time for each of the packets at the node. These are labeled *que_length* and *arrival_time*, respectively. The ***real*** fields *lambda* and *av_que_time* are used to store the mean arrival rate and the average queueing time for packets at the node.
    The complete program comprises nine procedures and the main program block.

Obviously some of the code is specific to the task of implementing the simulation of token passing. However, the only procedure that will significantly differ in alternative access protocol simulation programs is *allocate_token*. Hence the method employed is general to many communication networks, and it will be of benefit to the reader who wants to develop a simulation of their own system to understand the code in detail. The order in which procedures are called is useful in providing an overall view of the flow of program control, and this is depicted in Figure 4.6. It can be seen that the depth in terms of procedure call nesting only reaches a level of three.

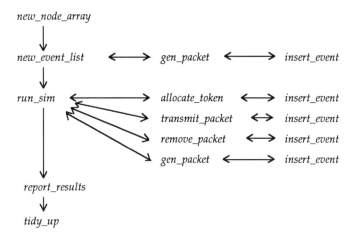

Figure 4.6 Order and nesting of procedure calls for token passing.

The first procedure to be called then is *new_node_array,* and its purpose is to establish an array of pointers to *node* types. Each of the fields are initialized with the value of *lambda* being set to the fraction of load chosen for the particular simulation run. In the most simple case values of *lambda* are set to be the same for all of the nodes, however, in some cases they may vary. The procedure is coded as follows:

```
procedure new_node_array;
begin
  for count := 0 to node_population - 1 do
  begin
    new(node_array[count]);
    with node_array[count]^ do
    begin
      lambda := load_fraction;
      tx_que.que_length := 0;
      av_que_time := 0;
      packet_count := 0;
```

end;
 end;
end;

      Within this procedure a pointer to each *node* is created in addition to the initialization of the fields in each of them. As a matter of fact the pointers are redundant in this simple example. They will be required later in other simulation programs, however, when being passed as an argument in some procedure calls. The next procedure to be executed is

procedure *new_event_list;*
begin
 new(event_que_front);
 event_que_front^.event_time := 2.3e37;
 for *count := 0 to node_population - 1* **do**
 begin
  with *an_event* **do**
  begin
   control_procedure := gen_packet;
   event_time := ((-1*ln(random))/(node_array[count]^.lambda*btu));
   node_id := count;
  end;
  insert_event(an_event);
 end;
end;

      The purpose of this procedure is to create an initial event list. The initial list will consist of a series of events that generates one packet, at a random point in time, for each node. The first line proper of the procedure creates an event pointer that is used to keep the location of the first event in the event queue. This is always the next event to be executed. A large event time is assigned to the effectively null event that will mark the end of the queue, calculated according to the capabilities of the machine on which the simulation is intended to be run. The fields of *an_event* are assigned suitable values in preparation for it to be passed to **procedure** *insert_event*. The values for *control_procedure* and *node_id* should be self-explanatory, however, the assignment for *event_time* is not so obvious.

      The *event_time* is calculated with the knowledge that packet generation events are inserted in the list as follows. The initial event list contains one packet generation event per node. During the simulation, when a packet generation event is encountered the arrival time and queue length in the nodes buffer are adjusted. Following this a new packet generation event is created and inserted in the event list. Hence subsequent events of this type are created with random inter-arrival times, in this case derived from the exponential distribution. Most PASCAL compilers provide a random number generator in the form of a function that returns a random number, u, between zero and one. The random variable that we require, t, is to be distributed exponentially, and it is shown later that this can be obtained using the formula

$$t = -\frac{1}{\lambda}\ln(1-u) \tag{4.6}$$

This is the expression that is incorporated in the line of code that assigns a value to *event_time*.

The next procedure to be executed is *run_sim* and this is the core of the simulation. It is the job of *run_sim* to inspect each event in the list and take appropriate action. The code that achieves this is

```
procedure run_sim;
begin
  transmitted_packets := 0;
  node_index := 0;
  allocate_token;
  repeat
    clock_time := event_que_front^.event_time;
    case event_que_front^.control_procedure of
      pass_token : allocate_token;
      tx_packet  : transmit_packet(event_que_front^.node_id);
      rx_packet  : remove_packet(event_que_front^.node_id);
      gen_packet : generate_packet;
    end;
    event_que_front := event_que_front^.que_front;
    dispose(event_que_front^.que_back);
  until transmitted_packets = max_packets;
end;
```

The first proper line of this procedure initializes the global variable *transmitted_packets*. This variable keeps a count of the total number of transmitted packets for all the nodes. The next two lines start the ball rolling by setting another global variable, labeled *node_index*, to zero. This variable is used to keep track of the identity of the node that is to receive the token next. The procedure *allocate_token*, which will be described shortly, carries out the necessary steps to accomplish the task of passing the token from the node that has current possession to the next logical recipient. As described in the introduction to this section, a repeated *case* statement is used to inspect each of the events in the linked list in chronological order. The *event_time* of the event that is at the front of the list is stored in the global variable *clock_time* on each occasion the *case* statement is repeated. Hence *clock_time* is in fact just that. A suitable procedure is called depending on the *control_procedure* of the current event. Each of these are described in ensuing paragraphs. When control has been returned to *run_sim* the front of the event queue is advanced and the space allocated to the previous one is discarded. Finally *run_sim* ends when the number of transmitted packets reaches a predetermined maximum.

The procedure called *allocate_token,* is mentioned twice in *run_sim.* The first occasion is to begin the token circulation, as described previously, and the next is within the **repeat** statement. The latter call is made each time the event *pass_token* is encountered.

```
procedure allocate_token;
begin
  a_node := node_array[node_index];
  if a_node^.tx_que.que_length > 0 then
  begin
   with an_event do
   begin
    control_procedure := tx_packet;
    event_time := clock_time + packet_length;
    node_id := node_index;
   end;
   insert_event(an_event);
  end
  else
  begin
   with an_event do
   begin
    control_procedure := pass_token;
    event_time := clock_time + propagation_delay + token_length;
   end;
   insert_event(an_event);
   node_index:= (node_index + 1) mod node_population;
  end;
end;
```

Essentially two tasks are carried out in this procedure. If the node currently in possession of the token, identified by *node_index,* has any packets awaiting transmission, then a *tx_packet* event is inserted in the event list. Otherwise the token is transmitted to the next node by inserting a *pass_token* event and incrementing *node_index.* Both cases are accomplished in the usual way by assigning suitable values to *an_event,* which is then passed to *insert_event.* Care has been taken to ensure that the correct values for event times are assigned. In the former case the transmission time of the packet is added, while in the latter propagation delay and token length are accounted for.

When a *tx_packet* is encountered at the front of the event queue the following code is executed:

```
procedure transmit_packet(tx_node_index: integer);
begin
```

```
a_node := node_array[tx_node_index];
with an_event do
begin
  control_procedure := rx_packet;
  event_time := clock_time + propagation_delay;
  node_id := tx_node_index;
end;
insert_event(an_event);
with an_event do
begin
  control_procedure := pass_token;
  event_time := clock_time + propagation_delay + token_length;
end;
insert_event(an_event);
node_index:= (node_index + 1) mod node_population;
end;
```

During this procedure the events *rx_packet* and *pass_token* are inserted into the event list. The *rx_packet* event is given a time that accounts for the propagation delay of the packet, and when it reaches the front of the event list the procedure *remove_packet* is called. At this time the length of the queue in the buffer of the transmitting node is decremented and the average queueing time at the node, over all packet transmissions, is calculated. The reader should inspect the code listing to confirm that these instructions are implemented.

Hence all the tasks required to carry out the simple token passing access scheme have been covered, with the exception of one remaining event called *gen_packet*. The purpose of the initial event list and how it is created has already been described. During this discussion it was noted that *gen_packet* is an event used to simulate the arrival of a packet at a node. The procedure associated with this event is

```
procedure generate_packet;
begin
  an_event := event_que_front^;
  a_node := node_array[an_event.node_id];
  with a_node^ do
  begin
    if tx_que.que_length = buffer_size then writeln('Buffer Overflow')
    else
    begin
      inc(tx_que.que_length);
      tx_que.arrival_time[tx_que.que_length] := clock_time;
    end;
    an_event.event_time := clock_time + ((-1*ln(random))/(lambda*btu));
    insert_event(an_event);
```

end;
end;

The *gen_packet* events essentially form the background task that is the arrival process of the system. Each time the prior procedure is called, as a result of the *gen_packet* event, a new *gen_packet* event is created and inserted into the list. The time associated with the new event is also derived using the random inter-arrival time generation algorithm. In addition, the queue length at the receiving node is compared with the predetermined buffer size. If the new packet causes the queue length to exceed the buffer size it is not accepted and a suitable comment is output to the screen. The astute reader may note here that additional code may be used to log the statistics associated with packets lost in this manner.

The majority of the description of the simulation procedures is now in place. The discussion of *insert_event* has been delayed until now. This is a procedure that has more to do with the technique of discrete events rather than the simulation of token passing.

```
procedure insert_event(an_event: event);
var
  search_ptr, temp_ptr: event_ptr;
  search_time: real;
begin
  new(temp_ptr);
  temp_ptr^ := an_event;
  search_time := temp_ptr^.event_time;
  if event_que_front^.event_time >= search_time then
  begin
    temp_ptr^.que_back := nil;
    temp ptr^.que_front := event_que_front;
    event_que_front^.que_back := temp_ptr;
    event_que_front := temp_ptr;
  end
  else begin
    search_ptr := event_que_front;
    while search_time > search_ptr^.event_time do
      search_ptr := search_ptr^.que_front;
    with temp_ptr^ do
    begin
      que_front := search_ptr;
      que_back := search_ptr^.que_back;
      que_back^.que_front := temp_ptr;
      que_front^.que_back := temp_ptr;
    end;
  end;
end;
```

end;

The integrity of the linked list that forms the event queue depends on the correct operation of *insert_event*. Fortunately this procedure is common to all simulations that use the technique described here. The event to be inserted is passed as an argument to the procedure. The essential value required by *insert_event* is stored in the *event_time* field of the event. Within *insert_event* this is assigned to a local variable labeled *search_time*. Its value may then be compared with each of the events in the existing list in order to locate the correct position for insertion. Two cases arise in this task and each require separate attention.

The first case is when the time of the event is before that of the event at the front of the existing event queue, and it is thus to be inserted at the front. Hence in the second case it is to be inserted somewhere in the body of the list. The former case is depicted in Figure 4.7 wherein the first two events of the existing list are shown with event times of t_1 and t_2 and the event to be inserted has a time $t < t_1$. A rectangular box is used to represent each event. The *true* portion of the *if* statement in the preceding procedure deals with this case. A local variable, *temp_ptr,* is assigned to point at the event to be inserted. Four pointer assignments are required to complete the process: the *que_front* and *que_back* of the new event, *que_back* of the event that was previously at the front, and *event_que_front* itself.

When the new event is destined for a location within the body of the list the pointer assignments are different and so have been placed in the *false* portion of the *if* statement. The required adjustments are illustrated in Figure 4.8. Now the new event has a time *t,* such that $t_2 < t < t_3$, and new pointer assignments are required in adjacent events as well as the new event. The reader should attempt to follow the code, with reference to

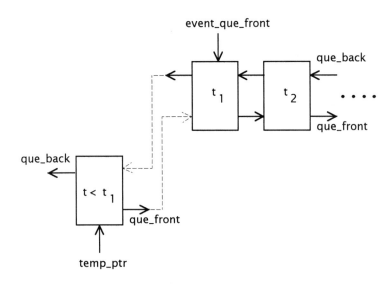

Figure 4.7 Inserting an event at the front of the list.

the diagram in Figure 4.6. In the case when $t = t_3$ the new event is inserted before the existing one. For our simple token passing simulation this choice is arbitrary, however, in more complicated systems it is important to bear this point in mind.

In Section B.1 of the appendix there are two procedures, called *report_results* and *tidy_up*, that the reader should inspect. These perform the tasks of presenting the results and disposing of pointer memory allocations prior to exiting the program. More will be said later about possible enhancements for the output data.

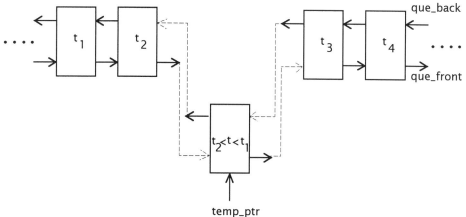

temp_ptr
Figure 4.8 Inserting an event in the body of the list.

4.3 RUNNING SIMULATIONS

The token passing simulation should compile and run on any machine with a PASCAL compiler. Possible corrections may be required to account for the maximum permissible real number or differences in the random number generator. We are using Borland's Turbo Pascal on a 486-based personal computer installed with a math coprocessor. This system permits real numbers in the range 2.9×10^{-39} to 1.7×10^{38}. Hence the dummy event that remains the last in the linked list was given an event time of 1.0×10^{38}. This provides for a running time that proves to be more than adequate. At 10 Mbit/s a simulated network lifetime of 1.0×10^{38}, which is in bit transmission time units, allows events to take place beyond 3×10^{23} years after the start of the simulation run.

The random number generator is accessed using the function *random(range)*, where if the range is not specified a value between zero and one is returned. With these possible exceptions accounted for the reader should have no problem running the program successfully.

In the first section there was some discussion regarding the validation and output analysis of data from simulation programs. Although there are some general principles that may be applied in these tasks, the actual methods implemented in carrying them out depend on the simulation. In the arrivals program there is no warm-up time, for example.

Moreover, it is easy to both validate the simulation itself and the output data by comparing the results obtained with the theoretical expectation for the mean inter-arrival time of the exponential distribution. In this case, however, there is no immediately obvious mechanism for validation and more emphasis may be imposed on the confidence intervals of the output as provided by statistical analysis. If the mean packet delay is required, for example, then the theoretical value is obtained using equations that are not immediately accessible.

4.3.1 Validating Token Passing

The following approaches can be implemented to validate the simple token passing algorithm. The first method is that which most programmers use for debugging, that is, by including statements that output the values of suitable variables during run time. A selection of *writeln* statements may be included in each of the procedures that are executed as a result of the occurrence of an event. Each statement may display the essential information about the event, and this can be cross-checked with what should be expected.

The second method is to investigate some results. The simulation was run with the following parameters, which correspond to those of a system with $N = 10$, a data transmission rate of 10 Mbit/s, 1000-bit packets, 20-bit tokens, and an end-to-end propagation distance of 1 km.

datarate = 10000000;
btu = 1/*datarate*;
propagation_delay = 1000/(*btu**2e8);
node_population = 10;
load_fraction = 0.05;
buffer_size = 10;
packet_length = 1000;
token_length = 20;
max_packets = 100;

Note that the value for *load_fraction* corresponds to the mean arrival rate at each node. The limiting capacity is 10,000 packets/s (10 Mbit/s and 1000-bit packets), hence the network load when *load_fraction* = 0.05 is 500 packet/s. The output obtained, after a run time of 1 min 28 sec, was a mean delay of 0.128 ms, at a throughput of 436 packets/s. The run was repeated with a maximum number of packets of 200 and the mean delay was 0.139 ms, at a throughput of 439 packet/s. This time the simulation took 2 min 53 sec. A series of runs produced the results tabulated in Table 4.2. In all cases there were no packets rejections, as it should be reasonable to expect with such low loads, and the throughput was the same as the offered load.

With most systems it is possible to estimate the expected mean delay at low loads, that is, when the queueing delay is negligible and the only significant contribution to the mean delay is the scheduling delay and service time. In this case the scheduling

Table 4.2
Simple token passing simulation runs

Max_packets	Mean delay (ms)	95% confidence interval (ms)	Throughput (packet/s)	Run time (min:sec)
100	0.128	0.027	436	1:28
200	0.139	0.018	439	2:53
300	0.140	0.012	442	4:13
400	0.141	0.011	458	5:23
500	0.141	0.010	465	6:36
1000	0.140	0.006	482	12:34

delay is, on average, the time taken for the token to be passed to half of the nodes. The *token rotation time* (*TRT*), is the time taken for the token to circulate around the whole network and is given by

$$TRT = N \times (\text{token transmission time} + \text{propagation delay}) \qquad (4.7)$$

where N is the number of nodes. The service time is just the packet transmission time plus the propagation delay. Hence the mean delay at low loads, D_{low}, is given by

$$D_{low} = \frac{TRT}{2} + \text{packet transmission time} + \text{propagation delay} \qquad (4.8)$$

For a system with $N = 10$, a data transmission rate of 10 Mbit/s, 1000 bit packets, 20 bit tokens, and an end-to-end propagation distance of 1 km, we find that $D_{low} = 0.14$ms. Hence the simulation is validated by the results when the load is small. In Chapter 7 other analytical approaches are used to validate the simulation over the full range of loads up to system capacity.

4.3.2 Processing Time

In terms of processing time, the simulation runs can be expensive. From the data in Table 4.2 it can be seen that the run with 1000 packet transmissions took over twelve and a half minutes. Though reasonably steady-state conditions appear to have been obtained with only 300 transmissions, this is not always the case. It is always good practice, therefore, to investigate the possibility of improving efficiency. One method for reducing the processing time in our simple token passing scheme is to check for future packet arrivals when the system is idle. Under low load conditions the majority of processing time will be used for token passing events. Since data regarding packet delay is only generated when packets are transmitted, this would seem to be wasteful.

Consider the new *allocate_token* procedure that follows. It avoids this excessive computation by looking ahead for the next packet generation event.

```
procedure allocate_token;
var
  active_node_found, event_found: boolean;
  next_event_time: real;
begin
  active_node_found := false;
  event_found := false;
  next_event_time := event_que_front^.que_front^.event_time;
  repeat
    a_node := node_array[node_index];
    if a_node^.tx_que.que_length > 0 then
    begin
      active_node_found := true;
      with an_event do
      begin
        control_procedure := tx_packet;
        event_time := clock_time + packet_length;
        node_id := node_index;
      end;
      insert_event(an_event);
    end
    else
    begin
      if (clock_time + token_pass_time) < next_event_time then
        clock_time := clock_time + token_pass_time
      else
      begin
        event_found := true;
        with an_event do
        begin
          control_procedure := pass_token;
          event_time := clock_time + token_pass_time;
        end;
        insert_event(an_event);
      end;
      node_index:= (node_index + 1) mod node_population;
    end;
  until active_node_found or event_found;
end;
```

Three new local variables— *active_node_found, event_found* and *next_event_time*—
have been introduced. The whole of the body of the old procedure has been encapsulated
in a **repeat** statement. If *node_index* is found to be active, then *active_node_found* is set
to be *true* and the simulation proceeds as before. Otherwise, providing there is no new

event, which could be a *generate_packet* scheduled to occur before the next node receives the token, a token pass is effected within the procedure. As a consequence the unnecessary insertion of *token_pass* events into the event list are avoided. This process is repeated, through the use of a nested *if* statement, until either an active node or a generate packet event is found. Thus event list manipulation, which results in a significant number of processor operations, is reduced to a minimum.

In the case when a generate packet event is found before an active node, which will be more significant when larger node populations are simulated in low load conditions, we could make a further saving by avoiding token passes to the idle nodes in between the node in current possession of the token and the one that is about to become active. This is left as an exercise for the reader with the hint that an additional global variable is required to store the total number of packets on the network. We repeated the simulation run using the preceding procedure with 1,000 packet transmissions and it took 4 min 11 sec. This compares with the previous time of 12 min 34 sec.

Similar and alternative techniques can be used to shorten the program run time for other simulations. The event graph technique, which is the subject of the next chapter, is used as a framework for the development of simulation programs. One of the objectives in this technique is to reduce the required number of unique events to a minimum. Thus event lists should be as short as possible and again the list processing times are reduced to a minimum. There are only four types of event in the token passing simulation program, so it is unlikely that this number can be reduced further. More complicated simulations, however, generally involve more types of event. In this case the event graph technique is useful, not only for the possible savings in processing time but also in providing a more disciplined method of program development.

4.3.3 Steady State

In Section 4.2.3, where the analysis of output data was discussed, it was observed that increasing the number of iterations in a simulation generally improves accuracy. When the results are derived as the average value of a parameter that is generated throughout the course of the simulation, it is important that the steady-state condition has been observed. Only then is it fair to say that the result is an indication of the true mean value. In the arrivals example of that section, each iteration consists of a packet arrival. The statistic observed, namely the average inter-arrival time, is independent of any start-up conditions. Hence there is no warm-up time, and the identification of steady state is relatively straightforward. In the token passing simulation, however, there are four types of event for each iteration. In this case we may be interested in the mean packet delay, for example, and this obviously depends on the start-up conditions in a less trivial manner. Thus the minimum number iterations required to observe steady state depends on the accuracy demanded and the complexity of the simulation. Moreover, there is a trade-off between the accuracy and the processing time.

The data in Table 4.2 shows that the simple token passing program gives the mean delay correct to three significant figures beyond around 300 packet transmissions, and the corresponding 95% confidence interval is ± 0.012 ms. The expected value is

0.140 ms; and since the value obtained is also 0.140 ms, the predicted confidence is clearly conservative. When 1000 packet transmissions are simulated the confidence interval is reduced to 0.006 ms. In this case, on average, each of the 10 nodes will have generated and transmitted 100 packets each. Hence, as a general rule of thumb, and when the processing time is not excessive, it should be fair to say that an accuracy of at least three significant figures is obtained when simulating 1000 iterations per node. The greater than tenfold increase over the requirements for the simple token passing algorithm should compensate for any significant increase in the complexity of other systems.

In many cases the output data is used in a quantitative analysis of performance characteristics that do not require a high degree of accuracy. Then, a good indication that sufficiently steady-state conditions have been obtained is the smoothness of the resulting performance characteristics. In Figure 4.9 we have plotted two curves that are the results obtained for mean delay over a range of values for throughput. The purpose of the graph in this case is to compare the characteristics for two cable lengths. It may be observed that there is a small reduction for the delay when the cable is shortest, as expected. Each of the points on the curve was obtained using max_packets = 1000, so it is known that the steady-state accuracy is better than the resolution of the vertical axis. The relative positions of the points that make up each curve corroborate the supposition that steady state has been obtained. In other words, the fact that the improvement is noticeable indicates that the averages are true. Otherwise, the curves may appear jagged to the extent that the relative positions of the characteristics might be indistinguishable.

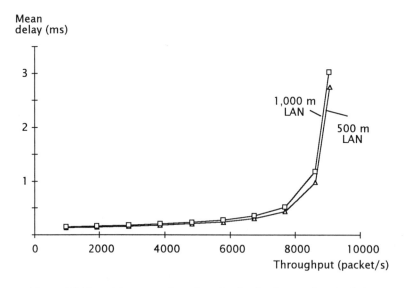

Figure 4.9 Mean delay versus throughput for simple token passing simulation.

4.4 SLOTTED SYSTEMS

Token passing is a protocol that has been implemented in LANs. The technique for simulating token passing may be applied to different types of network, equally successfully, however. In this section we describe the simulation of slotted systems that are more representative of telecommunication networks. Digital telecommunication systems that are based on the SDH and PDH formats, and even ISDN networks, rely on some form of *time division multiple access* (TDMA). In a TDMA system, time is divided into slots, normally of length equal to or at least related to packet length. We introduce here a simulation of fixed TDMA in which slots are permanently assigned for exclusive use by a particular node. This exercise also serves to illustrate how the simulation of different systems can be achieved by relatively minor modifications of the basic method.

4.4.1 Fixed Assigned TDMA

A simulation program for the fixed TDMA simulation, which operates as follows, may be constructed by modifying the token passing program. A network of nodes share a common transmission medium. Each of the nodes are synchronized to a common clock and time is divided into slots. All slots have the same length, which is equal to the transmission time of a packet. Each node on the network has the exclusive use of a particular slot, hence the term fixed assigned; and if there are N nodes, each is fixed assigned to use one in every N slots. This situation is depicted in Figure 4.10 wherein the time scale is divided into frames of N slots. When a node generates a packet for transmission on the network it utilizes one slot per frame. A flow chart of the program is presented in Figure 4.11.

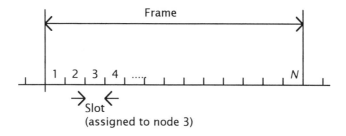

Figure 4.10 Frame structure of fixed assigned TDMA.

Upon inspection it may be noticed that only three elements of the flow chart are different compared to the one for token passing and that its overall structure is exactly the same. This gives some indication as to the amount of code replication and the comfort one can take in that having understood the operation of one simulation, the effort in developing new ones is significantly reduced. Similar to token passing, at the

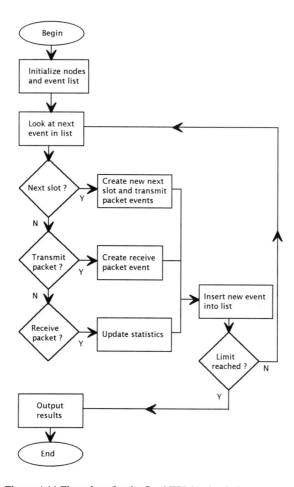

Figure 4.11 Flow chart for the fixed TDMA simulation program.

beginning of program execution the global constants, including data transmission rate, packet length, bit transmission time unit, propagation delay, and node population, are defined. The token length is obviously not required in this program; however, the slot length is an additional constant that is set to be equal to the packet length.

After this only two of the procedures in the fixed TDMA simulation differ significantly from the simple token passing program. The main one is as follows.

procedure allocate_slot;
var
   active_node_found, event_found: boolean;
   next_event_time: real;
begin
   active_node_found := false;

```
event_found := false;
next_event_time := event_que_front^.que_front^.event_time;
repeat
  a_node := node_array[node_index];
  if a_node^.tx_que.que_length > 0 then
  begin
    active_node_found := true;
    with an_event do
    begin
      control_procedure := tx_packet;
      event_time := clock_time + packet_length;
      node_id := node_index;
    end;
    insert_event(an_event);
  end
  else
  begin
    if (clock_time + slot_length) < next_event_time then
      clock_time := clock_time + slot_length
    else
      event_found := true;
  end;
  node_index:= (node_index + 1) mod node_population;
until active_node_found or event_found;
with an_event do
begin
  control_procedure := next_slot;
  event_time := clock_time + slot_length;
end;
insert_event(an_event);
end;
```

The *allocate_slot* procedure replaces *allocate_token,* and as might be expected it has the task of carrying out the fixed TDMA slot allocation. In a similar fashion as token passing, *node_index* is used to store the index of the node to which the current slot has been assigned. If its buffer queue length is greater than zero the first *if* statement in the procedure is *true* and a *tx_packet* event is entered in the event list to simulate a transmission during the slot. Otherwise a processing time saver that looks for the next event is executed and *node_index* is incremented to signal the passing of the current slot and to allocate possession of the next slot to the next node. In any case, once an active node or a new packet generation event is found, a *new_slot* event is created for the event queue.

The other procedure that has changed significantly from the simple token passing simulation is *transmit_packet.* Previously this procedure was required to create a new event for passing the token, as well for removing the packet, and clearly in the fixed TDMA program the token pass event is not required. Apart from these two procedures just a small number of obvious modifications are required to complete the program.

Recall that in general, when running simulations, we are concerned with a number of factors. Let us investigate the methods applied to the token passing simulation with regard to the fixed TDMA program. Some preliminary results, for similar parameters used in the simple token passing runs of the previous section are presented in Table 4.3.

datarate = 10000000;
btu = 1/datarate;
propagation_delay = 1000/(btu*2e8);
node_population = 10;
load_fraction = 0.5;
buffer_size = 10;
packet_length = 1000;
slot_length = 1000;

Table 4.3
Fixed TDMA simulation runs

Max_packets	Mean delay (ms)	95% confidence interval (ms)	Throughput (packet/s)	Run time (min:sec)
100	0.509	0.194	436	0:2
200	0.579	0.143	439	0:4
300	0.602	0.103	442	0:6
400	0.605	0.096	458	0:8
500	0.609	0.090	465	0:10
1000	0.606	0.058	483	0:18

Notice the significantly smaller run times compared with the token passing program. The discovery of the cause for this is left as an exercise for the reader. The results for mean delay, however, appear to be less stable. It is not clear that the steady-state solution has been obtained correct to three significant figures. Further runs showed that stability is reached above 200 packet transmissions per node, for which the mean delay is (0.605 ± 0.004) ms, with 95% confidence. This result was acquired well within the 1000 packets per node rule of thumb.

The fixed TDMA simulation may be validated in a manner similar to that of the token passing program. Again, a simple formula for calculating small load delays may be derived. Under small load conditions it may be assumed that normally the buffer is empty and, when a packet is generated, it is immediately placed at the front of the buffer queue where it is ready for transmission. In this case the only delays incurred are due to scheduling and service. For fixed TDMA the scheduling delay is, on average, the time taken for half of the effective frame length to circulate around the network. The frame length, L, is given by

$$L = N \times \text{slot length} \tag{4.9}$$

where N, as before, is the number of nodes. The service time is again just the packet transmission time plus the propagation delay. Hence the mean delay at low loads, D_{low}, is given by

$$D_{\text{low}} = \frac{L}{2} + \text{packet transmission time} + \text{propagation delay} \tag{4.10}$$

For the system with $N = 10$, 1000 bit packets, and a data transmission rate of 10 Mbit/s, a value of $D_{\text{low}} = 0.605$ ms precisely is obtained. The agreement with simulation is therefore quite good. Later in the text an analysis of fixed TDMA with variable loads is presented, and this may be used in a more rigorous process of mutual verification.

4.4.2 Random TDMA

A simple variation of fixed assigned TDMA, which is relevant in some slotted systems, is random TDMA. In this case each node may access any slot. The framing structure that was appropriate in the description of the fixed TDMA system is therefore not relevant here.

In order to simulate the random access of slots we can use the same program as fixed TDMA and, with the exception of one or two line additions and changes, only the *allocate_slot* procedure is required to be rewritten. The new *allocate_slot* procedure for random TDMA is as follows.

```
procedure allocate_slot;
var
  active_node_found, event_found, all_nodes_inspected, all_nodes_idle: boolean;
  nodes_inspected: integer;
  next_event_time: real;
begin
  active_node_found := false;
  event_found := false;
  all_nodes_inspected := false;
  nodes_inspected := 0;
  all_nodes_idle := true;
  next_event_time := event_que_front^.que_front^.event_time;
  repeat
    a_node := node_array[node_index];
    if a_node^.tx_que.state = active then
    begin
```

```
    a_node^.tx_que.state := transmit;
    active_node_found := true;
    with an_event do
    begin
      control_procedure := tx_packet;
      event_time := clock_time + packet_length;
      node_id := node_index;
    end;
    insert_event(an_event);
  end
  else
  begin
    inc(nodes_inspected);
    if nodes_inspected = node_population then all_nodes_inspected := true;
  end;
  node_index := (node_index + 1) mod node_population;
until active_node_found or all_nodes_inspected;
if all_nodes_inspected then
begin
  for count := 0 to node_population - 1 do
    if node_array[count]^.tx_que.state = transmit then
      all_nodes_idle := false;
  if all_nodes_idle then
    repeat
      if (clock_time + slot_length) < next_event_time then
        clock_time := clock_time + slot_length
      else
        event_found := true;
    until event_found;
end;
with an_event do
begin
  control_procedure := next_slot;
  event_time := clock_time + slot_length;
  node_id := node_index;
end;
insert_event(an_event);
end;
```

With random TDMA we have to account for the possibility that the *allocate_slot* procedure may be scheduled to execute again before a packet transmission is completed. This could, in certain circumstances, result in a second *tx_packet* event being created for the same packet. In fact, this situation may also arise in the fixed assigned TDMA simulation. A description of the circumstances and a solution to the problem are left as an exercise for the reader. Hence for the random method an additional field has been placed in the buffer type field of each node. This new field is an enumerated type called *buffer_state*, which has been defined in the type declaration section of the code as

buffer_state = *(idle, active, transmit);*

Now the preceding procedure is essentially made up of three parts. The first part has the task of inspecting a node, again identified as *node_index*, to see if it has a packet awaiting transmission. If it has, a suitable new *transmit_packet* event is created, otherwise the next node is inspected. The process is repeated until either an active node has been found or all the nodes have been inspected. The second part of the procedure is the processor time saving section, and the final part enters a new *next_slot* event in the linked list.

Under small load conditions a packet will arrive at the head of the buffer queue, on average, half way through the duration of a slot. Hence the mean scheduling delay is $S/2$, half of the slot length. The service time is again just the packet transmission time plus the propagation delay. Hence the mean delay at low loads is given by

$$D_{low} = \frac{S}{2} + \text{packet transmission time} + \text{propagation delay} \tag{4.11}$$

Using simulation, for a system with a data transmission rate of 10 Mbit/s and packets of 1000 bits, the low load mean delay is estimated to be (0.159 ± 0.007) ms, with 95% confidence. Using Eq. (4.11) we obtain $D_{low} = 0.155$ ms.

In Figures 4.12 and 4.13 we compare the mean delay/throughput and rejection probability/offered load characteristics obtained using the reservation TDMA simulation with those obtained using fixed assignment. Before analyzing the results it should be appreciated that, all things being equal, the capacity of fixed TDMA is the same as the capacity of random TDMA. In either case, the maximum throughput, in packets/sec, is the data transmission rate divided by the packet length. The same network parameters have been used in each case, and so it is fair to make a comparative performance analysis based on these results.

As it should be reasonable to expect, the delay for fixed TDMA is greater than for random access under low load conditions. In the former case, even though there are few packets awaiting transmission, those that are present must wait on average for half of one full frame. In the latter case they need only wait for half of one slot. Since the capacity of the two methods are comparable, the asymptotes to each delay curve should be coincidental and it appears that this may be the case. The rejection probabilities are significant when the offered load approaches capacity or is greater than the capacity. The rejection probability/offered load characteristics shown have thus been obtained using greater traffic intensities than for the mean delay. Again, since the capacities of the two systems are equal, it is fair to expect that the rejection probabilities of the two systems should not differ significantly, given that the buffer spaces are equivalent.

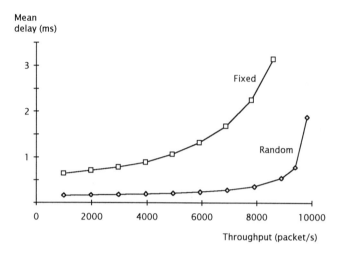

Figure 4.12 Mean delay versus throughput for fixed and random TDMA.

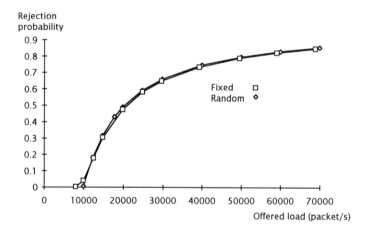

Figure 4.13 Rejection probability versus offered load for fixed and random TDMA.

4.5 SWITCHED TOKEN RINGS

In many engineering problems there is usually more than one way to implement a solution, and simulation programs are certainly no exception to this general observation. The reader who has been actively following the progress of the material in this chapter may have experimented with the programs and possibly even developed his or her own simulation. In this section we describe one of numerous possible methods for simulating multiple-segment systems. A popular method for expanding LANs is to interconnect them using bridges. At the medium MAC level a bridge effectively switches packets from one segment, or LAN, to another. In the following example the simple token passing algorithm, with which the reader now has some familiarity, is used as the LAN protocol.

The simulation of switched token rings presents a more complicated system that involves the inter-connection of two or more segments. The method of verifying the results with analysis is certainly not straightforward in this case. One reason for implementing multiple-segment LANs is that the volume of network traffic and the configuration of services is such that a large broadcast network becomes overloaded. When broken down into smaller units or segments, which are connected with a switch or bridge, the traffic is segregated. Thus packets that are not addressed to nodes on segments other than the one on which it was generated are not forwarded to any other segments. The complete code listing for the multiple-segment token passing simulation is given in Appendix B. A significant increase in the degree of complexity is reflected in the length of the program, which is nearly twice that of the original simple token passing.

The system operates in exactly the same fashion as the single-segment version, with the addition of a multiple-segment switching capability. Each packet is now generated with a destination address. If the destination segment is not the same as the segment address of the node that sourced the packet, then it is processed by the switch. The switch is effectively connected to all the segments and has a buffer at each link. The received packet is stored in the buffer corresponding to the destination segment.

A flow chart of the simulation program is given in Figure 4.14. In comparison with the simple token passing in Section 4.2, three additional event types and their associated procedures have been used. Namely, the events are *switch_packet*, *tx_switch_packet*, and *rx_switch_packet* and their respective procedures are *arrival_at_switch*, *transmit_switch_packet*, and *remove_switch_packet*. All the original procedures *allocate_token*, *run_sim*, and *report_results* have received considerable modifications and there are a number of additional types, constants, and variables, with some existing ones being redefined.

The constants *segment_population* and *hub_buffer_size* should be self-explanatory, as should the new types *address, packet, buffer, switch, and lan*, which are declared as follows:

```
address = record
  lan_id, node_id: integer;
end;

packet = record
  arrival_time: real;
  source, destination: address;
end;

switch = record
  packet_count, rejected_packets: longint;
  tx_que: array[0..segment_population] of buffer;
end;

lan_ptr = ^lan;
```

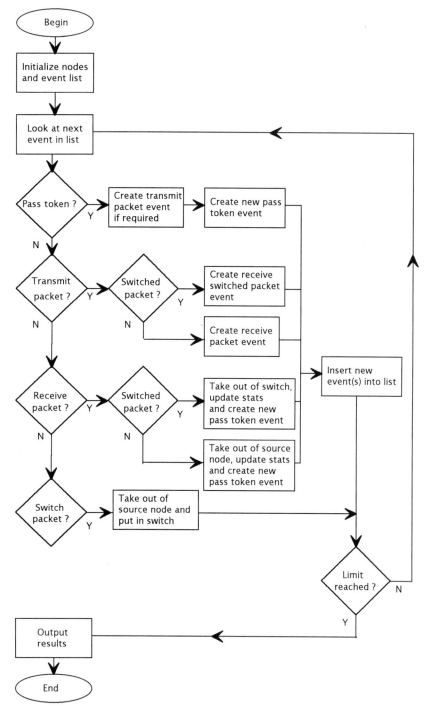

Figure 4.14 Flow chart for the simple multiple-segment token ring.

```
lan = record
  lan_population: longint;
  node_array: array[0..max_lan_population - 1] of node_ptr;
  token_id: integer;
end;
```

Two existing types have been modified. Node has an additional **longint** field, *lost_packets*, which is used to store the number of packets lost at the switch due to a full buffer, and the array in *buffer* has been redefined to contain *packet* types. Now each packet generated can be assigned values for the *source* and *destination address* types, which are simply integers identifying *lan_id* and *node_id* in each case. The switch type is similar to *node*, as might be expected, except that some of the longint fields are not required and additional *tx_ques* are included, one for each segment.

The procedure *allocate_token* has been modified to include the global variable of type *switch*, labeled *hub*, in the token passing process. It operates in the same way as for *token_simulation* by generating a *tx_packet* or *tx_switch_packet* event if required and a new *token_pass* event. The procedure *transmit_packet* has been modified to check the destination address field in the packet to be transmitted. In the case when the destination *lan_id* is not the same as the source *lan_id*, it becomes an inter-networked packet and this is implemented by creating a *switch_packet* event. Otherwise the *rx_packet* event is generated and the program executes in the usual way. When the *switch_packet* event has made its way to the front of the events list, the following procedure is executed.

```
procedure arrival_at_switch(the_source, the_destination: address);
var
  buffer_overflow: boolean;
begin
  buffer_overflow := false;
  inc(hub.packet_count);
  with hub.tx_que[the_destination.lan_id] do
  begin
   if que_length = hub_buffer_size then
   begin
     buffer_overflow := true;
     writeln('Buffer Overflow at hub');
     inc(hub.rejected_packets);
   end
   else
   begin
     inc(que_length);
     contents[que_length] :=
       network[the_source.lan_id]^.
            node_array[the_source.node_id]^.
            tx_que.contents[1];
   end;
end;
```

```
end;
a_lan := network[the_source.lan_id];
a_node := a_lan^.node_array[the_source.node_id];
with a_node^ do
begin
  if buffer_overflow then
  begin
   inc(lost_packets);
  end;
  dec(tx_que.que_length);
  if tx_que.que_length > 0 then
   for count1 := 1 to tx_que.que_length do
    tx_que.contents[count1] := tx_que.contents[count1+1];
 end;
end;
```

The flow chart in Figure 4.14 indicates that in this procedure the packet should be taken out of the source node and put in the switch, and this is indeed what happens. The order of execution is reversed, however. First the relevant buffer— that is, the one connected to the segment known as destination *lan_id*— is inspected to ensure that the buffer size is not exceeded. If the result is positive, then the packet is transferred by a suitable assignment statement using the contents field of *tx_que*. Otherwise the packet is lost and finally, in either case, the *tx_que* of the source is modified to effect the packets removal. In a similar fashion to the regular nodes the length of each of the queues in the switch is stored in an integer field, and it is this value that is inspected during *allocate_token*. If a switch packet is present during this procedure a *tx_switch_packet* event is created. The associated procedure *transmit_switch_packet* differs from the regular *transmit_packet*, in that it is not required to check source and destination addresses. The procedure *remove_switch_packet* also differs from the equivalent code for a regular packet in respect of the packet being removed from the switch.

The procedure *report_results* has been modified to output the statistics for each individual segment and the overall network. An additional performance criteria arises from the possibility that packets are lost at the switch due to a full buffer, and this is included in the output. The reader should be aware of precisely how the results are calculated so that they are correctly interpreted. For example, the packet rejection probability does not include those lost at the switch, as they are presented in a separate calculation. Multiple-segment network performance analysis is only recently receiving the attention of researchers, and at this time standard performance criteria have not emerged. It is apparent that many characteristics may be generated with multi segment systems through the many possible variable parameters. It is likely that individuals will exercise a preference for one or two characteristics of interest. One of the advantages with approaching simulation from first principles, using a high-level language, is the flexibility of being able to tailor the input and output required.

We have discussed a number of concerns when running simulations in previous sections. The first is with validating the simulation. As the system becomes more complex, so does this process. For example, the method of estimating low load delays is not straightforward in the multisegment case. We can, however, include *writeln* statements to output the information about each event as they occur and verify that events occur as expected.

The simulation was executed with the following constants, and the output obtained is presented in Table 4.4. Note that a system with just three segments was modeled and the values of the parameters for each of the segments, and the averages overall, are contained in the table.

datarate = 10000000;
btu = 1/datarate;
propagation_delay = 1000/(btu*2e8);
max_lan_population = 20;
max_buffer_size = 100;
segment_population = 3;
load_fraction = 1.0;
buffer_size = 10;
hub_buffer_size = 10;
packet_length = 1000;
token_length = 20;
token_pass_time = token_length + propagation_delay;
max_packets = 10 * max_lan_population * segment_population;

Table 4.4
Output of the multiple token ring simulation program

Parameter	Segment			Overall
	0	1	2	
Mean delay (ms)	7.017	4.587	4.407	5.337
Throughput (packet/sec)	2,684	4,963	2,481	1,0128
Offered load (packet/sec)	10,179	9,706	9,824	2,9709
Packet rejection probability	0.005	0.005	0.000	0.003
Packet loss probability	0.557	0.351	0.593	0.502
Mean queue length (packet)	4.70	3.40	3.95	4.02
Utilization	0.27	0.50	0.25	0.34

Hence the first thing to note is the amount of data available for analysis. Also we should expect the same figures for each segment, or LAN, since they were each modeled with the same parameters, with complete symmetry. This is clearly not the case and we look to increase the value of *max_packets* to obtain the steady-state solution. The preceding results were obtained with a simulation run length of just 10 packets per node on average. Intuitively we might expect that, compared with the single-segment case, around twice as many transmissions will be required due to the random nature of inter-network traffic.

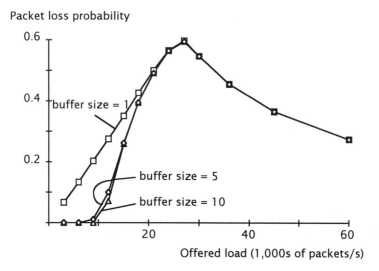

Figure 4.15 Packet loss probability at the switch as a function of offered load.

We have selected just one type of characteristic, concerning the switch, to illustrate the use of the multisegment token passing simulation. In Figure 4.15 the packet loss probability is plotted as a function of offered load, with switch buffer sizes of 1, 5, and 10.

4.6 THE INPUT PROCESS

So far in this chapter we have used exponentially distributed random variables to determine the inter-arrival times of messages at each node. The sources of randomness in communication networks and their statistical characteristics may be modeled using a variety of probability distributions. An important consideration in choosing the probability distribution for the random parameter is how closely the real process is modelled. Obviously the output data will depend on the probability distribution chosen, and the effect can be significant. Three methods for choosing suitable probability distributions are available. The first is to use actual data values, the second is to derive an empirical distribution, and the third is to use the best theoretical distribution. In the absence of data we are restricted to choosing the most suitable theoretical distribution, and we shall describe a number of suitable candidates in this section.

Families of probability distributions can usually, though often loosely, be described by one or more of three types of parameter. The location parameter specifies a suitable "x-value" for identifying the location of the distributions range of values. A change in the location parameter simply shifts the distribution on the abscissa. The scale parameter determines the unit of measurement for the values of x and thus changes the degree of compression or expansion. The shape parameter of a distribution changes the basic form, or shape, of its density function.

The process of generating random variables from a given probability distribution is not always straightforward. The basic ingredient for generating random variables from any distribution is a source of *independently and identically distributed* (IID) random variables. Since most high-level programming languages provide a standard function for returning IID variables between 0 and 1, we show how these can be used to generate variables from the required distribution. A number of techniques are available for achieving this, with the most popular and effective being the inverse transform method. A short algorithm describing the method for generating random variables using the random number function is given for each of the probability distributions.

4.6.1 The Random Number Generator

Before we continue with the statistical distributions in this section we should at least mention the random number generator itself. Though we do not wish to explore this subject in great detail the reader should be aware of some of the important factors that may affect the results of simulation. It is probably safe to say that manual methods of generating random numbers, such as throwing a dice, should produce purely random sequences. The use of computers, however, dictates that sequential methods have to be used where the next number must depend, at least to some extent, on one or more of the previous values. Using this process naturally gives rise to the question of how random, independent, and identically distributed such a sequence might be, and it is for this reason that computer-generated random numbers are often referred to as being pseudorandom.

It is generally reported that a good random number generator should possess a number of properties. Above all it should appear to generate independent, identically and uniformly distributed random numbers, usually between 0 and 1. Methods for assessing how well it does this range from visual inspection to rigorous statistical analysis. It is probably fair to say that modern generators incorporate well-developed algorithms that are perfectly adequate for the purposes of communication network simulation with which we deal in this text. The thorough reader who strives for peace of mind may, however, take the time to appraise their system. The test for goodness of fit, to a uniform distribution for example, may be accomplished using the chi-square test.

4.6.2 The Uniform Distribution

The simplest type of distribution is the uniform distribution, which gives an equal probability for the value of a random variable over a given interval. The continuous uniform distribution function is given by

$$F(x) = \begin{cases} 0 & \text{if } x < a \\ \dfrac{x-a}{b-a} & \text{if } a \le x \le b \\ 1 & \text{if } b < x \end{cases} \tag{4.12}$$

The corresponding density function is given by

$$f(x) = \begin{cases} \dfrac{1}{b-a} & \text{if } a \leq x \leq b \\ 0 & \text{otherwise} \end{cases} \qquad (4.13)$$

and this is graphically illustrated in Figure 4.16. The parameters of the distribution are the real numbers a and b, with $a < b$, such that either may be described as the location parameter and $b - a$ is the scale parameter.

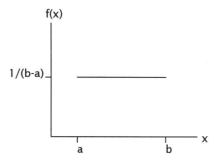

Figure 4.16 Density function of the continuous, uniform distribution.

The absence of shape in the uniform distribution provides intuitive evidence for the lack of a shape parameter. A more general form of distribution, known as the triangular distribution, is depicted in Figure 4.17. Here the shape parameter is c and clearly if $f(a) = f(b) = f(c)$ we obtain the uniform distribution.

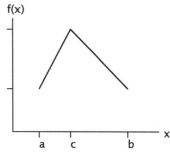

Figure 4.17 Density function of the triangular distribution.

The triangular distribution is probably not very useful in finding many applications in communication network traffic analysis, however, it does illustrate the use of a shape parameter quite well. It is easy to see how the value of c determines a number of the properties associated with the triangular distribution such as, for example, skewness. The skewness property of a distribution has been defined in a number of ways by using a combination of one or more moments of f. Since the location of c will have an impact on the moments and the skewness of a distribution will certainly affect the random variable, the shape parameter is an important concept.

The inverse transform method provides a simple algorithm for generating uniform random variables from a continuous distribution. If we put $u = F(x)$ in Eq. (4.12) and rearrange we obtain

$$x = F^{-1}(u) = a + (b-a)u \tag{4.14}$$

Hence given random variables between 0 and 1, in which case $0 \le u \le 1$, a uniform random variable between a and b may be obtained using Eq. (4.14).

The discrete version of the uniform distribution function is given by

$$F(x) = \begin{cases} 0 & \text{if } x < i \\ \dfrac{\lfloor x \rfloor - i + 1}{j - i + 1} & \text{if } i \le x \le j \\ 1 & \text{if } j < x \end{cases} \tag{4.15}$$

and its mass function, which is illustrated in Figure 4.18, is given by

$$p(x) = \begin{cases} \dfrac{1}{j - i + 1} & \text{if } x \in \{i, i+1, \ldots, j\} \\ 0 & \text{otherwise} \end{cases} \tag{4.16}$$

The integers i and j provide the location of the distribution and the value of $j - i$ determines the scale. In fact we have already used the discrete uniform distribution in Section 4. When generating traffic for the multisegment token ring simulation we arbitrarily chose the destination segment for each packet at random with equal probability. Let j be the segment number and the value of x be the chosen destination.

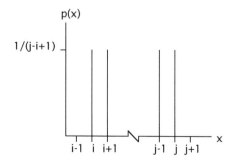

Figure 4.18 Mass function of the discrete uniform distribution.

Using the inverse transform method, if we put $u = F(x)$ and $i = 0$ in Eq. (4.15) and rearrange for x we obtain

$$\lfloor x \rfloor = F^{-1}(u) = (j+1)u - 1 \tag{4.17}$$

The line of code corresponding to the calculation of the destination segment, or *destination.lan_id* as it is written in the multisegment token passing simulation, does so according to Eq. (4.17).

4.6.3 The Exponential Distribution

So far in this chapter we have used exponentially distributed inter-arrival times exclusively. The exponential distribution is continuous and its function is given by

$$F(x) = \begin{cases} 1 - e^{-x/\beta} & \text{if } x \geq 0 \\ 0 & \text{otherwise} \end{cases} \tag{4.18}$$

The corresponding density function, which is illustrated in Figure 4.19, is given by

$$f(x) = \begin{cases} \dfrac{1}{\beta} e^{-x/\beta} & \text{if } x \geq 0 \\ 0 & \text{otherwise} \end{cases} \tag{4.19}$$

The location of the exponential distribution function on the abscissa is fixed and its scale may be changed by the variable β. The unique property of the exponential distribution is that it is the only continuous one with the memoryless property, and this is the reason why it is the most popular choice for generating inter-arrival times.

In a previous section we obtained the inverse transform using the density function of the exponential distribution. The same result is obtained if we put $u = F(x)$ in Eq. (4.18) and rearrange to give

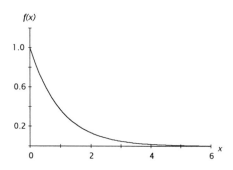

Figure 4.19 Density function of the exponential distribution.

$$x = F^{-1}(u) = -\beta \ln(1-u) \tag{4.20}$$

Hence given $0 \le u \le 1$ Eq. (4.20) can be used to calculate a continuous random variable that has been derived from the exponential distribution. Note that the subtract operation on the right-hand side of Eq. (4.20) may be eliminated by replacing $(1-u)$ with u since they have the same distribution. This results in a minor saving in computation when implemented in the simulation program.

4.6.4 The m-Erlang Distribution

If X_1, X_2, ... , X_m are m independent variables with exponential probability distributions, each with mean β/m, then $X_1 + X_2 + \cdots + X_n$ is an m-Erlang-distributed variable with mean β. The m-Erlang distribution function is given by

$$F(x) = \begin{cases} 1 - e^{-x/\beta} \sum_{j=0}^{m-1} \dfrac{(x/\beta)^j}{j!} & \text{if } x > 0 \\ 0 & \text{otherwise} \end{cases} \tag{4.21}$$

and its density function, plotted in Figure 4.20 for $m = 1$, 2, and 3, is given by

$$f(x) = \begin{cases} \dfrac{\beta^{-m} x^{m-1} e^{-x/\beta}}{(m-1)!} & \text{if } x > 0 \\ 0 & \text{otherwise} \end{cases} \tag{4.22}$$

The m-Erlang distribution is fixed in location with a scale parameter of β and shape parameter m. Notice that the $m = 1$ case is the same as the exponential distribution. One technique for generating m-Erlang-distributed variables illustrates the method of convolution. We have already stated that an m-Erlang random variable with a mean of β

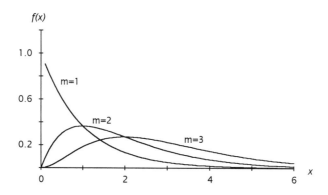

Figure 4.20 Density function of the m-Erlang distribution with $\beta = 1$.

is the same as the sum of m independent exponential variables each with a mean of β / m. Hence an m-Erlang variable is obtained from the sum of m variables generated using Eq. (4.20). The actual computation time for this algorithm may be reduced by noting that the sum of m logarithms factorize as follows:

$$\sum_{i=1}^{m} -\frac{\beta}{m}\ln(1-u) = -\frac{\beta}{m}\ln\left(\prod_{i=1}^{m} u\right)$$

(4.23)

again replacing $(1-u)$ with u.

4.6.5 The Weibull Distribution

The Weibull distribution is popularly applied to the time to failure of equipment and finds applications in network resilience. The Weibull distribution function is given by

$$F(x) = \begin{cases} 1-e^{-(x/\beta)^{\alpha}} & \text{if } x > 0 \\ 0 & \text{otherwise} \end{cases}$$

(4.24)

The corresponding density function is given by

$$F(x) = \begin{cases} \alpha\beta^{-\alpha}x^{\alpha-1}e^{-(x/\beta)^{\alpha}} & \text{if } x > 0 \\ 0 & \text{otherwise} \end{cases}$$

(4.25)

and the illustration in Figure 4.21 is the Weibull probability density functions with $\alpha = 0.5$, 1, 2, and 3 and $\beta = 2$. Again the position of the Weibull distribution on the abscissa is fixed and the scale and shape parameters are β and α, respectively.

The Weibull distribution function is easily inverted, and by substituting $u = F(x)$

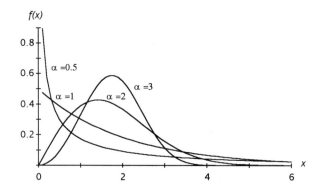

Figure 4.21 Density of the Weibull distribution with $\beta = 2$.

we obtain

$$x = F^{-1}(u) = \beta \left[-\ln(1-u) \right]^{1/\alpha} \tag{4.26}$$

Thus Eq. (4.26) provides a simple method for calculating a Weibull-distributed random variable.

4.6.6 The Normal Distribution

The normal distribution is often referred to in engineering disciplines as the Gaussian distribution and finds useful applications in modeling errors. There is no closed form for the distribution function because there is no primitive for the density function. In other words, it is not possible to solve the indefinite integral

$$F(x) = \int \frac{1}{\sqrt{2\pi\sigma^2}} e^{-(x-\mu)^2/2\sigma^2} dx$$

We have illustrated the normal distribution function in Figure 4.22 with $\mu = 0$ and $\sigma^2 = 1$.

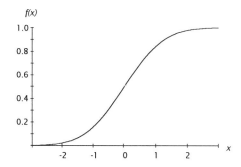

Figure 4.22 Cumulative function of the normal distribution.

The density function of the normal distribution is given by

$$f(x) = \frac{1}{\sqrt{2\pi\sigma}} e^{-(x-\mu)^2/2\sigma^2} \quad \forall x \in \{\text{real numbers}\} \tag{4.27}$$

and it is illustrated in Figure 4.23 with $\mu = 0$ and $\sigma^2 = 1$.

Because there is no closed form for the distribution function we cannot use the inverse transform method to generate normally distributed random variables, instead we use the so-called polar method, reported by Marsaglia and Bray, as follows. First we

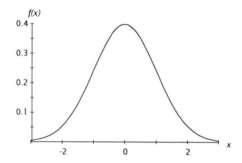

Figure 4.23 Density function of the normal distribution.

note that if the sample X is normally distributed with $\mu = 0$ and $\sigma = 1$, then $X' = \mu + \sigma X$ gives X' as a normally distributed sample with $-\infty < \mu < \infty$ and $\sigma > 0$. Now X can be generated using the following algorithm:

(i) Generate U_1 and U_2 as uniform IID variables with $0 < U_1, U_2 < 1$.
(ii) Let $V_{1,2} = 2U_{1,2} - 1$.
(iii) Let $W = V_1^2 + V_2^2$
(iv) If $W > 1$ go back to (i).
(v) Let $Y = \sqrt{-2\ln W / W}$
(vi) Let $X = V_{1,2}Y$

Note that two samples are generated from two random numbers for each execution of the algorithm.

4.6.7 The Lognormal Distribution

Another distribution that is useful for modeling the time to complete some task is the lognormal distribution. In the final section we utilize this distribution for the time to repair as it gives a more pronounced "spike" close to $x = 0$; and it may be fair to assume, in the absence of data, that this is likely to be the case. Again there is no closed form for the distribution function. Its density function is given by

$$f(x) = \begin{cases} \dfrac{1}{x\sqrt{2\pi}\sigma} e^{-(\ln x - \mu)^2 / 2\sigma^2} & \text{if } x > 0 \\ 0 & \text{otherwise} \end{cases} \tag{4.28}$$

In Figure 4.24 we plotted the density functions of the lognormal distributions with $\mu = 0$ and $\sigma = 0.5$, 1.0, and 1.5. The values of μ and σ determine the scale and shape, respectively.

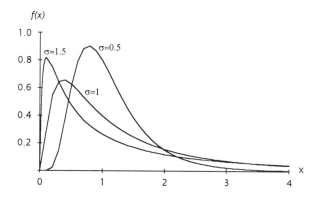

Figure 4.24 Density function of the lognormal distribution.

Lognormally distributed variables may be generated from normally distributed variables using the fact that if X is a normal sample, then $Y = e^X$ gives the lognormal sample Y.

4.6.8 The Binomial Distribution

The two simplest discrete probability distributions are the discrete uniform and Bernoulli distributions. We have already mentioned the uniform distribution that applies to random values that may take one of a finite number of possible values, each of which is equally likely. The Bernoulli distribution provides two possible outcomes and is usually thought of as generating random sequences of successes and failures. The binomial distribution provides a random number of successes in a certain number of independent trials, with a given probability of success or failure. If the number of trials is t and the probability of success is p, the distribution function of the binomial distribution is given by

$$F(x) = \begin{cases} 0 & \text{if } x < 0 \\ \sum_{i=0}^{\lfloor x \rfloor} \binom{t}{i} p^i (1-p)^{t-i} & \text{if } 0 \le x \le t \\ 1 & \text{if } t < x \end{cases} \tag{4.29}$$

and the probability mass function is given by

$$p(x) = \begin{cases} \binom{t}{x} p^x (1-p)^{t-x} & \text{if } x \in \{0,1,...,t\} \\ 0 & \text{otherwise} \end{cases} \tag{4.30}$$

In Figure 4.25 we have plotted the mass function for the four combinations with $t = 5$, 10 and $p = 0.1$, 0.5. The graphs serve to illustrate how t may be interpreted as either a scale or location parameter while p is certainly a shape parameter.

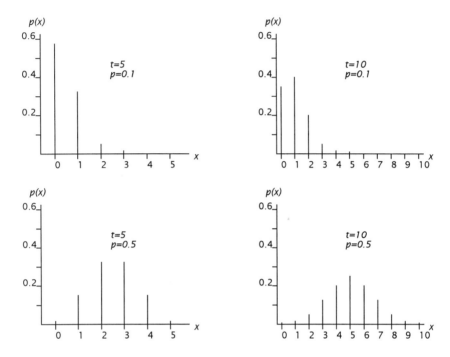

Figure 4.25 Mass functions of the binomial distribution.

A distribution closely related to the binomial distribution is that of the negative binomial. It describes the probability of a certain number of failures prior to a success. If the success occurs at the sth trial, then the distribution function of the negative binomial is given by

$$F(x) = \begin{cases} \displaystyle\sum_{i=0}^{\lfloor x \rfloor} \binom{s+i-1}{i} p^s (1-p)^x & \text{if } x \geq 0 \\ 0 & \text{otherwise} \end{cases} \tag{4.31}$$

and the probability mass function is given by

$$p(x) = \begin{cases} \displaystyle\binom{s+x-1}{x} p^s (1-p)^x & \text{if } x \in \{0,1,...\} \\ 0 & \text{otherwise} \end{cases} \tag{4.32}$$

In this case s has replaced t as the scale parameter while p remains the shape parameter.

4.6.9 The Geometric Distribution

The geometric distribution describes the number of failures before the first success in a sequence of independent Bernoulli trials. Again if the probability of success is p, then the distribution function for the geometric distribution is given by

$$F(x) = \begin{cases} 1-(1-p)^{\lfloor x \rfloor + 1} & \text{if } x \geq 0 \\ 0 & \text{otherwise} \end{cases} \tag{4.33}$$

and the probability mass function is given by

$$p(x) = \begin{cases} p(1-p)^x & \text{if } x \in \{0,1,\ldots\} \\ 0 & \text{otherwise} \end{cases} \tag{4.34}$$

Two examples of the mass function with $p = 0.25$ and 0.5 are presented in Figure 4.26. There is just one parameter associated with the geometric distribution. The value of p determines the shape of the distribution as it affects the eccentricity of the exponential envelope for the mass distribution.

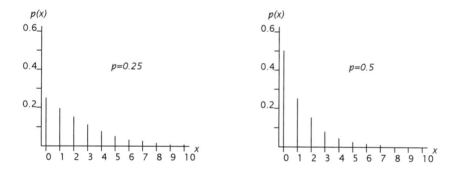

Figure 4.26 Mass functions for the geometric distribution.

4.6.10 The Poisson Distribution

A series of numbers generated from the Poisson distribution provides a sequence of independent random numbers with a prescribed mean value. It exhibits the memoryless property and is in this sense the discrete equivalent of the exponential distribution. The Poisson distribution function is given by

$$F(x) = \begin{cases} 0 & \text{if } x < 0 \\ e^{-\lambda} \sum_{i=0}^{\lfloor x \rfloor} \dfrac{\lambda^i}{i!} & \text{if } 0 \leq x \end{cases} \tag{4.35}$$

where λ is the mean value. Its mass function is given by

$$p(x) = \begin{cases} \dfrac{\lambda^x e^{-\lambda}}{x!} & \text{if } x \in \{0, 1, ...\} \\ 0 & \text{otherwise} \end{cases} \qquad (4.36)$$

and the graphs in Figure 4.27 illustrate the mass functions of the Poisson distribution with $\lambda = 0.5$, 1, 2, and 6. It is clear that the value of λ determines the shape of the distribution and so may be regarded as the shape parameter.

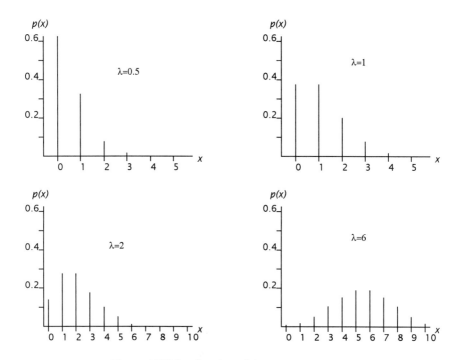

Figure 4.27 Mass functions of the Poisson distribution.

4.6.11 Use of Empirical Distributions

It is feasible the actual data obtained from real telecommunications networks could be used to specify an empirical distribution. This may be required in situations where a suitable standard distribution cannot be found. The derivation of continuous empirical distributions depends on the form of data given. As an example, imagine that data regarding the holding times of calls arriving at a telecommunications switch has been collected. The data has been used to produce the bar graph in Figure 4.28 (a), which shows the total number of calls of a certain duration in increments of 10 seconds. Each of the points on the distribution in (b) was obtained by summing the number of calls in

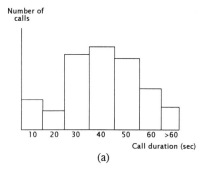
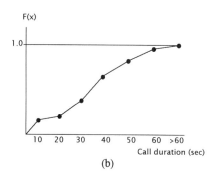

Figure 4.28   Data for call duration: (a) number of calls with a certain duration, (b) empirical distribution function for the duration of a call.

each interval and averaging over the total number of calls. A continuous distribution may be derived by linear interpolation, as shown.

Of course, when being used to model quantities based on samples, an empirical distribution still has the problems that any other distribution has. If it is based on too few observations, for example, then it may not be a true representation of the process that it is supposed to model. It is desirable that any distribution should be tested to determine how good the model is, and this may be acheived using, for example, the χ-squared test.

4.7 RELIABILITY

One of the important performance parameters of any system is its reliability. The reliability of a system is a measure of its resilience to failure. Strictly speaking reliability is not a measure with which the traffic analyst is concerned; however, when all or part of a communication network fails, there will certainly be some effect on the transmission of messages. In this section we will illustrate a method for introducing failures to simulation.

So far in this chapter the exponential distribution has been used to generate random inter-arrival times for data packets. Studies of reliability in systems have shown that equipment time to fail more closely follows Weibull-, lognormal-, beta-, and Pearson-shaped distributions, however. These distributions allow for the possibility that a system is likely to remain operational for at least some time. Similarly, the time to repair may be accurately modeled using these, with the lognormal distribution being a popular choice. Essentially, it is expected that there will be at least some delay before the repair can take place. Of course it may be anticipated that there will be a marked difference between the values of location and shape parameters for the distributions in each case.

4.7.1 Node Failures

Assume that the simulation of node failure and repair is to be included in a program. The program is to be designed using the discrete event-driven simulation method. The two additional procedures *down_node* and *up_node* will be used to simulate the actions that are part of these events. The events that execute these procedures are called *node_failure* and *node_repair*.

        The simulation of node failures may be accomplished as a background task, in the same manner as packet generation. When the initial event list is set up, prior to simulation execution, a *node_failure* event for each and every node is created. The code that follows provides an example of how this may be achieved:

```
with an_event do
begin
  control_procedure := node_failure;
  event_time := exp(ln(beta_fail) + (1/alpha_fail) * (ln(-ln(random)))) / btu;
  node_id := count;
end;
insert_event(an_event);
```

Note that this code resides in a *for* loop that is repeated *node_population* times. The line that assigns a value to *event_time* may be recognized as the condensed algorithm for generating random variables that follow the Weibull distribution. An example for a *down_node* procedure is

```
procedure down_node;
begin
  inc(node_failures);
  an_event := event_que_front^;
  a_node := node_array[an_event.node_id];
  with a_node^ do
  begin
   node_down := true;
   if tx_que.state = active then
   begin
    tx_que.state := idle;
    lost_packets := lost_packets + tx_que.que_length;
    tx_que.que_length := 0;
   end;
  end;
  with an_event do
  begin
   control_procedure := node_repair;
   event_time := clock_time + (lognormal(mu, sigma) / btu);
  end;
```

```
  insert_event(an_event);
end;
```

When the *down_node* procedure executes all the packets currently stored in the node, as identified by *node_array[an_event.node_id]*, are lost. A field in the node type, labeled *node_down*, is a Boolean value that is assigned to be *true* at this point. Any new packets caused by *generate_packet* being executed while *node_down* remains true are also lost. The final task of the *down_node* procedure is to create a *node_repair* event.

4.7.2 Node Repair

The time for repair is taken from the lognormal distribution, which is often used to model the time taken to complete some task because its density distribution has a more pronounced maximum close to the origin. The function code for generating lognormal-distributed random variables follows the algorithm described in the previous section and is as follows.

```
function lognormal(mu, sigma: real): real;
var
  R1, R2, V1, V2, W, X: real;
begin
  repeat
    R1 := random;
    R2 := random;
    V1 := (2 * R1) - 1;
    V2 := (2 * R2) - 1;
    W := sqr(V1) + sqr(V2);
  until W <= 1;
  X := V1 * sqrt((-2 * ln(W))/W);
  lognormal := exp(mu + (sigma * X));
end;
```

When the *node_repair* event is encountered at the front of the event list, the code in the following procedure *up_node* listed is executed. Two tasks are carried out in this procedure. The first assigns the negative Boolean value to the *node_down* field, and the second creates a new *node_failure* event. The time for this event is again calculated using the algorithm for Weibull-distributed random variables.

```
procedure up_node;
begin
  an_event := event_que_front^;
  a_node := node_array[an_event.node_id];
  with a_node^ do
  begin
```

```
   node_down := false;
end;
with an_event do
begin
  control_procedure := node_failure;
  event_time := clock_time +
                    (exp(ln(beta_fail) +
                    (1/alpha_fail) * (ln(-ln(random)))) / btu);
end;
insert_event(an_event);
end;
```

4.7.3 Performance Characteristics

As usual performance characteristics may be obtained using simulation programs that implement these types of procedure. With the introduction of node failures, however, we have presented more choices in the determination of suitable run parameters. A second termination criterion, based on the number of node failures, may be incorporated. The run time for a simulation that included the Weibull and lognormal distributions will depend on the values of α, β, μ, and σ, which are the parameters of the distributions that affect the node failure and repair mechanisms. Note that when choosing suitable values for these parameters the mean of the Weibull distribution is given by

$$W_{mean} = \frac{\beta}{\alpha} \Gamma\left(\frac{1}{\alpha}\right)$$

where Γ is the gamma function that simplifies to

$$\Gamma(k+1) = k!$$

for any positive integer k. The mean of the lognormal distribution is given by

$$LN_{mean} = e^{\mu + \sigma^2/2}$$

4.8 CONCLUDING REMARKS

The method of developing computer simulations in high-level languages, such as PASCAL, provides a flexible tool for performance prediction. The analytical models which that developed in the wider field, and in this text, generally require the imposition of restrictive assumptions. In the latter case, where the investigator is concerned with the operation of a system under conditions that do not satisfy these assumptions, a new analytical model has to be developed. A computer program that simulates the system, however, may be readily upgraded with extra lines of code or functions.

The processes in communication networks may be described as a series of events that are ordered by their time of occurrence. These events, along with the action of protocols, may be replicated in a type of computer program that is known as a discrete-event simulation. Three or four methods for implementing discrete-event simulation software have been identified. In this text we concentrated on the use of PASCAL as a high-level language. This is arguably the most flexible method for the individual because it allows complete control of the system design and the content and format of output data. Readers should now be aware of the general technique and the detail of more specialised methods that are required to develop a complete simulation experiment.

When running simulation experiments it is important that a process of verification is undertaken. Although the steps that should be taken are not clearly defined, there are a number of general techniques that may be adopted to increase the investigators confidence that the simulation replicates the intended system. Cross-checking the results with analytical solutions is one method— calculating the expected mean delay, for example. It may be the case, however, that the complexity of the simulation makes the analysis intractable. It may be possible to reduce the task into several smaller parts. In a reliability simulation, for example, a separate program could be used to verify the operation of the functions that simulate node failures and repair. Thus, combined with a method of checking the integration of these functions, a process of verification for the whole program has been performed.

Output analysis is also of concern to the investigator. There is a number of standard methods in statistics that can be used to provide confidence intervals for mean values, for example. It is also possible to generate extra data, to increase the levels of confidence, by repeating simulation runs with different random number generator seeds, for example. The degree of output analysis really depends on the requirements of the investigator. In the programs that have been developed as examples in this chapter, and those that have been used in later sections, satisfactory results are obtained using the rule of thumb that says generate 1000 packets per node. Generally, in this case, performance characteristics may be produced that permit the qualitative analysis of various performance metrics, including the mean delay, throughput, and loss probability. It should be noted, however, that such steady-state conditions may not be reached when the events of interest are infrequent. So-called "rare events" may require excessive processing times.

Exercises

4.1 Code the simulations for a source of traffic with exponentially distributed inter-arrival times using both event- and time-driven techniques, as given in Figures 4.1 and 4.2. Run the simulations using the same parameters and comment on any differences between the results you obtain and those quoted in the text.

4.2 Include additional lines in the program from question 4.1 such that the output is the result of averaging only the last 1000 arrivals out of a total of 2000 arrivals. How does the result compare with those previously obtained?

4.3 Include extra code in the same program that outputs the variance of the mean inter-arrival time. Also include a line that calculates the confidence that the mean obtained is within a specified range of the true mean, as predicted by Chebycheff's inequality. Determine approximately how many arrivals should be simulated in order to be at least 95% confident that the mean has been obtained within 0.02 seconds of its true value when the arrival rate is 10 messages per second.

4.4 (a) Write a program to simulate the arrival of messages. The messages arrive at fixed intervals of time and have a length in bits that is given by a random variable with a Poisson distribution. Provide output that gives the average message length. Run the program for 1000 arrivals. Calculate the expected result using the expression for the mean of the Poisson distribution, and comment on any differences between that obtained using the simulation. Include lines of code to output the variance, the confidence interval provided by Chebycheff's inequality, and the standard deviation. Experiment with the input parameters and investigate the accuracy of the predicted confidence intervals.

(b) Include lines of code that delay the collection of data for a fixed number of iterations. Experiment with different values for the delay.

4.5 Write a program that simulates an $M/M/1$ queue. Compare the results of simulation output data with those predicted by theory.

4.6 Write a simple token passing simulation program. Include lines of code in the program to save processing time, as suggested in Section 4.3.2.

4.7 Explain the difference between the run times observed for the simple token passing and fixed TDMA programs.

4.8 Consider the operation of the fixed TDMA simulation program. Under what circumstances is it possible that more than one *transmit_packet* is generated for the same packet. Design and implement a solution. *Hint:* Consider what happens at the first if statement in *allocate_slot* when there is only one active node. It is possible that the *que_length* field of the node is decremented after the next execution of *allocate_slot*.

4.9 Introduce nonsymmetric traffic loads to the simulations for random and fixed TDMA as follows. Divide the nodes into two groups and assign different values for λ to each group. Investigate the effects of different ratios for the traffic intensities by plotting mean delay versus throughput characteristics.

4.10 Derive an expression for the low load mean delay of all packets on the multiple-segment token passing system, described and simulated in Section 4.5. Assume that each packet is equally likely to be destined for any one of s segments. Compare the values obtained using this expression with the mean delay predicted by the simulation program.

4.11 The packet rejection probabilities at the switch of a multiple-segment token passing system are plotted as functions of the traffic intensity in Figure 4.15. Explain the apparent anomaly that as the intensity increases a point is reached where the rejection probability reduces.

4.12 Write down an algorithm for generating random variables from the empirical distribution function in Figure 4.27(b).

4.13 Investigate the effect of changing the parameters of the distributions for node failures and repairs in a simulation of reservation TDMA.

References

[1]   Law, A. M., and W. D. Kelton, *Simulation Modelling and Analysis*, second edition, New York: McGraw-Hill, Inc., 1991.
[2]   Pooch, U. W., and J. A. Wall, *Discrete Event Simulation, A Practical Approach*, Boca Raton, FL: CRC Press Inc., 1993.
[3]   Nelson, B. L., *Stochastic Modelling, Analysis and Simulation*, New York: McGraw-Hill, Inc., 1995.
[4]   Law, A. M., and M. G. McComas, "Simulation Software for Communication Networks," *IEEE Communications Magazine*, March 1994.
[5]   *IEEE Journal on Selected Areas in Communications*, Special Issues on Computer-Aided Modeling and Analysis of Communication Systems, Jan. 1984 and Jan. 1988.
[6]   Fishman, G. S., *Principles of Discrete Event Simulation*, New York: John Wiley and Sons, 1978.

Chapter 5

Event Graphs for Simulation

The event graph is a formal technique for constructing diagramatic models of discrete-event systems. It may be used to aid the process of developing computer simulations of communication networks using any high-level language. By following the complete set of algorithms involved in developing an event graph the investigator is provided with a structure for the program. In many cases it also produces the most computationally efficient approach. It should be clear from the previous chapter that positive contributions in these areas will be welcome.

The workings of any system are usually more easily understood when they are illustrated in a well-prepared diagram. A discrete-event model may be depicted in so-called event graphs [1], and this process could serve as a useful method for describing the system prior to implementing a simulation in code. Notation that requires the analyst to follow a well-defined sequence of steps has been developed, and this enables a quite rigorous approach [2].

5.1 METHOD

At this point, an overview of the technique, highlighting its benefits, will be instructive. There are three stages of development. First, when a simulation is being planned, all the possible events are listed along with their associated actions. Usually at least one of the actions will be to generate another event. A first event graph is then constructed from this list. Essentially, the system is depicted in a diagram as a group of discs and connecting edges. Each of the discs represent an event. Where two discs are connected by an edge, this indicates that the event associated with one of the discs may occur as a result of the event associated with the other disc; that is, one event causes another to be scheduled.

Second, the event graph is manipulated in such a way as to group the events that have certain properties. For example, where two events may occur simultaneously, and both modify the same variable, the order of execution may be important. This stage involves a number of steps, the details of which will be explained in the following subsections. The methodology is perhaps most easily understood when it is illustrated by example. In the following sections, each example has been chosen to illustrate one

155

particular mechanism. Since the code has been developed already, the reader should be able to concentrate on the techniques of event graph dvelopment.

In the final stage the event graph is manipulated in such a way as to reduce the number of unique events, in particular those that require entries in the event list, to a minimum. Recall that event list manipulation, in terms of processing time, is expensive. Thus reducing the number of events is a desirable feature of the process. The final graph should provide a clear picture of the overall structure for a simulation program. Generally, more complex simulations result in more elaborate graphs, and the process is likely to be more beneficial in such cases.

At all stages there are clearly defined algorithms that must be followed, and this provides a rigid framework of development for the investigator. In order to begin constructing an event graph, all of the processes that collectively make up the system to be simulated must have been described in detail. In the second stage the investigator accounts for the consequences of all possible event-scheduling anomalies. Again, the requirement for attention to detail serves to focus the development process. The event graph that is the result of the final stage provides an outline of the structure for the coded simulation program. Hence, if the event graph technique is applied correctly, the development of the actual simulation program should be more straightforward than if it had not been applied at all. Moreover, the resulting material may be retained as documentation, and this could prove to be useful during the process of validation, for example.

5.1.1 Event Graph Notation

Event graph notation is illustrated in Figure 5.1 where there are two events, j and k, depicted by two labeled discs or vertices. The events are connected by an arrow, or edge, which indicates that event k will occur as a result of event j. The figure more specifically states that k will occur t time units after j, given that i holds true. Edges may be attributed with both a condition and a time delay, one or the other, or neither. In the absence of a value for t, or a condition, then k will be scheduled to take place unconditionally and immediately following j. An example of a complete graph for simple token passing, which is described in detail in the next section, is given in Figure 5.6.

The first step in producing an event graph is to formally describe the system in terms of a set of variables, a list of events, the actions that take place in each event, and a description of the conditions that are used in conjunction with scheduling events. This

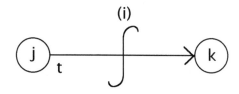

Figure 5.1 Event graph notation.

information provides the data required to construct an initial event graph. The process of choosing a set of events that model the system adequately and accurately is possibly the least straightforward task in using event graphs. Selecting the most suitable set of events is open to interpretation and the inexperienced reader should not expect to be able to complete this job without the benefit of having studied one or two of the examples in this chapter. In the early stages it is perhaps most important to appreciate that the main factor that determines the choice of system events is the time of execution. Any actions that do not occur simultaneously must be placed in separate events.

5.1.2 Formal Description

Let $V_1, V_2, ..., V_n$ be the system variables and let $VS_1, VS_2, ..., VS_n$ be their associated value sets. In the simple token ring system described in Section 4.2, for example, *clock_time* is a system variable that has a value set equivalent to the set of positive integers. Further, let the function $E(v_1, v_2, ..., v_n)$ denote the result of executing event E in the case when $V_1, V_2, ..., V_n$ take on the values $v_1, v_2, ..., v_n$. Let M be the set of all possible values $\{v_1, v_2, ..., v_n\}$, and let the variable S be the system state, which may be any one of these sets of values, at any given time. Note that each event does not necessarily require all the variables to evaluate its function nor does each event alter all the system variables. Hence an input variable of event E is defined as one whose value is required to calculate the outcome of the event. Similarly an output variable is one that may be altered by the execution of the event. Let the symbols I_E and O_E represent the sets of input and output variables for event E, respectively. Note also that the clock time and future event list are system variables and that the future event list is always a member of O_E.

Given an event graph G, an initial system state s_0, and a so-called end event, we can prescribe a computational sequence that proceeds as follows. In the first step, assign $S \leftarrow s_0$, and initialize the clock time and future event list.[1] Next the event with the earliest scheduled time, E_0, is selected from the future event list and processed. In the formal notation this is equivalent to executing the function $E_0(s_0)$. As a result of executing the function, the system state is now given by s_1 and a new next event, E_1, is taken from the future events list. Hence the simulation proceeds as $s_{n+1} = E_n(s_n)$ until the end event, or termination criterion, is met.

The major task in the event graph technique is the construction of an expanded event graph, G'. To demonstrate the purpose of the expanded event graph consider the section of unexpanded graph depicted in Figure 5.2(a). Here we have three events: X, Y, and Z. In this example Y is scheduled to occur immediately following the execution of X and Z to occur T_{YZ} time units after Y. Also the execution of Z results in X being scheduled to occur again. In Figure 5.2(b) event vertex X and the edge from X to Y of the unexpanded graph have been duplicated. A simulation following either the prescribed execution sequence of the graph in Figure 5.2(a) or 5.2(b), however, will compute in

---

[1] The $\leftarrow$ symbol is standard algorithmic notation that is used to indicate that the value on the right is assigned to the variable on the left.

precisely the same manner. The graph in (b) is an expanded version of that in (a) because there are more events. Now, since Z and X occur simultaneously and there is no time delay associated with the connecting edge, we can group these two events into a "super" event, or subgraph. Since Z is the first to be executed, it is known as the root event of the subgraph that contains Z and X. In the formal notation we say that Z is a member of the root set of G' and the two events Z and X form the subgraph SG_Z. The super event is depicted by the shaded area in Figure 5.2(c).

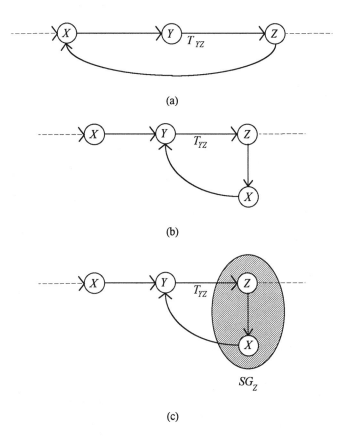

Figure 5.2 Event graph (a) before expanding, (b) after expanding, and (c) with the subgraph.

When a complete graph is expanded by following a procedure that will be described later, it will have the following properties associated with it. Each subgraph will have a single, unique event vertex called its root. All the events in a subgraph are reachable from its root via a path without a time delay. Only the root of the subgraph will have an incoming edge that originates from another subgraph. There will be no more than one subgraph with a particular root, and within each subgraph there will only be at most one copy of any event.

The advantage in using expanded graphs is the improved efficiency that results from the adjusted computational sequence, which proceeds as follows. As before, in the first step we assign $S \leftarrow s_0$ and initialize the clock time and future event list. Now only the root events may appear in the future events list, and the one with the earliest scheduled time, E_0, is selected. At this point all the events in SG_E are executed in the order determined by the subgraph. As before the simulation proceeds with the evaluation of $s_{n+1} = E_n(s_n)$, however, in this case only root events are placed in the future events list and the corresponding event list processing time is reduced. When implementing the simulation this implies that each event may be coded as part of the routine that corresponds to the super event.

There are two points here that are worthy of comment. First, the reader should by now appreciate that processing time is at a premium when running simulation programs. Even though linked lists are utilized, being the most efficient method of list processing, it is still the most processor time-consuming activity. The size of a linked list is therefore proportional to the simulation run time, and it is also directly proportional to the number of events that may be placed in it. Only the root events in an event graph are required to be entered into the list. Second, and following from the previous statement, the events that make up a complete super event, or subgraph, including the root event, may be coded as part of the same routine. Thus a single entry in the event list may be used to initiate the processing of all the events in a subgraph. There are two clear benefits of using the event graph technique: processing time is reduced to a minimum, and an overall design for the code is produced.

5.1.3 Initial Event Graph

Before the graph G can be expanded to form G', it has to be constructed, of course. Each event, identified by its index, is plotted as a vertex in a graph. An event that causes another to be scheduled is noted on the graph by connecting their vertices with a line or edge. An arrow, pointing to the resulting event, is included on every edge. Consider event X in the previous example. It contains an action that causes the immediate occurrence of event Y. Thus X and Y are drawn as two labeled discs with an adjoining edge beginning at X and ending at Y. Where the event is to be scheduled to occur after some time delay, such as Z is after Y, the time is indicated at the source of the edge.

It is possible for an edge to begin and end at the same event, in which case an event of the same type is scheduled. An event that is not the source of any edges, but only the end of one or more edges, is known as an end event. Any conditions that are associated with the secheduling of an event should be indicated on the edge that terminates at that event, as illustrated in Figure 5.1. Note that G may not be complete if all of the events listed do not appear on the graph at least once.

5.1.4 Expanding Event Graphs

The procedure for expanding an initial event graph may be conveniently described in the following steps. Note that not all the steps are always required. First identify the root events that make up the primary root set, P. In P place all the events from G that either have no entering edges or have an entering edge with a time delay. This collection of events is known as the primary root set since other events that also belong to the root set may be identified at a later stage. In the simple token passing system the primary root set is equal to the root set, in more complex simulations this is generally not the case. Next, construct the subgraph, or equivalently identify the vertex set, for each of the events in P. Any event that is not a member of P and is reachable from primary root event E via a path without a time delay is placed in the vertex set of E. This is the step that was carried out in the example of Figure 5.2.

In step two construct the secondary root set. These are additional root events that were not identified in the first step. There will be secondary roots, in certain circumstances, when event execution order priorities come into play. Execution order priority between two events E and F is important when the output variables of E are affected by the input variables of F, or visa versa, and the two events may be scheduled simultaneously. In this case the order of execution could affect the final outcome of one or more variables. It is said that events E and F may react with each other. Now any events that may be involved in priority conflicts must be made root events so that the computational scheme may account for the prioritization.

Consider the example of Figure 5.2(a), which has been modified to include event W, as in Figure 5.3(a). Now imagine that W and X react with each other in such a way that W must be executed first when the two events are scheduled simultaneously. As before event vertex X and the edge from X to Y of the unexpanded graph may be duplicated. In fact, if the process of identifying the events that make up the subgraph SG_Z is completed, then it is also apparent that Y may be duplicated, as in Figure 5.3(b). Hence, again, the computational sequence prescribed by the graph in (b) will be the same as that prescribed in (a). In this case, however, we are not allowed to group Z and X into a super event, since if W and Z were scheduled to occur simultaneously then Z may be executed first. In this case, since X would execute immediately after Z, before W, and in violation of the assigned priority, X instead becomes a secondary root event and the expanded graph in Figure 5.3(c) results.

Note that the procedure for computing the subgraphs of secondary roots is the same as for primary roots. A final modification is required because one of the properties of an expanded event graph is that there should be no more than one subgraph with a particular root. In (c) there are two copies of SG_X and we can simply remove one of these, with the result depicted in the graph in (d), without changing the computational sequence.

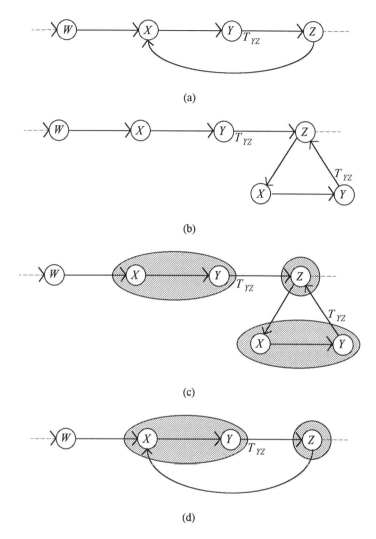

(a)

(b)

(c)

(d)

Figure 5.3   Event graph (a) before expanding, (b) after expanding, (c) with subgraphs, and (d) removing the unnecessary subgraph.

5.1.5 Merging Roots

It may be possible that subgraphs of G' with secondary roots can be merged with other subgraphs without disturbing the computational sequence. These are located in the final step. The process is best described with the aid of our example, which is redrawn in Figure 5.4(a), with an additional event V. Assume that the only priority conflict is between X and W, as was the previous case, and that V is a member of the primary root set. Following the method described we can obtain the subgraphs and draw the expanded graph depicted in Figure 5.4(b). Now a secondary root is mergeable if there is no event

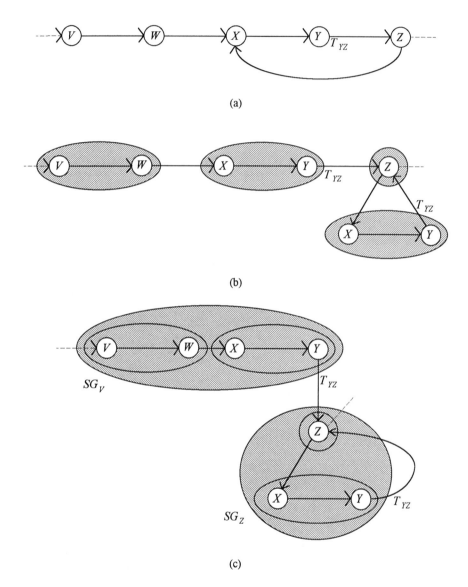

Figure 5.4 Event graph (a) before expanding, (b) after expanding, and (c) after merging.

in the root set with a higher execution order priority. Hence, since we have $P = \{V, Z\}$, X, the only secondary root, is a mergeable root.

To determine the subgraphs with which SG_X can be merged, if any, it is first necessary to identify any possible candidates by looking at the expanded event graph in its present state. If X is a mergeable root, then any subgraph, SG_Y, containing a vertex that is the source of an edge ending on X is a candidate for merging. The condition that must be satisfied to allow the merging of the two subgraphs is that there exists a path without a time delay from any vertex in SG_Y to the root of SG_X. Returning to the example in Figure 5.4(b) it can be seen that SG_V and SG_Z are two candidates for merging with SG_X. Moreover the condition for mergeablility is satisfied because of the two edges that begin at W and Z and end at copies of X. The ultimate form of the expanded event graph is illustrated in Figure 5.4(c).

By completing the process of expanding the event graph in (a) to the form in (c), the number of event types that requires event list processing has been reduced from five to two. The simulation program structure suggested by the sequence in the expanded graph will therefore exhibit a considerable saving in processing time as compared with that prescribed by the initial event graph. There are also implications for the overall structure of a coded simulation, and these will become clear when the examples are presented.

5.2 TOKEN PASSING REVISITED

The simple token passing simulation program that was developed in the previous chapter will be used as the first example to illustrate the event graph technique. A good way to begin constructing the initial event graph is to draw a simple diagram of the model. This will aid the process of developing the event structure before the formal process begins. The diagram should depict the path of some entity, which is the focus of the purpose for the simulation. The simple token passing model is illustrated In Figure 5.5, with arrows depicting the path of packets through the system.

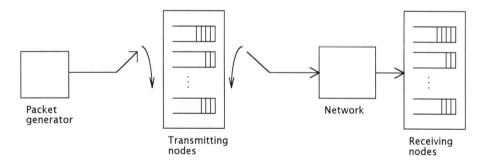

Figure 5.5 Simple token passing model.

Assuming that the collection of traffic statistics is the purpose for simulation, the packet is a suitable focus for the model. The packet generator is the part of the model that is responsible for generating network traffic. In a real system this might be the network adapter card in a personal computer, for example. When a packet has been generated it is then placed in a buffer of one of the transmitting nodes. Packets wait in the buffers until they are transmitted on to the network. Transmissions are ordered by the token passing method, so in the case of a first-come first-served queueing discipline the packet that is currently at the front of the queue is transmitted when the token arrives. Once the network transmission medium has carried the packets to their destination, the receiving node stores the data ready for processing.

The next step in describing the model is to list the system variables. The future events list is one variable that will be present in any simulation program, and the system clock time is likely to be another. The list of variables required for a particular simulation program may be updated as the model is developed. With hindsight, the complete list of variables required for simple token passing is presented in Table 5.1.

Table 5.1
Variable list for token passing

Variable name	Description
EL	The future events list
T	System clock time
Nodes	An array of node structures
TxBuffers	An array of node transmit buffers, includes *BufferLength*
RxBuffers	An array of node receive buffers
T_{ia}	Packet inter-arrival time
WP	Number of packets waiting for transmission
Token	Destination of the token
TPT	Total number of packets transmitted

Note that although these do not correspond exactly to the code used to declare the global variables in the token passing simulation, they are present for their stated purpose in some form. For example, *EL* has been implemented using a double linked list previously. A number of constants are is required, and these are listed in Table 5.2.

Table 5.2
Constants for token passing

Constant name	Description
NodePopulation	The number of nodes on the network
T_{pt}	Transmission time for a packet
T_{tt}	Transmission time for a token
T_{pd}	End-to-end propagation delay
MaxPT	Maximum number of packet transmissions

The events associated with the various processes in the system are given in Table 5.3. These events have been chosen almost arbitrarily, with the intention of including all the processes that collectively provide a complete description of the operational system. It may be the case that two or more of these events can be grouped into a single event without losing the accuracy of the simulation in its replication of simple token passing. One of the services provided using the event graph method is to reduce the number of

Table 5.3
Simple token passing events

Index	Description
1	Packet generated
2	Packet stored in buffer
3	Packet shuffled up in buffer
4	Packet arrives at front of buffer
5	Packet awaits transmission
6	Token received
7	Packet transmitted
8	Packet enters service
9	Packet received
10	Packet awaits processing
11	Token transmitted
12	Token enters service
13	Execution terminates

events to a minimum, and the cautionary approach of including more event types than may seem necessary is recommended.

As a general rule of thumb the time of execution and effects on system variables are the delimiting factors in choosing the types of event. For example, in events 5 and 6, which represent the packet awaiting transmission and token receipt, there are timely distinct actions. Now, the purpose of a simulation is to investigate progress in time, and the objective for delimiting the events is to determine the purpose of the code within the procedure that is associated with that event. Hence any processes that happen at different times must be placed in different events, and for events 5 and 6 this is the case.

The actions for each event, which will ultimately determine the coded procedures, are given in Table 5.4. The conditions referred to in the table are as follow, and the reader should take time to study them.

(i) *TxBuffer* not full: There is room in the nodes transmit buffer for the new packet.
(ii) Next memory location in *TxBuffer* is empty.
(iii) Front memory location in *TxBuffer* is empty.
(iv) *BufferLength* > 0: There is at least one packet remaining.
(v) *TPT* = *MaxPT*: Termination condition is reached.

Now the formal procedure begins with the construction of the initial event graph. As explained previously, this is a diagram that consists of event vertices and edges. Each of the events, identified by its index in Table 5.4, is plotted as a vertex in a graph. An event that causes another to be scheduled is noted on the graph by connecting their vertices with a line or edge. An arrow, pointing to the resulting event, is included on every edge. For example, consider event 1. This event contains two actions, each causing another event to be scheduled. It is therefore the source for two edges. One of these edges ends at itself due to action 1.1. The other, due to action 1.2, ends on a vertex representing event 2. Condition (i) is included with the latter edge. In the initial event graph only one vertex for each event is required. The complete graph for the

Table 5.4
Simple token passing event actions

Index	Actions
1	1.1 Schedule new event 1 at time $T = T + T_{ia}$.
	1.2 If condition (i) is true schedule event 2 at time T.
2	2.1 *BufferLength* $\leftarrow$ *BufferLength* $+1$
	2.2 If condition (ii) is true schedule event 3 at time T
3	3.1 If condition (iii) is true schedule event 4 at time T
4	4.1 Schedule event 5 at time T
5	5.1 *WP* $\leftarrow$ *WP* $+1$
6	6.1 If condition (iii) is false schedule event 7 at time $T = T + T_{pt}$
	6.2 If condition (iii) is true schedule event 11 at time $T = T + T_n$
7	7.1 *BufferLength* $\leftarrow$ *BufferLength* -1
	7.2 *WP* $\leftarrow$ *WP* -1
	7.3 If condition (iv) is true schedule event 3 at time T
	7.4 Schedule event 8 at time T
8	8.1 Schedule event 9 at time $T = T + T_{pd}$
	8.2 Schedule event 11 at time $T = T + T_{tt}$
9	9.1 *TPT* $\leftarrow$ *TPT* $+1$
	9.2 Schedule event 10 at time T
10	10.1 If condition (v) is true schedule event 13 at time T
11	11.1 *Token* $\leftarrow$ *Token* $+1$ mod *NodePopulation*
	11.2 Schedule event 12 at time T
12	12.1 Schedule event 6 at $T = T + T_{pt}$
13	13.1 Exit

simple token passing model is depicted in Figure 5.6.

The expanded event graph may be constructed by following the procedure described in the previous section. First, the primary root set is identified as the collection of events that are scheduled by an edge with a time delay. Thus, by inspecting the initial

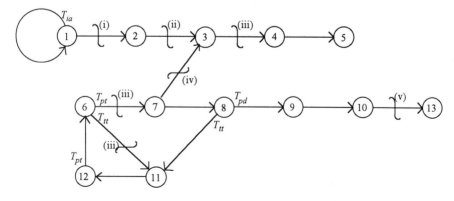

Figure 5.6 The initial event graph for simple token passing.

event graph, the primary root set for simple token passing is given by $P = \{1,6,7,9,11\}$. Next, the events that are members of the subgraphs that correspond to each element of P are obtained. Recall that in the trivial case event F is a member of SG_E if it is reachable from E via a path without a time delay and if it is not already a member of P. It may be verified that the subgraphs are found to be given by $SG_1 = \{1,2,3,4,5\}$, $SG_6 = \{6\}$, $SG_7 = \{7,3,4,5,8\}$, $SG_9 = \{9,10,13\}$, and $SG_{11} = \{11,12\}$.

In this case, as mentioned in the first section, the root set is the same as the primary root set, and this implies that the completion of step 1 is sufficient to derive the final expanded event graph. A sketch of the expanded graph is provided in Figure 5.7. Expanded graphs are constructed by drawing one super event for each subgraph. In each subgraph one event, identified using a disc, is used to represent each member of its vertex set. Ignoring the edges, this has been acheived in the figure by shading the area covered by a subgraph.

The edges are included as follows. For the events within a subgraph of G', the corresponding events in G are inspected. All the scheduling edges without a time delay that originate on the vertices in G, including their conditions, should be incorporated in G'. The edge that originates at event 7 and terminates at 3 is an example of such an edge. Note, however, that an edge that connects event 7 in SG_7 to event 3 in SG_1 is not included. At this stage we are only concerned with including edges which will be confined to the events within a subgraph.

In the case when there is only one event in the vertex set of a subgraph and there is a scheduling edge originating and ending at that event in G, this edge should be incorporated in G' irrespective of any time delay. In this case there are no examples of such an edge.

Finally, the subgraphs are connected by incorporating the edges that end at their roots. We refer here to edges that terminate at 1, 6, 7, 9, and 11. If there are any edges originating from events in G that do not yet appear in G', then these should be included along with their attributes. In the initial event graph of Figure 5.6, for example, there is an edge that begins at 8 and terminates at 9. This edge must be added to the expanded graph, as in Figure 5.7.

The formal procedure for the event graph technique is now complete. The expanded graph in Figure 5.7, which satisfies the properties associated with expanded graphs stated in the previous section, could be used as a guideline for coding a simulation program of simple token passing. We will compare the program structure suggested by the event graph technique with that discussed in the previous chapter.

The previous graph suggests separate event routines corresponding to SG_1, SG_6, SG_7, SG_9, and SG_{11}. To give the purpose of the routines some meaning, recall the descriptions associated with the events that are the roots of these subgraphs. From Table 5.3, for example, the root event of subgraph SG_1 is described as packet generated. Four more events are included in this subgraph, and each of them include tasks that should be carried out immediately following the generation of a packet. Hence a suitable procedure for implementing SG_1 may be labeled *generate_packet* and will include the code for actions 1.1 through 5.1, as described in Table 5.4. Similarly, a suitable label for the procedure that corresponds to SG_6 would be *receive_token*. This procedure will only

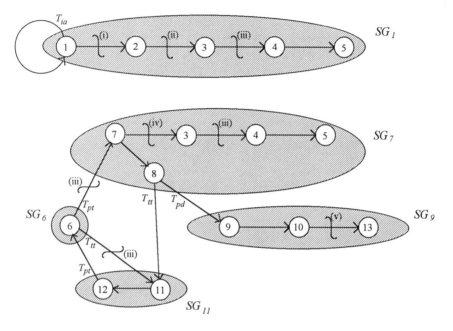

Figure 5.7 The expanded event graph for simple token passing.

include actions 6.1 and 6.2, since these are the actions associated with the root event that is the only vertex in SG_6. Suitable labels for SG_7, SG_9, and SG_{11} would be *transmit_packet*, *receive_packet*, and *transmit_token*, with the corresponding tasks easily found from Table 5.4.

A simulation program, having a structure suggested by the expanded event graph in Figure 5.7 and written in the same style as the simulations in the previous chapter, would therefore include a routine that identifies each event. The following code would be suitable for this task, and it compares directly with that which can be found in the *runsim* procedure of the token passing simulation program developed in the previous chapter.

```
repeat
  next_event := front_of_eventque^
  case next_event of
    generate_packet: generate_a_packet;
    transmit_token: tx_token;
    receive_token: rx_token;
    transmit_packet: tx_packet;
    receive_packet: rx_packet;
  end;
until packets_transmitted = limit
```

5.3 SIMULATING CSMA/CD

In this section the event graph technique is applied to develop a simulation program from scratch. Recall from the earlier description of CSMA/CD that each node on an Ethernet network continually senses the communication channel. If it is busy, then the node defers transmitting any packets until the channel becomes idle. Moreover, if the node senses another transmission during one of its own, it detects a collision and reschedules the corrupt packet for transmission at a later time. In this case we have chosen a randomized binary exponential backoff algorithm for the retransmission process.

5.3.1 The Event List

The first task to be undertaken is to list the events and actions from which an initial event graph may be constructed. For the CSMA/CD process, which is illustrated in the time diagram in Figure 5.8, we can begin with identifying a number of obvious events. In order to recognize the beginning and end of busy and idle periods time is divided into slots that have a length equal to the end-to-end propagation delay. This is convenient because a contention slot is twice this value and the length of the jamming signal following a collision is three times the value. Thus we begin with four events that may be conveniently labeled *start_contention_interval*, *start_contention_slot*, *channel_contention*, and *node_acquires_channel*.

The first event, *start_contention_interval*, occurs at the end of a successful transmission; and the second event, *start_contention_slot*, delimits the time taken for a node to determine whether a transmission has been successful. The event *channel_contention* occurs when a collision has been detected, and a *node_acquires_channel* event is scheduled following a successful attempt at transmission. In addition, two events will be required for the transmission and receipt of packets.

In order to determine the state of the channel at any time during the simulation so that we know whether a *channel_contention* or *node_acquires_channel* is to be scheduled, we will require some method for keeping track of nodes that are in the process of contending for the channel. This can be achieved using a collection of records, conveniently known as the contention queue.

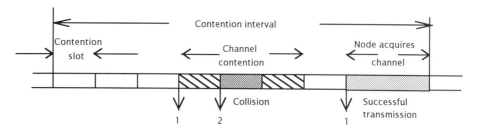

Figure 5.8 Time diagram for CSMA/CD.

When a node becomes active by generating a packet for its hitherto empty buffer, it is placed in the contention queue using one of these records. At this stage we can identify at least two fields that will be required in each record. One of these will store the identity of the slot during which the node became active. This will make it possible to ascertain the number of nodes wishing to transmit in the same slot. The other field will be required to store the value of the exponential backoff parameter if the node is involved in one or more collisions. When the node becomes idle, following a successful transmission that leaves the buffer empty, its record is deleted from the contention queue. Hence a dynamic construct is required for implementing the contention queue, and a linked list is appropriate in this case. Four events in total will be required to insert and delete entries and adjust and inspect the contention list. Along with events required for generating traffic at each node these are listed in Table 5.5.

Table 5.5
CSMA/CD events

Index	Description
1	Generate packet
2	Packet stored in buffer
3	Adjust Contention queue
4	Insert node into contention list
5	Take node out of contention list
6	Start contention interval
7	Start contention slot
8	Get contending devices
9	Channel contention
10	Node acquires channel
11	Transmit packet
12	Receive packet
13	Execution terminates

5.3.2 The Event Actions

The actions to be associated with each of the events are now required. As before, these are necessary to ensure that the simulated system reflects that which was required to be simulated in the first place. They should also provide the variables and structures that will enable the collection of data for analysis. For example, we may be interested in the number of packets rejected at full buffers. This may be easily accomplished by including a variable, say *rejected_packets*, that is incremented as a task in the *generate_packet* event if it occurs when the buffer of the node for which the packet was intended is full.

The acquisition of mean delay statistics, however, is a little more involved. In this case it is required that packet generation and receipt times are stored. Moreover, care should be taken to ensure that the packet receipt time, obtained within the event *receive_packet*, is associated with the correct time of packet generation, which will be set in *generate_packet*. This will require careful manipulation of the node buffer. A

Table 5.6

CSMA/CD event actions

Index	Actions
1	1.1 Schedule event 1 at time $clock\_time + random\_time$.
	1.2 If condition (i) is true schedule event 2 at $clock\_time$
2	2.1 If condition (ii) is true schedule event 3 at $clock\_time$
	2.2 $arrival\_time := clock\_time$
	2.3 $que\_length := que\_length + 1$
3	3.1 If condition (ii) is true schedule event 4 at $clock\_time$
	3.2 If condition (ii) is false schedule event 5 at $clock\_time$
4	4.1 $contention\_que\_length := contention\_que\_length - 1$
5	5.1 $contention\_que\_length := contention\_que\_length + 1$
6	6.1 $re\_tx\_factor := 1$
	6.2 $tx\_slot\_index := 1$
	6.3 $slot\_index := 1$
	6.4 Schedule event 7 at $clock\_time$
7	7.1 If condition (v) is true schedule event 8 at $clock\_time$
	7.2 If condition (iv) is true schedule event 10 at $clock\_time$
	7.3 If condition (v) is true schedule event 7 at $clock\_time + slot\_length$
8	8.1 $contending\_devices :=$ number of contention queue members with $tx\_slot\_index = slot\_index$
	8.2 If condition (vi) is true schedule event 9 at $clock\_time$
	8.3 If condition (vii) is true schedule event 10 at $clock\_time$
	8.4 If condition (viii) is true schedule event 7 at $clock\_time + slot\_length$
9	9.1 $re\_tx\_factor := re\_tx\_factor * 2$
	9.2 $tx\_slot\_index := tx\_slot\_index + 1 + (random * re\_tx\_factor)$
	9.3 $slot\_index := slot\_index + 1$
	9.4 Schedule event 7 at $clock\_time + jam\_time$
10	10.1 Schedule event 11 at $clock\_time + packet\_length$
11	11.1 $tx\_packet\_count := tx\_packet\_count + 1$
	11.2 Schedule event 12 at $clock\_time + propagation\_delay$
12	12.1 $que\_time := clock\_time - arrival\_time$
	12.2 $que\_length := que\_length - 1$
	12.3 If condition (ii) is true schedule event 3 at $clock\_time$
	12.4 Schedule event 6 at $clock\_time$
	12.5 If condition (ix) is true schedule event 13 at $clock\_time$
13	13.1 Exit

<u>Key to Conditions</u>
(i) $que\_length < buffer\_size$
(ii) $que\_length = 0$. (iii) $contention\_que\_length > 1$
(iv) $contention\_que\_length = 1$.(v) $contention\_que\_length = 0$.
(vi) $contending\_devices > 1$ (vii) $contending\_devices = 1$.
(viii) $contending\_devices = 0$ (ix) $tx\_packet\_count = max\_packets$.

Table 5.7
CSMA/CD variables and constants

Name	Description
clock_time	System clock time
random_time	Random inter-arrival time for new packets
arrival_time	The actual arrival time for new packets
que_length	Number of packets stored in a node buffer
contention_que_length	Number of nodes in the contention queue
re_tx_factor	The backoff parameter
tx_slot_index	Next slot for transmission
slot_index	Current slot
contending_devices	Number of nodes attempting transmission in the same slot
tx_packet_count	Number of packets transmitted
que_time	Queueing and transmission delay for a packet
slot_length	Time duration of a slot
jam_time	Duration of the jamming signal
packet_length	Time duration of a packet
propagation_delay	End to end transmission delay

complete list of event actions is given in Table 5.6 and followed by a key to the conditions. The variables and constants used in Table 5.6 are listed in Table 5.7.

So the requirements for constructing the initial event graph have been met, and the resulting graph, which may be constructed in the same fashion as for token passing in the previous section, is depicted in Figure 5.9. The reader should take the time required to verify the structure of the graph.

At this stage in the development of the token passing model the expanded event graph was produced. Before proceeding in this case, however, we must investigate one of the subtleties in using the event graph technique. Consider what would happen if events 3 and 12 were scheduled simultaneously. The course of action in both of these events depends on the value of *que_length*. Moreover, the value of *que_length* itself is changed in event 12. Hence it is possible that the order for execution of these two events could have an effect on the eventual outcome. Care must therefore be taken to ensure that, should these two events ever occur simultaneously, the order of execution is prescribed. All similar possible situations must be identified, and something known as the event interaction table may be used to assist in this process.

5.3.3 Event Interactions

The event interaction table should be created before the procedure for expanding the event graph is invoked. The task begins with identifying the input and output variables for each event. Recall from the formal description of event graphs that the input variable of an event is one that is required to calculate the result of executing that event and an output variable is one that may be affected. The input and output variable sets for

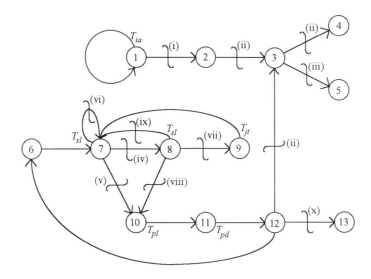

Figure 5.9 The initial event graph for CSMA/CD.

CSMA/CD are listed in Table 5.8. For example, the first action in event 9 is to calculate a new value for *re_tx_factor*. This is the variable used in the backoff algorithm following channel contention. The new value depends on the old value, thus *re_tx_factor* is both an input and output variable of event 9.

In the next step the events that may interact with each other are identified. This may be accomplished using an algorithm that will be described shortly. First, however, a

Table 5.8
The input and output variable sets for CSMA/CD

Index	I	O
1	*random_time*	∅
2	*que_length*	*arrival_time, que_length*
3	∅	∅
4	*contention_que_length*	*contention_que_length*
5	*contention_que_length*	*contention_que_length*
6	∅	*re_tx_factor, tx_slot_index, slot_index*
7	∅	∅
8	*tx_slot_index, slot_index*	*contending_devices*
9	*re_tx_factor, tx_slot_index, slot_index*	*re_tx_factor, tx_slot_index, slot_index*
10	∅	∅
11	*tx_packet_count*	*tx_packet_count*
12	*arrival_time, que_length*	*que_time, que_length*
13	∅	∅

number of terms and definitions are required. Let the closure of an event be defined as the set of events accessible from that event via a path without a time delay, including the event itself. Also, for two events, if one or more input variables of either are the same as output variables of the other, then these events may react with each other. Finally consider the closure of each event. If any of the events in the closure of one may react with any of the events in the closure of another, then the two events are said to interact. Note the subtle difference between reaction and interaction. Two events may react with each other if they share input and output variables. However, they may only interact if it is possible that they may be executed simultaneously.

The input and output variable sets in the preceding table, combined with the closure sets obtained from the initial event graph, result in the possible interaction sets given in Table 5.9. As an example consider the fact that event 8 is in the closure of event 6. This is so because 8 is accessible from 6 via two edges, neither of which incur a time delay. Also, tx_slot_index is an input and output variable of 9, and it is an input variable of event 8. Thus 8 and 9 may react with each other. Now, 9 is also in the closure of 6; therefore, 8 and 9 may interact. It so happens that tx_slot_index is an output variable of 6; hence, it also may interact with both 8 and 9.

Table 5.9
Event interaction table for CSMA/CD

Index	Closure	May react with	May interact with
1	1,2,3,4,5	Ø	2,3,4,5,12
2	2,3,4,5	12	1,3,4,5,12
3	3,4,5	Ø	1,2,4,5,12
4	4	5	1,2,3,5,12
5	5	4	1,2,3,4,12
6	6,7,8,9,10	8,9	7,8,9,12
7	7,8,9,10	Ø	6,8,9,12
8	8,9,10	6,9	6,7,9,12
9	9	6,8	6,7,8,12
10	10	Ø	Ø
11	11	Ø	Ø
12	12,3,4,5,6,7,8,9,10,13	2	1,2,3,4,5,6,7,8,9
13	13	Ø	Ø

5.3.4 Execution Order Priorities

When two events can interact it may be necessary to prescribe the order of execution. The execution order priority matrix should be constructed before proceeding to expand the event graph. It may take the form of a lower triangular matrix, with element i,j representing the relationship between events i and j. Conventionally n indicates that either events i and j do not interact or that they may never be scheduled simultaneously. A y indicates that they may interact, however their order of execution is not important. The values 1 and -1 mean that the events do interact in such a way that i takes priority over j and j takes priority over i, respectively.

An efficient method for completing an execution order priority matrix is to begin by setting the values of the elements for those events that may never interact to 'n'. For example, from the first row in Table 5.9, we can see that event 1 may never interact with 6, 7, 8, 9, 10, 11, or 13, and the first column in the matrix may be partially filled accordingly. Other elements may be set to n if the corresponding events may never be scheduled simultaneously. In this case, however, we are required to call on our knowledge of the process under scrutiny. For instance, we know that events 1 and 2 may never be scheduled at the same time because 2 always occurs uniquely as a result of 1.

For the empty elements that remain, it must be decided whether it is still important to assign an execution order priority. This is not a straightforward task and it requires an intimate knowledge of the process. For example, event 1 may interact with 3, 4, and 5, and they may also be scheduled simultaneously because of the edge that begins at 12 and ends at 3. In this case interaction is caused by a request from either 2 or 12 to adjust the contention queue. Since the order of entering or deleting nodes in the contention queue does not matter, the execution order priority is not important and the corresponding elements are set with the value y. The complete matrix is presented in Figure 5.10.

j	1	2	3	4	5	6	7	8	9	10	11	12	13
i													
1	n												
2	n	n											
3	y	y	n										
4	y	y	y	n									
5	y	y	y	y	n								
6	n	n	n	n	n	n							
7	n	n	n	n	n	n	n						
8	n	n	n	n	n	n	n	n					
9	n	n	n	n	n	n	n	n	n				
10	n	n	n	n	n	n	n	n	n	n			
11	n	n	n	n	n	n	n	n	n	n	n		
12	y	y	y	1	1	n	n	n	n	n	n	n	
13	n	n	n	n	n	n	n	n	n	n	n	n	n

Figure 5.10 Execution order priority matrix for CSMA/CD.

We can now proceed to expand the event graph, beginning with the task of identifying the events that make up the root sets. In this case we will be required to determine both the primary and secondary root sets. By following the procedure to identify the primary root set and inspecting Figure 5.9, we obtain $P = \{1, 7, 11, 12\}$. Now in computing the vertex set for each of the roots in P, we have to account for any execution order priorities. In the preceding table it was deduced that event 12 should take a higher execution order priority than events 4 and 5.

Recall that an event F is a member of the subgraph of E, SG_E, if it is not in the root set, if there is a path from E to F without a time delay, and if there is no other event with a higher execution order priority than F. The first two conditions are easily checked by inspecting the initial event graph, and the third condition is checked by examining the applicable element of the priority matrix. Any events that satisfy the first two conditions but not the third become secondary roots. As an example consider the subgraph represented by SG_1, which has event 1 as its root. The four events 2, 3, 4, and 5 are not members of the root set, and they are reachable from 1 via a path without a time delay. There are no other events with a higher execution order priority than 2 and 3, so they are all members of SG_1. Events 4 and 5 become secondary roots, however, since they have a lower priority than 12. It turns out that these two events make up the complete secondary root set.

The two root sets are combined and their vertex sets are determined as $SG_1 = \{1,2,3\}$, $SG_4 = \{4\}$, $SG_5 = \{5\}$, $SG_7 = \{7,8,9,10\}$, $SG_{11} = \{11\}$,   and $SG_{12} = \{12,3,6,13\}$. In the final step we investigate to see if any of the secondary roots are mergeable. Recall from Section 1 that a secondary root is mergeable if there is no event in the root set with a higher execution order priority. Since events 4 and 5 are the only secondary roots, these are the candidates for scrutiny in this case. Event 12 is a root event and it has a higher priority than both 4 and 5, however, it is still possible that they are mergeable. The special case here is that at any one time there may only be one occurrence of event 12 in the event list. As long as 4 and 5 are executed after 12, they may be merged with it.

By inspecting the graph in Figure 5.11 it can be seen that SG_1 and SG_{12} both contain vertices that are the sources of edges ending at 4 and 5 and are, therefore, possibilities for merging with SG_4 and SG_4. Further, since all of these edges are without time delays, both mergers are permitted. The final version of the expanded graph for CSMA/CD is presented in Figure 5.12.

5.3.5 Implementing the Code

The expanded event graph suggests that a simulation program can be implemented with just four event routines—one for each subgraph. Using suitable labels for these events, the following code may be used in the event inspection routine of the program.

```
repeat
  clock_time := event_que_front^.event_time;
  case event_que_front^.control_procedure of
    next_slot   : start_next_slot;
    tx_packet   : transmit_packet;
    rx_packet   : remove_packet;
    gen_packet  : generate_packet;
  end;
  event_que_front := event_que_front^.que_front;
```

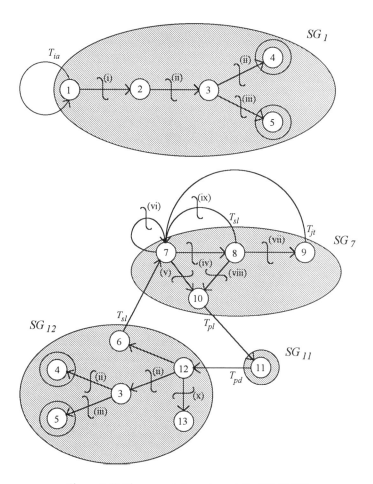

Figure 5.11 The expanded event graph for CSMA/CD.

dispose(event_que_front^.que_back);
until *tx_packet_count = max_packets;*

The structure of the event *gen_packet* is quite similar to the corresponding events in the previous example. In this case, however, the buffer manipulation routines, though still required, have been omitted for the sake of simplicity. The event *next_slot* encompasses 7, 8, 9, and 10 of the original list in Table 5.5. Thus in simple terms, if the original model were coded, four event list routines would have been used. It has been shown that one suffices. The subgraph that is represented by the event *rx_packet* encompasses an additional five events, and in total one may realize a saving of nine events.

5.4 CONCLUDING REMARKS

The event graph is a useful framework for developing computer simulations. By completing the various steps in constructing an event graph, the developer is required to follow a structured approach. The process of expanding an event graph results in a graphical representation of the most efficient program structure. In the final graph there may be two or more instances of the same event. Such events should be coded as a subroutine. Each subgraph may in turn be coded as a routine that is activated when the root event is scheduled. The goal of the technique that has been described is to reduce the number of subgraphs to a minimum. Hence the list processing time is reduced and the simulation run time should be significantly improved.

The use of the event graph technique is not essential. However, it will always provide a starting point for the structure of the program. It is generally accepted that a formal approach to any type of software development is preferable to coding from scratch. The documentation that has been produced in the process should also prove to be useful in the software maintenance tasks, and this is an added benefit.

Exercises

5.1 Draw the trivial event graph that represents the arrivals simulation in Section 4.1.

5.2 List and describe the major steps used to produce the expanded event graph for simple token passing.

5.3 Consider an early token release system whereby the token may be piggybacked on the transmission of a packet.
(i) Rewrite the relevant action(s) from Table 5.4. Include any condition(s) required to account for the possibility that the token may be received at the next node on or before the reception of the packet at its destination.
(ii) Draw the initial event graph.
(iii) Expand the event graph, making sure that execution order priority of token and packet receipt is preserved.
(iv) Modify a token passing simulation program to include early token release.

References

[1] Schruben, L., *Event Graph Modelling using SIGMA*, second release, San Francisco: The Scientific Press, 1992.
[2] Som, T. K., and R. G. Sargent, "A Formal Development of Event Graphs as an aid to Structured and Efficient Simulation Programs," *ORSA Journal of Computing*, Vol. 1, No. 2, pp. 107–125, 1989.

Chapter 6

Markov Analysis

In this chapter we will use discrete-time Markov chains to develop a self-contained method of network systems analysis. As with continuous-time Markov chains, which were dealt with in Chapter 3, the method is quite general in its application to communication networks and its solutions provide for the calculation of all the most useful performance indicators. Markovian analysis of even the most simple systems can give a detailed insight into the operation of the communications channel.

Our approach to presenting this material is intended to give the reader a methodology for developing models for analysis as well as utilizing the existing solutions. We begin with the fundamental concepts behind Markov chains and, in a similar fashion as Kleinrock, introduce a simple example to demonstrate the ideas behind this type of analysis. The chapter progresses with increasing complexity and covers methods that can be used for some quite complicated systems including access protocols with collisions and multisegment networks. In completing the course of this material it is hoped that the student will be armed with the capability to apply the analytical techniques to his or her own particular problems.

6.1 THE DISCRETE-TIME MARKOV CHAIN

Imagine a system that can be described as being in a particular quantifiable state at a particular time. As time elapses the processes within the system cause it to leave one state and enter another in some sequence. If the set of possible state values is discrete, then this sequence may be recorded as a series of numbers. If this series satisfies certain properties, then it is known as a discrete-time Markov chain and mathematicians have developed techniques for analyzing their predictable behavior. It would appear that this type of analysis is ideal for studying the behavior of communication networks. It is instructive to understand the properties that the sequence of state transitions must satisfy, and these are well-documented in most texts on the theory of stochastic processes and queueing. We will not attempt to cover this theory in depth. We will, however, introduce the terminology for stochastic processes and state the essence of the properties of Markov chains, a special kind of stochastic process, as they are required.

A stochastic process is a family of random variables, say $X(t)$, that are indexed by a time parameter, t. There are three quantities relating to a stochastic process that dictate how it is classified. First, the state space determines the values that $X(t)$ can take and may be discrete or continuous, finite or infinite. Second is the time parameter that also may be discrete or continuous. The terms X_n are normally used for processes with a discrete time series. Finally the statistical relationship between the values $X(t)$ is the property that provides the most distinguishing feature of a stochastic process. For example, if the relationship between the $X(t)$ remains constant with shifts in time the process is said to be stationary.

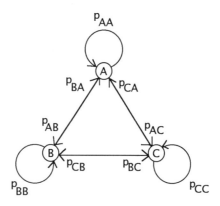

Figure 6.1 A system with three possible states: A, B, and C.

A Markov chain is a stochastic process with the memoryless property. It is memoryless because, like the Poisson, exponential, and geometric distributions, the probability for future events depends only on the present state of the system and not on its history. Without further delay we will look at a simple example that can then be used to illustrate the properties of Markov chains. Consider a system that has three possible states— A, B, and C— as depicted in Figure 6.1. The probability that the system leaves A and enters B at the next transition, given that it is already in A, is p_{AB}. The probability that it remains in A, given that it is already in A is p_{AA}. The terms p_{BA}, p_{BB}, and p_{BC}, for example, are similarly defined. The example in Figure 6.1 illustrates what is known as a state transition diagram. A matrix of the probabilities, P, known as the transition probability matrix, may be constructed as

$$P = \begin{pmatrix} p_{AA} & p_{AB} & p_{AC} \\ p_{BA} & p_{BB} & p_{BC} \\ p_{CA} & p_{CB} & p_{CC} \end{pmatrix} \qquad (6.1)$$

If we define the row vector π with elements π_i equal to the probability that the system can be found in state i, then the state distribution is given by

$$\pi = \begin{pmatrix} \pi_A & \pi_B & \pi_C \end{pmatrix} \tag{6.2}$$

Assume that initially the system is in state A, in which case $\pi_A = 1$, $\pi_B = 0$, and $\pi_C = 0$. The Eq. (6.2) becomes

$$\pi^{(0)} = \begin{pmatrix} 1 & 0 & 0 \end{pmatrix} \tag{6.3}$$

where the superscript is used to indicate the transition number; in this case, no transitions have taken place. The probability that the system ends up in A immediately after the first transition is given by $\pi_A p_{AA}$, which may be simply evaluated as p_{AA}. Similarly the probability that it ends up in B and C is given by p_{AB} and p_{AC}, respectively. At the beginning of the next step therefore, it is possible that the system may be residing in states A, B, and C with probabilities p_{AA}, p_{AB}, and p_{AC}, respectively. Hence we have a new state distribution given by

$$\pi^{(1)} = \begin{pmatrix} p_{AA} & p_{AB} & p_{AC} \end{pmatrix} \tag{6.4}$$

Note that Eq. (6.4) could have been obtained by multiplying Eq. (6.1) by Eq. (6.3).

Now the probability that the system will end up in state A immediately following the second transition is given by $p_{AA} p_{AA} + p_{AB} p_{BA} + p_{AC} p_{CA}$. Similar expressions for the probabilities of ending up in states B and C can be written and so the state distribution now becomes[1]

$$\pi^{(2)} = \begin{pmatrix} p_{AA} p_{AA} + p_{AB} p_{BA} + p_{AC} p_{CA} \\ p_{AA} p_{AB} + p_{AB} p_{BB} + p_{AC} p_{CB} \\ p_{AA} p_{AC} + p_{AB} p_{BC} + p_{AC} p_{CC} \end{pmatrix} \tag{6.5}$$

Again this expression could have been obtained from Eqs. (6.1) and (6.4). Hence the probability that the system will end up in a particular state immediately following the nth transition can be found from the product

$$\pi^{(n+1)} = \pi^{(n)} P \tag{6.6}$$

Imagine that the three possible states pertain to the buffer of a network node. States A, B, and C correspond to the buffer being idle, containing one packet and containing greater than one packet, respectively. Moreover, assume that the node is connected to a slotted channel such that state transitions occur at the slot boundaries. Let us assign some arbitrary values to P:

---

[1] The matrix is presented in transposed form for convenience.

$$P = \begin{pmatrix} 0.6 & 0.4 & 0 \\ 0.5 & 0.25 & 0.25 \\ 0 & 0.5 & 0.5 \end{pmatrix} \qquad (6.7)$$

In fact, the values of the elements of the matrix in Eq. (6.7) are not completely arbitrary. They have been chosen so that the rows all satisfy the total probability law. In other words, since the elements in each row of P represent the probabilities that the system either remains in the present state or leaves it to enter another one, they must add up to one. Closer inspection of P will reveal that it is impossible for the buffer to go from state A to state C in one step as $p_{AC} = 0$. That is, the arrival process dictates that messages consist of one packet and only one arrival may occur at a transition. Hence it is only possible for the system to enter the state where it has one packet or it remains idle given that it was already idle. Similarly only one packet may be serviced at any transition and so $p_{CA} = 0$. Further assume that initially the buffer was in state A, that is, it was empty on start up, and Eq. (6.3) gives

$$\pi^{(0)} = \begin{pmatrix} 1 & 0 & 0 \end{pmatrix} \qquad (6.8)$$

Now the state probability distribution immediately after the first transition is given by

$$\pi^{(1)} = \pi^{(0)}P = \begin{pmatrix} 1 & 0 & 0 \end{pmatrix} \begin{pmatrix} 0.6 & 0.4 & 0 \\ 0.5 & 0.25 & 0.25 \\ 0 & 0.5 & 0.5 \end{pmatrix} = \begin{pmatrix} 0.6 & 0.4 & 0 \end{pmatrix} \qquad (6.9)$$

Hence there is a significant possibility that a packet has arrived in the buffer and the event that two or more packets arrived is impossible. Similarly the distribution after the second step may be calculated as

$$\pi^{(2)} = \pi^{(1)}P = \begin{pmatrix} 0.6 & 0.4 & 0 \end{pmatrix} \begin{pmatrix} 0.6 & 0.4 & 0 \\ 0.5 & 0.25 & 0.25 \\ 0 & 0.5 & 0.5 \end{pmatrix} = \begin{pmatrix} 0.56 & 0.34 & 0.1 \end{pmatrix} \qquad (6.10)$$

Now there is a fair chance that there is indeed a packet stored in the buffer with a small possibility that there is more than one. Repeating this procedure, using Eq. (6.6), we find that

$$\pi^{(3)} = \begin{pmatrix} 0.506 & 0.359 & 0.135 \end{pmatrix} \qquad (6.11)$$

$$\pi^{(4)} = \begin{pmatrix} 0.483 & 0.36 & 0.157 \end{pmatrix} \qquad (6.12)$$

$$\pi^{(5)} = \begin{pmatrix} 0.47 & 0.362 & 0.168 \end{pmatrix} \qquad (6.13)$$

Clearly probabilities are tending to specific values. The distribution after the tenth step was found to be

$$\pi^{(10)} = (0.455\ 0.363\ 0.181) \tag{6.14}$$

In fact, the distribution in Eq. (6.14) was also obtained for $\pi^{(11)}$ and we can say that the system has reached what is known as the steady state. In other words, we have obtained, correct to two significant digits, the steady-state distribution of the system, $\pi = (0.46\quad 0.36\quad 0.18)$. Hence if we inspect the system at any time, the probabilities that the buffer is idle, contains one packet, and contains more than one packet are 0.46, 0.36, and 0.18, respectively. Notice that the sum of these probabilities is 1.0 and so the law of total probability is satisfied. Incidentally these figures give an indication of the required buffer size in the circumstances where the arrival and departure processes result in the given transition probability matrix P.

A mathematician would recognize the fact that π is an eigenvector of P, since $\pi = \pi P$; an alternative method of obtaining its value is to solve this equation. This fact arises when the Markov chain satisfies a number of properties as stated earlier. To understand the properties we need to introduce some terminology. The memoryless property we have discussed may be expressed as

$$\Pr[X_n = j / X_1 = i_1, X_2 = i_2, \ldots, X_{n-1} = i_{n-1}]$$
$$= \Pr[X_n = j / X_{n-1} = i_{n-1}] \tag{6.15}$$

In terms of our example this means that the state of the buffer at the end of a slot depends only on its state at the end of the previous slot. Given Eq. (6.6) this is clearly the case since $\pi^{(n)}$ describes the system before the transition and P is independent of n. If the transition probabilities are independent of n the Markov chain is said to be homogeneous, in which case

$$\Pr[i \rightarrow j] \stackrel{\Delta}{=} \Pr[X_n = j / X_{n-1} = i_{n-1}] \tag{6.16}$$

In our example the transition probabilities are given by Eq. (6.7) and as we have just stated these are independent of which slot is under inspection. It follows that for a homogeneous Markov chain the probability of reaching state j from state i after m steps, $\Pr[i \rightarrow j]^{(m)}$, is given by

$$\Pr[i \rightarrow j]^{(m)} = \Pr[X_{n+m} = j / X_n = i] \tag{6.17}$$

Now a Markov chain is said to be irreducible if there exists an integer m_0 such that

$$\Pr[i \rightarrow j]^{(m_0)} > 0 \tag{6.18}$$

Clearly the buffer system results in an irreducible chain because Eqs. (6.6) and (6.7) mean that for $n > 0$ the elements of $\pi^{(n+1)}$ are all greater than zero. In our example this is shown to be true in Eqs. (6.10) through (6.14). Further, if we define the probability that the first return to state j occurs n steps after leaving state j as $f_j^{(n)}$, then the probability that the system ever returns to j is given by

$$f_j = \sum_{n=1}^{\infty} f_j^{(n)} \tag{6.19}$$

In particular, if $f_j = 1$ the state j is said to be recurrent, and if $f_j < 1$ it is said to be transient. For recurrent states we may define the mean recurrence time as

$$M_j = \sum_{n=1}^{\infty} n f_j^{(n)} \tag{6.20}$$

and if $M_j = \infty$ the state j is recurrent null, whereas if $M_j < \infty$ it is recurrent nonnull. The states of an irreducible Markov chain are either all transient, all recurrent nonnull, or all recurrent null. Finally let the only possible steps the system can return to state j are $\gamma, 2\gamma, 3\gamma, \ldots$, where γ is the largest integer greater than one. The state is said to have a period γ, and if $\gamma = 1$ it is aperiodic. It is easy to show that the states of the buffer are recurrent nonnull and aperiodic. This means that there is a nonzero probability of finding the buffer in any state and that there is no restriction on the required number of steps taken to get there.

Now, for an irreducible and aperiodic homogeneous Markov chain the limiting probabilities

$$\pi_j = \lim_{n \to \infty} \pi_j^{(n)} \tag{6.21}$$

always exist and are independent of the initial state probability distribution. In the case where the system is transient or recurrent null $\pi_j = 0$ for all j. Otherwise the system is recurrent nonnull and π_j are uniquely determined through the equations

$$\pi_j = \sum_i \pi_i \Pr[i \to j] \tag{6.22}$$

and

$$\sum_i \pi_i = 1 \tag{6.23}$$

In the case of our buffer we have, from Eqs. (6.22) and (6.7), the following three equations:

$$\pi_A = 0.6\pi_A + 0.5\pi_B$$
$$\pi_B = 0.4\pi_A + 0.25\pi_B + 0.5\pi_C \qquad (6.24)$$
$$\pi_C = \phantom{0.4\pi_A + {}}0.25\pi_B + 0.5\pi_C$$

Also, from Eq. (6.23) we have

$$\pi_A + \pi_B + \pi_C = 1 \qquad (6.25)$$

Note that there is a linear dependence among Eqs. (6.24). Hence, discarding one of these we are left with three equations in three unknowns and the simultaneous solution is found to be

$$\pi^{(\infty)} = (0.46 \ \ 0.36 \ \ 0.18)$$

Thus the equilibrium solution obtained earlier is the same as the limiting probabilities. In summary, if we can determine the values of the transition probabilities for a system that has the properties of a discrete, irreducible, and aperiodic homogeneous Markov chain we can use Eqs. (6.22) and (6.23) to find the steady-state distribution. In subsequent sections we will use this to evaluate the useful performance indicators for a variety of systems.

6.2 SLOTTED COMMUNICATION SYSTEMS

In this section we will look at a slightly more complicated yet still quite general system. Assume that a network of nodes shares a common communication channel and each contains a single capacity buffer. The nodes are synchronized with the channel that has its time divided into equal-length slots, as depicted in Figure 6.2. The length of each slot is the same as the transmission time for a packet.

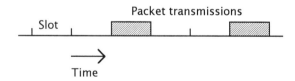

Figure 6.2 A slotted communication channel.

In the first analysis that follows we will consider what may be described as one of the simplest access control mechanisms. Packet transmissions are scheduled at the beginning of slots, such that packets originating from different nodes have an arbitrary order and are contiguous. This is commonly known as random TDMA. In this scheme each node that has a packet ready for transmission utilizes the next available slot for its own purposes. Further, we will assume that no contention or collisions occur in any of the slots in order to keep the analysis simple. In practical broadcast networks (excluding point-to-point links) this is in fact clearly not feasible and some mechanism of reservations or contention resolution would be required. We will move on to look at these more complex systems in due course.

Let us describe the state of our network system using the number of active nodes, that is, the number of nodes for which there are currently one or more packets awaiting or in the process of transmission. If packets arrive at each node randomly and independent, of each other, then the state of the system is also a random variable. We can generate a Markov chain by inspecting the system at the same instant in every slot, since the state of the system will depend only on the number of active nodes in the previous slot and the arrival/departure rates. If the average arrival and departure rates remain constant, then the chain is homogeneous. It can also be shown that it is irreducible and aperiodic.

Consider now a networked system of three nodes. Further, let the elements of the transition probability matrix be defined as the probabilities that at the end of slot k the system is in state j, given that at the end of slot k-1 the system was in state i as follows

$$p_{i,j} = \text{Pr}\,[\text{state} = j \text{ at end of slot } k \,/\, \text{state} = i \text{ at end of slot } k] \tag{6.26}$$

where $i = 0,1,2,3$ and $j = 0,1,2,3$. Notice that the notation for subscripts in the previous section have been replaced with i and j as is the usual and more convenient practice. Packets arrive at the nodes in each slot with a probability σ. Those packets that arrive at active nodes, whose buffer already contains a packet ready for transmission, are rejected and do not return. In such a scenario it is likely that the rejections will be of interest.

Now, if the state of the system is 0 at the beginning of a slot, then the probability that the state remains at 0 at the end of the slot, which is equivalent to that for which no packets arrive during that slot, is simply given by

$$p_{0,0} = (1-\sigma)^3 \tag{6.27}$$

This is known as the one-slot transition probability for $i = 0, j = 0$. The probability that the state transits from 0 to 1 is equivalent to the joint probability of one of the three nodes becoming active and the other two remaining inactive. Hence the one-slot transition probability $i = 0, j = 1$ is given by

$$p_{0,1} = 3\sigma \cdot (1-\sigma)^2 \tag{6.28}$$

Next, the one-slot transition probability for $i = 0, j = 2$ is the joint probability that two nodes become active and the other remains idle (an idle node is inactive), which is given by

$$p_{0,2} = 3\sigma \cdot (1-\sigma) \tag{6.29}$$

and similarly the one-slot transition probability for $i = 0, j = 3$ is given by

$$p_{0,2} = \sigma^3 \tag{6.30}$$

Eqs. (6.27) through (6.30) are given by the binomial distribution, and the general expression for the state of the system ending up in j given that the slot started life in state 0 is given by

$$p_{0,j} = \binom{3}{j} \cdot \sigma^j \cdot (1-\sigma)^{3-j} \tag{6.31}$$

where $j = 0, 1, 2, 3$.

The one-slot transition probabilities for $i = 1, j = 0, 1, 2, 3$ are also related by the binomial distribution. However, in this case the number of active nodes at the end of the slot is affected by the fact that one node was active at the beginning of the slot. That node will utilize the slot by transmitting its packet and will become inactive. Now this node is not permitted to become active again during this slot, since arrivals are restricted to occur at the end of slots. Hence the transition from $i = 1$ to $j = 0$ occurs with a probability equivalent to that for which the remaining two nodes stay inactive and is given by

$$p_{1,0} = (1-\sigma)^2 \tag{6.32}$$

The transition from $i = 1$ to $j = 1$ is the event that while one of the nodes is busy transmitting a packet, one of the remaining two nodes generates a packet and the other remains idle. The corresponding one-step transition probability is thus given by

$$p_{1,1} = 2\sigma \cdot (1-\sigma) \tag{6.33}$$

Next, the value of $p_{1,2}$ is equivalent to the probability that while one of the nodes is busy transmitting a packet, the two remaining nodes both generate a packet each; it is simply given by

$$p_{1,2} = \sigma^2 \tag{6.34}$$

The remaining state transition for a slot that begins with one active node is in fact impossible. The transition from $i = 1$ to $j = 3$ requires that all three nodes generate a packet during a slot in which one of the nodes is busy transmitting, and we have already stated that this cannot occur. Hence

$$p_{1,3} = 0 \tag{6.35}$$

Using the binomial distribution Eqs. (6.32) through (6.35) can be written in the more general form as

$$
p_{1,j} = \begin{cases} \binom{2}{j} \cdot \sigma^j \cdot (1-\sigma)^{2-j} & \text{for } j \le 2 \\ 0 & \text{for } j > 2 \end{cases}
\tag{6.36}
$$

It can be similarly shown that the general expression for the slot transition probabilities $i = 2, j = 0,1,2,3$ are given by

$$
p_{2,j} = \begin{cases} \binom{1}{j-1} \cdot \sigma^{j-1} \cdot (1-\sigma)^{2-j} & \text{for } j = 1,2 \\ 0 & \text{for } j = 0,3 \end{cases}
\tag{6.37}
$$

And the expression for $i = 3, j = 0,1,2,3$ is given by

$$
p_{3,j} = \begin{cases} \binom{0}{j-2} \cdot \sigma^{j-2} \cdot (1-\sigma)^{2-j} & \text{for } j = 2 \\ 0 & \text{for } j = 0,1,3 \end{cases}
\tag{6.38}
$$

It can be said that the last two expressions are a little overcomplicated. This is true, in particular, for Eq. (6.38) since the only nonzero term is $p_{3,2}$, which evaluates to 1. This is exactly what should be expected since if all the nodes are active at the beginning of a slot, then the only possibility is that a packet is transmitted and the system state reduces by one at the end of that slot. However, by writing the probabilities in this form, it is easier to see that a more general form for the transition probabilities can be written as

$$
p_{i,j} = \begin{cases} \binom{3-i}{j-i+1} \cdot \sigma^{j-i+1} \cdot (1-\sigma)^{2-j} & \text{for } i > 0 \\ \binom{3}{j} \cdot \sigma^j \cdot (1-\sigma)^{3-j} & \text{for } i = 0 \end{cases}
\tag{6.39}
$$

If we give σ a value, say 0.1, then the matrix P is calculated to be

$$
P = \begin{pmatrix} 0.729 & 0.243 & 0.027 & 0.001 \\ 0.81 & 0.18 & 0.01 & 0 \\ 0 & 0.9 & 0.1 & 0 \\ 0 & 0 & 1 & 0 \end{pmatrix}
$$

Remember that in order to preserve the law of total probability each of the rows must add to one, and this is in fact the case. Now in order to find the steady-state solution, from Eqs. (6.22) and (6.23) we are required to solve the simultaneous equations formed by

$$\pi = \pi \cdot P \quad \text{and} \quad \sum_{s=0}^{3} \pi_s = 1$$

where π is a row vector of elements π_s, $s = 0,1,2,3$, the steady-state probability distribution for the system. Since the equations are linearly dependent, they can be solved using the formula

$$\pi = \begin{pmatrix} 1 & 0 & 0 & 0 \end{pmatrix} \cdot (P'-I)^{-1} \tag{6.40}$$

where P' is the same as P with $p_{0,j} = 1$ for $j = 0,1,2,3$. The result for the case $\sigma = 0.1$ is

$$\pi = \begin{pmatrix} 0.73 & 0.244 & 0.025 & 7.297 \times 10^{-4} \end{pmatrix}$$

Hence if we observe the system at an arbitrary point in time, the probability that there will be no active nodes, given by π_0, is quite high at 0.73. This should be expected since each of three nodes only generate a packet during a slot with a probability of 0.1. The solution obtained when $\sigma = 0.5$ is

$$\pi = \begin{pmatrix} 0.136 & 0.475 & 0.373 & 0.017 \end{pmatrix}$$

Now there is a one in two chance that every node generates a packet for every slot, and so the probability that we will find the system in the condition where all three nodes are idle is just 0.136. However, there is a probability of $\pi_1 + \pi_2 = 0.848$ that the system will contain one or two active nodes. The chance of all the nodes being active, π_3, is still small because our ideal access mechanism is highly efficient and new packets generated at a node that is utilizing the current slot are rejected.

We can go on to calculate a number of performance criteria that might be of interest. First, the throughput of the system, S, is given by the percentage of time the channel is involved in transmitting packets. Here this is given by the sum of the steady-state probabilities that the system has one or more active nodes, or

$$S = \pi \cdot J \tag{6.41}$$

where J is a column vector with elements $j_0 = 0$ and $j_k = 1$ for $k = 1,2,3$. The throughputs for $\sigma = 0.1$ and 0.5 are calculated to be 0.27 and 0.864, correct to three significant figures, respectively.

A plot of traffic intensity for offered load and throughput as a function of packet generation probability is given in Figure 6.3. As the figure shows, the actual throughput of the system is less than the offered load, due to the rejection of new packets at busy nodes. As the packet generation probability increases, more packets are rejected and the difference between actual and ideal throughput increases. As the generation probability increases to one, so does the probability that all the users will be found active and the actual throughput reaches the capacity of the network. The ideal throughput, being the

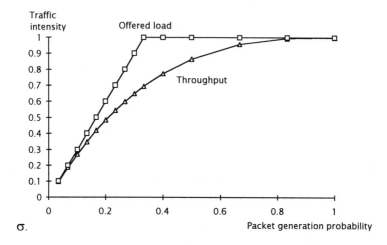

Figure 6.3 Network traffic as a function of packet generation probability.

number of packets generated, is directly proportional to σ. Hence it is easy to show that the rejection probability is given by

$$RP = 1 - \frac{S}{N\sigma} \tag{6.42}$$

Figure 6.4 shows a plot of the rejection probability as a function of the packet generation probability given by Eq. (6.42). As predicted by the ideal and actual throughputs, the rejection probability steadily increases. When each node generates a

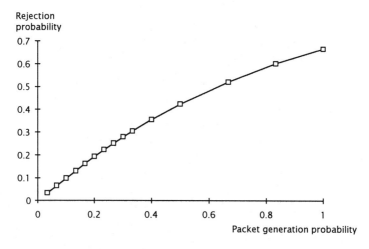

Figure 6.4 Rejection probability as a function of packet generation probability.

packet for every slot, that is, for $\sigma = 1.0$, the probability that it is rejected is a considerable 0.67.

Another performance criteria that is often of interest is the expected queue lengths at nodes. This gives an indication of the buffer occupancy and can be used to determine the required capacity for a particular system. Here the capacity of each node is just one and we have already clearly demonstrated, for this simplified system, that for only moderate traffic intensity the rejection probability is likely to be intolerable. Even so, it is instructive to look at a parameter that is closely related to the queue length at each node, namely, the number of packets in all the nodes, or the backlog. This is easily calculated using the formula

$$Q = \pi \cdot \beta \tag{6.43}$$

where β is a column vector with elements $\beta_k = k$ for $k = 0,1,2,3$. In effect, Q here is the expected state of the system if it was observed at an arbitrary time, but this is not always the case. The backlogs for $\sigma = 0.1$ and 0.5 are calculated to be 0.297 and 1.271, respectively, correct to three significant figures. Finally we can write an expression for the mean delay of transmitted packets, using Little's result in Eq. (3.70), noting the redefined terms, such that

$$D = \frac{Q}{S} \tag{6.44}$$

The values of Q and D given by Eqs. (6.43) and (6.44) are plotted as functions of packet generation probability and throughput in Figures 6.5 and 6.6. The underlying trend of the characteristics are as expected, and it is reassuring to note that the maximum possible backlog and mean delay are obtained for both maximum possible packet

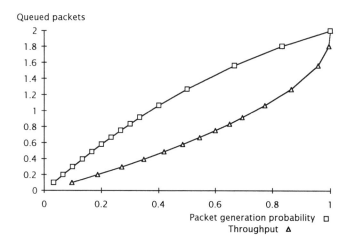

Figure 6.5 Backlog as a function of packet generation probability and throughput.

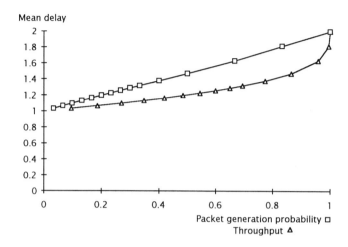

Figure 6.6 Mean delay as a function of packet generation probability and throughput.

generation probability and throughput.

Because we have studied a very simple, idealized system, it is not worth continuing a discussion of the results here to any great depth. At the outset we have already determined that this network has a high rejection probability and so the delay characteristics, which are only relevant to the packets that were allowed access to the system, are not really a useful performance criteria.

It is instructive, however, to investigate alternative applications of this simple technique. Next we will look at a way of modeling a slightly modified access strategy. It has already been stated that the random TDMA mechanism used for the previous analysis would in fact be impossible to implement in a real network. Perhaps the simplest modification that would permit this would be to assign particular nodes the exclusive use of particular slots in a fixed assigned TDMA fashion. There is now no question of any contention arising, and no collisions will take place that would require resolving.

In this case we distinguish between slots that remain idle and slots that are utilized. It is possible for a slot to remain idle even if at its beginning there is one or more active nodes. Previously this was not necessary because a slot was always utilized, providing at least one node had a packet ready for transmission. Now it is possible that the node that is assigned to the current slot may be inactive, in which case even if one of the other nodes were active then the slot remains unused. On average, it can be said that each slot is utilized with probability $i/3$, given that there were i busy nodes at the beginning of the slot. Hence the elements of the transition probability matrix for active slots are given by

$$
pa_{i,j} = \begin{cases} \dfrac{i}{3}\dbinom{3-i}{j-i+1}\cdot \sigma^{j-i+1}\cdot(1-\sigma)^{2-j} & \text{for } i > 0 \\ 0 & \text{for } i = 0 \end{cases}
$$

(6.45)

and the corresponding elements of the matrix for idle slots, which occur with probability $(1-i/3)$, are given by

$$pi_{i,j} = \begin{cases} \left(1-\dfrac{i}{3}\right)\left(\dfrac{3-i}{j-i+1}\right)\cdot\sigma^{j-i+1}\cdot(1-\sigma)^{2-j} & \text{for } i > 0 \\ \left(1-\dfrac{i}{3}\right)\left(\dfrac{3}{j}\right)\cdot\sigma^{j}\cdot(1-\sigma)^{3-j} & \text{for } i = 0 \end{cases}$$ (6.46)

where $j = 0,1,2,3$. These expressions were obtained simply by imposing the active and idle slot probabilities on the expressions obtained for the transition probabilities of the random TDMA system in Eq. (6.39). For $\sigma = 0.1$ the matrices are calculated to be

$$PA = \begin{pmatrix} 0 & 0 & 0 & 0 \\ 0.27 & 0.06 & 0.003 & 0 \\ 0 & 0.6 & 0.067 & 0 \\ 0 & 0 & 1 & 0 \end{pmatrix} \qquad PI = \begin{pmatrix} 0.729 & 0.243 & 0.027 & 0.001 \\ 0 & 0.54 & 0.12 & 0.007 \\ 0 & 0 & 0.3 & 0.033 \\ 0 & 0 & 0 & 0 \end{pmatrix}$$

The system transition probability matrix is calculated as the sum

$$P = PA + PI$$ (6.47)

and it is reassuring to note that again the law of total probability is observed since, if H is the unit column vector, using the values of PA and PI in Eq. (6.47) we calculate

$$P \cdot H = \begin{pmatrix} 1 \\ 1 \\ 1 \\ 1 \end{pmatrix}$$

We can solve for the steady-state distribution, π, using Eq. (6.40) in the same manner as the previous analysis. The throughput of the system is the probability that an arbitrary slot is utilized, and this is given by the expression

$$S = \pi \cdot PA \cdot H$$ (6.48)

The throughputs at $\sigma = 0.1$ and 0.5 are calculated to be 0.231 and 0.6, respectively, and as expected these values are lower than for random TDMA. The throughput is plotted as a function of packet generation probability for both schemes in Figure 6.7. The characteristics clearly show that the random access method is more efficient than fixed assignment.

The rejection probability is given by the same expression as for random TDMA. It is calculated to be 0.231 and 0.6 for $\sigma = 0.1$ and 0.5, respectively, and it is interesting

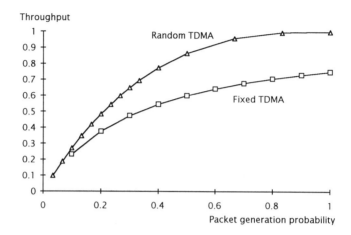

Figure 6.7 Throughput as a function of packet generation probability.

to note that these values are the same as throughput. The backlog and mean delay are also calculated using the same expressions as for random TDMA. In Figure 6.8 the backlog is plotted as a function of packet generation probability for both random and fixed TDMA. Again it is clear that random TDMA exhibits an improvement over the fixed assignment scheme, as the backlog is on average always the smaller. In Figure 6.9 the same parameters are plotted as a function of throughput and a similar characteristic performance is evident. Another interesting point is gleaned from the plot of backlog against throughput for fixed TDMA; namely, that there is a directly proportional relationship. In fact, it transpires that in general

$$Q = N \cdot S \tag{6.49}$$

Thus, in our case with $N = 3$ in Eq. (6.49) the fixed TDMA characteristic in Figure 6.9 is obtained.

Finally we note that the mean delay of packets in our fixed TDMA system is calculated to be equivalent to three slots for all nonzero values of σ and S. Put in simple terms, when a packet is generated it must wait on average for three slots before it is permitted to access the channel.

In the first section of this chapter we looked at an arbitrary transition probability matrix for the state of a buffer in a single node. In a similar fashion to the previous methods for constructing P, we can calculate system matrices for the buffer state with the two access mechanisms we have covered. Instead of using the number of busy nodes as the state descriptor, we can use the number of packets stored in a buffer, that is, the buffer occupancy. Assume a buffer capacity of three and the possible system states $i = 0$ (buffer empty) and $i = 1, 2, 3$. Again assume that the node accesses a communication channel using transmit when ready with no contention or collision. The system can be described by a transition probability matrix P as

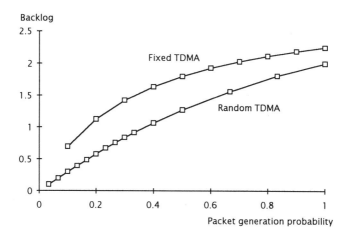

Figure 6.8 Backlog as a function of packet generation probability.

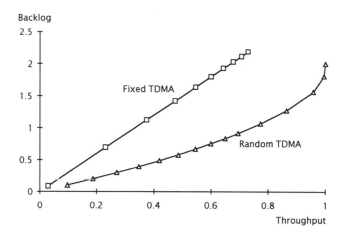

Figure 6.9 Backlog as a function of throughput.

$$P = \begin{pmatrix} 1-(\sigma+\sigma^2+\sigma^3) & \sigma & \sigma^2 & \sigma^3 \\ 1-(\sigma+\sigma^2+\sigma^3) & \sigma & \sigma^2 & \sigma^3 \\ 0 & 1-(\sigma+\sigma^2) & \sigma & \sigma^2 \\ 0 & 0 & 1-\sigma & \sigma \end{pmatrix} \qquad (6.50)$$

where σ is the probability that a packet arrives during a slot, σ^2 is the probability that two packets arrive, and so on. The steady-state solution can be obtained as before. For $\sigma = 0.1$ and $\sigma = 0.5$ it is calculated to be

$$\pi_{(\sigma=0.1)} = \begin{pmatrix} 0.877 & 0.11 & 0.012 & 0.001 \end{pmatrix} \qquad \pi_{(\sigma=0.5)} = \begin{pmatrix} 0.036 & 0.25 & 0.429 & 0.286 \end{pmatrix}$$

Throughput, backlog, rejection probability, and mean delay can also be obtained with similar methods to those used previously. However, this is left as an exercise for the reader. It is perhaps interesting to note that the system matrix in Eq. (6.50) has been calculated assuming that packets may be accepted at a node during a slot in which it is currently transmitting a packet. If we take the alternative case in which the packet is rejected, the system matrix is given by

$$P = \begin{pmatrix} 1-(\sigma+\sigma^2+\sigma^3) & \sigma & \sigma^2 & \sigma^3 \\ 1-(\sigma+\sigma^2) & \sigma & \sigma^2 & 0 \\ 0 & 1-\sigma & \sigma & 0 \\ 0 & 0 & 1 & 0 \end{pmatrix} \qquad (6.51)$$

The steady-state solutions obtained using Eq. (6.51) are

$$\pi_{(\sigma=0.1)} = \begin{pmatrix} 0.878 & 0.109 & 0.012 & 8.78 \times 10^{-4} \end{pmatrix}$$

and

$$\pi_{(\sigma=0.5)} = \begin{pmatrix} 0.14 & 0.491 & 0.351 & 0.018 \end{pmatrix}$$

Compared with the solutions obtained using Eq. (6.50), we find that, as expected, the probability that the system will be found in a higher state is reduced from the previous case when arrivals at a busy node were permitted.

These systems have limited the number of states to $N+1$ and are useful mechanisms for studying the methods involved by providing manageable equations. However, we can allow the number of states to vary and investigate perhaps more realistic systems. We have calculated the characteristics using the random TDMA analysis at larger values of N, and the results for throughput are presented in Figure 6.10. Clearly the size of the system will affect the results obtained.

This analysis requires evaluating expressions with $(N+1)$ by $(N+1)$ matrices, and the computation time can become significant. The number of operations increases exponentially with the number of possible states, a phenomenon known as state-space explosion, and implies that a practical limit is imposed on the analysis. The actual limits depend on the method of computation and the computing platform. Software packages for mathematical applications and programming languages impose limits on the size of arrays, for example.

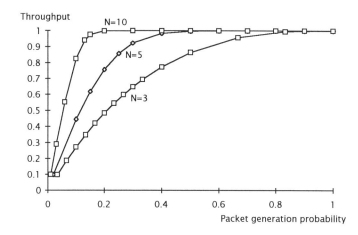

Figure 6.10 Throughput as a function of Packet generation probability for N = 3,5, and 10.

6.3 MULTIDIMENSIONAL MARKOV CHAINS

A multidimensional Markov chain is used when the system to be analyzed is so complex as to require additional state descriptors. In previous sections the system was described by one variable that has represented the number of active nodes or the number of packets in a buffer. Clearly a more realistic situation is for a communication system to consist of both a varying number of active nodes with finite buffer capacities greater than one. This can be modeled using what has been termed a multidimensional Markov chain. The state descriptor for a Markov chain with n dimensions is given by the vector $S = (s_1, s_2, ..., s_n)$. When applied to some real system each variable s_k represents some parameter of that system and may take on appropriate discrete values. For example, a more realistic model for a communication system might use one variable, or dimension, for each node, with the value taken by that variable being the number of packets stored in the buffer. If the system has N nodes, this would give rise to a chain with N dimensions. We have already explained how the increasing number of states gives rise to unmanageable calculations, and clearly the use of more than one variable will exacerbate the problem. A system of N nodes each having a buffer capacity L gives rise to $(N+1) \times (L+1)$ possible states, requiring the solution of as many simultaneous equations. Often it is possible to make reasonable assumptions that can reduce the number of states significantly while retaining the ability to investigate more complex systems, as we shall see.

In the first example we begin with a simple system that incorporates a two-dimensional chain. Consider a channel that uses the fixed TDMA access method as before. Previously the state of the system was described by a single variable $i = 0, 1, 2, ..., N$ that represented the number of active nodes. Now we introduce a second variable and express the state descriptor, s, as the vector $s = (i, j)$ with the additional variable $j = 0, 1$. We will use the value of j, taken to be 0 if a particular node is idle and 1 if it is active, in order to replicate a model described for fixed TDMA in the previous section. The particular node in question, which we will refer to as the tagged node, may be chosen arbitrarily due to the fact that the arrival and departure process is the same for all N, a property known as equivalent statistical behavior. The state transition probability matrix now looks a little more complicated as it takes on the form

$$P = p_{s,s'} = \Pr[\text{state transits from } s = (i,j) \text{ to } s' = (i',j')] \tag{6.52}$$

and the first problem arises as to how the matrix can be formed. One method is to choose a suitable transform that, when applied to the state vector, gives a unique index for each possible combination of i and j. In this case we choose

$$w = (2 \times i) + j$$
$$\tag{6.53}$$
$$w' = (2 \times i') + j'$$

as the transform pair $s \to w$, $s' \to w'$.

This is illustrated in Table 6.1 where the transform is applied to our three-node system. The matrix P is then constructed with elements $p_{w,w'}$. For example, the element $p_{3,2}$ corresponds to the probability that the system transits from the state of having one busy node and an active tagged node ($i = 1, j = 1$) to the state where there is again one busy node while the tagged node has become idle ($i = 1, j = 0$).

Table 6.1
Matrix indices

i	j	$w=2i+j$
0	0	0
0	1	1
1	0	2
1	1	3
2	0	4
2	1	5

Effectively we are examining a system where the slots are grouped into frames as illustrated in Figure 6.11. In each frame there are as many slots as there are nodes, three in this case, and each slot is assigned for the exclusive use of one particular node as indicated by the slot number. In the figure we have illustrated a sample time slot of the system in which four packets are transmitted over a cycle of three frames: one from node one, two from node two, and one from node three. The memoryless property of the system at each slot has been lost because the system state now depends on up to three transitions, one for each slot in a frame. However, we can imbed a Markov chain at the end of each frame when we inspect the state of the system with respect to our tagged node.

Now let us evaluate the expressions for the elements of P in terms of i, j, and σ.

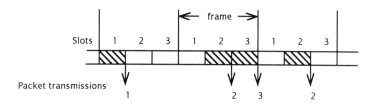

Figure 6.11 Frame structure for the fixed TDMA model.

First, we must distinguish between slots that are assigned to the tagged node and slots that are not. Let the probability transition matrices corresponding to these slots be identified by T and C, with elements $t_{s,s'}$ and $c_{s,s'}$. The transition probability for a whole frame, or the system transition matrix, is then given by

$$P = T \cdot C^2 \tag{6.54}$$

The term on the right-hand side of Eq. (6.54) consists of two types of transition probability matrix with contributions from one slot for the tagged node and two for the remaining nodes. Now the probabilities $t_{s,s'}$ are made up of the joint probability

$$t_{s,s'} = \Pr[i \to i' \quad \text{and} \quad j \to j'] \tag{6.55}$$

and, since these are independent,

$$t_{s,s'} = \Pr[i \to i'] \cdot \Pr[j \to j'] \tag{6.56}$$

The first factor on the right-hand side of Eq. (6.56) is given by the binomial distribution to be

$$\Pr[i \to i'] = \binom{2-i}{i'-i} \sigma^{i'-i} (1-\sigma)^{2-i'} \tag{6.57}$$

where the tagged node has been subtracted from the node population. The second factor is to account for the activity of the tagged node. There are two possibilities for the value of j, the state of the tagged node at the beginning of the slot. If it begins idle, then it will not utilize the slot and it remains idle with probability $1 - \sigma$

$$\Pr[j = 0 \to j' = 0] = 1 - \sigma \tag{6.58}$$

Similarly it will become active with probability σ

$$\Pr[j = 0 \to j' = 1] = \sigma \tag{6.59}$$

Alternatively, if the tagged user is active at the beginning of its slot, then it utilizes the slot and transits to the idle state with probability 1. Hence

$$\Pr[j=1 \to j'=1]=1 \tag{6.60}$$

We can combine the individual contributions of Eqs. (6.58), (6.59), and (6.60) more conveniently in the expression

$$\Pr[j \to j'] = \delta(j,0)\{\delta(j',0)(1-\sigma)+\delta(j',1)\sigma\}+\delta(j,1)\delta(j',0) \tag{6.61}$$

where

$$\delta(x,y) = \begin{cases} 1 & \text{if } x=y \\ 0 & \text{if } x \neq y \end{cases} \tag{6.62}$$

Thus Eqs. (6.57) and (6.61) may be used to calculate T. The probabilities $c_{s,s'}$ are similarly given by

$$c_{s,s'} = \Pr[i \to i'] \cdot \Pr[j \to j'] \tag{6.63}$$

However in this case we are required to account for slots in which active nodes other than the tagged users transmit a packet and slots in which they do not. Averaging over a frame, slots not assigned to the tagged node are utilized with probability $i/2$, in which case the number of active nodes is reduced by one and we have

$$\Pr[i \to i'] = \frac{i}{2}\binom{2-i}{i'-i+1}\sigma^{i'-i+1}(1-\sigma)^{1-i'} \tag{6.64}$$

while for slots that are not utilized, which occur on average with probability $1-i/2$, we have

$$\Pr[i \to i'] = \left(1-\frac{i}{2}\right)\binom{2-i}{i'-i+1}\sigma^{i'-i+1}(1-\sigma)^{1-i'} \tag{6.65}$$

The contribution of the second factor in the right-hand term of Eq. (6.63) has to account for the fact that if the tagged node is active at the beginning of a slot that is assigned to another user, then it must remain active such that

$$\Pr[j \to j'] = \delta(j,0)\{\delta(j',0)(1-\sigma)+\delta(j',1)\sigma\}+\delta(j,1)\delta(j',1) \tag{6.66}$$

Now P may be calculated. For example, with $\sigma=0.5$ we obtain

$$P = \begin{pmatrix} 0.025 & 0.178 & 0.074 & 0.52 & 0.025 & 0.178 \\ 0.051 & 0.152 & 0.148 & 0.445 & 0.051 & 0.152 \\ 0.027 & 0.191 & 0.07 & 0.492 & 0.027 & 0.191 \\ 0.055 & 0.164 & 0.141 & 0.422 & 0.055 & 0.164 \\ 0.031 & 0.219 & 0.063 & 0.438 & 0.031 & 0.219 \\ 0.063 & 0.188 & 0.125 & 0.375 & 0.063 & 0.188 \end{pmatrix}$$

and in the usual way we can reassure ourselves by confirming that

$$P \cdot H = \begin{pmatrix} 1 & 1 & 1 & 1 & 1 & 1 \end{pmatrix}^{\mathrm{T}}$$

Solving for the steady state in the usual fashion, for this example we obtain

$$\pi = \begin{pmatrix} 0.049 & 0.173 & 0.123 & 0.432 & 0.049 & 0.173 \end{pmatrix}$$

The throughput of the system is given by

$$S = \frac{1}{3}\pi \cdot J \tag{6.67}$$

with the elements of the column vector J taking on values

$$j_{2i+j} = i + j \tag{6.68}$$

for $i = 0,1,2$ and $j = 0,1$. It is calculated to be 0.205 and 0.593 for $\sigma = 0.1$ and 0.5, respectively. Let us recall the values we obtained using the one-dimensional model for fixed TDMA in the previous section.

It appears that there is some discrepancy since we have predicted a slightly more conservative estimate for the throughput at these packet generation probabilities. In fact, the previous analysis allowed each node to randomly select one of every three slots, hence the slight improvement. Even in this analysis we are allowing the nodes other than the tagged one to randomly select from the slots in the frame other than that assigned to the tagged node and we could predict a further reduction in the throughput for an exact model.

The throughput is plotted as a function of traffic generation probabilities for each of the models in Figure 6.12. At higher packet transmission probabilities the situation reverses because active nodes on average are required to wait for three slots before being allowed to accept new traffic in the previous analysis while for the two-dimensional model this factor is only relevant to the two nodes other than the tagged one.

The rejection probability, backlog, and mean delay may be obtained in a similar manner to the previous analyses. Rejection probability is plotted as a function of packet generation probability in Figure 6.13. The characteristic for both models of fixed assignment are included and compare in a similar fashion as the throughput in Figure

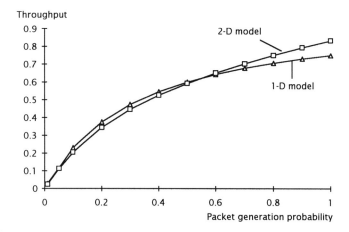

Figure 6.12 Throughput as a function of packet generation probability

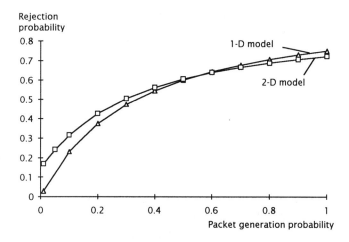

Figure 6.13 Rejection probability as a function of generation probability.

6.12. The system backlog for each model is depicted in Figure 6.14, and the agreement in this case is clear to see.

Since our main purpose here is the method of analysis and not the results themselves, we will proceed without further comment on these results. In the next section, by allowing ever-increasing complexity, we will look at a system that allows us to model nodes with a finite buffer capacity greater than one.

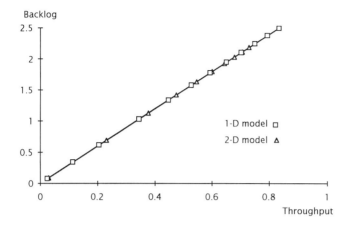

Figure 6.14 Backlog as a function of throughput.

6.4 BUFFERED SLOTTED COMMUNICATION SYSTEMS

Assume a random access slotted system with N nodes. The arrival rate of packets is given by the probability σ that an arrival occurs in a slot. Since the system is fair and symmetric, we can assume that the model may be completely analyzed by considering the behavior of just one node; that is, the system exhibits the property known as the equivalent statistical behavior of all nodes. We will again identify this arbitrarily chosen node as the tagged node. The two-dimensional state vector is represented by $s = (i, j)$, where i is the number of busy nodes, except the tagged one, and j is the queue length at the tagged node.

A Markov chain may be constructed if we examine the state of the system immediately following the transmission of a packet. In this analysis we account for contention and collisions such that the cycle in between each transition will consist of a contention period followed by a packet transmission time, as depicted in Figure 6.15. Hence a chain is imbedded at the end of each cycle. Because we are studying the behavior of the tagged node, we must distinguish between transmissions from that node

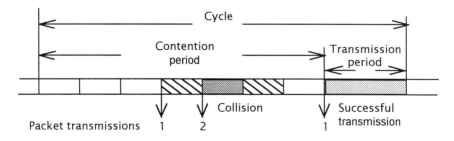

Figure 6.15 The contention and transmission period cycle.

and those from other nodes. Hence each cycle consists of two possible events: a contention period followed by a transmission from the tagged node or a contention period followed by a transmission from another node.

We can define $c_{ss'}$ as being the probability that the system transits from the state s at the beginning of a cycle to s' at the end of the contention period, for a cycle in which a node other than the tagged one is about to transmit a packet. The probability $ct_{ss'}$ is the corresponding value for a cycle in which the tagged user transmits a packet. Similarly $t_{s's''}$ is the transition probability from state s' at the beginning of the transmission period to state s'' at the end of the cycle given that the transmission originated from a node other than the tagged one, and $tt_{s's''}$ is the corresponding transition probability given that the transmission originated from the tagged node. The transition probability matrix for the Markov chain is thus given by

$$P = C \cdot T + Ct \cdot Tt \tag{6.69}$$

where C, Ct, T, and Tt are the matrices whose elements are $c_{ss'}$, $t_{s's''}$, $ct_{ss'}$, and $tt_{s's''}$, respectively.

We will first investigate the calculation of C. During a contention period that ends with the beginning of a transmission from a user other than the tagged one, there are two possible events that may occur in each slot, and these have to be accounted for. Either (i) all nodes including the tagged one remain idle or at least one unsuccessful transmission occurs or (ii) a node other than the tagged one acquires the channel.

Let Q be the matrix of elements $q_{ss'}$, the probabilities that the system transits from state s to s' during a single slot, given that all nodes including the tagged one remain idle or are involved in an unsuccessful transmission. Also let Q' be the corresponding matrix for a slot during which any node other than the tagged one acquires the channel. It is evident that, given that the contention period lasts for k slots, the values of $c_{ss'}$ may be calculated from the fact that for k-1 of the transitions the nodes including the tagged one remain idle or are involved in an unsuccessful transmission. Also, during the last slot, a transition occurs along with the event of a node other than the tagged one acquiring the channel. Hence

$$C = \sum_{k=0}^{\infty} Q^k Q' \tag{6.70}$$

which can be simplified to

$$C = (I - Q)^{-1} Q' \tag{6.71}$$

A similar argument leads us to the corresponding relationship for a contention period that ends with the tagged node acquiring the channel

$$Ct = (I - Q)^{-1} Q'' \tag{6.72}$$

Here Q'' is the transition probability matrix for a slot in which the tagged user acquires the channel. Now in order to construct C and Ct we are required to evaluate the matrices Q, Q', and Q'' whose elements are $q_{ss'}$, $q'_{ss'}$, and $q''_{ss'}$, respectively.

The value of $q_{ss'}$ is the probability that the system transits from $s = (i, j)$ to $s' = (i', j')$ during a single slot given that the channel remains idle or one or more nodes including the tagged one are involved in an unsuccessful transmission. The latter probability is given by $1 - s(i*)$, where $s(i*)$ is the probability of a successful transmission given that there are $i*$ busy nodes. The former transition probabilities may be evaluated as follows. From the binomial distribution the probability that the number of busy nodes, excluding the tagged one, increases from i to i' is given by

$$P[i \to i'] = \binom{N-i-1}{i'-i} \sigma^{i'-i} (1-\sigma)^{N-i'-1} \tag{6.73}$$

where $i, i' = 0, 1, 2, \ldots, N-1$. The probability that the number of packets in the buffer of the tagged user increases from j to j' is given by

$$P[j \to j'] = \begin{cases} \sigma & \text{for } j' = j+1, j \neq L \\ 1-\sigma & \text{for } j' = j \\ 1 & \text{for } j = j' = L \end{cases} \tag{6.74}$$

where $j, j' = 0, 1, 2, \ldots, L$ and L is the buffer capacity. In this expression we have accounted for the case when the buffer is full at the beginning of the slot.

Hence the elements of Q may be calculated using Eqs. (6.73) and (6.74) with

$$q_{ss'} = [1 - s(i*)] \cdot P[i \to i'] \cdot P[j \to j'] \tag{6.75}$$

The term $s(i*)$ will be dealt with in due course. Similarly the elements of Q', which are the transition probabilities when any node other than the tagged one acquires the channel during a single slot, are given by

$$q_{ss'} = i \frac{s(i*)}{i*} \cdot P[i \to i'] \cdot P[j \to j'] \tag{6.76}$$

Finally the elements of Q'', the transition probabilities when the tagged user acquires the channel, are given by

$$q_{ss'} = \begin{cases} \dfrac{s(i*)}{i*} \cdot P[i \to i'] \cdot P[j \to j'] & \text{for } j > 0 \\ 0 & \text{for } j = 0 \end{cases} \tag{6.77}$$

In this expression we have accounted for the fact that the tagged user will not attempt to acquire the channel if its buffer is empty.

Now in order to compute the matrix P we are still required to evaluate T and Tt. The method for doing this is not unlike that shown above for Q, Q', and Q'' and will be dealt with henceforth. First, concerning the probability transition matrix T, which pertains to the transmission period of a cycle in which a node other than the tagged one transmits. Let the transmission period consist of m slots, during each of the first $m-1$ slots the only possible events are the arrival of new packets at any of the nodes. Let R be the matrix of elements $r_{ss'}$, the probabilities that the system transits from state s to s' during each of the first $m-1$ slots; and let R' be the matrix of elements $r'_{ss'}$, corresponding to the transition probabilities of the last final slot, which includes a departure from one of the nodes other than the tagged one. Then we can write

$$T = R^{m-1} \cdot R' \tag{6.78}$$

It follows from previous arguments that the elements of the matrix R are given by

$$r_{ss'} = P[i \rightarrow i'] \cdot P[j \rightarrow j'] \tag{6.79}$$

where the factors on the right-hand side are given by Eqs. (6.73) and (6.74), respectively. Note that this expression is the same as that in Eq. (6.75) for $q_{ss'}$ but without the first factor, which accounts for the possibility that an unsuccessful transmission attempt has taken place.

The corresponding expression for $r'_{ss'}$ is not as straightforward because the state of the transmitting node is unknown. That is, we do not know if the transmission will leave the node with an empty buffer and, hence, reduce the number of active nodes by one or not. In order to facilitate this exception we introduce the variable $x(i^*)$, which is the probability, given i^* active nodes other than the tagged one, that any node has exactly one packet remaining in its buffer at the beginning of the last slot in the transmission period. The values for $x(i^*)$ may be computed for the tagged user and assumed to be the same for all users, as follows.

Let f be a row vector whose elements, $f_{(i,j)}$, are the probabilities that the system is in state (i, j) at the beginning of the last slot in the transmission period, given that the tagged user transmits. These are given by

$$f = \pi \cdot Ct \cdot R^{m-1} \tag{6.80}$$

where as usual π is the steady-state probability distribution. Now the probability that there are i^* busy users, including the tagged node, is equivalent to the sum of probabilities for each i^*-1 state with $j > 0$, as given by

$$f_{i^*} = \sum_{j=1}^{L} f_{(i^*-1,j)} \tag{6.81}$$

Hence by definition

$$x(i^*) = \frac{f_{(i^*-1,1)}}{f_{i^*}} \tag{6.82}$$

We can now return to evaluating $r'_{ss'}$. Recall that these are the transition probabilities of the final slot in the transmission period, which includes a departure from one of the nodes other than the tagged one. Now there are two possibilities here. First, the node ends up with an empty buffer with probability $x(i^*)(1-\sigma)$, and second, the node ends up with one or more packets in its buffer with probability $1-x(i^*)(1-\sigma)$. Hence

$$r'_{ss'} = \begin{cases} \{x(i^*)(1-\sigma)P'[i \to i'] \\ +(1-x(i^*)(1-\sigma))P[i \to i']\} \cdot P[j \to j'] & \text{for } i > 0 \\ 0 & \text{for } i = 0 \end{cases} \tag{6.83}$$

where $P[i \to i']$ is as defined previously and $P'[i \to i']$, accounting for the fact that the buffer of a node other than the tagged one becomes empty and reduces the number of active nodes by one, is given by

$$P'[i \to i'] = \binom{N-i-1}{i'-i+1}\sigma^{i'-i+1}(1-\sigma)^{N-i'} \tag{6.84}$$

The $x(i^*)$ in Eq. (6.83) may be calculated using Eqs. (6.81) and (6.82) using an iterative process with a seed value for π.

The method for obtaining the elements of Tt, which pertains to the transmission period of a cycle in which the tagged node transmits, is fortunately more straightforward. Not surprisingly the first $m-1$ slots are the same as for T, and during the final slot we are simply required to account for the fact that there has been a departure from the tagged node. Hence,

$$Tt = R^{m-1} \cdot R'' \tag{6.85}$$

where the elements of the matrix R'' are given by

$$r''_{ss'} = \begin{cases} P[i \to i']P'[j \to j'] & \text{for } j > 0 \\ 0 & \text{for } j = 0 \end{cases} \tag{6.86}$$

with $\Pr[i \to i']$ given by Eq. (6.73) and in order to account for the departure from the tagged node we have

$$P'[j \to j'] = \begin{cases} \sigma & \text{for } j' = j \\ 1-\sigma & \text{for } j' = j-1 \end{cases} \tag{6.87}$$

We are now in a position to be able to solve for the steady-state probability distribution using $\pi = \pi P$ and $\sum_i \pi_i = 1$. Recall that the $x(i^*)$ were found using a seed for π and the correct solution is obtained using an iterative process.

Normally, once this stage has been reached, the computation of the performance metrics is a straightforward task. A one-dimensional Markov chain, usually taking the number of packets in the system as the state descriptor and assuming either a single or infinite buffer space, will result in the complete knowledge of the buffer state. In this case a simple application of Little's result gives the delay characteristic. In dealing with an extra dimension here we have complicated the matter. The mean delay is arrived at in the following manner. Note that we do not account for rescheduling unsuccessful transmission attempts, which will give misleading results at high throughputs.

Hence, beginning with Little's result, we can write the delay with respect to traffic throughput, S, at each node as

$$D = \frac{J}{S} \tag{6.88}$$

where J is the mean queue length. The traffic throughput at each node is easily calculated as the percentage of time that there is a transmission on the channel, equivalent to the ratio m/F, where F is the mean cycle length.

In order to calculate the mean cycle length let $\mathbf{F}$ be the column vector of elements F_s, the cycle length given that the state of the system at the beginning of the cycle is s. Hence,

$$F = \pi \cdot \mathbf{F} \tag{6.89}$$

It can be shown that

$$\mathbf{F} = \sum_{k=1}^{\infty} kQ^{k-1} \cdot (Q'+Q'') \cdot H + mH \tag{6.90}$$

where H is the unit column vector with $N(L+1)$ elements equal to 1. Using the fact that

$$\sum_{k=0}^{\infty} kQ^{k-1} = (I-Q)^{-2}$$

and

$$(I-Q)^{-1} \cdot (Q'+Q'') \cdot H = H$$

we can simplify Eq. (6.90) to give

$$F = (I-Q)^{-1} \cdot H + m \cdot H \tag{6.91}$$

Hence using Eqs. (6.89) and (6.91) we have

$$F = \pi \cdot (I - Q)^{-1} \cdot H + m \tag{6.92}$$

The average queue length at a node is given by

$$J = \sum_{j=1}^{L} j \Pr[\text{queue length at node} = j] \tag{6.93}$$

where the probability term evaluates to the same figure for each user and can be taken as being that of the tagged node, which is given by

$$\Pr[\text{queue length at node} = j] = \sum_{i=0}^{N-1} \pi_{(i,j)} \tag{6.94}$$

The final task in this analysis is the calculation of $s(i*)$. Recall that this is the probability of a successful transmission given $i*$ busy users, including the tagged node. Thus we have

$$i* = i + u(j) \tag{6.95}$$

where

$$u(j) = \begin{cases} 1 & \text{if } j > 0 \\ 0 & \text{if } j = 0 \end{cases} \tag{6.96}$$

Now $s(i*)$ depends on the access scheme. In fact, the analysis can be applied to any system that can be described in terms of the contention and transmission period cycles and for which $s(i*)$ is known. For perfect random TDMA we have

$$s(i*) = 1 \tag{6.97}$$

since any transmission is successful, and no collisions or contention occurs. For fixed TDMA we have

$$s(i*) = \frac{1}{N} \tag{6.98}$$

We should be able to compare this analysis, using $L = 1$, with the previous analyses for fixed TDMA in Sections 2 and 3. This is left as an exercise for the interested reader. Remember that the definition of slot length is different in each case. Compensating for this, however, is straightforward.

We will illustrate the analysis here with the type of results that can be obtained for the CSMA/CD protocol for LANs. In this case the slot length is dependent on the end-to-end propagation delay of the LAN. The throughput for CSMA/CD depends on the transmission probability, which is given by

$$\text{Pr[node attempts transmission]} = \frac{1}{i\,*}$$

Hence the probability that a node defers transmission is $(1 - 1/i\,*)$. The optimum throughput is obtained when $i\,* - 1$ nodes defer, allowing one successful transmission. Thus

$$s(i\,*) = \left(1 - \frac{1}{i\,*}\right)^{i\,* - 1} \tag{6.99}$$

We used this analysis to generate a number of characteristics and demonstrate the type of performance parameters that may be obtained. The characteristics were calculated for a 10-node system with packet lengths of 20 slots. They are presented in Figure 6.16 and show the expected queue lengths at a node with varying buffer capacities as the offered traffic or packet generation probability increases.

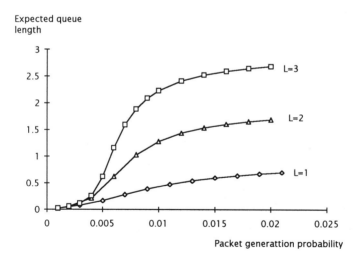

Figure 6.16 Expected queue length as a function of packet generation probability.

We are avoiding a detailed description of the results here, however, it is worth remarking that with random access systems that allow unsuccessful transition attempts, the offered load is in fact greater than the traffic throughput since it consists of rescheduled packets as well as new ones. Hence the throughput will not increase linearly with packet generation probability, which is directly proportional to the intensity of new packets. This effect is clearly illustrated in the characteristics of Figure 6.17.

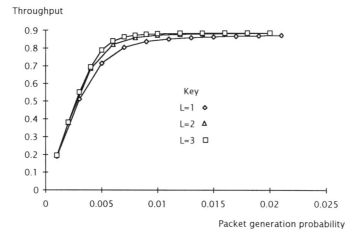

Figure 6.17 Throughput as a function of packet generation probability.

The mean delay is plotted as a function of both throughput and packet generation probability in Figure 6.18. The probability that a packet is rejected due to the fact that it arrives at a full buffer is another performance metric that is of potential interest. This probability is directly proportional to that of the buffer being full, which is plotted as a function of throughput and packet generation probability in Figure 6.19.

6.5 MULTISEGMENT SYSTEMS

The analyses we have described so far in this chapter may be applied to single-segment systems with uniform traffic distributions. It is possible to introduce further dimensions to the Markov chain to account for nonuniform traffic load distributions in single segments and also to examine multisegment systems. An example of a multisegment system is a WAN, implemented perhaps using ATM switched Ethernets.

Consider a network with M segments, as depicted in Figure 6.20. Each segment consists of a finite number of nodes, one of which is equivalent to the connection of that segment to the central switch. The switch consists of M connections, one for each segment. The method of analyzing the system involves considering the solution of M independent segments, following the methods described in previous sections, and using an iterative method to estimate the parameters of the whole interconnected system. A number of additional performance issues is generated by this situation in relation to the potential point of congestion at the central switch. It is of interest therefore to be able to change the arrival patterns and the service discipline for the switch.

Let the number of nodes in segment be N_i, $i = 1, 2, ..., M$, each having unit buffer capacity and arrival rate governed by the probability σ that a packet arrives in a slot. The probability that a packet generated on one segment is destined for another segment is i_s. One of the nodes in each segment is the connection to the switch and by

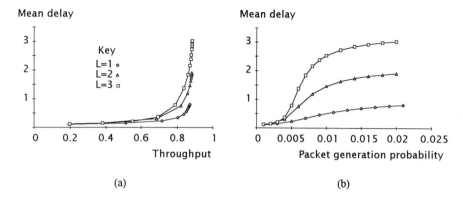

Figure 6.18 Mean delay as a function of (a) throughput, and (b) packet generation probability.

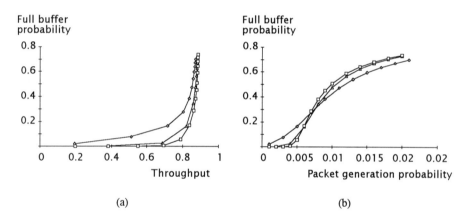

Figure 6.19   Probability that node buffer is full as a function of (a) throughput, and (b) packet generation probability.

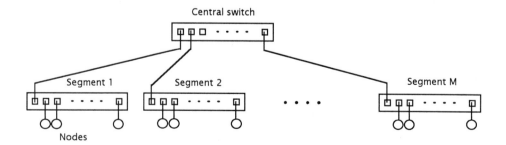

Figure 6.20 A multisegment network.

its nature requires a buffer capacity, $L \geq 1$, used to store packets destined for that segment generated on another. The probability that a packet arrives at the switch in a slot is σ_s. The channel operates synchronously with slots that have a length τ equal to one propagation delay, and the packet transmission time is $Tx + 1$ slots. Hence a successful packet transmission occupies $t + 1$ slots, beginning with the start of transmission and ending with receipt at the destination. The transmission time of a collided packet is $R + 1$ slots, and this is calculated to be sufficient for all the nodes to detect the collision and clear the channel. In this analysis we are able to evaluate each segment and the overall system performance.

The method of the previous section is extended using a three-dimensional Markov chain to account for the addition of the switch node. The three-dimensional state vector is represented by $s = (i, j, k)$ where as usual i is the number of busy nodes. Now j is the queue length at the switch node, and k is the state of the channel. There are six possible channel states: idle; collision; successful acquisition of the channel by the switch; successful transmission from the switch; successful acquisition of the channel by a regular node; and successful transmission from a regular node.

A Markov chain may be constructed if we examine the state of the system immediately following the transmission of a packet from either one of the regular segment nodes or the switch node. In this analysis we are able to restrict the size of transition probability matrices to $(N+1)(L+1) \times (N+1)(L+1)$ elements, which normally provides for a maximum of $(N+1)(L+1)$ possible states. We are able to do so only at the expense of requiring more types of transition, and hence more transition probability matrices, to account for the additional dimension with six possible channel states. In addition, the process of developing expressions for throughput and delay is more involved.

The cycle between each transmission will consist of a contention period during which the state of the channel may be idle or in collision followed by a slot during which a successful channel acquisition by one of the regular nodes or the switch node occurs, as depicted in Figure 6.21. The transition probabilities can be defined in a manner similar to the analysis in the previous section as follows. Ten matrices are involved:

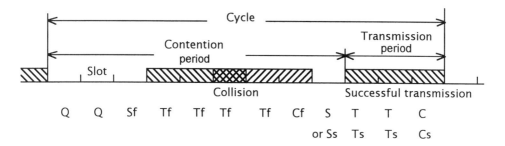

Figure 6.21 The transitions cycle for a multisegment system.

$$Q_{ss'} = P[i',j',k' = \text{Idle}/i,j,k = \text{Idle}] \quad \text{for} \quad i' \geq i, j' \geq j \tag{6.100}$$

$$Sf_{ss'} = P[i',j',k' = \text{Collision}/i,j,k = \text{Idle}] \quad \text{for} \quad i+u(j) \geq 1, i' \geq i, j' \geq j \tag{6.101}$$

$$Tf_{ss'} = P[i',j',k' = \text{Collision}/i,j,k = \text{Collision}] \quad \text{for} \quad i+u(j) \geq 1, i' \geq i, j' \geq j \tag{6.102}$$

$$Cf_{ss'} = P[i',j',k' = \text{Idle}/i,j,k = \text{Collision}] \quad \text{for} \quad i+u(j) \geq 1, i' \geq i, j' \geq j \tag{6.103}$$

$$S_{ss'} = P[i',j',k' = \text{Success}/i,j,k = \text{Idle}] \quad \text{for} \quad i > 0, i' \geq i, j' \geq j \tag{6.104}$$

$$T_{ss'} = P[i',j',k' = \text{Transmit}/i,j,k = \text{Success}] \quad \text{for} \quad i > 0, i' \geq i, j' \geq j \tag{6.105}$$

$$C_{ss'} = P[i',j',k' = \text{Idle}/i,j,k = \text{Transmit}] \quad \text{for} \quad i > 0, i' \geq i-1, j' \geq j \tag{6.106}$$

$$Ss_{ss'} = P[i',j',k' = \text{Success(switch)}/i,j,k = \text{Idle}] \quad \text{for} \quad j > 0, i' \geq i, j' \geq j \tag{6.107}$$

$$Ts_{ss'} = P[i',j',k' = \text{Transmit(switch)}/i,j,k = \text{Success(switch)}] \quad \text{for} \quad j > 0, i' \geq i, j' \geq j \tag{6.108}$$

$$Cs_{ss'} = P[i',j',k' = \text{Idle}/i,j,k = \text{Transmit(switch)}] \quad \text{for} \quad j > 0, i' \geq i, j' \geq j-1 \tag{6.109}$$

where $i,i' = 0,1,2,\ldots,N; \; j,j' = 0,1,2,\ldots,L;$ and the six possible channel states are Idle, Collision, Success, Transmit, Success(switch), and Transmit(switch). Idle and collision are self-explanatory. Success and Transmit occur when one of the segment nodes successfully acquires the channel. Similarly Success(switch) and Transmit(switch) apply to the switch node successfully acquiring the channel. The function $u()$ that appears in two of the boundary conditions is given by Eq. (6.96).

Now, the system transition matrix consists of three possible cycles: transmissions that collide, successful transmission from a node, and successful transmission from the switch. In terms of the matrices defined in Eqs. (6.100) through (6.109) it can be written as

$$P = Id \cdot Sf \cdot Tf \cdot Cf + Id \cdot S \cdot T \cdot C + Id \cdot Ss \cdot Ts \cdot Cs \tag{6.110}$$

where each of the cycles begins with an Idle period. The probability transition matrix for the Idle period is given by

$$Id = \sum_{k=0}^{\infty} Q^k$$

which, as before, simplifies to

$$Id = (I - Q)^{-1} \tag{6.111}$$

The elements of the transition probability matrices may be calculated as follows. Following the previous similar reasoning for Q, we have

$$q_{ss'} = SI(s) \cdot P[i \to i'] \cdot P[j \to j']$$ (6.112)

where

$$P[i \to i'] = \binom{N-i}{i'-i} \sigma^{i'-i}(1-\sigma)^{N-i'}$$ (6.113)

and

$$P[j \to j'] = \begin{cases} \sigma_s & \text{for } j' = j+1, \ j \neq L \\ 1-\sigma_s & \text{for } j' = j, \ j \neq L \\ 1 & \text{for } j = j' = L \end{cases}$$ (6.114)

where $i, i' = 0, 1, 2, ..., N$ and $j, j' = 0, 1, 2, ..., L$. Notice that the expression for the probability that the number of active nodes increases from i to i' accounts for the fact that if we are choosing $i'-i$ nodes from a possible $N-i$, then $i'-i$ become active with a probability σ and $N-i$ become idle with a probability $1-\sigma$. The first factor on the right-hand side of Eq. (1.112) is the probability that there is no transmission, given that the system is in state s.

Next, Sf is the transition probability matrix for a slot that begins with an idle channel and ends with it in the collision state. Hence the elements of Sf are given by

$$sf_{ss'} = \{1 - S(s) - Ss(s)\} \cdot P[i \to i'] \cdot P[j \to j']$$ (6.115)

where $S(s)$ and $Ss(s)$ are the probabilities that any of the segment nodes and the switch, respectively, successfully transmit a packet given that there are i nodes active and there are j packets queued in the buffer of the switch. The elements of Tf are simply given by

$$tf_{ss'} = P[i \to i'] \cdot P[j \to j']$$ (6.116)

since during any transmission slot there is a change of state only due to the arrival of packets that can affect the number of active nodes and the queue length at the switch. This is also true for T and Ts, hence the elements of these matrices may be calculated using the same equation. Similarly slots that include the transition from the state of channel collision to channel idle involves only packet arrivals, and Cf is also given by this equation.

Next we will deal with the matrix S concerning the transition probabilities for slots that begin in the channel Idle state and end with a node involved in a successful packet transmission. These probabilities are simply given by

$$s_{ss'} = S(s) \cdot P[i \to i'] \cdot P[j \to j']$$ (6.117)

The intermediate slots for the transmission period of a segment node have been dealt with above. The final slot has probability transition matrix C with elements

$$c_{ss'} = P[i \to i'] \cdot P[j \to j']$$ (6.118)

where in this case

$$P[i \to i'] = \binom{N-i}{i'-i+1} \sigma^{i'-i+1}(1-\sigma)^{N-i'-1}$$ (6.119)

for $i, i' = 0, 1, 2, ..., N$. This is the probability that the number of active nodes increases from i to i', accounting for the fact that if we are choosing $i'-i+1$ nodes from a possible $N-i$, then $i'-i+1$ become active with a probability σ. Also $N-i-1$ become idle with a probability $1-\sigma$, since during this slot the active node that is involved in the transmission will become idle.

Similarly the elements of Ss and Cs, the equivalent probabilities for the switch node, are given by

$$ss_{ss'} = Ss(s) \cdot P[i \to i'] \cdot P[j \to j']$$ (6.120)

and

$$cs_{ss'} = P[i \to i'] \cdot P[j \to j']$$ (6.121)

In the last expression the calculation of $P[i \to i']$ does not have to account for the switch node becoming idle and its value is that given previously in Eq. (6.113). This fact does, however, affect $P[j \to j']$, which becomes, for the expression in Eq. (6.121) only,

$$P[j \to j'] = \begin{cases} \sigma_s & \text{for } j'= j, j \neq 0 \\ 1-\sigma_s & \text{for } j'= j-1, j \neq 0 \\ 0 & \text{for } j'= j = 0 \end{cases}$$ (6.122)

where $j, j' = 0, 1, 2, ..., L$.

Taking the preceding into account we can rewrite the expression for P in the more convenient form

$$P = (I-Q)^{-1} \cdot [Sf \cdot T^{r+1} + S \cdot T^t \cdot C + Ss \cdot T^t \cdot Cs]$$ (6.123)

In Eq. (6.123) we replaced Id using Eq. (6.111) and used the fact that Tf, Cf, and Ts are equivalent to T. Each of the terms in the square brackets represent the contributions from the periods of failed transmissions, successful transmissions from a segment node, and successful transmissions from the switch node in that order. Hence we constructed a Markov chain and derived the system transition probability matrix which can be used to solve for the steady-state distribution in the normal manner.

Expressions for the performance metrics will now be derived. As with the previous section we require the average frame length, or cycle length, which is obtained from the contributions of contention and transmission periods, successful or otherwise. Let Fc and Ft be the column vectors whose elements Fc_s and Ft_s are the lengths of the contention and transmission periods given that they begin in the state s. If the length of the contention period is $k+1$ slots, then it consists of k slots with transitions of the type given by Eq. (6.100), followed by one of the three possibilities given by Eqs. (6.101), (6.104), or (6.107). Thus we have

$$Fc = \sum_{k=0}^{\infty} (k+1)Q^k \cdot (Sf + S + Ss) \cdot H \tag{6.124}$$

The length of the transmission period of the cycle depends on the state of the channel at the beginning of the period. The row vector of the probabilities that the state of the channel at the beginning of the transmission period is unsuccessful is given by $\sum_{k=0}^{\infty} Q^k \cdot Sf \cdot H$, and the length of the period is then $R+1$ slots. Similarly the probabilities of the successful transmission period are given by $\sum_{k=0}^{\infty} Q^k \cdot (S + Ss) \cdot H$, and in this case the length of the transmission period is $Tx+1$ slots. The combined probabilities give

$$Ft = \sum_{k=0}^{\infty} Q^k \cdot \{(R+1)Sf + (Tx+1)(S+Ss)\} \cdot H \tag{6.125}$$

Hence, the cycle length is given by the sum of Eqs. (6.124) and (6.125). Using the fact that

$$\sum_{k=0}^{\infty} (k+1)Q^k = (I-Q)^{-2}$$

$$\sum_{k=0}^{\infty} Q^k = (I-Q)^{-1}$$

and

$$(I-Q)^{-1} \cdot (Sf + S + Ss) \cdot H = H$$

we have

$$\mathbf{F} = (I-Q)^{-1} \cdot H + (I-Q)^{-1} \cdot \{(R+1)Sf + (Tx+1)(S+Ss)\} \cdot H \tag{6.126}$$

The mean frame length is thus given by

$$F = \pi \cdot \mathbf{F} \tag{6.127}$$

As usual the throughput is the fraction of time with which the channel is involved in successful transmission. It can easily be shown that

$$S = \frac{T}{F} \cdot \pi \cdot \{(I - Q)^{-1} \cdot S \cdot H\} \tag{6.128}$$

and

$$Ss = \frac{T}{F} \cdot \pi \cdot \{(I - Q)^{-1} \cdot Ss \cdot H\} \tag{6.129}$$

give the throughput for regular segment nodes and the switch node, respectively. The total throughput for the segment may be obtained using the sum of Eqs. (6.128) and (6.129).

In order to calculate the average backlogs for the segment and switch nodes we need to find the contributions of all the slots for all the possible sequences of slots that may form a cycle. If the sum of the contributions is X it can be shown that

$$X = (I - Q)^{-1} \cdot \{I + Sf \cdot \sum_{k=0}^{R} T^k + (S + Ss) \cdot \sum_{k=0}^{Tx} T^k \tag{6.130}$$

and thus we have for the backlog of the regular segment nodes, or the number of active nodes,

$$J = \frac{1}{F} \pi \cdot X \cdot \alpha \tag{6.131}$$

and for the backlog of the switch node

$$Js = \frac{1}{F} \pi \cdot X \cdot \beta \tag{6.132}$$

where α and β are the column vectors with elements $\alpha_{(i,j)} = i$ and $\beta_{(i,j)} = j$. Rejection probability and mean delay may easily be calculated in the same manner.

The results that follow demonstrate the type of performance characteristics that may be obtained using the multisegment analysis. The average number of active segment nodes and expected queue length at the switch node is plotted as a function of traffic load in Figure 6.22. We used $N=9$, $R=2$, and $Tx=30$ with a switch buffer capacity of 1, 2, and 3 packets. Similarly, results obtained for throughput, rejection probability, and mean delay are presented in Figures 6.23, 6.24, and 6.25, respectively. In general, and as

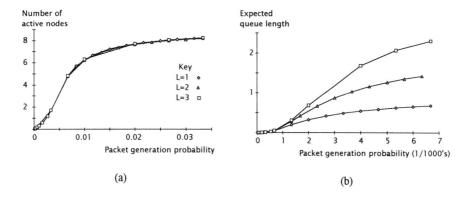

Figure 6.22   Number of active nodes and mean queue length at switch node as functions of packet generation probability.

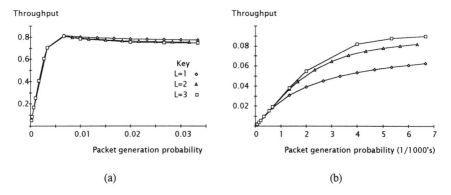

Figure 6.23   Throughput as a function of packet generation probability for (a) nodes and (b) the switch.

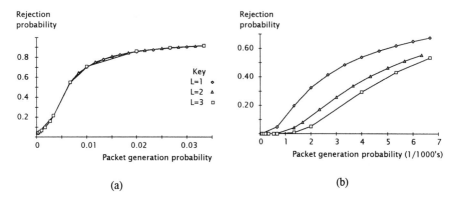

Figure 6.24   Packet rejection probability as a function of packet generation probability for (a) regular nodes and (b) the switch node.

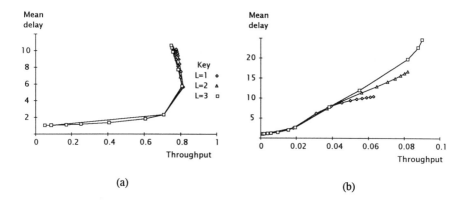

Figure 6.25 Mean delay versus throughput for (a) regular nodes and (b) the switch node.

expected, the buffer length at the switch does not affect the characteristics of the regular nodes.

Without entering into too much detail, something should be said of the nature of the characteristics in Figure 6.25(a). First appearances may give the impresion that the delay is reduced as the throughput increases. This is not in fact the case, rather, the delay increases while the throughput is reduced. This is a well-known phenomenon in so-called loss systems, which result from the loss of packets due to collisions. Essentially, as the offered load increases, so does the throughput. However, there becomes a point when the network is clogged with retransmitted packets and the throughput begins to reduce. Thus interesting characteristics result, such as those in Figure 6.25, which demonstrate this bistable behavior.

Switches may incorporate more complex access mechanisms such as in ATM networks where the traffic matrix affects the service offered to the switch. In many situations the switch port will see more traffic, and it is therefore suitable to give the switch a higher priority for access. This can be accomplished by providing a gated service to the switch, whereby it is allowed to transmit more than one packet at a time. It therefore has the opportunity to take more of the available bandwidth to meet its increased demand. We can adjust the previous analysis to account for this situation.

Now, each successful packet transmission from the switch is followed immediately by another until the buffer at the switch node is empty. Hence the part of the cycle in which the switch successfully acquires the channel consists of one or more packet transmissions. This may be accounted for using the same probability transition matrices defined in the previous section with the final matrix for the transmission period of a cycle in which the switch successfully acquires the channel, Cs, adjusted as follows. We have

$$csl_{ss'} = \begin{cases} P[i \to i'] \cdot P[j \to j'] & \text{for } j' \geq 1 \\ 0 & \text{for } j' = 0 \end{cases} \tag{6.133}$$

and

$$cs0_{ss'} = \begin{cases} P[i \to i'] \cdot P[j \to j'] & \text{for } j' = 0 \\ 0 & \text{for } j' \geq 1 \end{cases} \tag{6.134}$$

where Eqs. (6.133) and (6.134) are the elements of the matrices that represent the state transition probabilities for the final slots of a successful packet transmission that leaves the buffer active and idle, respectively.

Following previous similar arguments the factors on the right-hand side of these equations are given by

$$P[i \to i'] = \binom{N-i}{i'-i} \sigma^{i'-i}(1-\sigma)^{N-i'} \tag{6.135}$$

and

$$P[j \to j'] = \begin{cases} \sigma_s & \text{for } j' = j, j \neq 0 \\ 1-\sigma_s & \text{for } j' = j-1, j \neq 0 \\ 0 & \text{for } j' = j = 0 \end{cases} \tag{6.136}$$

We can now write a new expression for the contribution of the successful switch transmission period to the cycle time as

$$\sum_{k=0}^{\infty}(Ts^{Tx} \cdot Cs1)^k \cdot (Ts^{Tx} \cdot Cs0)$$

Again, as previously, the summation can be simplified and we arrive at a new expression for the transition probability matrix for the Markov chain as

$$P = (I-Q)^{-1} \cdot [Sf \cdot T^{R+1} + S \cdot T^{Tx} \cdot C + Ss \cdot (I - Ts^{Tx} \cdot Cs1)^{-1} \cdot Ts^{Tx} \cdot Cs0] \tag{6.137}$$

The performance metrics may also be derived. Now $T^{Tx} \cdot Cs1$ gives the transition probabilities when the switch transmits another packet. Hence the contribution of a switch transmission period to the mean cycle time is given by

$$(I-Q)^{-1} \cdot Ss. Tx. \sum_{k=0}^{\infty}(k+1)(T^{Tx} \cdot Cs1)^k \cdot T^{Tx} \cdot Cs0 \tag{6.138}$$

So Eq. (6.125) in this case becomes

$$Ft = \sum_{k=0}^{\infty}Q^k \cdot \{(R+1)Sf + (Tx+1)S + (Tx+1)S \cdot \sum_{k=0}^{\infty}(k+1)(T^{Tx} \cdot Cs1)^k \cdot T^{Tx} \cdot Cs0\} \cdot H \tag{6.139}$$

Now we have

$$\sum_{k=0}^{\infty}(k+1)(T^{Tx}\cdot Cs1)^k = (I - T^{Tx}\cdot Cs1)^{-2}$$

and

$$(I - T^{Tx}\cdot Cs1)^{-1}\cdot T^{Tx}\cdot Cs0\cdot H = H$$

so

$$\sum_{k=0}^{\infty}(k+1)(T^{Tx}\cdot Cs1)^k \cdot T^{Tx}\cdot Cs0 = (I - T^{Tx}\cdot Cs1)^{-1} \qquad (6.140)$$

Hence we can simplify Eq. (6.139) using Eq. (6.140) to give the following modified version of Eq. (6.126):

$$\mathbf{F} = (I - Q)^{-1}\cdot H + (I - Q)^{-1}\cdot\{(R+1)Sf + (Tx+1)[S + Ss\cdot(I - T^{Tx}\cdot Cs1)^{-1}]\}\cdot H \qquad (6.141)$$

Again the frame length is given by Eq. (6.127) and the throughputs by Eqs. (6.128) and (6.129). Also, the backlogs are given by Eqs. (6.131) and (6.132) with the computation of X modified to account for the switch transmission period as follows:

$$X = (I - Q)^{-1}\cdot\{I + Sf\cdot\sum_{k=0}^{R}T^k + S\cdot\sum_{k=0}^{Tx}T^k + Ss\cdot(I - T^{Tx}\cdot Cb1)^{-1}\cdot\sum_{k=0}^{Tx}T^k\} \qquad (6.142)$$

We will end this section with a selection of results that were obtained for the switch priority mechanism using the preceding analysis. The characteristics compare with those obtained using the previous analysis in which the switch accesses the channel using the same protocol as the segment nodes. The results obtained for the number of active segment nodes and queue length at the switch, throughput, packet rejection probability, and mean delay are presented in Figures 6.26 through 6.29. We assumed the particular case when $\sigma_s = 0.2\sigma$, and since this is likely to be a significant parameter, the results obtained for different values of σ_s, and indeed the other parameters of the network, may be of interest.

It is possible then to produce many types of characteristics that indicate various performance trends, however, in this chapter we are avoiding detailed descriptions of the results obtained. The overall performance of multisegment systems can be examined by considering the individual contribution of each segment, as we have indeed already done, or by averaging over the whole network.

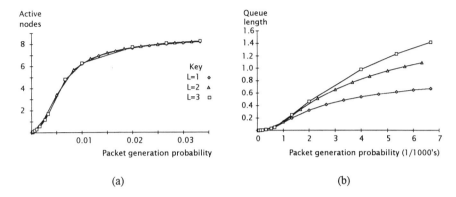

Figure 6.26   Number of active nodes and mean queue length at switch node as functions of packet generation probability.

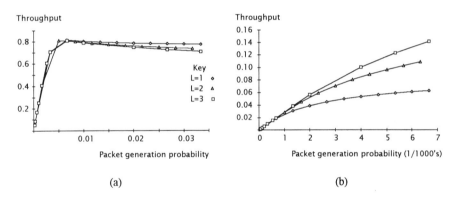

Figure 6.27   Throughput as a function of packet generation probability for (a) nodes and (b) the switch.

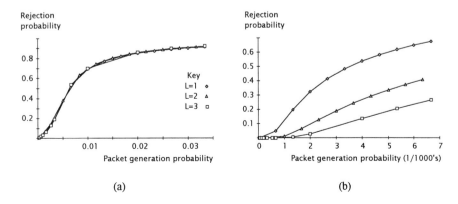

Figure 6.28   Packet rejection probability as a function of packet generation probability for (a) regular nodes and (b) the switch node.

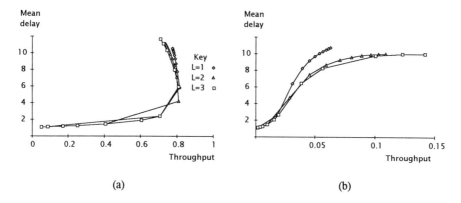

Figure 6.29 Mean delay versus throughput for (a) regular nodes and (b) the switch node.

6.6 SYSTEMS WITH NONSYMMETRIC TRAFFIC

In the analysis of the models we have discussed so far in this chapter we made the assumption that the packet generation probability is the same for all the nodes on a single segment. With the exception of the multisegment system this symmetrical property has allowed us to reduce the state space and give a tractable solution. However, in real life systems it is likely to be the case that the packet generation probability, or load distribution across the network, will vary quite dramatically. In fact, it is highly unlikely that the load will ever be perfectly symmetrically distributed.

It is possible to vary the load distributions, not to be confused with statistical distributions, using a variety of functions. In Figure 6.30 five single-step functions with varying degrees of asymmetry are displayed for a network of 100 nodes. Each of the

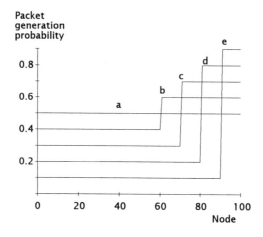

Figure 6.30 Step functions for nonsymmetric traffic.

functions contains two groups of nodes, each with corresponding packet generation probability. Function a corresponds with the symmetric case, while function b is split into two groups of 60 and 40 nodes with a 4:6 traffic load ratio. The functions a to e contain increasingly asymmetric distributions, with e the most asymmetric at 90:10 grouping with a 1:9 traffic ratio. Clearly the single-step function is one of many ways of distributing the traffic, but a thorough treatment is beyond the scope of this text.

Assume that we have a common communication channel for N nodes using the random TDMA without contention access method. Let the number of users in groups 1 and 2 be N_1 and N_2, respectively, and let the corresponding packet generation probabilities be σ_1 and σ_2. For the purpose of developing the Markov process the system can be viewed as consisting of three types of transition. The first type of transition occurs if, at the beginning of a slot, all the nodes in both groups are idle. The second type occurs if only one or more of the nodes in group 1 is active, and the third if at least one node from each group is active.

In order to derive a workable expression for the latter case it is assumed that priority is given to the group of nodes with the higher packet generation probability or greater traffic load. A two-dimensional Markov chain will be used, each dimension representing the number of active users in a group. Let the state descriptor be $s = (i, j)$ at the beginning of a slot and $s' = (i', j')$ at the end of it, where i, i' and j, j' are the numbers of active nodes in groups one and two, respectively. For the first type of transition we have

$$\Pr[i \to i', j \to j'] = bin(N_1, i', \sigma_1) \cdot bin(N_2, j', \sigma_2) \quad \text{for} \quad i = 0, j = 0 \tag{6.143}$$

where

$$bin(N, i, \sigma) = \binom{N}{i} \sigma^i (1-\sigma)^{N-i} \tag{6.144}$$

is the binomial function. For the second type of transition one of the active nodes in group 1 will transmit a packet and we have

$$\Pr[i \to i', j \to j'] = bin(N_1 - i, i' - i + 1, \sigma_1) \cdot bin(N_2, j', \sigma_2) \quad \text{for} \quad i > 0, j = 0 \tag{6.145}$$

Finally in the case where at least one node from both groups are active and priority is given to the group with higher traffic load, we have

$$\Pr[i \to i', j \to j'] = bin(N_1 - i, i' - i, \sigma_1) \cdot bin(N_2 - j, j' - j + 1, \sigma_2) \quad \text{for} \quad i > 0, j > 0 \tag{6.146}$$

assuming that $\sigma_2 \geq \sigma_1$. Calculation of the system transition matrix is therefore relatively straightforward, and we can solve for the steady-state distribution in the normal way.

The performance measures can be evaluated using the expressions that will now be derived. First, the throughput, which as usual is the fraction of time with which the channel is involved in successful transmission of data, may also now be calculated for individual groups. The throughput for group 1 is given by the sum of the probabilities that if the system were inspected at any time it is found to be in a state where one or more nodes from that group is active while all the nodes in the other group are idle. This can be expressed as

$$S_1 = \pi \cdot J_1 \tag{6.147}$$

with the column vector J_1 given by

$$J_1 = \begin{cases} 1 & \text{for } i > 0, j = 0 \\ 0 & \text{otherwise} \end{cases} \tag{6.148}$$

A similar expression gives the throughput for group 2 with corresponding column vector J_2 given by

$$J_2 = \begin{cases} 1 & \text{for } j > 0 \\ 0 & \text{otherwise} \end{cases} \tag{6.149}$$

In the latter expression we account for the fact that active nodes in group two access slots with priority over group one nodes.

With $N_1 = 5, N_2 = 5, \sigma_1 = 0.04$, and $\sigma_2 = 0.06$ the values for S_1 and S_2 are calculated to be 0.188 and 0.266, respectively. If we compare the ratios S_1/σ_1 and S_2/σ_2 this will give some indication as to the effect of the priority mechanism. In this example they are calculated to be 0.213 and 0.225, respectively, and as expected the nodes in group two have the greater success rate in terms of both overall throughput and as a fraction of traffic generated.

If we set $\sigma_1 = \sigma_2$ this results in a symmetric traffic load and we should expect to get the same results as we obtained with the analysis for random TDMA, using a one-dimensional Markov chain, in Section 6.2. Figure 6.31 illustrates the throughput characteristics obtained using each method with a system of 10 nodes, and reassuringly the results are in agreement.

Since there is a priority mechanism it is not expected that the throughput for each group will be the same. This is clearly shown in Figure 6.32 in which the throughputs for each group are plotted on the same axes. Above a small packet generation probability the priority group 2 packets swamp the channel and at high throughputs dominate the utilization of its bandwidth. If we take the ratio of throughputs as a measure of fairness, with a value of one being the most fair, below $\sigma_1 = \sigma_2 = 0.1$ it is close to 1 while at $\sigma_1 = \sigma_2 = 0.5$ it is 0.03. Quite unfair! As we vary the traffic symmetry, using a range of single steps such as those illustrated in Figure 6.30, the overall throughput characteristic will change, and calculations summarized in Figure 6.33 show this to be true. This is the case with the fairness characteristic, as defined here.

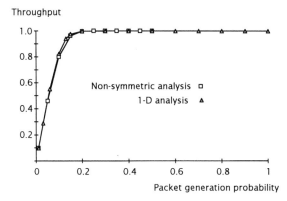

Figure 6.31 Throughput for random TDMA; comparison of analyses.

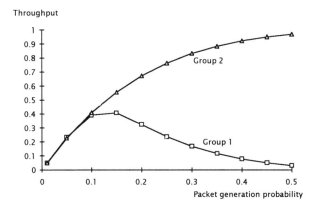

Figure 6.32 Comparison of throughput for each group.

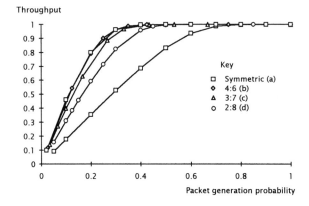

Figure 6.33 Overall throughput characteristics for nonsymmetric traffic.

The results for each group are affected, however, and in Figure 6.34 the throughput for group 1 at each nonsymmetric traffic distribution given in Figure 6.30 is presented. The corresponding characteristics for group 2 nodes are presented in Figure 6.35. As expected we can see from these two figures that, since the traffic is more asymmetrically distributed, the priority mechanism works in favor of the more heavily loaded group 2 nodes. While the throughput of group 1 nodes is reduced, the reverse is true for the other group. It is also interesting to note that in the most asymmetric case e, the throughput is equal to the packet generation probability and we should find that the rejection probability is zero.

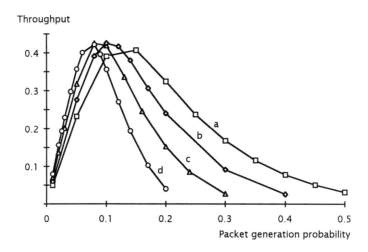

Figure 6.34 Throughput for group 1 nodes with nonsymmetric traffic.

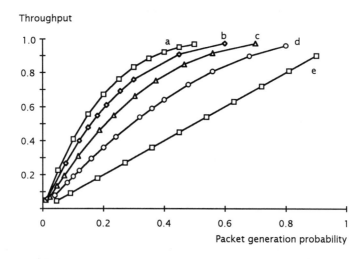

Figure 6.35 Throughput for group 2 nodes with nonsymmetric traffic.

The rejection probability for each group may be calculated with the usual expression

$$RP_g = 1 - \frac{S_g}{N_g \sigma_g} \tag{6.150}$$

with the subscript g identifying the group index. In Figure 6.36 the rejection probability characteristics are presented for each group. As predicted for group 2 the rejection probability with nonsymmetric distribution e was found to be zero at all packet generation probabilities, and so this data was not included in the figure.

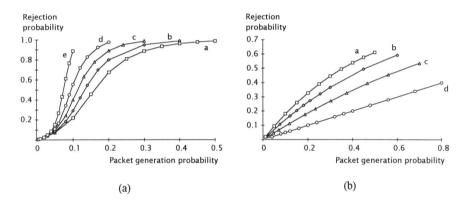

(a)

(b)

Figure 6.36 Rejection probability characteristics for (a) group 1 nodes, and (b) group 2 nodes.

The system backlog is given by $Q = Q_1 + Q_2$ with

$$Q_g = \pi \cdot \beta_g \tag{6.151}$$

The column vectors β_g, $g = 0,1$ are given by $\beta_1 = i$ and $\beta_2 = j$. The backlog characteristics of each node group for nonsymmetric distributions a, b, and c are presented in Figure 6.37.

Finally delay is calculated using Little's result in the usual manner. In Figure 6.38 we have chosen to present the results of the overall mean delay for both groups as functions of throughput. Within reasonable error, and as should be expected, this characteristic is independent of the traffic distribution. The delays for individual node groups may be calculated and, in certain circumstances, may prove to be useful performance indicators. In this text, however, we are primarily concerned with the method of analysis and not the results themselves.

The analysis for fixed TDMA presented in the second section of this chapter may also be modified to account for nonsymmetric traffic, assuming the same system parameters as for the random TDMA without contention access method. Let the number

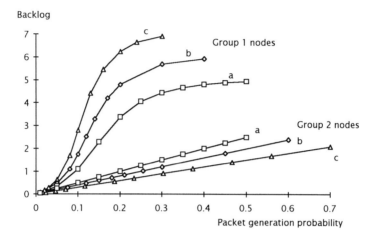

Figure 6.37 System backlog characteristics.

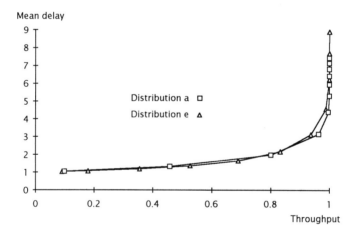

Figure 6.38 Mean delay versus throughput characteristics.

of users in groups 1 and 2 be N_1 and N_2, respectively, and let the corresponding packet generation probabilities be σ_1 and σ_2. The system can be modeled with the same two-dimensional Markov chain. The state descriptor is $s = (i, j)$ at the beginning of a slot, and $s' = (i', j')$ at the end of it, where i, i' and j, j' are the number of active nodes in groups 1 and 2, respectively.

In this case, however, we are required to construct a system matrix with imbedded points at the end of frames that consist of $N1+N2$ slots—one for each node. Further, due to the nature of fixed assignment, the transition probabilities $\Pr[i \rightarrow i']$ and $\Pr[j \rightarrow j']$ are independent, and separate expressions for different ranges of values of i

and j are not required. As far as transition probability matrices are concerned each frame consists of three types and the system transition matrix is given by

$$P = (T_1 + T_2 + Id)^{N_1 + N_2} \tag{6.152}$$

The first type, T_1, is for a slot in which one of the active nodes in group 1 may transmit a packet. Averaging over the length of a frame, we have a probability $i/N1 + N2$ that the slot in question is utilized. Hence the elements of T_1 are given by

$$\Pr[i \rightarrow i', j \rightarrow j'] = \frac{i}{N_1 + N_2} bin(N_1 - i, i' - i + 1, \sigma_1) \cdot bin(N_2 - j, j' - j, \sigma_2) \tag{6.153}$$

Similarly the elements of T_2, the transition probabilities for slots in which one of the j active nodes in group 2 may transmit, are given by

$$\Pr[i \rightarrow i', j \rightarrow j'] = \frac{j}{N_1 + N_2} bin(N_1 - i, i' - i, \sigma_1) \cdot bin(N_2 - j, j' - j + 1, \sigma_2) \tag{6.154}$$

Finally the transition probability matrix Id, for slots that are idle, has elements

$$\Pr[i \rightarrow i', j \rightarrow j'] = \left(1 - \frac{i+j}{N_1 + N_2}\right) \cdot bin(N_1 - i, i' - i, \sigma_1) \cdot bin(N_2 - j, j' - j, \sigma_2) \tag{6.155}$$

It is easy to show that the throughput, rejection probability, backlog, and mean delay for the individual node groups and the system overall are given by

$$
\begin{array}{lll}
S_1 = \pi \cdot T_1 \cdot H & S_2 = \pi \cdot T_2 \cdot H & S = S_1 + S_2 \\
RP_1 = 1 - \dfrac{S_1}{N_1 \sigma_1} & RP_2 = 1 - \dfrac{S_2}{N_2 \sigma_2} & RP = 1 - \dfrac{S_1 + S_2}{N_1 \sigma_1 + N_1 \sigma_1} \\
Q_1 = \pi \cdot \beta_1 & Q_2 = \pi \cdot \beta_2 & Q = Q_1 + Q_2 \\
D_1 = \dfrac{Q_1}{S_1} & D_2 = \dfrac{Q_2}{S_2} & D = \dfrac{Q}{S}
\end{array}
$$

where, similar to the random TDMA case, the column vectors β_g, $g = 0, 1$, are given by $\beta_1 = i$ and $\beta_2 = j$.

Evidently we could calculate a variety of characteristics and provide a detailed performance analysis for fixed TDMA. However, this is not the aim of this text. Figures 6.39 and 6.40 provide a number of throughput characteristics that serve to illustrate the type of results that can be obtained. The graphs may be compared with those obtained previously for random TDMA.

Recall that we presented an alternative and perhaps more realistic analysis for fixed TDMA in Section 6.3, and this approach may also be used for the model with

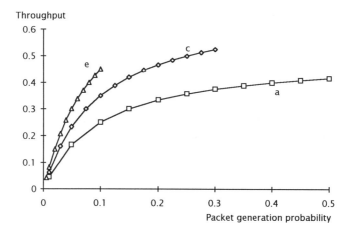

Figure 6.39 Fixed TDMA throughput characteristics for group 1 nodes.

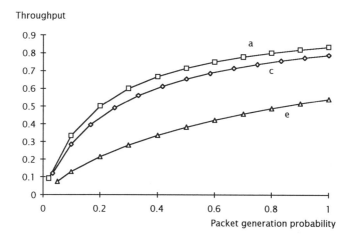

Figure 6.40 Overall system throughput for fixed TDMA with nonsymmetric traffic.

nonsymmetric traffic. In this case, however, we will be required to use a Markov chain with four dimensions, and this will involve the solution of no less than $2N_1 \times 2N_2$ simultaneous equations—100 in the case of a ten-node system evenly split into two groups.

Let the state descriptor be $s = (i,a,j,b)$ where i and j are the numbers of active nodes in each group and a and b may take on the values 0 and 1, representing the activity of a tagged node from groups 1 and 2, respectively. The system transition matrix will consist of contributions from four types of transition arising from two slots being available for the tagged node in each group and two slots available for the remaining nodes in each group. With corresponding transition probability matrices T_1, T_2, C_1, and C_2 we have

$$P = T_1 \cdot C_1^{N_1-1} \cdot T_2 \cdot C_2^{N_2-1} \tag{6.156}$$

The following expressions may be used to calculate the elements of T_1 ($^1t_{s,s'}$) and C_1 ($^1c_{s,s'}$) and are presented without comment. The complete analysis is left as an exercise for the reader.

$$^1t_{s,s'} = \Pr[i \to i'] \cdot \Pr[a \to a'] \cdot \Pr[j \to j'] \cdot \Pr[b \to b'] \tag{6.157}$$

with

$$\Pr[i \to i'] = bin(N_1 - 1, i' - i, \sigma_1)$$

$$\Pr[a \to a'] = \delta(a,0)\{\delta(a',0)(1-\sigma_1) + \delta(a',1)\sigma_1\} + \delta(a,1)\delta(a',0)$$

$$\Pr[j \to j'] = bin(N_2 - 1, j' - j, \sigma_2)$$

$$\Pr[b \to b'] = \delta(b,0)\{\delta(b',0)(1-\sigma_2) + \delta(b',1)\sigma_2\} + \delta(b,1)\delta(b',1)$$

Similarly

$$^1c_{s,s'} = \Pr[i \to i'] \cdot \Pr[a \to a'] \cdot \Pr[j \to j'] \cdot \Pr[b \to b'] \tag{6.158}$$

with

$$\Pr[i \to i'] = \frac{i}{(N_1 - 1) + (N_2 - 1)} bin(N_1 - 1, i' - i + 1, \sigma_1)$$
$$+ \left(1 - \frac{i}{(N_1 - 1) + (N_2 - 1)}\right) bin(N_1 - 1, i' - i, \sigma_1)$$

$$\Pr[a \to a'] = \delta(a,0)\{\delta(a',0)(1-\sigma_1) + \delta(a',1)\sigma_1\} + \delta(a,1)\delta(a',1)$$

$$\Pr[j \to j'] = bin(N_2 - 1, j' - j, \sigma_2)$$

$$\Pr[b \to b'] = \delta(b,0)\{\delta(b',0)(1-\sigma_2) + \delta(b',1)\sigma_2\} + \delta(b,1)\delta(b',1)$$

6.7 CONCLUDING REMARKS

In this chapter we studied methods of obtaining various network performance metrics using discrete-space, discrete-time Markov chains. Simple systems can be modeled with one- or two-dimensional chains while more complex models are required for more sophisticated access mechanisms and traffic loads. The complexity of these analyses can lead to solutions that give quite different results for what appear to be similar systems.

This was demonstrated for fixed TDMA. However, it was also shown how this approach can give a whole range of measures for performance that should be useful in communication network analysis.

Exercises

6.1 (a) Write down the transition probability matrix for the homogeneous Markov chain whose state transition diagram is depicted in the following figure.

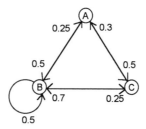

Figure 6.41 A system with three possible states, A, B, and C.

(b) If the system is initially in state A, what is the probability, after two transitions, that it can be found in state C ?

(c) Solve for the steady-state solution.

6.2 A discrete-space, discrete-time Markov chain has the transition probability matrix

$$\begin{pmatrix} 1-\alpha & \alpha & 0 \\ \beta & 1-\beta & 0 \\ 0 & 0 & 1 \end{pmatrix}$$

Under what conditions will the chain be irreducible and aperiodic?

6.3 Explain why the Markov chain described for the random TDMA system, at the beginning of Section 6.2, is irreducible and aperiodic.

6.4 Derive the four components of Eqs. (6.37) and (6.38).

6.5 The steady-state probability distribution, π, is obtained by solving the system of linearly dependent, simultaneous equations given by $\pi = \pi P$ and $\sum \pi_i = 1$. Equation (6.40) was obtained by replacing the first row of P with the latter expression. Write down the equivalent expression when the second row is replaced. Verify that the same solution is obtained for either of the cases when $\sigma = 0.1$ or 0.5.

6.6 A Markov chain is used to model a random TDMA channel. N nodes are attached to the channel via the multiplexor. Assume that each node has a unit capacity buffer and may access the channel without contention or collision. Write down the general expression for the elements of the system transition matrix.

6.7 For the same system as the previous question, if σ is the per slot packet generation probability and S is the throughput, show that the probability that a packet arrives to find a node idle is given by $S/N\sigma$. Hence derive Eq. (6.42).

6.8 Verify that the elements of the matrices in Eqs. (6.50) and (6.51) are correct. Using the same principles and assuming similar system characteristics, write down the matrix that represents the state transition probabilities for a node with a buffer capacity of four. Calculate and comment on the values of throughput and mean delay for steady-state conditions when $\sigma = 0.1$ and 0.5.

6.9 Write down a suitable transform that could be used to reference the elements of a square matrix in the case when a three-dimensional Markov chain is required. In what circumstances might a three-dimensional Markov chain be utilized ?

6.10 Derive Eq. (6.72). Explain why the infinite sum converges to the finite expression.

6.11 Derive Eq. (6.90) by summing the contributions of the mean contention period when the tagged node acquires the channel, the mean contention period when a node other than the tagged one acquires the channel, and the transmission period.

6.12 Develop a method for calculating the expected queue length of systems that can be analyzed using the technique described in Section 6.4. Compare the results obtained for the fixed and random TDMA methods with those obtained previously using alternative analyses.

References

[1] Apostolopoulos, T. K., and E. N. Protonotarios, "Queueing Analysis of Buffered CSMA/CD Protocols," *IEEE Transactions on Communications*, Vol. COM-34, No. 9, pp. 898–905, Sept. 1986.

[2] Apostolopoulos, T. K., E. D. Sykas, and E. N. Protonotarios, "Analysis of a New Retransmission Control Algorithm for Slotted CSMA/CD LANs," *IEEE Transactions on Computers*, Vol. C-36, No. 6, pp. 692–701, June 1987.

[3] Kleinrock, L., *Queueing Systems, Volume 1: Theory*, New York: John Wiley and Sons, 1979.

[4] Sykas, E. D., D. E. Karvelas, and E. N. Protonotarios, "Queueing Analysis of some Buffered Random Multiple Access Schemes," *IEEE Transactions on Communications*, Vol. COM-34, No. 8, pp. 790–798, Aug. 1986.

[5] Sykas, E. D. and G. L. Lyberopoulos, "Performance Analysis of Interconnected CSMA/CD Local Area Networks," *IEE Proceedings, Part I*, Volume 139, No. 2, pp. 181–197, April 1992.

Chapter 7

Local Area Networks

In this chapter we will concentrate on the traffic analysis relevant to LANs. There is a number of distinguishing features of LANs in this respect. One is the geographical extent of the LAN, which has an impact on the length of the transmission path, and another is the topology. Perhaps, as it may be fair to expect, one of the most important parameters is the type of MAC protocol. The access protocol certainly brings a strong influence to bear on LAN performance. However, it will be seen that in any particular set of circumstances one of a host of LAN parameters can have a profound influence. The data transmission rate, packet length, node population, and traffic arrival patterns are also parameters that should be accounted for. In turn, the higher layer protocols, which dictate some of these parameters, may distinguish themselves by characteristic effects on the performance. However, we do not intend to deal with them in this text.

Methods for analyzing LAN performance vary from simple models that predict, for example, the maximum capacity with a given set of parameters, to complex models that describe the time-varying statistics for individual data packets. In time-honored tradition we begin with the simple ideas and progress with increasing complexity. Throughout the chapter we will introduce a number of different techniques for the mathematical analysis of LAN performance, and these will be compared with each other and the results of computer simulation where suitable. In most cases the access protocol dictates the method of analysis, and in order to carry through the algebra we are often required to impose a number of assumptions. It is probably fair to say that the analysis becomes more complex when assumptions are relaxed. Throughout the chapter we will assume that the physical layer remains fully operational and that the error rate is negligible or dealt with by higher layer protocols.

7.1 THE EFFECTIVE CHANNEL LENGTH

William Stallings has provided us with a suitable starting point for LAN performance analysis through a number of articles that loosely predict the capacity of the *carrier sense multiple access with collision detection* (CSMA/CD) and token ring access methods [1], [2]. His work is based on the observation that, all things being equal, the performance of a LAN as measured by the channel utilization depends on the effective channel length, a.

If the data transmission rate is D bit/s and the end-to-end propagation delay is P s, then the effective channel length, or normalized propagation delay, is given by

$$a = \frac{DP}{L} \tag{7.1}$$

where L is the packet length in bits. This expression can be derived by inspecting the units or by recognizing that L/D is the time taken to transfer a packet from a node onto the transmission medium. From the latter statement we can rewrite Eq. (7.1) in the form that expresses a as being the ratio of the propagation and transmission times for the channel, thus

$$a = \frac{\text{propagation time}}{\text{transmission time}} \tag{7.2}$$

Now, assuming that the propagation delay and packet lengths remain constant, the value of a determines an upper bound on the channel utilization of a LAN that does not allow more than one packet to be in transit on the medium at any one time. In stating that the propagation delay remains constant it is intended that all the nodes effectively require the same propagation time across the network, equal to the maximum time and independent of their physical location. The CSMA/CD and simple token passing scheme are two access protocols that do not allow more than one packet on the medium at any time. We will refer to these methods as single-packet protocols.

For the time being let us make the further assumption that the single-packet protocol under consideration is perfect, and as soon as a transmission is complete then another one may begin. When the traffic is sufficiently heavy, or intense, the LAN is being utilized at a value given by the throughput divided by the data transmission rate. That is

$$U = \frac{\text{throughput}}{D} \tag{7.3}$$

where the throughput is the useful network time, measured in bit/s, given by $L/(P + L/D)$. Using this and Eq. (7.1) in Eq. (7.3), we obtain

$$U = \frac{1}{1+a} \tag{7.4}$$

Hence the utilization is inversely proportional to the effective channel length.

This relationship is intuitive because if the packet is small and the propagation delay is large, then we should expect the utilization to be small. Thus we refer to a as the effective channel length; as the packet length becomes, then the effective channel length increases and, as we have seen, the channel efficiency is reduced.

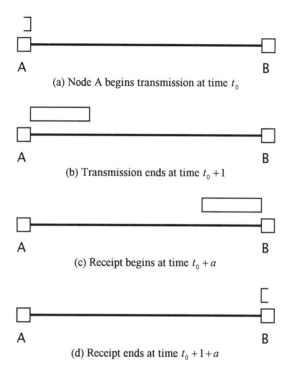

(a) Node A begins transmission at time t_0

(b) Transmission ends at time $t_0 + 1$

(c) Receipt begins at time $t_0 + a$

(d) Receipt ends at time $t_0 + 1 + a$

Figure 7.1 Packet transmission on a simple bus LAN.

Following Stalling's explanation, consider the process as depicted in Figure 7.1, which illustrates a bus with two nodes, A and B, at the extreme ends. Time in the figure is normalized with respect to the packet transmission time. Again, assuming that the traffic arrival rate is sufficient, the end of a transmission from either node corresponds with the beginning of a new transmission. Hence time t_0, the beginning of a transmission from A as in Figure 7.1(a), corresponds with the end of a previous transmission. In (b) the transmission has just been completed and the time is now $t_0 + 1$. Packet receipt begins at $t_0 + a$ and the propagation of the whole is complete by $t_0 + 1 + a$, at which time a new transmission begins. The utilization, as given Eq. (7.4), is easily verified. Note that the result is the same if the packet transmission time is greater than the propagation delay, that is, if $a \leq 1$ or if $a \geq 1$.

The same simple model can be applied to a ring LAN as depicted in Figure 7.2. In this case we have chosen to illustrate the case for which the packet transmission time is greater than the propagation delay, that is, $a < 1$, and the packet receipt begins before its transmission has ended. A similar argument could be applied to star topology LANs and so an upper bound for the utilization, as given by Eq. (7.4), is applicable to any simple topology.

The utilization for our simple LAN efficiency model is plotted in Figure 7.3 as a function of throughput for a selection of typical values for a. Note that below the upper bound we have plotted the offered load, as given by $U = $ throughput. For example, with

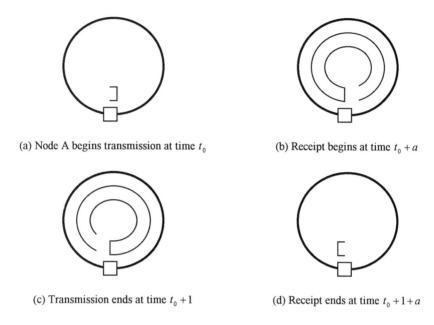

(a) Node A begins transmission at time t_0

(b) Receipt begins at time $t_0 + a$

(c) Transmission ends at time $t_0 + 1$

(d) Receipt ends at time $t_0 + 1 + a$

Figure 7.2 Packet transmission on a simple ring LAN.

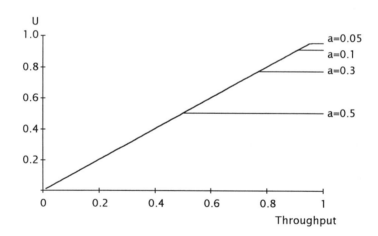

Figure 7.3 Simple LAN model utilization as a function of throughput.

$D = 10$ Mbit/s, 1000 bits, and a cable length of 1000 m, we have $a = 0.05$.[1] In this case the upper bound for utilization is close to one (0.95). If $L = 100$ bits, then $a = 0.5$ and the upper bound is exactly 0.5. This is the same as the effect of increasing the data transmission rate to 100 Mbit/s.

---

[1] Assuming a propagation speed of 2×10^8 m/s.

The efficiency of popular LAN systems such as Ethernet and token ring, which operate with similar parameters such as those given in the preceding examples, may therefore provide a source of concern. An access protocol will introduce overheads to the process such that the upper bound given by Eq. (7.4) may be overconservative. For example, in the CSMA/CD method there should be time allocated to resolving collisions, which under the heavy traffic conditions will certainly occur, and this will have the effect of reducing throughput. A similar reduction in throughput is observed for token passing, which requires that a special packet is transmitted between data packets. In any case, it is obvious that small values for the a parameter are desirable for single-packet protocols.

The upper bound on utilization is not the same for access methods that permit the simultaneous propagation of two or more packets. Consider the same perfect protocol as previously. This time we give the transmitting node a gated service that allows it to transmit more than one packet at a time, in succession. Thus, transmissions from other nodes are delayed until the privileged node has transmitted all the data that it is allowed to send in one go. In the extreme case this node continually generates data and uses the whole channel bandwidth. The network utilization, in this case, is always a maximum. However, this is achieved at the expense of other nodes that are unfairly denied any access to the facility.

7.2 SIMPLE MODELS FOR TOKEN PASSING AND CSMA/CD

In the previous section we made a number of assumptions in order to investigate one of the interesting performance parameters for LANs. We even ignored the effects of any overhead that might be introduced by different access protocols. In this section we will relax one or two assumptions and probe the mechanisms of two of the most popular LAN types in more detail. The material closely follows Stalling's previous work in [3]. This should provide a basis of understanding for the more complex models that can be used to develop rigorous performance analyses presented later in the chapter.

The first assumption to be relaxed is that which concerns the overhead of the access mechanism. First consider a simple token ring system. Again assume that the traffic is heavy with a view to investigating the maximum throughput. Let there be N nodes connected in a ring with the possibility that the packet transmission time may be greater than the propagation delay, as in Figure 7.2, or less than it. In our simple system the propagation delay for the token is just the time taken to travel to the nearest neighbor and not a complete end-to-end journey. Assuming the nodes are equally spaced, the propagation delay for the token is given by a/N where, as before, a is the effective channel length, that is the end-to-end propagation delay normalized with respect to the packet transmission time. There are still four possible variations of this simple system as follows.

The first two cases arise when the packet transmission time is greater than the end-to-end propagation delay. Normalizing with respect to packet transmission time again, we can say these are the cases for which $a < 1$. In either case, with reference to Figure 7.2, the transmitting node must wait at least until the end of the packet transmission, that is, until time $t_0 + 1$, before it has the opportunity to transmit the token.

In the first case consider the token is transmitted immediately following the beginning of packet receipt, at time $t_0 + a$; and in the second case it waits until the complete packet has been received, at time $t_0 + 1 + a$. Now the throughput, S, being the fraction of time that the system spends transmitting useful data, is given by the ratio

$$S = \frac{\text{packet transmission time}}{\text{cycle time}} \tag{7.5}$$

where the cycle time is the time required to complete the packet transmission and to propagate the token to the next logical recipient. The packet transmission time is simply one. In the first case the cycle time is $1 + a/N$, assuming that the token transmission time is negligible, and we obtain

$$S = \frac{1}{1 + a/N} \tag{7.6}$$

In the second case the cycle time includes the additional a seconds required for the propagation of the data packet and the throughput becomes

$$S = \frac{1}{1 + a + a/N} \tag{7.7}$$

The other two cases arise when $a > 1$. So the third case is when token transmission begins at the same instant that the beginning of the data packet is received, and the fourth is when the complete packet has been received. The advantage in choosing the latter mechanism, even though it may appear to be the least efficient, is that the node may verify the correct transmission of the data packet prior to releasing the token. For the third case we obtain

$$S = \frac{1}{a + a/N} \tag{7.8}$$

and the fourth case is the same as for $a < 1$ as given by Eq. (7.7).

Throughput is plotted as a function of the normalized propagation delay, using Eqs. (7.6) to (7.8), in Figure 7.4. Note that, as should have been expected, the throughput is improved, providing a more efficient service, when the token is released earliest, over most of the range of values for a. Also note that in the cases for which Eqs. (7.6) and (7.8) hold the throughput is greater than the upper bound predicted in the previous section. The reason for this is that, in the previous section, we limited the network service to one packet at any one time. Now if the token is released at the beginning of a packet receipt, then it will be received at the next node before the packet has completed transmission, provided, of course, that $a/N < 1$. As soon as the next recipient takes possession of the token, it begins the transmission of a packet of its own,

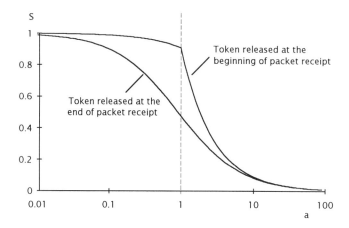

Figure 7.4 Simple token passing throughput as a function of normalized propagation delay.

with the result that more than one packet may be in transit simultaneously. Of course, the packets are not transmitted on the same section of cable. The network consists of N separate links, each transmitting and receiving signals independently.

We noted previously that the transmitting node must wait at least until the end of the packet transmission before it releases the token. If this is indeed the case, then, using popular jargon, we say that the token is piggybacked onto the packet. Assuming that the token transmission time is negligible, as we have been doing, and that the next recipient may transit another packet as soon as it receives the token, then under heavy traffic conditions there will be contiguous packets in transit on the ring. Effectively the LAN is now operating with a time division multiplexing mechanism. That is, at the same instant as the end of an existing packet transmission passes a node, a new packet is released on to the ring. This appears to be the perfect access mechanism for a multiple-packet LAN and the normalized throughput is always a maximum at one. We carefully avoid the temptation to declare this as the definitive perfect protocol since we have not considered any performance measure other than throughput.

Next we consider the throughput of a CSMA/CD LAN under the heavy traffic assumption. The analysis is a little more complex than for the simple token ring scheme. It is convenient to split time into equal length slots, as is often the case for random access methods such as CSMA/CD, and the length of a slot is set to be equal to twice the end-to-end propagation delay. This is the maximum time required to detect a collision.

As before the starting point is Eq. (7.5) and we progress by calculating the transmission and cycle times, expressed in numbers of slots. It is easily shown that a successful transmission occupies $1/2a$ slots. A cycle time, however, now includes the possibility that collisions have occurred and this will certainly be the case when all $N > 1$ nodes are permanently active. In fact, we must restrict each node to transmit with probability p in each slot, otherwise the network will be occupied solely with the task of dealing with colliding packets. Thus a cycle consists of two types of interval: a successful packet transmission, or transmission interval $T = 1/2a$, and a sequence of slots that contain either collisions or no transmissions, a contention interval C. Thus we have

$$S = \frac{T}{T + \overline{C}} \tag{7.9}$$

where the average length of a contention interval is given by

$$\overline{C} = \sum_{i=1}^{\infty} i \cdot \Pr[C = i] \tag{7.10}$$

The probability term inside the summation is the probability that there are i contiguous slots that contain collisions or no transmissions, followed by one slot with a single transmission. The latter, which we will denote by A, is equivalent to the probability that any one of N nodes transmits while the other $(N-1)$ nodes refrain. Thus

$$A = Np(1-p)^{N-1} \tag{7.11}$$

Now Eq. (7.10) may be written as

$$\overline{C} = \sum_{i=1}^{\infty} i \cdot (1-A)^i A \tag{7.12}$$

which simplifies to

$$\overline{C} = \frac{1-A}{A} \tag{7.13}$$

Hence replacing the variables in the quotient on the right-hand side of Eq. (7.9) using Eq. (7.13) and the fact that $T = 1/2a$, we have

$$S = \frac{1}{1 + 2a(1-A)/A} \tag{7.14}$$

The maximum throughput for CSMA/CD, under assumptions that we have made, may therefore be calculated using Eqs. (7.11) and (7.14). As with token passing we can select a value for the node population, N, and the effective channel length a. In addition we are required to assign a value for the transmission probability p.

In Figure 7.5 we plotted throughput as a function of a for three different values of p, with $N = 10$. It may be seen that the protocol is operating most efficiently when $p = 0.1$ as compared with $p = 0.05$ and 0.2. In fact, the throughput is a maximum for this value of p when there are 10 nodes on the network; we could have predicted this scenario, as follows. Equation (7.11) gives the probability of successful transmission in

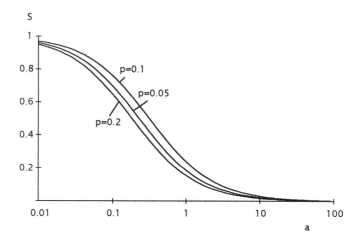

Figure 7.5 Throughput as a function of *a* for CSMA/CD with heavy traffic.

terms of p and N, and it is a maximum when $p = 1/N$. Note that due to Eq. (7.14), for $N > 1$, the throughput of CSMA/CD is always bounded by the upper limit that we determined in the previous section.

It is interesting to compare the throughputs of simple token passing and CSMA/CD in the same graph. The characteristics obtained for two different node populations are presented in Figure 7.6. For CSMA/CD we have chosen p to give the maximum throughput. In both cases CSMA/CD is out-performed by both of the token passing variants. We will see later that the honors are reversed when the traffic is light. In Figure 7.7 we plotted the throughputs as a function of N for two values of a. In all cases the throughput quickly approaches some limiting value.

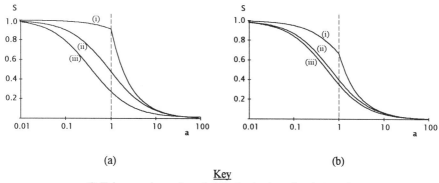

(a)   (b)

<u>Key</u>
(i) Token passing; released at the beginning of packet receipt
(ii) Token passing; released at the end of packet receipt
(iii) CSMA/CD

Figure 7.6 Throughput as a function of *a* with (a) $N = 10$, (b) $N = 2$.

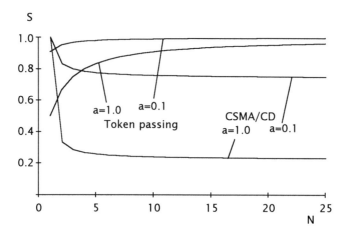

Figure 7.7 Throughput as a function of N with $a = 1.0$ and 0.1.

It is usual practice, where possible, to verify traffic performance analysis results with those obtained using computer simulation. We can accomplish this task here using the simple token passing simulation program described in Chapter 4. The program requires modifications from three respects so that it will provide us with the results we require. The first is to set the packet generation times so that we conform with the heavy traffic assumption. A convenient way of doing this is to change the line that assigns the *gen_packet* event time so that the inter-arrival time is negligible. This must be done in two places: when the initial event list is constructed and following packet removal from the LAN. The second respect concerns the operation of the token passing protocol. In the original program we implemented the case for which the token is released after the whole packet has been received at the transmitting node. We have changed just two lines to implement the alternative described previously, whereby the token is released at the same instant as the leading edge arrives at the transmitting node, and included an *if* statement to deal with the cases for $a < 1$ and $a \geq 1$. Finally we had to include a line in the results procedure to calculate the utilization, or throughput, as defined in the preceding analysis.

The reader is encouraged to develop their own code and implement the required modifications. It should be realized that the equivalent statement for $a < 1$ in code is propagation_delay $<$ packet_length. The characteristics in Figure 7.8 show that the results of the analysis are in good agreement with the simulation programs. In fact, all the throughputs obtained using each method were the same up to at least five significant figures. The simulations were executed with 1000 packet transmissions per node and seven different values of a were used in each variant by adjusting the packet length.

In Figure 7.9 we plotted the simulation results for the CSMA/CD algorithm obtained with $N = 10$ and $N = 2$. Again we obtained a very good agreement between the two methods for calculating the throughput under heavy traffic conditions. In order to obtain these results, we significantly modified the original program. Notably, just one

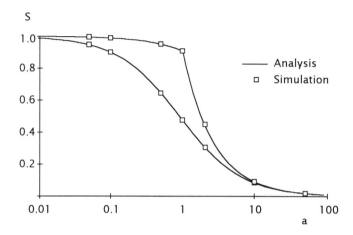

Figure 7.8 Verifying the simple token passing analysis with simulation.

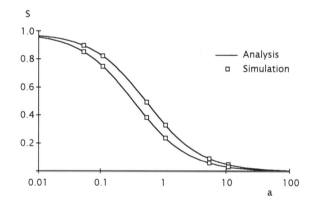

Figure 7.9 Verifying the CSMA/CD analysis with simulation.

event type was utilized, and there were no requirements to store information about individual node or packet statistics.

7.3 TOKEN PASSING ANALYSIS

In the last section we discovered that token passing can be more efficient than CSMA/CD under certain circumstances. Now we look to provide more detailed analyses of these mechanisms that will allow us to change one or more of the various network parameters and construct models for alternative performance measures. The throughput of a token passing system, through its determinate nature, is generally equal to the offered load up to network capacity. The analysis is therefore trivial, provided that the token overhead is neglected. The delay incurred by traffic is less obviously deduced and therefore provides the focus in this section. The material is based on the popularly quoted paper written by Sethi and Saydam [4].

Rejection probability is another characteristic of interest, and its derivation will also be covered. It should be noted that the intention is not to provide a thorough and rigorous analysis of token passing or polling systems. Such a work would constitute a sizable volume in its own right. However, it is intended that the analyses in this section provide the material for an indepth study of the token passing system. An alternative approach to Sethi and Saydam, which permits the observation of asymmetric traffic loads, is therefore included. This is based on methods that are presented in a paper by Ibe and Cheng [5].

In the first instance we will assume that all arrivals at each of the N network nodes consist of single, fixed-length packets. The delay of a packet on a token passing LAN is the sum of the waiting times in a queue, or buffer, and the time taken to transmit and propagate the packet. The mean delay is therefore given by

$$\overline{D} = \overline{W} + x \qquad (7.15)$$

where $\overline{W}$ and x represent the contributions of the waiting time and transmission and propagation times, respectively. The value of x depends on the packet length, data transmission rate, and the propagation delay. If it is assumed that the delay calculation is based on a complete round trip, then the calculation of x is trivial. We will assume that the buffer capacity at each node is infinite, so the waiting time depends on the specific token passing algorithm and its calculation is a little more involved. The waiting time, in turn, is the sum of two variables that may be calculated independently.

The timing diagram in Figure 7.10 depicts the arrival and departure of an arbitrary packet at an arbitrary network node. The value of $\overline{T}$ is the average time taken for the token to visit all the nodes once, or the token rotation time. The packet may arrive at any point in one of these cycles and the residual token rotation time is denoted by T_r. If $\overline{Q}$ is the number of packets already queueing, then the time $\overline{QT}$ is the additional waiting time for the arbitrary packet. Thus

$$\overline{W} = T_r + \overline{QT} \qquad (7.16)$$

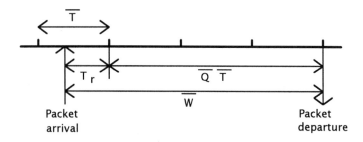

Figure 7.10 Timing diagram for token passing.

In the example illustrated the packet arrives to find that it must wait for three rotations of the token before it reaches the front of the queue, that is, $\overline{Q} = 3$. Hence the system we are analyzing allows for just one transmission per token visit. Using Little's result we have that

$$\overline{Q} = \lambda \overline{W} \qquad (7.17)$$

where λ is the packet arrival rate, assumed to be the same for each node.

In general, the value of $\overline{T}$ depends on the average number of active nodes, $\overline{N_a}$, and is given by

$$\overline{T} = \overline{N_a}x + Nr \qquad (7.18)$$

where r is the constant that represents the time taken to pass the token. Here again we are placing a constraint on the operation of the LAN. By taking the product of $\overline{N_a}$ and x to calculate the delay contribution for active stations, we are assuming that the token is released at the instant that the leading edge of the packet is received at the node from which it originated. Further, by including the second product on the right-hand side of Eq. (7.18), it is implied that the time taken to pass the token is r seconds, whether the node releasing the token is active or not. We could analyze alternative strategies using simple modifications.

The value of $\overline{N_a}$ is easily calculated using

$$\overline{N_a} = N\lambda\overline{T} \qquad (7.19)$$

Eliminating $\overline{N_a}$ from Eq. (7.18) using Eq. (7.19) and rearranging, we obtain

$$\overline{T} = \frac{Nr}{1 - N\lambda x} \qquad (7.20)$$

We plotted the average token rotation time as a function of the throughput, for a 10-Mbit/s LAN with 1000-bit packets and 20-bit tokens, in Figure 7.11. The distance between the stations was taken to be 1000m.[2] As expected, the value of $\overline{T}$ increases asymptotically, toward the network capacity, with increasing throughputs. At first glance, it may appear that the capacity of a 50-node LAN is double that of the 100-node LAN. However, since we used the throughput per node and the network throughput is a multiple of the figures in the graph, we deduce that in fact the network capacities are the same. Note that simulation results again show excellent agreement with the analysis. During the simulation run for the result with the highest throughput in the 50-node network a number of packets were lost at full buffers. Close inspection of the point on

---

[2] If the LAN was implemented using a central cabling concentrator this implies a ring with a radius of 500 m.

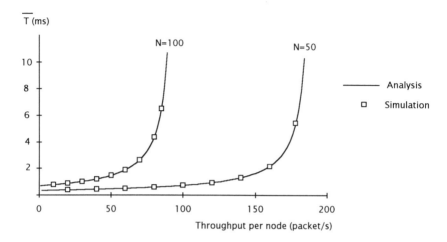

Figure 7.11 Average token rotation time as a function of throughput.

the preceding figure will reveal a minor discrepancy between the values obtained because the analysis, in assuming infinite buffers, has not accounted for this.

Moving on to calculate the waiting times, combining Eqs. (7.16) and (7.17) we can write

$$\overline{W} = \frac{T_r}{1 - \lambda \overline{T}} \tag{7.21}$$

So all that remains for us is to determine the residual token rotation time, which is quite simply half of the token rotation time, on average.

Mean delay characteristics, obtained using Eqs. (15), (20), and (21) with $T_r = \overline{T}/2$, are plotted as a function of throughput for the same LAN in Figure 7.12. This time we used the overall network throughput on the horizontal axis in (a) and network utilization in (b), and a population of 100 nodes is held at a constant for all the curves. We presented the results for networks with data transmission rates of 4, 10, and 16 Mbit/s, respectively. In (a) we can see that the greater throughput is obtained with the higher data transmission rate. In (b) however, it is apparent that the lower data transmission rate is in fact the most efficient. This reversal of fortunes is a direct result of the effective channel length, or normalized propagation delay, that we discussed in the previous section. Lower data transmission rates decrease the effective channel length, which in turn improves the network utilization. The actual values for the mean delay become important when discussing the type of traffic that is being transmitted.

In Figure 7.13 we plotted the mean queue lengths for the same network parameters. Given the relationship between queue length and waiting time in Eq. (7.17) we should expect the characteristics to be similar and this is indeed the case. The most notable difference is that the mean queue lengths are zero when the load is very small. Recall that in the case of token passing we may invariably use the terms throughput and

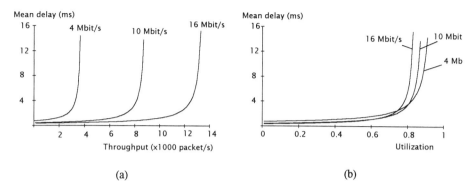

Figure 7.12 Mean delay as a function of (a) network throughput and (b) network utilization.

offered load, or just load, interchangeably. Using these characteristics we can estimate the buffering requirements for nodes that are expected to operate on networks with the specific parameters and assumptions stated previously. For example, from Figure 7.13(a), we can see that a 16-Mbit/s ring with a total traffic load of 12,000 packet/s, evenly distributed amongst 100 nodes, require buffer storage capacities for up to around 30 packets, or about 4 kbytes. Anything significantly smaller than this will result in the loss of data.

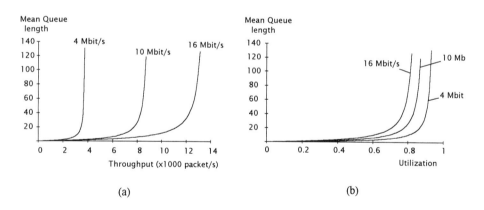

Figure 7.13 Mean queue length as a function of (a) network throughput and (b) network utilization.

So far in this section we assumed that messages consist of single, fixed-length packets of 1000 bits. Further, we presumed that individual nodes are statistically indistinguishable or that the traffic is symmetrically distributed across the network. For fixed-length packets arriving with random inter-arrival times, this simply means that the generation rates are the same at each node. Since it is clearly unlikely that this will be the case for real networks, we will present methods for investigating the performance of token passing when these assumptions are relaxed.

First, consider the case for which arrivals consist of packets that have random lengths, governed by some probability distribution. Now the token rotation time is given by

$$T = x_1 + x_2 + \cdots + x_{N_a} + Nr \tag{7.22}$$

where the x_1, x_2, ..., x_{N_a} are N_a independent, identically distributed random variables with mean $\overline{x}$ and N_a is itself a random variable with mean $\overline{N_a}$. The mean token rotation time is then given by

$$\overline{T} = \overline{N_a} \overline{x} + Nr \tag{7.23}$$

which is simply Eq. (7.18) with the constant x replaced by the mean $\overline{x}$. As before, since Eq. (7.19) is still valid, we obtain

$$\overline{T} = \frac{Nr}{1 - N\lambda \overline{x}} \tag{7.24}$$

The residual token rotation time in this case is given by ([6], p. 173)

$$T_r = \frac{\overline{T}}{2} + \frac{\sigma^2}{2\overline{T}} \tag{7.25}$$

where σ^2 is the variance of the token rotation time.

The variance can be found by taking the Laplace transform of the distribution of T from Eq. (7.22), which is, for exponentially distributed message lengths, given by

$$\mathcal{T}(s) = e^{-sNr} \left[1 - \frac{\lambda \overline{T} \overline{s} \overline{x}}{1 + s\overline{x}} \right]^N \tag{7.26}$$

So using the facts that

$$\sigma^2 = \overline{T^2} - \overline{T}^2 \tag{7.27}$$

and[3]

$$\overline{T^2} = \frac{d^2}{d^2 s} \mathcal{T}(s) \Big|_{s=0} \tag{7.28}$$

---

[3] The notation $f(x)\big|_{x=x_1}$ indicates that the function $f(x)$ is to be calculated using the value x_1.

we obtain

$$\sigma^2 = N\lambda\overline{T}(2 - \lambda\overline{T})\overline{x}^2 \qquad (7.29)$$

Hence the waiting time for the token passing LAN with exponentially distributed message lengths may be calculated using Eq. (7.21) with the residual and mean token rotation times given by Eqs. (7.24) and (7.25), respectively. Again the mean delay is calculated using Eq. (7.15) and the mean queue length is given by Eq. (7.17). Assuming that a fair comparison is obtained using a mean message length equal to the constant packet length, the only difference in calculation is the additional term on the right-hand side of Eq. (7.25). The difference is negligible, as can be seen in Figure 7.14, which displays the characteristics obtained at 10 Mbit/s using similar network parameters as before and with mean packet lengths of 1000 bits.

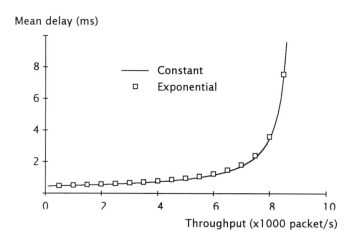

Figure 7.14 Token passing delay with constant and exponentially distributed message lengths.

Second, consider the case for which the traffic is asymmetrically distributed across the network. In the following, which is adapted from Ibe and Cheng [5], we account for the contributions of individual nodes. Denote the service times for a message that originates from node i, by x_i, $i = 1, 2, ..., N$. Similarly the message arrival times are denoted by λ_i, thus enabling us to investigate the effects of varying traffic intensities and message lengths across the network.

We begin with an expression, equivalent to that of the symmetric system in Eq. (7.16), for the average or expected waiting time, $E[W_i]$, at node i, in terms of the residual and complete token rotation times. Consider what happens to an arbitrary message arriving at node i and assume that it arrives to find that there are l messages already waiting for transmission. Then we can write

$$E[W_i / Q_i = l] = \quad l \cdot \{x_i + E[T_i]\}$$
$$+ \sum_{j=1}^{N} p_{xj}(x_{oj} + E[U_{ij}]) \tag{7.30}$$
$$+ \sum_{j=1}^{N} p_{rj}(r_{oj} + E[V_{ij}])$$

where T_i is the time taken for the token to complete one rotation originating and ending at node i, U_{ij} is the time required for the token to reach node i given that node j is being served, and V_{ij} is the token transit time to i given that j is the next to receive it.

The first term on the right-hand side of Eq. (7.30) is the delay incurred due to the l messages already waiting. This is simply l times the sum of the service time and average token rotation time for station i. The second and third terms account for the contribution of the residual token rotation time. Their values depend on which node is being serviced, or which node the token is about to service, as follows.

If p_{xj} is the probability that node j is being served when our message arrives, and if x_{oj} is the residual life of that service time, then the second term on the right-hand side of Eq. (7.30) is the expected time taken for the token to reach node i, given that any node was being serviced at the time of the message arrival.

Similarly if p_{rj} is the probability that node j is about to receive the token and r_{oj} is its residual time, then the third term is the expected time taken for the token to reach node i, given that a node was about to receive the token at the time of the message arrival.

If we remove the condition from the left-hand side, then Eq. (7.30) may be written as

$$E[W_i] = E[Q_i] \cdot \{x_i + E[T_i]\} + \sum_{j=1}^{N} p_{xj}(x_{oj} + E[U_{ij}]) + \sum_{j=1}^{N} p_{rj}(r_{oj} + E[V_{ij}]) \tag{7.31}$$

Using Little's result we can replace $E[Q_i]$ with $\lambda_i E[W_i]$ and rearranging we obtain

$$E[W_i] = \frac{\sum_{j=1}^{N} \{p_{xj}(x_{oj} + E[U_{ij}]) + p_{rj}(r_{oj} + E[V_{ij}])\}}{1 - \lambda_i \{x_i + E[V_i]\}} \tag{7.32}$$

In order to calculate the unknown quantities we begin with the average token rotation time for a complete rotation, which is given by

$$\overline{T} = \sum_{k=1}^{N} (r_k + p_k x_k) \tag{7.33}$$

where $\overline{T}$ is the familiar label for the mean token rotation time, or cycle time; r_i is the token passing time for node i; and p_i is the probability that it has at least one packet awaiting transmission. The latter probability is equivalent to the traffic intensity at the node that in steady-state conditions is given by $\lambda_i \overline{T}$. Thus we can write

$$p_j = \lambda_j \sum_{k=1}^{N} (r_k + p_k x_k) \tag{7.34}$$

and rearranging to find the expression for p_j we have

$$p_j = \frac{\lambda_j \sum_{k=1}^{N} r_k}{1 - \sum_{k=1}^{N} \lambda_k x_k} \tag{7.35}$$

In deriving this expression we made use of the fact that

$$\frac{p_k}{p_j} = \frac{\lambda_k}{\lambda_j} \tag{7.36}$$

Now we can easily determine the probability that node j is being serviced, or is about to receive the token, in terms of the previous expressions. The former is dependent on the fraction of the token rotation time dedicated to serving j and may be written

$$p_{xj} = p_j \frac{x_j}{\overline{T}} \tag{7.37}$$

The probability that j is about to receive the token is equal to the fraction of token rotation time taken transmitting the token to j, which is

$$p_{rj} = \frac{r_j}{\overline{T}} \tag{7.38}$$

The terms $E[V_i]$, $E[U_{ij}]$, and $E[V_{ij}]$ remain to be evaluated. The former is the expected cycle time given that a message is transmitted from i during that cycle. In order to determine this quantity we define q_{ji} to be the probability that j has at least one message during a cycle in which i transmits a message. Then, due to the steady-state conditions,

$$q_{ji} = \lambda_j \left\{ x_i + \sum_{k=1}^{N} r_k + \sum_{\substack{k=1 \\ k \neq i}}^{N} q_{ki} x_k \right\} \qquad \text{for } j \neq i \tag{7.39}$$

where the term in the curly brackets is the relevant cycle length. Taking the factor q_{ji} out of the last summation and using the fact that

$$\frac{q_{ji}}{q_{ki}} = \frac{\lambda_j}{\lambda_k}$$

(7.40)

we can rewrite Eq. (7.39) for q_{ji} in terms of known quantities as

$$q_{ji} = \frac{\lambda_j \left\{ x_i + \sum_{k=1}^{N} r_k \right\}}{1 - \sum_{\substack{k=1 \\ k \neq i}}^{N} \lambda_k x_k}$$

(7.41)

Now the expected length of a cycle in which i makes a transmission is easily deduced. In fact, it has already been written in Eq. (7.39). Explicitly, we can write

$$E[V_i] = \sum_{k=1}^{N} r_k + \sum_{\substack{k=1 \\ k \neq i}}^{N} q_{ki} x_k$$

(7.42)

The term $E[U_{ij}]$ is the expected time required for the token to reach node i given that node j is currently in possession of it. Define u_{ij} to be the probability that a node $l \neq j$ has at least one message during a cycle in which a message from j was in the process of being transmitted when the message on which we are concentrating arrived at i. The length of such a cycle, C_u, is given by

$$C_u = 2x_{0j} + \sum_{k=1}^{N} r_k + \sum_{\substack{k=1 \\ k \neq j}}^{N} u_{kj} x_k$$

(7.43)

because the service time at j is the sum of the residual service time, x_{0j}, and the age of the service time at j when our message arrived at i, which is also x_{0j}. In equilibrium, $u_{lj} = \lambda_l C_u$; thus, we have

$$u_{lj} = \lambda_l \left\{ 2x_{0j} + \sum_{k=1}^{N} r_k + \sum_{\substack{k=1 \\ k \neq j}}^{N} u_{kj} x_k \right\}$$

(7.44)

Again we make use of a simple relationship in order to obtain an expression for the unknown probabilities. This time the fact that the ratio of the arrival rates at l and k is equivalent to the ratio of the probabilities that each has at least one message in a buffer, u_{lj}/u_{kj} , and so

$$u_{lj} = \frac{\lambda_l \left\{ 2x_{0j} + \sum_{k=1}^{N} r_k \right\}}{1 - \sum_{\substack{k=1 \\ k \neq j}}^{N} \lambda_k x_k} \qquad (7.45)$$

We can easily deduce that

$$E[U_{ij}] = \sum_{k=j+1}^{i} r_k + \sum_{k=j+1}^{i-1} u_{kj} x_k \qquad (7.46)$$

Note that when evaluating this equation care must be taken to ensure that the cases for which the node indices give $i < j$ are accounted for.

Using similar arguments we obtain the following expression for the expected length of time elapsed from the moment when our message arrives at i and the token is in transit to node j until the token is next received at i:

$$E[V_{ij}] = \sum_{k=j+1}^{i} r_k + \sum_{k=j}^{i-1} v_{kj} x_k \qquad (7.47)$$

where the v_{lj} are the probabilities that node l has at least one message in its buffer during a cycle in which the token is in transit to node j when a specific message arrives at i. It is left as an exercise for the reader to show that

$$v_{lj} = \frac{\lambda_l \left\{ 2r_{0j} + \sum_{\substack{k=1 \\ k \neq j}}^{N} r_k \right\}}{1 - \sum_{k=1}^{N} \lambda_k x_k} \qquad (7.48)$$

Again, when evaluating Eq. (7.47), care must be taken to ensure that the cases for which the node indices give $i < j$ are accounted for.

The x_{0j} and r_{0j}, being the residual message transmission and token passing times respectively, are given by

$$x_{0j} = \frac{\overline{x}}{2} + \frac{\sigma_x}{2\overline{x}} \qquad (7.49)$$

and

$$r_{0j} = \frac{\bar{r}}{2} + \frac{\sigma_r}{2\bar{r}}$$ (7.50)

where the notation $\bar{a}$ and σ_a is used to indicate the mean and variance of a, respectively.

Hence the mean delay for asymmetric token passing LANs may be calculated by summing the delays obtained for each node and averaging over the network. The waiting times are obtained using Eq. (7.32) with the unknown probabilities given by the various expressions derived previously. This analysis provides for selecting the message arrival rates, transmission times, and token passing times for each of the nodes on an individual basis. In Figure 7.15 we plotted the mean delay versus throughput characteristics for various distributions of arrival rate on a 20-node LAN running at 10 Mbit/s. For convenience, the message lengths and token passing times were held constant.

The three characteristics in (a) were obtained by splitting the nodes into two evenly populated groups, that is, 10 in each. In (b) the nodes were split into groups of 5 and 15. The total network traffic was split in the ratios 1:1, 1:3, and 1:5, with the aggregate arrival rate in each group shared evenly among the nodes. The 1:1 ratio is the symmetric case, and the 1:3 and 1:5 ratios represent cases that are increasingly asymmetric. It may be seen that the capacity is reduced as the level of asymmetry increases. This effect is more apparent in (b) where the group sizes have been chosen to exacerbate the degree of asymmetry.

7.4 CSMA/CD ANALYSIS

In Section 7.2 we looked at the throughput of CSMA/CD and token passing under heavy traffic conditions. Because CSMA/CD can be inefficient under these circumstances, token passing demonstrated superior performance characteristics. In the previous section we developed analyses that can be used for more detailed investigations of the mechanisms that affect the performance of token passing systems. In this section we aim to complete the equivalent task for CSMA/CD and the random access protocols.

One of the fundamental differences between the two methods is a result of the fact that random access methods, in general, including CSMA/CD, are susceptible to packet loss for reasons other than limited buffer space. Different throughput and offered load characteristics are direct results of this. Moreover, since it is the case that throughput is directly proportional to offered load, or utilization, in token passing systems with adequate buffering, the delay characteristics may be plotted as functions of either variable without changing the performance characteristic. This is not the case for random access protocols and CSMA/CD.

To begin we will determine the throughput of a basic random access method for which collision detection is implicit. For simplicity we will assume that the propagation delay is negligible. A similar treatment is given by Tanenbaum [7]. In the ALOHA system, which is traditionally regarded as the original network access protocol, a node transmits a fixed-length packet as soon as it is generated. A successful transmission is acknowledged, so the lack of acknowledgment within a suitable time-out implies that the packet was involved in a collision, given that the channel is error-free. The colliding

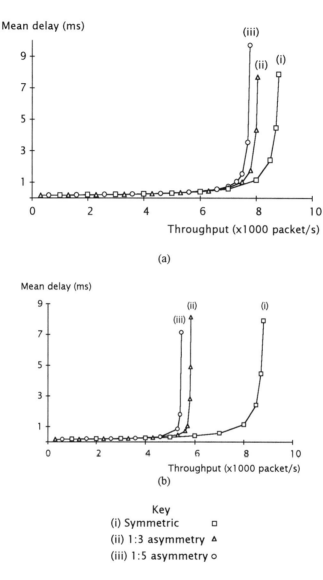

Figure 7.15   Token passing with asymmetric traffic loads for (a) 10 nodes in each group, and (b) 15 in one group and 5 in the other.

packets are retransmitted after a random time interval. Assume that traffic is generated according to the Poisson distribution with average rate λ packet/s.

The total traffic on the channel consists of new packets that are attempting transmission for the first time and retransmitted packets that have been involved in one or more collisions. Let the average rate of total traffic, including new and retransmitted packets, be γ packet/s. If the packet length is x, then $S = \lambda x$ and $G = \gamma x$ represent the throughput and offered load, respectively. The collisions and total traffic are also assumed to follow a Poisson distribution, though this is not strictly true.

Consider the timing diagram in Figure 7.16, which illustrates the transmission of a packet, depicted with shading, at time t_0. Thus any packet transmitted in the interval $t_0 - 1 < t < t_0 + 1$, as depicted in the figure without shading, is vulnerable to a collision. The duration of the interval, or collision window, is $2x$; and the probability that there are k packets transmitted in a vulnerable period is given by

$$\Pr[\,k \text{ packets in } 2x \text{ seconds}\,] = \frac{(2G)^k}{k!} e^{-2G} \qquad (7.51)$$

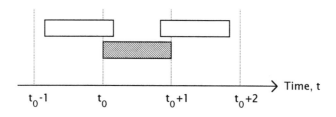

Figure 7.16 Timing diagram showing a collision.

The throughput is equivalent to the combined probability that exactly one packet is transmitted in x seconds and that no packets are transmitted in $2x$ seconds. The former probability is simply G, and the latter is calculated using Eq. (7.51) with $k = 0$. Thus we have

$$S = Ge^{-2G} \qquad (7.52)$$

This function is plotted in Figure 7.17 with the label pure ALOHA. Clearly the throughput will always be less than the offered load and the maximum throughput of $1/2e$, around 0.18, is obtained when $G = 0.5$. The second characteristic in the figure shows the throughput of a slotted ALOHA system, that is, the system whereby the transmission of a packet is restricted to occur on a slot boundary. The length of a slot in this case is x seconds. The collision window is reduced to the interval $t_0 - 1 < t < t_0$, which is equivalent to the slot length. Hence it is easily shown that the throughput for slotted ALOHA is given by

$$S = Ge^{-G} \qquad (7.53)$$

and this is a maximum when $G = 1.0$, at which point the throughput is $1/e$.

The delay for ALOHA traffic is the time elapsed between the first transmission attempt and the successful transmission of a message. If the end-to-end propagation delay is a, normalized with respect to the message transmission time, then the time taken

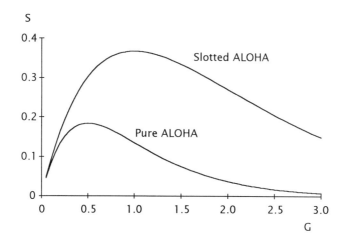

Figure 7.17 Throughput as a function of offered load for pure and slotted ALOHA.

for an unsuccessful transmission attempt is $1+2a+r$, where $2a$ is the maximum time required to detect a collision and r is the random delay before retransmission. The time required for a successful attempt is $1+a$; hence, the mean delay is given by

$$E[D] = E[k]\{1+2a+\bar{r}\}+1+a \tag{7.54}$$

where k is the number of collisions and $\bar{r}$ is the mean delay before retransmission. For pure ALOHA the probability that a message does not suffer a collision is e^{-2G} and the probability of a collision is thus $1-e^{-2G}$. The number of collisions therefore follows a geometric distribution, and the mean value is given by

$$E[k] = \frac{1-e^{-2G}}{e^{-2G}} \tag{7.55}$$

and Eq. (7.54) simplifies to

$$E[D] = e^{2G} + a(2e^{2G}-1) + \bar{r}(e^{2G}-1) \tag{7.56}$$

For slotted ALOHA we get

$$E[D] = e^{G} + a(2e^{G}-1) + \bar{r}(e^{G}-1) \tag{7.57}$$

Equations (7.56) and (7.57) were used to plot the curves in Figure 7.18. The units of mean delay on the vertical axis are normalized with respect to message transmission time, or slot length, and the typical values $a = 0.05$ and $\bar{r} = 10$ were used. Note that the characteristics are unlike the equivalent ones for token passing type algorithms. Here, the mean delay is plotted as a function of throughput, which as we have already seen is not directly proportional to offered load. The offered load consists of new messages as well as old messages that are in the process of being retransmitted. When the offered load is greater than that which gives the maximum throughput, the utilization becomes increasingly small. Hence the collisions, which become more intense as the offered load increases, cause the mean delay to increase. Meanwhile the throughput is reduced— hence, the shape of the characteristics.

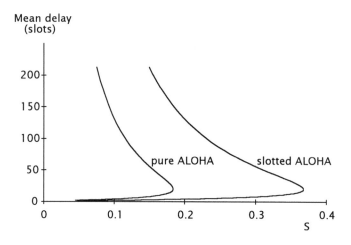

Figure 7.18 Mean delay versus throughput characteristics for ALOHA.

As a consequence of this effect the system exhibits a form of instability, where there are two possible values of delay at any given throughput. In order to determine which delay value is applicable at any given time, it is also necessary to know whether the offered load is high or low. All random access protocols that allow collisions are subject to this phenomenon, which has been well studied [8]. We may thus conclude that LANs that are expected to be subject to persistently high traffic loads should not employ such methods. However, this statement is made in the knowledge that the node population is large and that the traffic is symmetrically distributed.

The CSMA/CD protocol was proposed to improve the performance characteristics of random access LANs [9]. Now when a node has a message ready for transmission it senses the channel before transmission. If the channel is idle the message is sent immediately. The node continues to sense the channel during the transmission time to determine whether the message was involved in a collision. If it was, the message is scheduled for retransmission following a random period of time in the usual way. Otherwise, if the channel was sensed to be busy, then the transmission attempt is delayed for a random period of time after which the channel activity is assessed again.

A number of variants on the basic method is possible. The method we described is known as the nonpersistent method, and this is the one analyzed next. Alternatively,

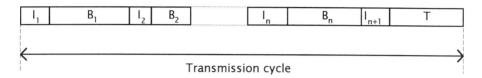

Figure 7.19 A transmission cycle for nonpersistent CSMA/CD.

on sensing the channel busy, the active node may continue sensing and transmit a message as soon as the channel becomes idle. This is the 1-persistent CSMA/CD protocol. The p-persistent method reduces the transmission probability to p.

The following analysis, similar to that provided by Vo-Dai [10], is more straightforward than that in [9]. As usual the throughput is calculated as the fraction of time for which the channel is involved in a successful transmission, as given by Eq. (7.5). The cycle for one successful transmission is depicted in Figure 7.19. In general, such a cycle consists of a series of idle and busy periods with various lengths, ending with an idle period, followed by a transmission period. Hence the throughput is given by

$$S = \frac{T}{E[n+1] \cdot E[I] + E[n] \cdot E[B] + T} \tag{7.58}$$

where n is the number of unsuccessful transmission attempts. If the transmissions are restricted to begin on slot boundaries, then the collision window is equal to the end-to-end propagation delay, A. Hence the probability of a collision, p, is

$$p = \int_0^A p(t)dt \tag{7.59}$$

where the function $p(t)$ is the inter-arrival time distribution. Since the total traffic is assumed to be Poisson, with parameter γ as before, we obtain

$$p = 1 - e^{-\gamma A} \tag{7.60}$$

The probability that there is no collision, q, is therefore

$$q = 1 - p = e^{-\gamma A} \tag{7.61}$$

and the number of unsuccessful transmissions is geometric with mean p/q such that

$$E[n] = e^{\gamma A} - 1 \tag{7.62}$$

An idle period is one for which there is no activity on the channel. Thus if γ is the total traffic, which has a Poisson distribution, then the inter-arrival times are exponential with mean $1/\gamma$, and we have

$$E[I] = \frac{1}{\gamma} \tag{7.63}$$

The remaining unknown in the denominator of Eq. (7.58) is the mean duration of a busy period, which is one in which there is a collision between two or more messages. The timing diagram for a collision between two messages is depicted in Figure 7.20. The end of an idle period begins with the start of a transmission. The length of a contention interval, X, is the time taken for the transmitting node to detect a collision. Obviously this must occur before the collision window has passed. At this time the jamming signal, of duration σ, is transmitted; and the busy period is completed with the two end-to-end propagation delays required to achieve this.

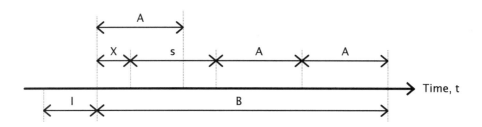

Figure 7.20 Timing diagram for a busy period with a collision.

Thus we can write

$$E[B] = E[X] + 2A + \sigma \tag{7.64}$$

The first term on the right-hand side of Eq. (7.64), the expected length of the contention interval, may be evaluated as follows. X is a random variable with distribution function, $F(x)$, defined as the probability that there is a collision in the interval $(0,x)$, given that there is more than one arrival in the interval $(0,A)$. Hence, using the fact that $P[A/B] = P[AB]/P[B]$, we can write

$$F(x) = \frac{\Pr[\text{collision in } (0,x) \text{ and } \geq 1 \text{ arrivals in } (0,A)]}{\Pr[\geq 1 \text{ arrivals in } (0,A)]} \tag{7.65}$$

The denominator on the right-hand side is easily calculated using Eq. (7.60). The numerator, $N(x)$, may be written as a summation:

$$N(x) = \sum_{k=1}^{\infty} \Pr[\text{collision in } (0,x) \text{ and } k \text{ arrivals in } (0,A)] \tag{7.66}$$

Now the channel must be clear at the end of the busy period, before the next idle period commences, and to satisfy this condition all k transmissions must begin in $(0, x)$. Hence, assuming the arrivals are uniformly distributed in $(0, A)$, we have

$$\Pr[\text{collision in } (0, x) \text{ given } k \text{ arrivals in } (0, A)] = \left(\frac{x}{A}\right)^{k} \tag{7.67}$$

Thus, using $P[A/B] = P[AB]/P[B]$ again, Eq. (7.66) may be written as

$$N(x) = \sum_{k=1}^{\infty} \left(\frac{x}{A}\right)^{k} \cdot \Pr[k \text{ arrivals in } (0, A)] \tag{7.68}$$

with the probability that there are k arrivals in the interval $(0, A)$ being given by the Poisson distribution with parameter γA. Using these arguments Eq. (7.65) may be written as

$$F(x) = \frac{\displaystyle\sum_{k=1}^{\infty} \left(\frac{x}{A}\right)^{k} \frac{(\gamma A)^{k}}{k!} e^{-\gamma A}}{1 - e^{-\gamma A}} \tag{7.69}$$

which simplifies to give

$$F(x) = \frac{e^{\gamma x} - 1}{e^{\gamma A} - 1} \tag{7.70}$$

The previous argument applies when the length of a contention interval is smaller than the collision window. The probability that the contention interval is less than the collision window has to be unity, and the complete distribution function for X is thus given by

$$F(x) = \begin{cases} 0 & \text{for } x < 0 \\ \dfrac{e^{\gamma x} - 1}{e^{\gamma A} - 1} & \text{for } 0 \le x \le A \\ 1 & \text{for } A < x \end{cases} \tag{7.71}$$

Differentiating we obtain the density function as

$$f(x) = \begin{cases} \dfrac{\gamma e^{\gamma x}}{e^{\gamma A} - 1} & \text{for } 0 \le x \le A \\ 0 & \text{otherwise} \end{cases} \tag{7.72}$$

and then the mean is given by

$$E[X] = \int_0^A x \frac{\gamma e^{\gamma x}}{e^{\gamma A} - 1} dx \tag{7.73}$$

Evaluating the integral and replacing $E[X]$ in Eq. (7.58), along with the other terms using the expressions derived previously, we obtain

$$S = \frac{T\gamma e^{-\gamma A}}{\gamma A + e^{-\gamma A}(1 + T\gamma) + \gamma(1 - e^{-A\gamma})(2A + \sigma)} \tag{7.74}$$

Normalizing with respect to T, the message transmission time, and using G to denote the total traffic as before, Eq. (7.74) may be written in the more traditional form as

$$S = \frac{Ge^{-aG}}{aG + e^{-aG}(1 + G) + G(1 - e^{-aG})(2a + \sigma)} \tag{7.75}$$

where a is the normalized end-to-end propagation delay, as previously defined.

A similar expression may be derived for CSMA without collision detection. Utilizing a less complex version of the previous analysis it should be straightforward to show that in this case we obtain

$$S = \frac{Ge^{-aG}}{G(1 + 2a) + e^{-aG}} \tag{7.76}$$

We plotted the functions in Eqs. (7.75) and (7.76) in Figure 7.21, along with the curve for slotted ALOHA for comparison. As expected the carrier sensing mechanism significantly increases the traffic throughput of the random access channel. Moreover, the throughput is greater still when collision detection is employed. In all cases, however, the bistability associated with such access mechanisms is clearly demonstrated. The results for $a = 0.05$ and 0.005, with and without collision detection, are presented in the figure. The effective channel length was discussed at length in the first section of this chapter, and it may be seen that the trend exhibited by these characteristics confirms our previous statements.

As always the delay of traffic may be a primary concern, and we now continue to find an expression for the mean delay, $\overline{D}$, of traffic on the CSMA/CD network. Essentially, $\overline{D}$ has two components, one of which depends on the number of retransmissions expected for an arbitrary message. The expected number of retransmissions required before a message is successful in its quest is p_f/p_s, where p_f and p_s are the transmission failure and success probabilities, respectively. The latter is equivalent to S/G, so the former is $1 - S/G$ and we can write

$$\overline{D} = \left(\frac{G}{S} - 1\right)\overline{d_r} + 1 + a \tag{7.77}$$

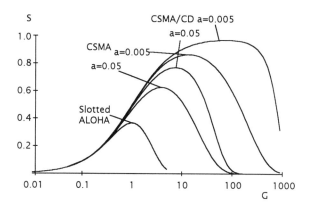

Figure 7.21 Throughput of CSMA with and without collision detection.

The first factor on the right-hand side is the simplified expression for p_f/p_s, and $\overline{d}_r$ is the expected delay for each retransmission attempt. The remaining two terms on the right-hand side of Eq. (7.77) represent the component of delay due to the message transmission and propagation.

There are three contributions to the retransmission delay, $\overline{d}_r$. A message that must be rescheduled because the channel is sensed busy experiences an average retransmission delay $\overline{r}$, normalized with respect to message transmission time, with probability S. A message that finds the channel idle, with probability $(1-S)$, experiences a delay through collision, with probability p_c, and a nonpersistent retransmission delay $\overline{r}$, with probability $(1-p_c)$. Thus we may write

$$d_r = S\overline{r} + (1-S)\left\{ p_c\overline{d}_c + (1-p_c)\overline{r} \right\} \tag{7.78}$$

where $\overline{d}_c$ is the mean delay caused by a collision. Now the probability that a message suffers a collision is given by the fraction of busy time occupied by the collision window. Hence making use of Eq. (7.64) we have

$$p_c = \frac{A}{E[X] + 2A + \sigma} \tag{7.79}$$

where $E[X]$ may be calculated using Eq. (7.73). Finally the value of $\overline{d}_c$ depends on the retransmission algorithm adopted following a collision.

Some methods have been proposed that account for the number of active nodes in order to reduce the probability of further collisions. As discussed in Chapter 2, the so-called back-off algorithm can have a significant effect when the traffic load is heavy. Here we will assume that messages are retransmitted as if the channel had been sensed busy such that $\overline{d}_c = \overline{r}$.

Mean delay versus throughput characteristics for two different effective channel lengths are presented in Figure 7.22. Note that the vertical axis has a logarithmic scale and the delays incurred by traffic when the network is in the unstable condition are considerable, if not intolerable. The curve for $a = 0.05$ shows the most rapid deterioration; and as expected, the performance is enhanced when the effective channel length is small. The curve for $a = 0.005$ demonstrates that a higher throughput is obtained.

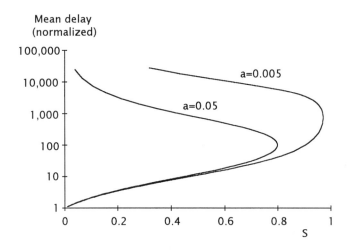

Figure 7.22 Mean delay versus throughput for CSMA/CD with $a = 0.05$ and 0.005.

A secondary effect is also apparent, though less obvious. The distance between the lower and upper limbs of the same curve is an indication of how stable the system is. That is, at any given throughput, if the distance between the two limbs is high, then the probability that the system can switch between states is small. This is shown at the lower values of throughput on both characteristics. Conversely, if the distance is small, as it is when the throughput is close to the maximum, then the probability that the network may become unstable is increased. Thus we see that the distance is greater for $a = 0.005$ than it is for $a = 0.05$, and the system is more stable in the former case. The improvement is by a factor that appears to be roughly equivalent to the ratio of effective channel lengths.

7.5 FDDI

The FDDI is intended to cover larger geographical areas than the token passing and CSMA/CD protocols. It has also been designed with some consideration of the different service requirements of certain traffic types. The data transmission rate for FDDI networks is fixed at 100 Mbit/s, and each node has a mechanism for imposing a maximum delay on time-constrained data. The algorithm is based on token passing. With a simple token passing ring using exhaustive service it is possible for the delay to increase without limit. The FDDI protocol uses a method of limiting the token rotation time, by incorporating a timed token, to guarantee that a maximum waiting time can be achieved for at least a portion of the traffic.

The following analysis is a good example of one that requires numerical techniques. It is based on the work of Tangemann and Sauer [11]. The system is modeled by a set of equations for which a closed-form solution has not been obtained. A closed-form solution is one that results in one or more equations that may be evaluated directly by substituting the values of the system parameters. It accounts for the buffer size, and it is not assumed that all the nodes are identical. First a method for calculating the token rotation time is given, followed by the delay analysis.

Due to the timed token rotation part of the algorithm it is possible that a varying number of packets can be served at each token visit. For this reason we approach the analysis in quite a different fashion to that for token passing in the previous section. Here we must account for both the number of packets waiting in a node and the maximum number that may be transmitted, during each token visit, or service time. Let A_i^n be the number of packets waiting in node i at the beginning of the nth token visit. Further, let $a_i^n(j)$ be the probability that $A_i^n = j$. Similarly B_i^n is the maximum number of packets that can be served and the probability that it is j is denoted by $b_i^n(j)$. Now if the actual number of packets that are transmitted during the nth service period is given by C_i^n, which takes on the value j with probability $c_i^n(j)$, we have

$$C_i^n = \min\left[A_i^n, B_i^n\right] \tag{7.80}$$

The token rotation time seen by node i, $T^n_{\mathrm{TRT}_i}$, is the time between the $(n-1)$th and the nth token arrivals, which is given by

$$T^n_{\mathrm{TRT}_i} = \sum_{k=i}^{n-1} T^{n-1}_{S_k} + \sum_{k=1}^{i-1} T^n_{S_k} \tag{7.81}$$

where $T^n_{S_i}$ is the total service time, including packet transmissions and token switchover time, for node i at the nth token visit. The first summation on the right-hand side represents the contributions of the service time for node i and those that remain to be visited by the token, in the $(n-1)$th cycle. Under steady-state conditions we can drop the dependency on n to find the average token rotation time that is then the sum of the average service times for all the nodes. The average service times may be calculated using the values $c_i^n(j)$ that depend on $a_i^n(j)$ and $b_i^n(j)$ as follows.

The actual number of packets waiting in a node just after the arrival of the token for the nth time is the sum of two values. The first of these values is the number of packets that were left behind after the previous token visit, and the second is the number of arrivals that occurred between times. Let D_i^n represent the former random variable, which takes on the value j with probability $d_i^n(j)$. Using similar notation let $e_i^n(j)$ be the probabilities for the latter. Hence the probabilities $a_i^n(j)$ are given by

$$a_i^n(j) = d_i^n(j) \otimes e_i^n(j) \tag{7.82}$$

which is the discrete convolution of the $d_i^n(j)$ and $e_i^n(j)$ and, if m_i is the capacity of node i, may be evaluated using

$$a_i^n(j) = \begin{cases} \displaystyle\sum_{k=0}^{j} d_i^n(k) \cdot e_i^n(j-k) & \text{if } 0 \le j < m_i \\ \displaystyle\sum_{k=0}^{m_i} \sum_{l=m_i-k}^{\infty} d_i^n(k) \cdot e_i^n(l) & \text{if } j = m_i \end{cases} \tag{7.83}$$

The number of packets left behind is the difference

$$D_i^n = A_i^n - C_i^n \tag{7.84}$$

which may be alternatively stated in terms of arrivals and number of packets served as

$$D_i^n = \max\left[A_i^n - B_i^n, 0 \right] \tag{7.85}$$

The associated probabilities are given by

$$d_i^n(j) = \sum_{k=j}^{m_i} a_i^n(k) \cdot b_i^n(k-j) \tag{7.86}$$

for $0 < j \le m_i$. The case for which the node buffer was left empty may then be calculated as one minus the sum of the other probabilities, which may be written as

$$d_i^n(0) = 1 - \sum_{k=1}^{m_i} d_i^n(k) \tag{7.87}$$

The probability that j packets arrived during the time taken for two successive token visits to i is given by

$$e_i^n(j) = \int_0^\infty \frac{(\lambda_i t)^j}{j!} e^{\lambda_i t} f_{\text{TRT}_i}^n(t) dt \tag{7.88}$$

where $f_{\text{TRT}_i}^n(t)$ is the distribution function for the nth token rotation time at i and we have assumed Poisson arrivals with rate λ_i.

Now the service time for node i is composed of C_i^n packet transmissions and a single switch-over time. The probabilities for C_i^n are obtained using the fact that the number of packets actually served is the smaller of the number of packets in the buffer and the maximum number that may be served. The probability that there are one or more packets in i when the token arrives for the nth time is $1 - a_i^n(0)$ and the probability that at least one packet may be served is $1 - b_i^n(0)$. Hence the probability that at least one packet is transmitted is $(1 - a_i^n(0)) \cdot (1 - b_i^n(0))$ and we have

$$c_i^n(0) = 1 - (1 - a_i^n(0)) \cdot (1 - b_i^n(0)) \qquad (7.89)$$

Similarly for $j > 0$

$$c_i^n(j) = 1 - \Pr[C_i^n \neq j] \qquad (7.90)$$

wherein

$$\Pr[C_i^n \neq j] = \Pr[C_i^n < j] + \Pr[C_i^n > j] \qquad (7.91)$$

The first term on the right-hand side is actually $\sum_{k=0}^{j-1} c_i^n(k)$. The second term is equivalent to the combined probability that both the number of packets in the buffer and the maximum number of packets to be transmitted are greater than j, which can be expressed as

$$\Pr[C_i^n > j] = (1 - \Pr[A_i^n \leq j]) \cdot (1 - \Pr[B_i^n \leq j]) \qquad (7.92)$$

Thus, in summary, and replacing the variables A_i^n and B_i^n with their respective probabilities, we can write

$$c_i^n(0) = \begin{cases} 1 - (1 - a_i^n(0)) \cdot (1 - b_i^n(0)) & \text{for } j = 0 \\ 1 - \left\{ \left(1 - \sum_{k=0}^{j} a_i^n(k)\right) \cdot \left(1 - \sum_{k=0}^{j} b_i^n(k)\right) + \sum_{k=0}^{j-1} c_i^n(k) \right\} & \text{for } 0 < j \leq m_i \end{cases} \qquad (7.93)$$

The values of $b_i^n(j)$ may be calculated using the given parameters of the system. If the target token rotation time for circuit-switched traffic is implemented in terms of the maximum rotation time, or priority threshold time, for each station, then if the token arrives at station i before the priority threshold, T_{PR_i}, is exceeded, then it may proceed to transmit packets until either the threshold is reached or the buffer is emptied. Otherwise the timed token must be passed on straight away. Hence, if T_{P_i} is the packet transmission time for i, we have

$$B_i^n = \begin{cases} 0 & \text{if } T_{PR_i} \leq T_{TRT_i}^n \\ j & \text{if } T_{TRT_i}^n + (j-1)T_{P_i} < T_{PR_i} \leq T_{TRT_i}^n + jT_{P_i} \\ m_i & \text{if } T_{TRT_i}^n + m_i T_{P_i} < T_{PR_i} \end{cases} \qquad (7.94)$$

and the associated probabilities are easily found to be

$$b_i^n(0) = \begin{cases} 1 & \text{for} \\ 0 & \text{otherwise} \end{cases} \qquad T_{PR_i} \leq T_{TRT_i}^n$$

(7.95)

for $j = 0$,

$$b_i^n(j) = \begin{cases} 1 & \text{for} \\ 0 & \text{otherwise} \end{cases} \qquad T_{TRT_i}^n + (j-1)T_{P_i} < T_{PR_i} \leq T_{TRT_i}^n + jT_{P_i}$$

(7.96)

for $0 < j < m_i$ and

$$b_i^n(m_i) = \begin{cases} 1 & \text{for} \\ 0 & \text{otherwise} \end{cases} \qquad T_{TRT_i}^n + m_i T_{P_i} < T_{PR_i}$$

(7.97)

for $j = m_i$.

We now have the expressions necessary to calculate the average token rotation time using an iterative method. First we are required to provide initial values for the average token rotation time itself and the probabilities $a_i^n(j)$. A reasonable first approximation for the latter is given by assuming that every station has one packet in its buffer or

$$a_i^n(j) = \begin{cases} 1 & \text{if } j = 1 \\ 0 & \text{otherwise} \end{cases}$$

(7.98)

In this case the token rotation time should be the sum of N packet transmissions and switch-over times, and our first estimate of the mean token rotation time is

$$T_{TRT_i} = N(T_{P_i} + T_{S_i})$$

(7.99)

where T_{S_i} is the switch-over time for i and we have dropped the dependency on the identity of the cycle, or token rotation, n. Next the $e_i^n(j)$ are calculated using Eq. (7.88).

Given the mean token rotation time and arrival rate we have

$$e_i(j) = \frac{(\lambda_i T_{TRT_i})^j}{j!} e^{\lambda_i T_{TRT_i}}$$

(7.100)

Using these values and Eqs. (7.86) and (7.87) a first estimate of the $d_i^n(j)$ may be calculated, and the probabilities $a_i^n(j)$ are obtained using Eq. (7.83). Finally we can calculate the first estimate for the $d_i(j)$ and the token rotation time.

The two graphs in Figure 7.23 show how the average token rotation time

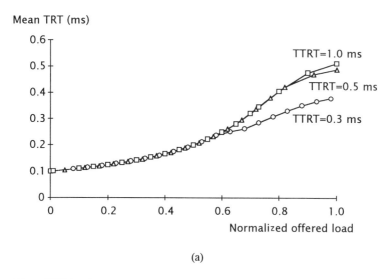

(a)

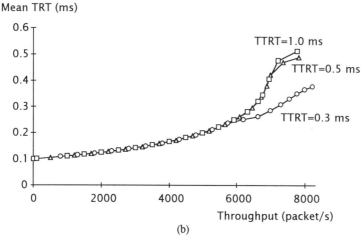

(b)

Figure 7.23 Token rotation times as functions of (a) offered load, and (b) throughput.

increases with offered load and throughput. Using this analysis we obtain a variation of offered load and throughput because the buffer space is limited and the rejection probability is greater than zero at significant traffic levels. The results were obtained for a 10-node network with packet service time and switchover times of 10 μs and with a buffer size of 5 packets. The target token rotation times that were set are shown to have the desired effect.

The mean delay of traffic may be calculated by deriving the probability distribution for the number of packets in the buffer, conditioned on the number of packets about to be served when the token arrives. Since we already know the distribution of the number of packets served, through the values of $c_i^n(j)$, the condition may be removed to facilitate the calculation of the mean queue length. The mean delay follows using Little's result.

In order to obtain these conditional probabilities we need to account for each stage of the service process in which the queue length changes. Let the steady-state probability that there are j packets at a particular node, given that there will be l packets serviced and that z of them have already been transmitted, be denoted by $p_{z,l}(j)$, for $j = 0, 1, 2, ..., m$. Note that, because we are considering the steady state of an arbitrary node, the previous notation using n and i is not required. Thus $p_{0,l}(j)$ is the said probability given that the token has just arrived and, since it is impossible that any of the packets have been transmitted at this time, we have

$$p_{0,l}(j) = 0 \quad \text{for } 0 \le j < l \tag{7.101}$$

For $l \le j \le m$ the $p_{0,l}(j)$ are obtained from the threefold product of the probability that the node is in a cycle for which l packets are served, given by $1/c(l)$, the probability that there are j packets in the node buffer in such a cycle, given by $a(j)$, and the probability that the node is in a cycle for which up to j packets may be served. The latter is given by $\sum_{k=j}^{m} b(k)$ for $j = l$ and $b(l)$ when $l < j \le m$. Thus in summary we can write

$$p_{0,l}(j) = \begin{cases} 0 & \text{for } 0 \le j < l \\ \dfrac{1}{c(l)} a(j) \sum_{k=j}^{m} b(k) & \text{for } j = l \\ \dfrac{1}{c(l)} a(j) b(l) & \text{for } l < j \le m \end{cases} \tag{7.102}$$

After the transmission of one packet there will be one less in the buffer and a number of arrivals. The probability that there were j arrivals is given, in an equivalent fashion to that of Eq. (7.100), by

$$h(j) = \frac{(\lambda T_p)^j}{j!} e^{\lambda T_p} \tag{7.103}$$

Hence the values of $p_{1,l}(j)$ are given, in a similar fashion as the convolution in Eq. (7.83), by

$$p_{1,l}(j) = \begin{cases} \displaystyle\sum_{k=1}^{j+1} p_{0,l}(k) \cdot h(j - k + 1) & \text{if } 0 \le j < m \\ \displaystyle\sum_{k=1}^{m} \sum_{l'=m-k+1}^{\infty} p_{0,l}(k) \cdot h(l') & \text{if } j = m \end{cases} \tag{7.104}$$

The probabilities $p_{z,l}(j)$ are thus obtained by replacing $p_{1,l}(j)$ and $p_{0,l}(j)$ in Eq. (7.104) with $p_{z,l}(j)$ and $p_{z-1,l}(j)$, respectively. It is required that the state probabilities at arbitrary instants in the cycle are known so that the dependency on z can be removed. These are obtained using the fact that when $z = l$ the duration of time relevant for the calculation of the number of arrivals consists of the remainder of the token rotation time as well as the service time for the last packet. In queueing theory terminology the remainder of the token rotation time is referred to as the server vacation time and is the time taken for the token to return to a specific node following its departure from that node. Denoting the state probabilities at arbitrary instants using a superscript asterisk we may write

$$p^*_{z,l}(j) = \begin{cases} p_{z,l}(j) \otimes h(j) & \text{for } 0 \le z < l \\ p_{z,l}(j) \otimes h_V(j) & \text{for } z = l \end{cases} \tag{7.105}$$

where $h_V(j)$ is the probability that there are j arrivals during the servers vacation. The vacation time, T_V, may be calculated as the sum of N switch-over times and $(N-1)$ total service times, T_S and the $h_V(j)$ may be calculated using Eq. (7.103) with T_P replaced by T_V. The dependency on z may now be removed by averaging over the complete cycle time. For $l = 0$ the solution is trivial since there are no packets serviced. Otherwise the complete cycle time is the sum of the expected vacation time and l packet transmission times. Moreover, the node spends a time $T_P \cdot \sum_{z=0}^{l-1} p^*_{z,l}(j)$ transmitting packets and a time $T_V \cdot p^*_{l,l}(j)$ waiting for the token to return. Thus we have

$$p^*_l(j) = \begin{cases} p^*_{0,l}(j) & \text{for } l = 0 \\ \dfrac{T_P \cdot \sum_{z=0}^{l-1} p^*_{l,i}(j) + T_V \cdot p^*_{l,l}(j)}{l \cdot T_H + T_V} & \text{for } 0 < l \le m \end{cases} \tag{7.106}$$

Finally the state probabilities are obtained by removing the condition that l packets are served using

$$p(j) = \sum_{l=0}^{m} c(l) \cdot p^*_l(j) \tag{7.107}$$

and the mean queue length is given by

$$Q = \sum_{j=0}^{m} j \cdot p(j) \tag{7.108}$$

The mean delay may then be calculated using Little's result.

The characteristics in Figure 7.24 provide an example of the delay performance of FDDI using the same parameters as previously. The delay is limited by the target

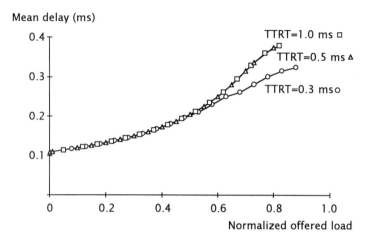

Figure 7.24 Mean delay.

token rotation time as required.

The FDDI-II standard defines mechanisms for reserving the channel bandwidth required for the portion of traffic that is time limited. The timed token protocol is used to service this traffic. However, the reduced delay has a trade-off with increased packet loss probability, since packets are lost when they arrive at a full buffer. Thus, when FDDI is heavily loaded and the target token rotation time is small, only a fraction of the total traffic will be serviced, regardless of its requirements.

7.6 RESERVATION PROTOCOLS

CSMA/CD, token passing, and FDDI are three popular methods that have been widely utilized in commercial broadcast data communication systems. A great many more protocols have been described in various works, and just a summary of their analyses could fill a number of volumes. In Harman R. Van As's review [12] there are well over two hundred references. A number of classification schemes have been suggested for these methods. Considering the performance aspect alone, however, it is possible to recognize a small number of groups: random access, deterministic, and slotted, for example. The random access protocols include ALOHA and CSMA/CD, and these are generally inefficient at high-traffic intensities. Deterministic protocols include token passing schemes, and these show improved capacities while remaining inefficient. The slotted protocols are more efficient because a greater number of packets may be in transmission at the same time.

Within each group the protocols are modified to enhance a particular performance criteria. The FDDI method, for example, is a deterministic protocol based on token passing. A large number of the slotted methods are based on some form of time division multiplexing. It is a method that has been incorporated in a number of the analyses of previous chapters. In this section we provide a relatively straightforward method for analyzing slotted systems that incorporate a reservation scheme.

In the previous chapter various discrete-time Markov models were used to analyze fixed and random access TDMA. As was discussed the highly simplistic fixed assigned TDMA can be inefficient and the random access TDMA, assuming that no collisions occur, would be impossible to implement in practice. Of course, random TDMA with collisions is in fact the same as ALOHA. As a compromise some portion of the bandwidth in TDMA, or synchronous time-slotted systems, may be allocated for the use of reservations, and these will be examined in this section.

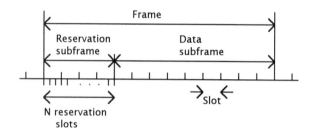

Figure 7.25 Frame structure of a basic reservation TDMA channel.

A timing diagram of the frame structure for a basic reservation TDMA scheme is presented in Figure 7.25. The network channel is viewed as a consecutive sequence of frames that is implemented in practice using synchronized clocks in each node. The frame consists of two subframe types. The first is a collection of slots that are used for reservation and the second contains the actual data packets. In its very simplest form each node has the opportunity to reserve just one slot in the data subframe portion of each frame. Hence the length of the data subframe can vary between zero and N packet transmission times

The system will be analyzed as a Markov process with the state of the system at the end of each frame being the number of active nodes. Since the buffer capacity of each node is assumed to be one, the state of the system is also equal to the total number of packets awaiting transmission on the network. The Markov chain is discrete and the state of the system is obtained by calculating the transition probabilities for each of the two types of slot that occur in the reservation and data subframe.

As usual N is the number of nodes on the network. Let $r_{i,j}$ be the probability that the system enters the state j at the end of a reservation slot given that it was already in state i. During a reservation slot only arrivals can occur in the system. Hence, if the arrival pattern is random and the probability of an arrival at each slot is σ, we have

$$r_{i,j} = bin(N-i, j-i, \sigma) \tag{7.109}$$

for $i, j = 0, ..., N$. The function $bin()$ is used to denote the binomial function and

$$bin(N-i,j-i,\sigma) = \left(\frac{N!}{i!(N-i)!} \right) \sigma^j (1-\sigma)^{N-i} \tag{7.110}$$

is given by the binomial distribution. If $r_{i,j}$ are the elements of the matrix R, then the transition matrix for the reservation subframe, RS, is given by

$$RS = R^k \tag{7.111}$$

where k is the number of slots in the reservation subframe. The actual value of k will be determined by the value of N, the number of reservation bits assigned to each node, the packet length, and data transmission rate and should remain constant. The elements of D, the transition matrix for a data subframe slot, are similarly given by

$$d_{i,j} = bin(N-i,j-i+1,\sigma) \tag{7.112}$$

wherein the departure of a packet has been taken into account. Hence the system transition matrix for the complete frame is given by[4]

$$[P]_{i,j} = [RS \cdot D^i]_{i,j} \tag{7.113}$$

Hence the values of P may be easily computed; since it is a proper transition matrix, because the system state transitions are memoryless, its validity may be checked during the calculation by making sure that the law of total probability is obeyed. The solution of the system of linearly dependent equations given by

$$\pi = \pi \cdot P \tag{7.114}$$

and

$$\sum_i \pi_i = 1 \tag{7.115}$$

provides the steady-state distribution π. It is easily shown that the average frame length is given by

$$\overline{F} = k + \pi \cdot J \tag{7.116}$$

where J is a vector whose elements are given by $j_i = i$. Each of the terms on the right-hand side of Eq. (7.116) represent the contributions from the reservation and data subframes. The system throughput, defined as the fraction of time the channel is involved in data transmission, is given by

---

[4] $[\ ]_{i,j}$ denotes the i,j element of the matrix.

$$S = \frac{\overline{F}}{\pi \cdot P} \tag{7.117}$$

Since we have assumed a buffer capacity of one at each node, the average number of packets in the system is the same as the expected number of slots in the data subframe, πJ. Hence the expected queue length is the same as the probability that the buffer is occupied as given by

$$Q = \frac{\pi J}{N} \tag{7.118}$$

The rejection probability can be obtained from one minus the acceptance probability and is given by

$$rp = 1 - \frac{S}{N\sigma} \tag{7.119}$$

Finally the mean delay may be calculated using the expression

$$D = \frac{Q}{S} \tag{7.120}$$

This analysis may appear to be complete and correct, however, it is only approximate. The average frame length was calculated using the assumption that the solution of Eqs. (7.114) and (7.115) provides the state distribution at arbitrary instants during the frame. This is clearly not the case because the system transition matrix was calculated assuming that the state of the system is examined at the end of the frame.

A computer simulation of the Reservation TDMA scheme was produced using the method of discrete events, as described in Chapter 4. Analytical and simulated mean delay versus throughput characteristics are presented in Figure 7.26 for a system of 10 nodes operating at a data transmission rate of 10 Mbit/s with 1000 bits in each packet. It may be observed that there is a close agreement between the characteristics obtained by the two methods; therefore, in this case the approximation is a good one.

7.7 MULTIMEDIA TRAFFIC

Much attention has been given to the range of services that can be provided on communication networks. These include LANs that are used to transport voice and video traffic as well as computer terminal data, and they are generally known as multimedia systems. The variation of traffic types will have an impact on the performance analysis and the effects may be significant. Again it is not possible to provide a thorough, in-depth, treatment of this subject in the subsection of one chapter. In the next few pages it is hoped that a small selection of due considerations will be addressed. Having identified three broad categories of network traffic types as data,

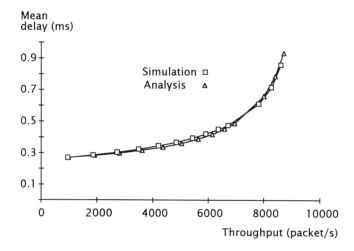

Figure 7.26 Comparison of analysis and simulation for basic Reservation TDMA.

voice, and video it would seem appropriate to deal with these on an individual basis.

First, it is appropriate that we review the traffic generation models. Multimedia systems are described by their traffic characteristics in a number of ways. Just as broadcast systems, two general categories of multimedia interaction include the interactive and retrieval processes [13]. Each of these include varying degrees of traffic intensity between the service user and provider. In both cases there can be a mix of data, audio, and video information. The performance constraints vary in each of these categories. Interactive processes are more sensitive to delay and delay variations, or jitter. Video telephony is an example of this. Thus the choice of traffic model is a critical one; and since any one or a combination of the following may be chosen, the modeling process is complex. The traffic models may then be applied to the calculation of performance measures as part of an analytical model or as the background task in a simulation program.

7.7.1 Source Modeling

Simple traffic models consist of single packet generators. As described in Chapter 3, the arrival pattern of a simple source is described by the inter-arrival time distribution. If this is fixed, the arrivals occur at a constant rate. Random patterns may be described, for example, by exponential inter-arrival times; and the average rate of arrival determines the overall traffic intensity. An alternative way of describing this is in terms of a counting process. The number of arrivals in a certain interval is considered in this case, and if they are Poisson, then again we have a completely random and memoryless pattern.

Compound and batch arrivals are two terms used to describe the arrival of different amounts of information at each arrival instant. A second distribution is required to specify the pattern of batch sizes. Hence there are effectively two dimensions to the arrival process, and any of the standard distributions, such as those described in Section 4.6, or an empirical relationship, may be applied to either. It is therefore possible to construct any number of traffic source models, and the terminology that has been constructed around the subject is quite involved.

Naturally, discrete- and continuous-time traffic processes are described by discrete and continuous probability distributions, respectively. Historically the completely random processes are known as renewal processes with independent identically distributed variables. One of the expected characteristics for multimedia traffic is that a degree of burstiness will prevail and great care should be taken to describe the term accurately. In Chapter 3 the peak to average arrival rate was considered, and this was shown to vary in different ways for the Poisson renewal process. The autocorrelation is also used to measure burstiness, however, and the autocorrelation is zero for all renewal processes.

Arrival patterns are often more formerly referred to as point processes and stochastic processes, for which a classification is well established. Thus simple arrival patterns are in fact homogeneous renewal processes. Nonhomogeneous arrival patterns introduce some statistical dependence in the sequence of arrivals. These are generally referred to as Markov and Markov renewal processes. In this case the arrival rate or the batch size can depend on the state of the system. An example of this is the popular *Markov Modulated Poisson Process* (MMPP) for which the arrivals are Poisson with rate λ_k when the state is k. An MMPP model can be used to characterize an on/off source, for example, when there are just two possible system states. Such models are extremely useful. In [14] the authors use a *Markov Modulated Deterministic Process* (MMDP) to model video sources that result from MPEG-2 coding.[5]

7.7.2 Data, Voice, and Video

Data traffic can originate from a wide variety of devices and network services. Shared disk file retrieval and printing, to name just two. This means that the task of finding a general model to accurately represent anything but a very specific setup is difficult. For example, the traffic on a token ring that consists of a certain number of idle networked personal computers and a file server should be completely deterministic. That is, the only packets in circulation will be a result of the tasks for the ring management protocol in maintaining the correct operation of the ring. These are intended to monitor the status of the ring, so, assuming the nodes remain in a constant state, the only transmissions will be token passes. If the file server is installed with a network operating system there will be additional packets, and even if these are transmitted in a logical, determinate fashion, the characteristics of the traffic on the network will become complex when users of the terminals become active.

In previous sections we made various assumptions about the nature of the traffic on the network in order to derive some performance measures. It is probably fair to say

---

[5] MPEG is the acronym for Moving Pictures Expert group. MPEG-2 is a standard coding scheme for digital broadcast television.

that the effect of particular parameters on one or more performance indicators should be dealt with on an individual basis. For example, one may wish to compare the variation of delay with throughput of a token ring and an Ethernet when all the packets are the same length. Indeed this task may be carried out using the methods described in various parts of this text. As we have seen, a specific inter-arrival time distribution is invariably required to make a mathematical analysis tractable. On the other, hand a computer simulation program may be used that incorporates any traffic generation model desired. The trade-off here is probably the relative convenience of each method, though where time permits it is reassuring, and often satisfying, to validate the results of one using the other.

Works on the study of voice traffic are probably more readily available than any other specific media type due to the history of telecommunications. The equations associated with the name of Erlang have long been used as a tool for the modeling of telecommunications networks intended for the transmission of speech. Their usefulness in modern digital transmission systems, as well as analogue lines, is readily demonstrated. The Erlang is a unit of measurement used in teletraffic analysis to represent the intensity of traffic on a line. For example, if calls arrive at a rate of two per minute and each has a duration of 45 seconds, then the intensity is $2 \times (45/60) = 1.5$ Erlangs. One of the parameters of interest in capacity planning is the probability that a call may be blocked given that a certain intensity of traffic is expected to prevail. This may be calculated using Erlang's B formula, which is given by Eqs. (3.125) and (3.126). Figure 3.10 showed that the loss, or blocking probability, increases with traffic intensity for a given number of lines. It also shows that for a given traffic intensity the blocking probability is reduced when the number of lines is increased, and this is what should be expected. Another parameter of interest is the utilization, which is the probability that all of the lines are in use. In fact, this is directly related to the blocking probability. Hence the capacity planner is presented with the task of trading improved utilization, which is desirable, against increased blocking probabilities, which are not.

The preceding properties are relevant for point-to-point links where the call connection, once obtained, is guaranteed for its duration. And the same argument applies whether the transmission is digital or analogue. Voice transmission on a LAN, which cannot provide such a service, gives rise to two additional design problems. The first is the preparation of the speech for transmission on the LAN by way of packetization. The second is the actual transmission of the packets on the LAN and their legible reconstruction for the listener. Hence the speech must be digitized no matter which method is used for signal propagation on the LAN. It is possible to improve efficiency with packet voice communications by detecting and utilizing silent intervals.

One of the important characteristics of packet voice systems is the amount of speech that is contained in each packet. The factors that affect this choice include the probability that packets are lost and the number of packets generated. The former is of concern when the packets are large and the replayed speech becomes broken. On the other hand, if the packets are too small there may be adverse effects on the throughput and delay performance of the LAN traffic. Typical packet sizes for LANs are in the region of multiples of thousands of bits. If the speech is sampled at 64 kbit/s, then 50 ms corresponds with 3200 bits. Hence ten packets of this size would be sufficient to transport half a second of dialogue. If the network runs at 10 Mbit/s the maximum possible number of simultaneous two-way conversations that could be supported is[6]

$$\left\lfloor \frac{10,000,000}{2 \times 64,000} \right\rfloor = 78$$

Of course, there will be some inefficiency due to the access mechanism and other overheads that will reduce this figure.

The mean packet delay and its variation will affect the quality of the reassembled speech at the receiver. In addition to the delay caused by the access protocol we must account for what is known as the reconstitution delay, that is, the time required to buffer the incoming packets until a reasonable amount of speech has accumulated and before the actual sound is generated.

Computer simulation provides a readily available method for investigating the performance of voice traffic. The simple token passing simulation program described in Chapter 4 has been modified to provide an example. The program that was used to obtain the results in Figures 7.27 and 7.28 may be found in the relevant directory on the disc provided. An additional variable, *active_nodes*, has been used to set the number of active voice stations. Thus *active_nodes* = 10, for example, corresponds with five simultaneous conversations. The initial event list has been constructed in a way that initiates each voice station at a random point in time. Subsequently packets are generated at a constant rate to provide a 64-kbit/s channel. Hence the traffic is deterministic as the inter-arrival time and length of each packet is fixed. The inter-arrival time of packets that are generated at a station is the same as the sample time. Hence 50-ms speech samples correspond with packets that are $64,000 \times 0.05 = 3,200$ bits in length, and throughout a conversation these are generated every 50 ms.

The mean delay versus throughput characteristics presented in Figure 7.27 are the results obtained with 50-, 40-, and 30-ms sample times. The packet sizes used were 3200, 2560, and 1920 bits, respectively, with a propagation distance of 1 km and a 20-bit token. As expected the capacity reduces when the packet size becomes smaller.

In Figure 7.28 the mean delay is plotted as a function of the number of simultaneous conversations. It is not clear what is the maximum delay that can be tolerated, and its determination is beyond our present scope. For example, the reconstitution delay, which is an important factor in the quality of replay, is ignored here. It is probably fair to say, however, that delay in the region of hundreds of milliseconds are unacceptable. There is a standard that sets a maximum end-to-end delay of 250 ms. Thus, from the figure, it may be deduced that the simple system modeled by the simulation program cannot support many more than 50 conversations.

The CSMA/CD program described in Chapter 5 has been modified in a similar way and the new one is also provided on the disc. In general, the number of packets rejected on a voice channel is not as critical as for data channels. If the number rejected is excessive, however, the quality of the replayed audio signal may become very poor. The packet rejection probability is plotted as a function of the number of active sources

---

[6] The notation $\lfloor x \rfloor$ is used to identify the largest integer less than or equal to x.

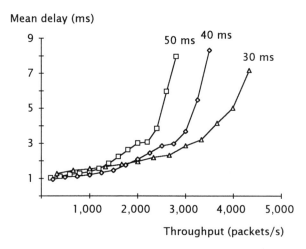

Figure 7.27 Mean delay against throughput for speech on a token passing LAN.

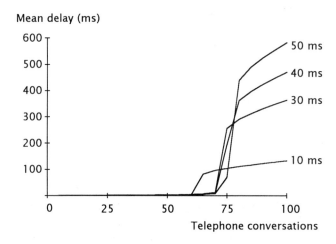

Figure 7.28 Mean delay as a function of the number of conversations on a token passing LAN.

on a CSMA/CD network in Figure 7.29. Rejection probabilities greater than around 0.1, or one-tenth of the actual speech, will significantly reduce the playback quality. Thus the capacity of the network at each of the three sample times is clearly shown. Note that a two-way conversation requires two active nodes, so using 100-ms samples the network may support around 100 active nodes or 50 simultaneous conversations. It may be surprising that, on a CSMA/CD network, the rejection probability is still less than 0.5 when there are 150 active sources and the samples are 100 ms. Recalling previous arguments relating to the effective channel length and realizing that the normalized propagation delay in this case is less than 0.008, this figure should seem reasonable. A

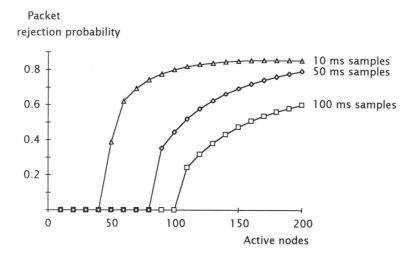

Figure 7.29   Packet rejection probability as a function of the number of active nodes on a CSMA/CD network.

comparable figure should be obtained using these parameters in the analysis of Section 7.4.

A number of final remarks are stated here to close the discussion of voice traffic. First it should be clear that the simulations are modeling very simple systems. For example, they do not account for the overhead bits that are required for timing and the fact that telephone conversations between two active nodes begin and end at some time. Second, a number of research papers have investigated the effect of silence suppression, or avoiding the transmission of packets that contain silent periods, and it has been shown that this can improve the efficiency. Finally the transmission of speech using time-slotted systems has become widespread in the telecommunications network through the use of digital switching. A number of the simulations described elsewhere in the text are suitable for investigating these systems and the interested reader may utilize these.

A treatment of packet video transmission could follow a similar line to that of voice transmission. There is a number of characteristics that are common to both voice and video traffic. For example, the raw stream of digits produced by a video signal is likely to consist of frames of equal length, generated at fixed intervals. Perhaps two of the most distinguishing features of video transmission are the increased bandwidth requirements and the simplex nature of most applications. In fact, some high-specification video signals require data transmission rates in the region of tens of Mbit/s, and in this case IEEE standard token passing and CSMA/CD LANs are clearly unsuitable. Slotted protocols can support high data transmission rates, as illustrated by the following results.

The characteristics in Figure 7.30 were produced using the reservation TDMA simulation described in the previous section. It is assumed that a scan rate of 50 Hz is acceptable and a new frame is produced every 20 ms. Figures 7.30(a) and (b) show the mean delay as a function of the number of active sources and rejection probability as a function of capacity, respectively, with an overall data transmission rate of 10 Mbit/s in both cases. Figures 7.30(c) and (d) show the corresponding results with a transmission rate of 20 Mbit/s. Characteristics for packet sizes of 5,000 and 10,000 bits are presented in each figure. The capacity is calculated as the ratio of offered load with the theoretical limit. For example, the limit for 10,000 bit packets transmitted at 10 Mbit/s is 1000 packets per second. Thus a capacity of 1.0 corresponds with 1000 packets per second in this case and 2000 packets per second when the packet size is 5000 bits. The mean delay and rejection probability are therefore acceptable at either transmission rate when the channel is loaded close to capacity. It appears that more active sources are supported when the packet size is small. The actual amount of data transmitted, however, is proportionately smaller, and the picture size or quality will be reduced.

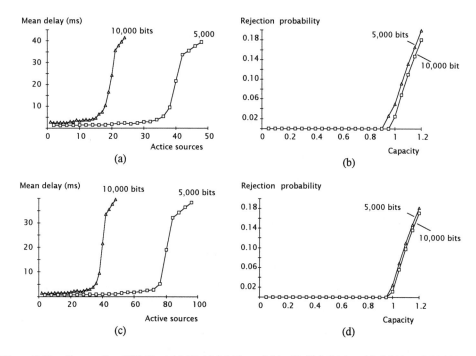

Figure 7.30   Reservation TDMA at (a),(b) 10 Mbit/s and (c), (d) 20 Mbit/s, with 5,000 and 10,000 bits per packet. (a,c) mean delay as a function of active sources and (b,d) packet rejection probability as a function of capacity.

7.8 CONCLUDING REMARKS

In this chapter a number of methods for investigating LAN performance were described. The focus was on four access mechanisms that are representative of those implemented in real systems. Single-packet protocols, such as token passing and CSMA/CD, are dependent on the effective channel length or normalized propagation delay. There are a number of well-established analytical methods for investigating their performance, and these were described in detail. The analysis is complicated when the traffic model is nonsymmetric. Similarly, more complex analytical models are required when the protocols are refined. The basic FDDI mechanism, which incorporates timed tokens, illustrates this point.

Time-slotted systems, characterized by the time division multiple access method, generally utilize bandwidth more efficiently. Fixed and random TDMA systems were analyzed in previous chapters, and the reservation process was briefly dealt with here. A simulation program was utilized for validating analytical results in this case, as with CSMA/CD and token passing. The final section provides an insight into the traffic modeling and performance implications for multimedia systems.

Exercises

7.1 Derive Eq. (7.4).

7.2 Assume that a LAN access method allows for the simultaneous propagation of two packets. What is the upper bound on the utilization in terms of the effective channel length?

7.3 A simple token passing system is implemented with the token being passed immediately following packet transmission. The system consists of a 10-node ring that transmits data at the rate of 4 Mbit/s and has an end-to-end transmission length of 1 km. Assume that all data packets are 1500-bytes long and that each node is permanently busy. Calculate the throughput, in packet/s, for the two cases when the token length is 0 bytes (i.e., not accounted for) and 20 bytes. Repeat the exercise for the case when all data packets are just 50-bytes long.

7.4 Explain the characteristics in Figure 7.7.

7.5 A token passing LAN is implemented as a physical ring with 100 nodes equally spaced 10m apart. Only one packet transmission per token visit is allowed, and the node releases the token when it detects the receipt of its own packet transmission. The token is 20-bits long, the data packets are 1000-bits long, and the data transmission rate is 4 Mbit/s. Assuming a propagation speed of 2×10^8 m/s, plot a graph of mean delay versus throughput. From the graph deduce an approximate value of the network capacity. Repeat the exercise at data transmission rates of 10 and 16 Mbit/s. Comment on the results by comparing them with Figure 7.12.

7.6 Modify the token passing simulation program so that each node may be assigned different arrival rates. Verify that simulation produces the expected trend when the degree of asymmetry is increased.

7.7 Show that the throughput for slotted ALOHA is given by $S = Ge^{-G}$, where S is the throughput and G is the total offered traffic.

7.8 Derive an expression, from first principles and stating any required assumptions, for the throughput of the carrier sense multiple access technique. Hence verify Eq. (7.76).

7.9 Explain why Little's result cannot be used in delay calculations for CSMA/CD.

7.10 Consider the CSMA/CD system. Write down an expression for the component of mean delay that is due to retransmission. Assume that the throughput is S and the collision probability is p_c. Calculate the collision probability when the CSMA/CD bus is 1-km long and transmits 1000 bit packets at 3000 packet/s with a data transmission rate of 10 Mbit/s. Assume that the jamming signal is twice the end-to-end propagation delay. Also calculate the mean delay assuming that the mean retransmission delay is four times the end-to-end propagation delay.

Help: $E[x] = \int_0^A x \frac{\gamma e^{\gamma x}}{e^{\gamma A} - 1} dx = \frac{\gamma A e^{\gamma A} - e^{\gamma A} + 1}{e^{\gamma A} - 1}$

7.11 The mean delay characteristics for FDDI show that reducing the target token rotation time improves the performance. Discuss the trade-off that exists between mean delay and packet rejection probability when the target token rotation time is changed.

7.12 Suggest a simple method for estimating the delay of both types of traffic in an FDDI-II system. State any approximations or assumptions that are required to validate the results obtained using the estimates.

7.13 Discuss the effects of placing reservation slots in different parts of the frame in reservation TDMA.

7.14 Modify the reservation TDMA program to simulate the transmission of voice traffic. Compare results obtained using the simulation with those of token passing and CSMA/CD in the last section. Suggest a method for introducing suppressed transmission of silent periods.

References

[1]   Stallings, W., "Local Network Performance," *IEEE Communications Magazine*, Vol. 22, No. 2, pp. 27–36, Feb. 1984.
[2]   Stallings, W., *Local Networks, An Introduction*, second edition, New York: MacMillan, 1987.
[3]   Stallings, W., *Data and Computer Communications*, New York: MacMillan, fourth edition, 1994.
[4]   Sethi, A. S., and T. Saydam, "Performance Analysis of Token Ring Local Area Networks," *Computer Networks and ISDN Systems*, Vol. 9, pp. 191–200, 1985.
[5]   Ibe, O. C., and X. Cheng, "Approximate Analysis of Asymmetric Single-Service Token-Passing Systems," *IEEE International Conference on Communications '87*, Seattle, WA, pp. 580–584, June 1987

[6]   Kleinrock, L., *Queueing Systems, Volume 1: Theory*, New York: Wiley-Interscience, 1975.

[7]   Tanenbaum, A. S., *Computer Networks*, second edition, Englewood Cliffs, NJ: Prentice-Hall, 1989.

[8]   Kleinrock, L., and S. S. Lam, "Packet Switching in a Multiaccess Broadcast Channel: Performance Evaluation," *IEEE Trans. on Commun.*, Vol. COM-23, No. 4, pp. 410–423, April 1975.

[9]   Tobagi, F. A., and V. B. Hunt, "Performance Analysis of Carrier Sense Multiple Access with Collision Detection," *Computer Networks*, Vol. 4, No. 5, pp. 245–259, 1980.

[10]   Vo-Dai, T., *Throughput-Delay Analysis of the Non-Slotted and Non-Persistent CSMA/CD Protocol*, North-Holland: Local Computer Networks, 1982.

[11]   Tangemann, M., and K. Sauer, "Performance Analysis of the Timed Token Protocol of FDDI and FDDI-II," *IEEE Journal on Selec. Areas in Commun.*, Vol. 9, No. 2, pp. 271–278, Feb. 1991.

[12]   van As, Harman R., "Media Access Techniques: The Evolution Towards Terabit/s LANs and MANs," *Computer Networks and ISDN Systems*, Vol. 26, pp. 603–656, 1994.

[13]   Bunn, W., "Multimedia in Interconnected LAN Systems," *British Telecom Technology Journal*, Vol. 13, No. 4, Oct. 1995.

[14]   Ni, J., T. Yang, and D. H. K. Tsang, "Source Modelling, Queueing Analysis, and Bandwidth Allocation for VBR MPEG-2 Video Traffic in ATM Networks," *IEE Proceedings on Communications*, Vol. 143, No. 4, pp. 197–205, Aug. 1996.

[15]   Asatani, K., and S. Nogami, "Trends in the Standardisation of Telecommunications on GII, Multimedia, and other Network Technologies and Services," *IEEE Communications Magazine*, Vol. 34, pp. 32–46, June 1996.

[16]   Frost, V. S., and B. Melamed, "Traffic Modelling for Telecommunications Networks," *IEEE Communications Magazine*, Vol. 32, pp. 70–81, March 1994.

Chapter 8

Wide Area Networks

An assortment of techniques that are applicable to networks covering large geographical areas are discussed in this chapter. Invariably some method of switching, or routing, is involved and the analysis of such systems is therefore the focus for much of this material. Again it will not be possible to address all the areas for study that could be placed under the title of WANs. The intention here is to provide some detailed aspect of the major areas that have been identified.

The first section deals with interconnected LANs. The CSMA/CD local access method is analyzed because it is probably the most widespread. In the next section we describe some of the standard techniques for analyzing networks of queues with respect to switching and routing. A small network is used to illustrate a simple application of the main technique. In the third section the analysis of buffering techniques for packet switching nodes is described in detail, and the theme is continued into the fourth section, which is entitled telecommunication networks. In this section a number of standard methods that are part of the field of teletraffic engineering are covered. In the final section of the chapter a model for a simple integrated services system is described.

8.1 INTERCONNECTED LANS

Larger data networks may be formed by interconnecting LAN segments using repeaters, bridges, and routers, as described in Chapter 2. Such multiple-segment networks are generally known as MANs and WANs. In Chapter 6 multiple-segment networks were used as the subject for an application of discrete-time Markov chain analysis. The general technique is more widely applicable, and since one or two details were not thoroughly investigated, these will be dealt with in more detail here. Specifically, it is possible to employ alternative algorithms for first transmissions and retransmissions. Recall the system that described in Section 6.5. The basic structure of the network is illustrated in Figure 6.20, and the analytical cycle depicted in Figure 6.21 is the same in this case.

In the analysis of multiple-CSMA/CD segments the conditional probabilities for the slot activity are denoted by $SI(s)$, $S(s)$, and $Ss(s)$, representing idle, successful transmission from a node and successful transmission from a switch, respectively, given that the state of the system at the beginning of the slot was s. Recall that these probabilities refer to the activity of slots on an individual segment. Moreover, they are calculated in a particular way, depending on the specific transmission control algorithm employed. The results already presented in Section 6.5 pertain to the case when the optimal ALOHA rule is implemented. Alternative, simplified algorithms could have a dramatic effect on the performance of the network.

When the first transmission is immediate, or the so-called 1-persistent CSMA/CD protocol is in operation, a node that generates or receives a packet for transmission senses the channel as usual. If the node senses that the channel is idle, then it transmits the packet immediately, as described in Section 2.3.1 and analyzed in Section 6.5.

Now the probability that a slot is idle, given that the state of the system at the beginning of the slot was $s = (i, j)$, is contributed to by two factors. The first is the probability that a node does not attempt a transmission, and the second is the probability that the switch does not attempt a transmission on that particular segment. The former consists of the probability that any backlogged nodes refrain from transmitting the packets awaiting retransmission. If the retransmission probability is v, then the probability that i nodes do not transmit is given by $(1-v)^i$. In addition, it is required that none of the remaining nodes generate a packet that will be transmitted immediately, and this is given by $(1-\sigma)^{N-i-1}$. Note that this expression accounts for the fact that one of the N nodes is assigned to the switch queue. The latter factor, concerning the probability that there is no transmission from the switch, consists of two possibilities: either the switch is awaiting retransmission, or it is idle and waiting for the generation of a packet. Hence this factor is the sum of two probabilities involving the terms v_s, the retransmission probability for a backlogged switch packet, and σ_s. Combining the two factors we obtain

$$SI(s) = \begin{cases} (1-v)^i(1-\sigma)^{N-i-1}[(1-v_s)u(j)+(1-\sigma_s)(1-u(j))] & \text{for } i < N \\ (1-v)^i[(1-v_s)u(j)+(1-\sigma_s)(1-u(j))] & \text{for } i = N \end{cases} \tag{8.1}$$

Note that in Eq. (8.1) the possibility that all of the nodes are backlogged is accounted for. The probability that the state of the slot is such that a node is successfully transmitting also consists of two factors. Following arguments similar to those for Eq. (8.1) we obtain

$$S(s) = \left[iv(1-v)^{i-1}(1-\sigma)^{N-i-1} + (N-i-1)\sigma(1-\sigma)^{N-i-2}(1-v)^i\right]$$
$$\times \left[(1-v_s)u(j)+(1-\sigma_s)(1-u(j))\right] \tag{8.2}$$

This equation holds for $i < N-1$. In the other cases, the factor that is raised to the power of $N-i-2$ disappears due to the fact that only one node remains to possibly become active.

Similarly, the probability that a switch packet is being successfully transmitted is given by

$$Ss(s) = (1-v)^i (1-\sigma)^{N-i-1}\left[v_s u(j) + \sigma_s (1-u(j))\right] \tag{8.3}$$

Again we must place the restriction that $i < N$. In the case when $i = N$ the second factor on the right-hand side of Eq. (8.3) is effectively unity.

An alternative algorithm introduces a delay before the first transmission. This time a node that becomes active joins the backlogged ones, whether the channel is idle or not. In other words, a node that has just received a packet for transmission behaves as if the channel were sensed busy. This mechanism is widely known as the p-persistent CSMA/CD protocol. In this case, the probabilities for the state of a slot are found to be

$$SI(s) = v_s(1-v)^i u(j) \tag{8.4}$$

$$S(s) = (1 - v_s u(j))iv(1 - v)^{i-1} \tag{8.5}$$

$$Ss(s) = (1 - v_s)^{u(j)}(1 - v)^i \tag{8.6}$$

The third option that has been identified is known as the optimal-ALOHA rule. In this case the transmission probability is chosen to maximize the probability of successful transmission. Let the probability of successful transmission in a slot, given that k is the number of busy users, be represented by $Su(k)$. The number of busy users includes the possibility that the switch queue is active such that

$$k = i + u(j) \tag{8.7}$$

In order that a successful transmission takes place it is required that $k-1$ nodes refrain from attempting access to the channel while just one makes an attempt. If the probability that a transmission is attempted is p, then this is given by

$$Su(k) = kp(1-p)^{k-1} \tag{8.8}$$

The maximum value of this function is obtained when $p = 1/k$, and this value is therefore chosen to be the retransmission probability. Now the slot state probabilities can be written as

$$SI(s) = 1 - Su(k) \tag{8.9}$$

$$S(s) = \frac{i}{k} Su(k) \tag{8.10}$$

$$Ss(s) = \frac{u(j)}{k} Su(k) \qquad\qquad (8.11)$$

In the figures that follow the results obtained for the performance of the optimum algorithm are compared with those of the delayed first transmission, or p-persistent method, as an illustration of the type of results that may be obtained. For consistency with the characteristics presented in Section 6.5, the number of nodes on a segment was 9 and the length of a successful transmission, that is, a packet, was 30 slots. The retransmission probability and the busy case first transmission probability for the p-persistent algorithm were set to be $1/3$.

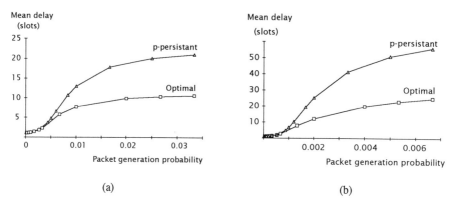

Figure 8.1   Mean delay as a function of packet generation probability for (a) regular nodes and (b) the switch queue.

Mean delay for the regular nodes is plotted as a function of packet generation probability in Figure 8.1(a). According to Little's result the mean delay is directly proportional to the number of active nodes since the nodes each have unit buffer capacity and may be viewed collectively as a single queue, and the packet generation probability is directly proportional to the offered traffic. It is possible, therefore, to qualitatively compare the charcteristics in Figure 8.1 with those in Figure 6.22, for example. The results obtained for the switch are plotted in Figure 8.1(b). In all cases the delay increases less dramatically as the offered load increases. The evidence in Figure 8.2, however, shows that there is a very high probability of rejection, and this should be expected since the queueing capacity is small and the CSMA/CD algorithm has been shown to be inefficient when the load is significant.

As in previous cases, when the delay or backlog is plotted as a function of throughput, or carried traffic, the instability of the system becomes evident. From Figure 8.3 (b) it can be seen that the maximum possible throughput for the regular nodes is around 0.8, with the optimal access scheme providing a small premium. In (b), where the results for the backlog in the switch are presented, there is a marked

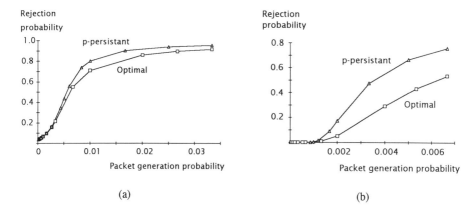

Figure 8.2   Rejection probability as a function of packet generation probability for (a) regular nodes and (b) the switch queue.

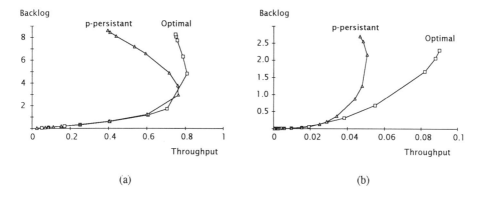

Figure 8.3   Backlog as a function of throughput for (a) regular nodes and (b) the switch queue.

difference between the two methods, however.

In all cases the optimum algorithm demonstrates a superior performance for regular nodes and the switch. It is also possible to compare these results with similar ones for the 1-persistent protocol, and there is considerable scope for observing the effects of adjustable parameters. The retransission control probability, or protocol, will certainly change the results, as would the priority given to switch queues, for example.

There are many possible combinations of protocols that can be implemented in multiple-segment networks. It is fair to say that the detailed analysis of such systems are complex. We have only looked at the connection of CSMA/CD segments using a single switch. Indeed it has even been assumed that the switching process takes place instantaneously and that the switch can deal with all the queues connected to it simultaneously. It should also be possible to carry through a similar method of analysis for multiple-segment token rings. In this case, however, the point in time for investigating the state of the system, and the structure of the system state itself, requires careful attention so that the properties of a Markov chain are preserved. This work has been reported by just a limited number of authors, and for an example the interested reader is referred to Takine et al. [1].

The nonperfect switch can be modeled by introducing an overhead, in the form of a time constant, for each packet that is processed by the queue which is connected to the switch. Let the processing time be denoted by t_p. Returning to the interconnected CSMA/CD network, in this case the system transition matrix that was previously given by Eq. (6.123) is modified to account for the extra number of slots required for processing as

$$P = (I - Q)^{-1} \cdot [Sf \cdot T^{r+1} + S \cdot T^i \cdot C + Ss \cdot T^{t+t_p} \cdot Cs] \qquad (8.12)$$

Note that the only change is in the power of T in the last term on the right-hand side. A similar modification is required in the calculation of the average frame length.

It may also be incorrect to assume that the switch can process the packets from each segment simultaneously. This factor is dictated by the processing speed of the switch in comparison with the data transmission speed of the connections. At one extreme the switch processor operates at a rate that exceeds the aggregate of all the channels, and in this case the packets may be effectively dealt with simultaneously, with only a constant delay introduced, as previously. At the other extreme it may only be possible for the switch to deal with one packet at a time and in this case the state of the system must be accounted for. A modification such as this may be significant as the properties of the cycle would be affected, as was the case for the bridge priority mechanism described in Section 6.5.

8.2 SWITCHES, ROUTERS, AND BRIDGES

Networks are interconnected using switches, routers, bridges, and repeaters. The repeater device does not, or at least it should not, change the flow of traffic and is therefore of no concern in this text. The other three devices make decisions about the forwarding of packets along interconnected point-to-point links however and are, therefore, sources of investigation for traffic analysis. The connection of these links in a nonuniform pattern are known as mesh topology networks and are the subject of analysis for so-called networks of queues.

The diagram in Figure 8.4 depicts the packet flow through an arbitrary network of queues. Packets enter the switched network from the top and may flow through according to the direction of the arrows until they leave the system, ready for delivery to the destination, at the bottom. The source of the packets, for example, may be a collection of personal computers on a LAN connected to some form of WAN interface. Similarly the destination may be a server on another remote LAN.

In their most simple form WANs are made up of single point-to-point links connecting two sites. Normally these will involve dedicated lines rented from a

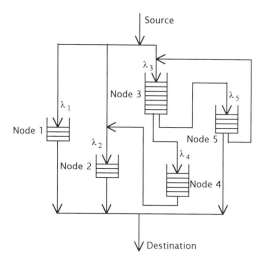

Figure 8.4 An arbitrary network of queues.

telecommunications company. In this case the analysis of traffic can be relatively straightforward since there is no competition for channel bandwidth. Such a two-node link is depicted in Figure 8.5.

Figure 8.5 A two-node network.

Some attention has been given to the analysis of the traffic at a single node in Chapter 3. The output of the single node is now the input of a second. With a simple traffic model the dynamics of such a system are quite trivial. For example, providing the transmission rates of the channel in each stage are sufficient to support the total traffic from the source, all the packets will reach the destination without delay, except for the transmission delay of course, as if there were no buffering at the nodes. It is likely that this will not be the case in practice. Typical transmission rates for leased line connections are less than around 2 Mbit/s, and these may be connecting LANs that run up to 16 Mbit/s and beyond. As usual, if the operating parameters of the system are changed, then this will probably have an effect on the traffic. For example, the system may be subject to the constraint that if one node is active then another must remain idle. This would be the case if each message is to be acknowledged before the next is transmitted.

Assume that the input to the first node is a stream of messages with exponential inter-arrival times. Let the mean arrival rate be λ. Further assume that the messages are variable in length such that the transmission time is exponentially distributed with mean length $1/\mu$. Since the output of node 1 is the input for node 2, provided the bit-rates are the same, the transmission time for the messages at node 2 will also be exponential with the same mean. Hence, a knowledge of the inter-arrival times at node 2 will provide a complete picture of its traffic activity. Again, since the output from one is the input to two, if the inter-departure time distribution from one is obtained, then we also have the inter-arrival time distribution at two.

There are two possibilities when a message departs from node one. Either there is another message waiting in the output buffer, or it is empty and the node will wait for a random time interval until another message arrives. In the former case, which occurs with probability λ/μ, the message that is left behind will be transmitted immediately following the current message. Hence the inter-departure time will be exponential with mean $1/\mu$. In the latter case, which occurs with probability $1 - \lambda/\mu$, the inter-departure time will be the sum of the service time and the time interval before the next arrival. Thus combining the two possibilities gives the inter-arrival time distribution at two as

$$d_2(t) = \frac{\lambda}{\mu}b(t) + \left(1 - \frac{\lambda}{\mu}\right)\{d_1(t) * b(t)\} \tag{8.13}$$

where $d_{1,2}(t)$ are the arrival time distributions at nodes one and two and $b(t)$ is the service time distribution.

The factor on the far right-hand side is the convolution of two distributions that are most easily evaluated by taking Laplace transforms. Thus, transforming both sides of Eq. (8.13) we obtain

$$\mathcal{D}_2(s) = \frac{\lambda}{\mu}\mathcal{B}(s) + \left(1 - \frac{\lambda}{\mu}\right)\{\mathcal{D}_1(s) \cdot \mathcal{B}(s)\} \tag{8.14}$$

Since all the distributions on the right-hand side are exponential, the following expressions are easily obtained

$$\mathcal{B}(s) = \frac{\mu}{s + \mu} \tag{8.15}$$

$$\mathcal{D}_1(s) = \frac{\lambda}{s + \lambda} \tag{8.16}$$

Replacing the transforms in Eq. (8.14) using these expressions and simplifying we obtain

$$\mathcal{D}_2(s) = \frac{\lambda}{s + \lambda} \tag{8.17}$$

which gives exactly the same inter-arrival distribution at two as at one. This is known as Burke's theorem.

The transform is easily inverted and we have a complete description of the traffic pattern in the two-node system. Note, however, that in utilizing the exponential distribution for the service time we have the small possibility that large messages will be created; therefore, as usual, the system is only approximately described by the analysis. Further, a more realistic situation may arise for the case when the data transmission rate on the intersite link is not the same as that on the link from node two to the destination, and this will result in different service time distributions at each node. This analysis and sample calculations are left as exercises for the reader.

Presume now that there are three nodes in the switched section of the WAN. Again it is assumed that the buffer size in each node is infinite. Consider the schematic diagram in Figure 8.6(a), which corresponds with the network topology illustrated in (b). Each of the three nodes is located at a different site, and one of the nodes is connected to the other two.

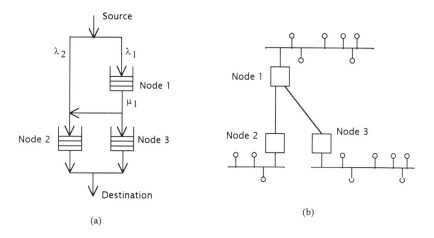

(a)

(b)

Figure 8.6 A three-node network: (a) schematic, and (b) topology.

The dynamics of this network can be described by three integers that represent the number of messages stored at each node. Thus the state (i, j, k) corresponds with the condition that there are i packets stored in node one, j packets in node two, and k in three. Let the arrival and departure rates for node x be denoted by λ_x and μ_x, respectively. It is generally not the case that the arrivals and departures are independent because a departure from one node may be destined for another. In special circumstances, however, this assumption is accurate [2].

The analysis proceeds in a similar fashion as for the Markov chain sequences presented earlier where the balance equations are written down and solved. As before these equations are most easily derived when a sketch of the state transitions is available for scrutiny. The state transition diagram for the three-node system is depicted in Figure 8.7. In Chapter 3 the Markov chains were used to model systems with one state variable and the associated transition diagrams may be thought of as being one-dimensional. In this case we have three state variables and so the most appropriate transition diagram is three-dimensional. The axis that is normally associated with a change in the x variable represents the discrete changes in the state of node one. Similarly the y- and z-axes are used to graph the changes in state of nodes two and three, respectively. Thus, for example, the edge that begins at state $(0,0,0)$ and ends at state $(1,0,0)$ represents a transition from an empty system to one in which node one has a single message while the other two remain empty. The length of each axis and also the size of the state space are limited by the size of the buffers in each node.

Balance equations equate the rate of flow in and out of each state. By inspecting Figure 8.7, the balance around the state $(0,0,0)$ is given as

$$(\lambda_1 + \lambda_2 + \lambda_3)P(0,0,0) = \mu_1 P(1,0,0) + \mu_2 P(0,1,0) + \mu_3 P(0,0,1) \tag{8.18}$$

The term on the left-hand side represents the flow out of the state, which occurs with probability $P(0,0,0)$, and each of the terms on the right-hand side represents the contributions of the flow back into the state through the departure of a message when the system is in one of three particular alternative states.

Similarly, the balance about the state $(1,0,0)$ is given by

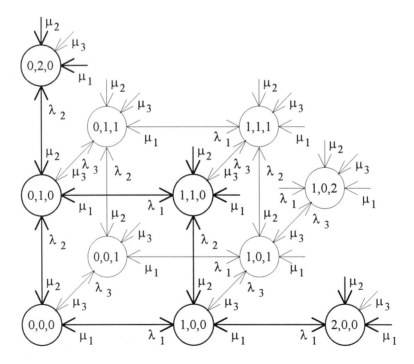

Figure 8.7 State transition diagram for the three-node network.

$$(\lambda_1 + \lambda_2 + \lambda_3 + \mu_1)P(1,0,0) = \mu_1 P(2,0,0) + \mu_2 P(1,1,0) + \mu_3 P(1,0,1) \\ + \lambda_1 P(0,0,0) \tag{8.19}$$

In general, we have

$$(\lambda_1 + \lambda_2 + \lambda_3 + \mu_1 + \mu_2 + \mu_3)P(i,j,k) \\ = \mu_1 P(i+1,j,k) + \mu_2 P(i,j+1,k) + \mu_3 P(i,j,k+1) \\ + \lambda_1 P(i-1,j,k) + \lambda_2 P(i,j-1,k) + \lambda_3 P(i,j,k-1) \tag{8.20}$$

wherein the obvious boundary conditions, namely, that i, j, and k must be positive, have to be taken into account.

It can be shown that the solution to these equations is given by [3]

$$P(i,j,k) = \left(\frac{\lambda_1}{\mu_1}\right)^i \left(\frac{\lambda_2}{\mu_2}\right)^j \left(\frac{\lambda_3}{\mu_3}\right)^k P(0,0,0) \tag{8.21}$$

where

$$P(0,0,0) = (1 - \lambda_1/\mu_1)(1 - \lambda_2/\mu_2)(1 - \lambda_3/\mu_3) \tag{8.22}$$

This is known as the product form solution, and the result for an n-node network follows to be

$$P(i_1, i_2, \ldots, i_n) = \prod_{j=1}^{n} \left(\frac{\lambda_j}{\mu_j}\right)^{i_j} P(0,0,\ldots,0) \tag{8.23}$$

where

$$P(0,0,\ldots,0) = \prod_{j=1}^{n} (1 - \lambda_j/\mu_j) \tag{8.24}$$

Note that one may have assumed that each of the nodes behave as if they were independent, $M/M/1$ queues, and this is a significant result that is known as Jackson's theorem.

Hence, if the arrival and departure rates for each of the queues are known or estimated, then the average statistics for the network may be obtained. For example, returning to the three-node system in Figure 8.6, it may be noted that the total input is shared between nodes one and two and that the output of node one is shared between two and three. For simplicity, assume that the sharing in both cases is equal so that $\lambda_1 = \lambda/2$, $\lambda_2 = \lambda/2 + \mu_1/2$, and $\lambda_3 = \mu_1/2$. The state probabilities may be obtained using Eqs. (8.23) and (8.24), and the average values for the system parameters may be calculated. The expected queue length, for example, at node one is given by

$$Q = \sum_i \sum_{j,k} i \cdot P(i,j,k) \tag{8.25}$$

Similar expressions can be written for the other two nodes.

It has been assumed that the buffers are infinite, so the values of i, j, and k in Eq. (8.25) have no limit. It is impossible to make an infinite number of calculations; therefore, simple numerical solutions for this system involve some form of approximation. Let us use an example to illustrate the accuracy of such approximations. Recall that we assumed the nodes form a system of independent, $M/M/1$ queues. Hence the expected queue lengths obtained with a good approximation should agree with those obtained using queueing theory. For the purposes of demonstration, let us choose what may be expected to be a poor approximation and investigate the consequences.

The queue length characteristics for nodes 2 and 3 are presented in Figure 8.8. Two of the curves in the figure were obtained using Eq. (8.25), with the upper limit for i, j, and k as just 3. These have been labeled as approximate. The other two curves were obtained using the standard results for an $M/M/1$ queue, and these have been labeled as accurate. It should be expected that the relative queue lengths in the nodes correspond with the relative rates of arrival, at least under low-load conditions. By inspecting the figure, this is indeed the case, since the initial assumptions give $\lambda_3 = \lambda_2/3$. It should also be expected that the mean queue length in each node continues to increase with traffic load, however, and clearly in the approximate case this does not happen. As the traffic load becomes heavy the probability that the queue length is greater than 3 will increase. Hence the approximation will become less accurate. The remedy is to increase the upper limit for i, j, and k in the calculation of Eq. (8.25).

It should be noted that less general analyses may be derived for more specific systems, and there are of course a great number of possibilities that may be of interest. As usual, the mathematics required for their solution may become complex. The option to develop computer simulations, however, is always available.

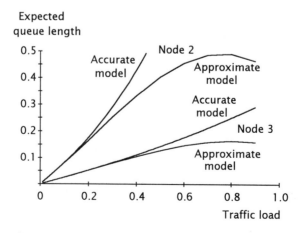

Figure 8.8 Expected queue lengths as functions of traffic load.

8.3 SWITCHING

The heart of any WAN is the process of switching the path for data from one output channel to another. A number of systems, using a wide variety of techniques, are used to achieve this function. The buffering strategies for these switches have a great impact on the traffic statistics, and this will be the subject of the material in this section.

An $N \times N$ space division switch in which any one of N inputs may be connected to any of the N outputs as depicted in Figure 8.9. Such a configuration is nonblocking because there is a switch, or crosspoint, for every possible combination of input and output pairs. Hence the number of crosspoints is N^2. Where N is large, the simple nonblocking configuration is not practical and uneconomical. It is unlikely that it will ever be fully utilized because this would require that each and every input, independently, make a connection to a unique output at the same time. Hence larger switches consist of smaller arrays connected in stages.

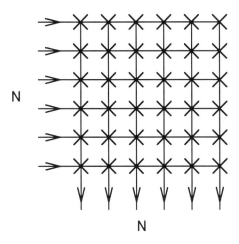

N

N

Figure 8.9 An $N \times N$ space division switch.

The two-stage configuration in Figure 8.10(a), which again has N inputs and N outputs, consists of two columns of k arrays. Each of the arrays is an $n \times k$ switch, and the total number of crosspoints in the system is therefore $2nk^2$. Since $k = N/n$, in terms of the number of inputs and outputs, we have $2Nk$ crosspoints. Also, since k will always be chosen as a factor of N, the number of crosspoints in the two-stage case is considerably less than for the nonblocking switch. Of course, there is an increased risk that a connection request is unsuccessful now because the maximum number of connections in this case is k^2. In other words, since k is less than N, and there are still the same number of inputs and outputs, there is a greater possibility that an outgoing line is found busy and a corresponding increase in the probability that an attempt to connect to an output fails.

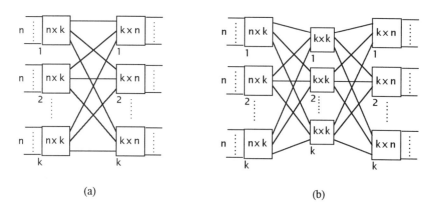

(a)   (b)

Figure 8.10 Multiple-stage switches.

The number of stages may be greater than two, and it is possible to construct nonblocking, multiple-stage switches, with considerably less than N^2 crosspoints. Consider the three stage switch, which is equivalent to inserting a column of k arrays between the two stages, as illustrated in Figure 8.10(b). Now there are k possible paths for a packet at any one input and in order for the switch to be nonblocking there must be a minimum value for k. This is found to be $2n-1$, and it can be further shown that the optimum value for n is approximately [4] given by

$$n \approx (N/2)^{1/2} \tag{8.26}$$

In this case the number of crosspoints, N_x, is given by

$$N_x = 4N\left[(2N)^{1/2} - 1\right] \tag{8.27}$$

So, for example, in the case for which $N = 128$, using Eq. (8.27) it is found that a nonblocking three-stage switch requires 7680 crosspoints compared with a single array that would require $16,384$.

Space division switches probably best describe the type of switches, normally referred to as crossbar switches, that are used in telecommunication networks. Providing that the switch is nonblocking, the only effect that the space division switch will have on any traffic is the introduction of a delay that may be considered to be a constant. Certainly this will be the case for digital data transmission, which uses a fixed number of bits for addressing. In this case a microprocessor, which is used to activate the crosspoints, requires a fixed amount of time to read a particular field in a message prior to closing the required switch. Generally there are considered to be two basic types of switch, and the other is known as a time division switch.

Time division switching, which is a combination of time division multiplexing and slot interchanging, requires that data that is destined for a particular output is placed in the time slot associated with that output. Switches may be purely space dividing, time dividing, or a combination of both. A purely time dividing switch must be capable of interchanging data from one slot on the input side to another slot on the output. A simple time slot interchanger is illustrated in Figure 2.12. In a hybrid switch a particular time slot is associated with a particular input, or output line, and in any of these cases there may be a requirement for buffering.

Establishing the buffering requirements for traditional circuit-switched networks is relatively straightforward since the communication links are point to point and are fixed throughout the duration of a call. Using the digital transmission of speech as an example, in a space division switch the signal simply traverses the matrix without delay or hindrance and only the length of a single sample is required to be stored in any part of memory at a time. In a perfect time division switch a particular one of n inputs may have to wait for up to $2n-1$ slots in order to be released in the correct output slot. Hence the time dividing switch requires a buffer with space for n samples.

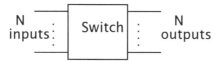

Figure 8.11 A fast packet switch.

More complex switching networks, incorporating so-called fast packet switching, are capable of providing virtual circuit switching, multicast and broadcast services. Now calculating the traffic statistics and buffering requirements is more complex because there is the additional possibility for conflicting output destination requests. Different types of buffering have been identified for this purpose and analyses based on the work of Karol et al. in [5] and [6] will be presented forthwith. For the purposes of each of the following subsections it is sufficient to view the switch as a box with N inputs and N outputs, as illustrated in Figure 8.11.

8.3.1 Output Buffering

When the incoming packets are switched immediately each output requires some buffering in order to store the incoming traffic from more than one source. The situation is depicted in Figure 8.12 wherein each output buffer is explicitly allocated to one particular output. The buffers therefore look like queueing systems and may be analyzed as such. A number of methods for developing the analysis of certain queueing systems have been described in this text, and these may be applied in this case.

First we are looking to form a Markov type model of the system, so a number of parameters have to be defined. Let the size of each buffer be sufficient to store N packets. This choice simplifies the analysis. It does make some sense, however, since there may be up to N arrivals in a single slot that are destined for the same output. Also

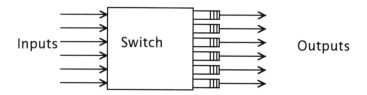

Figure 8.12 A switch with output buffers.

let a_x be the probability that x packets arrive. If the state of the system is the number of packets in a particular buffer, which seems to be convenient, then a discrete-time model may be developed by writing the balance equations as follows. The state transition diagram is illustrated in Figure 8.13. State n, for example, may be entered directly from any of the states 0 through to $n+1$, and there is also the possibility that the state remains at n. From this state the system may transit to any of the states $n-1$ through N. Note that the system is slotted and the state of the system describes the number of packets in an arbitrary buffer at the end of a slot. The probabilities for each transition are labeled on the appropriate arrow in the figure.

So, by inspecting the state transition diagram, it can be seen that the probability of entering state 0 is given by $(a_0 + a_1)p_0 + a_0p_1$. Further, the probability of leaving state 0 is given by $(a_0 + a_1)p_0 + (a_2 + a_3 + \cdots + a_N)p_0$. Thus, equating the two terms, which must be the case when the system is in steady state, and rearranging, we obtain

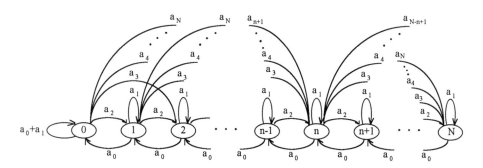

Figure 8.13 State transition diagram for an output buffer.

$$p_1 = \frac{1}{a_0}(a_2 + a_3 + \cdots + a_N)p_0 \tag{8.28}$$

The a_is must sum to one, so Eq. (8.28) may be expressed as

$$p_1 = \frac{1}{a_0}(1 - a_0 - a_1)p_0 \tag{8.29}$$

Similarly the probability flow about state 1 gives

$$P_2 = \frac{1}{a_0}\{(1-a_1)P_1 - a_2P_0\}$$

(8.30)

In general, about state n $(1 < n < N)$, we have

$$P_{n+1} = \frac{1}{a_0}\left\{(1-a_1)P_n - \sum_{i=2}^{n+1} a_i P_{n-i+1}\right\}$$

(8.31)

and finally about N

$$P_N = \frac{1}{a_0}\sum_{j=1}^{N-1}\sum_{i=1}^{j} a_{N-i+1}P_j$$

(8.32)

Thus we have obtained N equations, given by Eqs. (8.29) to (8.32), with $N+1$ unknowns. Another equation may be used to complete the system if the fact that the p_is must sum to one is used. Then

$$P_0 = 1 - \sum_{i=1}^{N} P_i$$

(8.33)

If it is assumed that the arrivals are random and memoryless, then the transition probabilities may be modeled using the binomial distribution such that

$$a_i - \binom{N}{i}(p/N)^i(1-p/N)^{N-i}$$

(8.34)

where p is the probability that a packet is generated in a slot. Note that if the number of inputs to the switch were assumed to be infinite, then the input traffic to each output queue would be Poisson and the previous analysis would be the same as for the $M/D/1$ queue, which is in fact a special case. Now we have a system of equations that may be solved numerically to give the steady-state probability distribution of the system and various performance characteristics may then be calculated.

The probability that a packet is lost because it arrives at a full buffer is easily found, for $p < \rho$, to be given by

$$P_L = 1 - \frac{\rho}{p}$$

(8.35)

The quotient on the right-hand side is the probability of successful transmission, which is equivalent to the packet generation probability, p, as a fraction of utilization, ρ. The utilization is easily calculated here as it is given by $(1 - a_0 P_0)$.

The closed-form solution for the state of the system, as obtained for various queueing disciplines in Chapter 3, is usually more convenient; Karol et al. have derived the generating function for output queueing as [5]

$$Q(z) = \frac{(1-p)(1-z)}{A(z)-z}$$

(8.36)

where $A(z)$ is the z-transform of the distribution of arrival times. This result assumes, however, that the buffer has an infinite capacity. Multiplying both sides of Eq. (8.34) by z^n and summing over all possible values we obtain

$$A(z) = \left(1 - \frac{p}{N} + z\frac{p}{N}\right)^N$$

(8.37)

Replacing this expression for $A(z)$ in Eq. (8.36), differentiating with respect to z, and taking the limit as $z \to 1$ give the mean number of packets in the output buffer as

$$\overline{Q} = \frac{N-1}{N}\frac{p^2}{2(1-p)}$$

(8.38)

The mean waiting time in the queue is easily obtained from Eq. (8.38) using Little's result. A comparison of the results obtained using the finite and infinite buffer assumption is left as an exercise for the reader.

8.3.2 Input Buffering

The obvious alternative to output buffering is obtained by placing the buffers at the input stage of the switch, as illustrated in Figure 8.14. In this configuration the switch operates by inspecting the destination address for the packet at the head of the queue. It then closes the appropriate connection and the packet is propagated through the output port of the switch. If the speed of the output trunk is sufficient the packet will incur no further waiting time other than that required to reach the head of the input queue and for the switch to establish the connection. Similarly, if the processing speed of the switch is sufficient, then the packet may not have to wait in the input queue and it will incur no queueing delays at all. This will require a processing speed at least equal to the sum of the data transmission rates for all the input lines, however, and this may not be suitable. Indeed if the switch was capable of keeping up with the maximum aggregate input, then there would be no need for input queueing at all.

It is probably fair to assume that the speed of each input and the switch itself will be equal to one another. In this case the switch imposes a maximum throughput for the system. Karol et al. [6] described a method for calculating the maximum throughput assuming that the system is saturated, and we will describe this here. Define A_m^i to be the number of new arrivals at the head of the inputs during the mth slot, destined for output

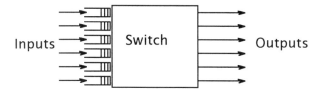

Figure 8.14 A switch with input buffers.

i. Also define B_m^i to be the number of packets at the head of the inputs that were not able to be switched during the *m*th slot. Thus

$$B_m^i = \max\left(0, B_{m-1}^i + A_m^i - 1\right)$$ (8.39)

If it is assumed that the arrivals are binomial, then we have

$$\Pr[A_m^i = k] = \binom{F_{m-1}}{k}(1/N)^k (1-1/N)^{F_{m-1}-k}$$ (8.40)

where F_{m-1} is the number of vacant inputs at the end of slot $m-1$. The expression $1/N$ is used for the probability of success in Eq. (8.40) because each of the packets at the head of N input queues are destined for any particular one of N outputs with equal probability. The system is saturated, so there will always be a packet available at the head of each input.

Since the number of arrivals is binomial, the arrival time distribution is geometric and the process described by Eq. (8.39) is a *Geom/D/1/N* queue. In the limit, as $N \to \infty$, the arrival time distribution becomes exponential and so the A_m^i become Poisson. The appropriate queueing system for modeling this case is the $M/D/1$ queue. Using standard queueing theory results then, for $N \to \infty$, we obtain the following expression for the mean number of blocked packets:

$$\overline{B^i} = \frac{\rho^2}{2(1-\rho)}$$ (8.41)

where ρ is the utilization of output *i*. Moreover, the following intuitive relationship between the number of blocked packets and the output utilization is true because the inputs are saturated

$$\overline{B^i} = 1 - \rho$$ (8.42)

Whence the maximum utilization, given by equating the right-hand sides of Eqs. (8.41) and (8.42) is found to be 0.586.

Karol et al. calculated the maximum utilization when N is finite, and the results are summarized in Table 8.1.[1] It may be observed that even for small N the utilization is not much greater than 0.6 and the value quickly converges to the maximum for $N \to \infty$.

Table 8.1
Maximum throughput for input buffering

N	Utilization
1	1.0000
2	0.7500
3	0.6825
4	0.6553
5	0.6399
6	0.6302
7	0.6234
8	0.6184
∞	0.5858

Essentially the throughput for input buffer switching is reduced because packets that are destined for idle outputs may be held up behind blocked packets. This, of course, assumes that the queueing discipline is strictly first-come first-served. Using alternative disciplines it is possible to show that the throughput will be improved. Dropping blocked packets is one crude method for achieving this. For example, if all the blocked packets at the end of a slot are dumped, then the memory at the front of all the input buffers is freed up at the end of every slot. Hence in this case F_{m-1} in Eq. (8.40) is replaced with N and the utilization of an output queue, which is equivalent to $\Pr[A_m^i > 0]$, is given by

$$\rho = \sum_{k=1}^{N} \binom{N}{k} (p/N)^k (1-p/N)^{N-k} \qquad (8.43)$$

where p is the probability that a packet is generated in a slot, which can be simplified to give

$$\rho = 1 - (1 - p/N)^N \qquad (8.44)$$

Hence a plot of the utilization as a function of offered load will show that the throughput of the switch is reduced when the number of input/output pairs increases, and this is what we should expect. However, the throughput will always be more satisfactory than for the random selection policy. Taking the worst case, as $N \to \infty$, from Eq. (8.44) the maximum throughput is obtained as

---

[1] Permission to print kindly given by the IEEE.

$$\rho = 1 - e^{-p} \qquad (8.45)$$

So a direct comparison with the throughput for the random selection policy under saturation (0.586) may be calculated using $p = 1.0$ in Eq. (8.45). The throughput for the dropped packets scheme is then 0.632, and so there is a noticeable improvement. Of course, there will be a point when the number of packet losses outweigh the benefit of a higher throughput; this is a trade-off for comparing the performance of random selection and dropping packets.

There are perhaps more elegant methods for improving the throughput of input buffering. For example, it should be possible for the switch to determine the longest queue length at each input buffer. When there are a number of inputs contending for the same output priority could be given to the most congested queue. It is not clear whether the throughput will always improve in this case because the two queues may continue requesting connection to the same output. The packet loss probability will be smaller, however, because the aggregate queue length at the inputs will be reduced.

Traffic smoothing [5] is an interesting method for input queueing in which the buffer collects a fixed number of number packets, say b, before accessing the switch. All b packets are then switched at the same time. Such a method effectively requires a matrix of $Nb \times Nb$ cross points, and the implications for a space division switch are that its physical size will be significantly increased. Hluchyj and Karol described a method of analysis that we will use here. As usual the arrivals are modeled using a Bernoulli process with probability of success p. The number of arrivals destined for output i is therefore given by

$$\Pr[A^i = k] = \binom{Nb}{k}(p/N)^k (1 - p/N)^{Nb-k} \qquad (8.46)$$

Now, a packet will be lost when more than b enter the switch at the same time and they are all destined for the same output. The total number of dropped packets can be calculated using the probabilities in Eq. (8.46) for which $k > b$. On average the total number of packets that arrives during b slots is bp. Hence the probability that a packet is lost is given by

$$L = \frac{1}{bp} \sum_{k=b+1}^{Nb} (k - b) \binom{Nb}{k}(p/N)^k (1 - p/N)^{Nb-k} \qquad (8.47)$$

Similarly the probability of successful transmission, which is the same as the utilization, is given by the sum of the probabilities for which $k < b$. Thus

$$\rho = \frac{1}{bp} \left\{ b - \sum_{k=0}^{b-1} (b - k) \binom{Nb}{k}(p/N)^k (1 - p/N)^{Nb-k} \right\} \qquad (8.48)$$

Here the terms in the summation represent the number of slots, out of a possible total of b, that are not occupied by successfully switched packets. We may compare the throughput for smoothing with the other input buffer queueing disciplines. As $N \to \infty$ the binomial coefficients in Eq. (8.48) will become Poisson and so the throughput becomes

$$\rho = \frac{1}{bp}\left\{b - \sum_{k=0}^{b-1}(b-k)\frac{(bp)^k}{k!}e^{-bp}\right\} \qquad (8.49)$$

Evaluating this expression with $p = 1.0$ gives the throughput under saturation and this is plotted as a function of b in Figure 8.15. As expected the throughput improves with increasing "smoothness," which is a result of larger values for b. Note that the special case $b = 1$ is the same as for the dropped packets scheme and using Eq. (8.49) we obtain the same saturation throughput of 0.632.

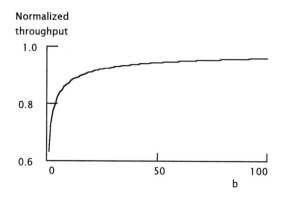

Figure 8.15 Saturation throughput as a function of b for input smoothing.

It would appear that, at least under certain conditions, the smoothing scheme is the input queueing method that provides the best throughput. Indeed this should be expected since it effectively involves increasing the size of the switch and thereby reducing the blocking probability and the associated packet loss.

Intuitively, the waiting time of the packets that are not dropped for input smoothing is given by

$$\overline{W} = \frac{b-1}{2} + \frac{\displaystyle\sum_{k=1}^{b-1}\frac{k-1}{2}k\,\Pr[A=k] + \frac{b-1}{2}b\,\Pr[A \geq b]}{\displaystyle\sum_{k=1}^{b-1}k\,\Pr[A=k] + b\,\Pr[A \geq b]} \qquad (8.50)$$

The first term on the right-hand side is the average time that elapses from the moment the packet arrives to the point at which b packets have accumulated. The second term is the mean time taken to multiplex the packet onto the output trunk. The numerator of this term is the sum of the individual times for each packet in the frame, and the denominator is the number of packets in the frame. The mean delay for input smoothing and output buffering is compared in Figure 8.16.

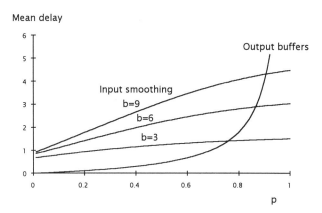

Figure 8.16 Mean delay for input smoothing and output buffers.

8.3.3 Shared Memory

A third method for switch buffering is known as shared memory. This case, which is illustrated in Figure 8.17, is similar to output buffering in that all the new arrivals are immediately presented to the switch crosspoints. If, in any particular slot, more than one arrival is destined for the same output port, then one is transferred to that port while the remainder enter a pool of memory that is shared by all the ports. This memory is fed back to the input of the switch so that during the next slot both the new arrivals at the input port and the previously blocked packets contend for access to the outputs. Shared buffering is a method of switching that offers the throughput performance of output buffering while reducing the buffer space required.

A number of configurations for shared memory is realizable. That depicted in the illustration shows one additional port for input and output. Then the size of the switch itself is $N+1$ squared. The most efficient configuration, from the traffic performance statistics point of view, will be that for which all the inputs and outputs have a separate connection to the shared memory pool. Then the packets may be represented to each of the outputs simultaneously. However, the size of the switch in this case is $2N$ squared.

If the shared memory is sufficiently large, then all the traffic will eventually arrive at the required destination port and the saturation throughput is the same as for output queueing. Even though the memory space has to be finite, the fact that it is shared means that it will be more efficiently utilized than the dedicated memory of output buffering. A simple analytic model for shared buffering is available if it is assumed that the buffer space is infinite. In this case the number of packets in the system destined for output i at the end of slot m, represented by Q_m^i, may be written in terms of the new arrivals, A_m^i,

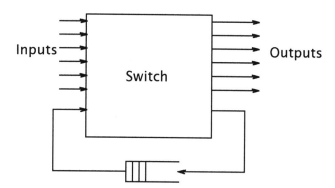

Figure 8.17 A switch with shared input and output memory.

using an expression similar to that in Eq. (8.39) as follows

$$Q_m^i = \max\left\{0, Q_{m-1}^i + A_m^i - 1\right\} \tag{8.51}$$

Whence, in steady-state conditions, the mean number of packets in the buffer is given by

$$\overline{Q} = \sum_{i=1}^{N} Q^i \tag{8.52}$$

This system may be modeled as an N-fold convolution of $M/D/1$ queues. In Chapter 3 we presented the expression for the transform of the distribution of the system size of an $M/M/1$ queue in Eq. (3.128) that may be modified, using $\mu = 1$, to give the equivalent expression for a single $M/D/1$ queue as follows

$$P(z) = \frac{(1-\lambda)(1-z)}{1-z-\lambda z + \lambda z^2} \tag{8.53}$$

This expression simplifies, by canceling the factors in $(1-z)$, to give

$$P(z) = \frac{1-\lambda}{1-\lambda z} \tag{8.54}$$

Hence the distribution of the number of packets in the shared buffer, being the N-fold convolution of $M/D/1$ queues, is given by

$$Q(z) = \left\{\frac{1-\lambda}{1-\lambda z}\right\}^N \tag{8.55}$$

This transform is easily inverted to give the probabilities

$$q_n = (1-\lambda)^N \left\{ \frac{1}{(N-1)!}(n+N-1)(n+N-2)\cdots(n+1)\lambda^n \right\} \tag{8.56}$$

and the performance metrics are then easily calculated.

Essentially, the throughput for input buffering is reduced, compared with that of output buffering and shared buffering, because packets that are destined for idle outputs may be held up behind blocked packets at the head of the queue. Hence, output and shared buffering provide superior throughput performance. The latter method benefits from a reduction in memory requirements at the expense of an increase in the switch size.

8.4 TELECOMMUNICATION NETWORKS

Telecommunication networks consist of different types of switches that are interconnected in a variety of configurations and over a range of distances. Essentially there are two types of switch that differ in respect of the effect on the network traffic. A space division switch connects a number of distinct cables, input lines, or trunks, at the input, to another set of lines at the output. A time division switch connects a number of channels at the input and output and may consist of just one physical cable. Another method of switching may be identified if the frequency division multiplexing technique for data transmission is included in the discussion. From the traffic analysis point of view, however, a device that switches data from one frequency at the input to another at the output is the same as a space division switch. If the data transmission and switching rates of a single input to a space division switch are the same as for one of the frequency carriers in a frequency switch, then the traffic performance of both devices will be identical.

Teletraffic engineering thus concentrates on the analysis of time and space division switching systems, of which there is a large variety. The capacity of a switch is probably one of the most important performance measures. At the outset the capacity of any type of switch depends on the data transmission speed of the receivers and transmitters and the processing speed of the switch itself. It also depends on many other parameters such as the intensity and distribution of the load across the inputs; in traffic analysis these are the parameters in which we are interested. Traffic intensity is measured in a unit known as the Erlang, and it will be used on a number of occasions in this section.

The Erlang was introduced in the previous chapter in discussing voice transmission. It is more properly defined as the ratio of the average amount of time that a device is busy to the total time that the device is available. Hence, if a device is busy for a total time t during a period T, then the traffic intensity is t/T Erlang, and this quantity has no dimensions. If there are on average λ calls per sec with a mean duration of c sec, then the traffic intensity is $(\lambda T)c/T$, or λc Erlang. It may also be used to quantify the amount of traffic flow through a number of devices. The traffic, in Erlangs, for multiple devices can be found by summing the traffic for each individual device. Thus if t_x is the sum of the times during which exactly x devices out of N are busy during the period T, then the total available time is effectively NT, the total busy time is effectively $\sum_{x=1}^{N} xt_x$, and the traffic flow is $\sum_{x=1}^{N} xt_x/NT$ Erlang. Intuitively, this expression may be interpreted as the average number of devices that is busy during the specified period.

8.4.1 Blocked Call Systems

A single-stage switch with as many inputs as outputs and a crosspoint for each and every possible connection is nonblocking. Normally it is not expected that all the outputs of a switch will be utilized at the same time, however, and economics dictate that the number of outputs should be less than the number of inputs. One of the simplest models for a blocking switch is provided by the $M/M/m/m$ queue. This is equivalent to one for which there is an infinite population of sources, or callers, and there are m outputs that correspond to the m servers in the queueing model. Since this queueing system permits only one customer to be present in each server at any given time, there is no waiting room. The analysis of this system, resulting in the Erlang distribution, was provided in Chapter 3; and the probability that a call is blocked is given by Eq. (3.130) with $n=m$, as

$$p_m = \frac{\left(\dfrac{\lambda}{\mu}\right)^m \dfrac{1}{m!}}{\sum_{k=0}^{m}\left(\dfrac{\lambda}{\mu}\right)^k \dfrac{1}{k!}} \tag{8.57}$$

Recall that this is known as Erlang's B formula, or loss formula, usually denoted by $E_{1,m}(\lambda/\mu)$. Note also that, in using it to model a switch, we are assuming that no routing function is provided. In other words, a call may choose any output to complete a successful connection. If a new call finds any output idle, then it may be utilized. Only when all the outputs are busy will a new call be blocked, or lost. This function is plotted in Figure 3.10 with $m = 1, 2, 4$, and 8.

The infinite source model may be suitable for approximating the performance of switches in a local exchange where the number of telephones at the input will be large compared with the number of output trunks. Intermediate switches connecting local and tandem offices, however, may be more appropriately modeled using the $M/M/m/k/s$ queue, for which the number of inputs and outputs will be given by s and m, respectively. Again it will be assumed that there is no waiting room such that $k = m$. The $M/M/m/k/s$ queue was analyzed in Section 3.4.2, so the solution to the $M/M/m/m/s$ system is provided by Eqs. (3.137) and (3.138) using $k = m$ as

$$P_n = \left(\frac{\lambda}{\mu}\right)^n \binom{s}{n} P_0 \tag{8.58}$$

and

$$p_0 = \left\{ \sum_{n=0}^{m} \left(\frac{\lambda}{\mu} \right)^n \left(\frac{s}{n} \right) \right\}^{-1} \tag{8.59}$$

These equations permit the calculation of the number of calls in progress and are collectively known as the Engset distribution. Again, the probability that a new call is blocked is the same as the probability that there are m busy outputs, or m calls in progress, and this may be calculated using Eqs. (8.58) and (8.59) with $n = m$.

Care must be taken here not to confuse the blocking probability with the loss probability. The latter is defined as the ratio of calls lost to the total number of attempts, and this may not be the same as the blocking probability. In fact, the two measures turn out to be the same when the Erlang distribution is assumed and this is because the arrival rates, or the number of new calls, are not dependent on the state of the system. The Engset distribution on the other hand predicts the state probabilities when the arrival rates are dependent on the number of busy output channels since no arrivals may occur when all the inputs are busy; whence, the probability that a call is blocked is not the same as the probability that it is lost. It is interesting to note that in order for the arrivals to be independent we must let $s \to \infty$ and $\lambda \to 0$ in the Engset, and it can be shown that Eqs. (8.58) and (8.59) in this case are equivalent to the Erlang distribution.

In previous analyses we replaced the ratio λ/μ with ρ, the traffic intensity, and this quantity may adopt the Erlang unit. Since the utilization per output is ρ/m, and this number must be less than one for the system to remain stable, it is apparent that the number of outputs should be chosen to be greater than the traffic intensity in Erlangs, or the Erlang rating. Moreover, the greater the number of outputs chosen the less becomes the probability of blocking, and losing calls. Again care is required with the precise definition of a measure since the Erlang rating of a trunk is not the same as the Erlang rating of the switch. The latter will be m times that of the trunk.

The switches for which the number of outputs is reduced to economize on the number of crosspoints are also cascaded into switching stages, as was described in the previous section. In fact, time and space division switches are connected in a variety of configurations. The resulting network of smaller switches may be designed as nonblocking. However, the economic argument for reducing the number of crosspoints again results in systems for which blocking, or congestion, may occur. Moreover, the blocking occurs within the switch itself.

A typical three-stage switch is depicted in Figure 8.18. This particular configuration consists of time-slot interchangers in the first and third stages with a space division switch connecting them in the second stage. Such a configuration is referred to as TST. Time-slot interchange is the term often given to a time division switch wherein the incoming data is placed into a particular slot, depending on the output destination. In the diagram each of the n inputs to the time-slot interchangers are multiplexed into k slots. With $k < n$ the interchangers are concentrating a number of inputs into less outputs and blocking may occur. This means that the number of crosspoints in the space switch may be reduced to $N/n \times N/n$ at the expense of the k-fold increase in data transmission

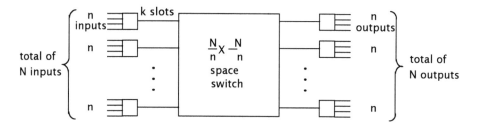

Figure 8.18 Three-stage TST switch.

rate and processing speeds and the increase in blocking probability in the time switches due to the concentration of n inputs into k. The blocking probability may be calculated as follows.

Begin with the probability that an input is busy, p_i, which is the fraction of time a call spends in service the system, and is given by $(1/\mu)/(1/\lambda + 1/\mu)$. This may be simplified to give

$$p_i = \frac{\lambda}{\lambda + \mu} \tag{8.60}$$

Through symmetry this is the same as the probability that an output is busy. Hence the probability that one of the inter-stage link time slots on either side of the space switch is busy, p_1, is

$$p_1 = p_i \frac{n}{k} \tag{8.61}$$

In order for the call to be successfully connected it must find idle time slots in two links: one on either side of the space switch. It does so with probability $(1-p_1)^2$. Assuming that the probabilities for the links are independent, the probability that a call is blocked, p_b, is given by the probability that all k slots are busy. Thus

$$p_b = \{1 - (1 - p_1)^2\}^k \tag{8.62}$$

Note that the same argument applies to any combination of time and space switches in a similar three-stage configuration. If the time-slot interchangers in Figure 8.18 were replaced with space switches, for example, then the k slots would be referred to as k lines, or trunks, instead. Note also that the independence assumption implies that the probability predicted by Eq. (8.62) will be approximate.

The blocking probability is more accurately obtained using Jacobaeus's combinatorial methods [7]. In fact, the call loss probability, p_L, is obtained, since in the following analysis the independence assumption is dropped. We begin with the following general expression for the loss probability in terms of the conditional probabilities that the links are busy:

$$P_{\mathrm{L}} = \sum_{l=0}^{k} H(k-l)G(l) \tag{8.63}$$

where $G(l)$ is the probability that any l of the k links terminating at a switch in the third stage are busy and $H(k-l)$ is the probability that the remaining $k-l$ links connecting the first stage are also busy. If the links are chosen randomly, then

$$H(k-l) = \sum_{x=k-l}^{k} J(x)\frac{D(k-l,x)}{C(k,x)} \tag{8.64}$$

where $J(x)$ is the probability that x links connecting the first stage are busy, $C(k,x)$ is the number of ways that x links may be selected from the total of k links in the first stage, and $D(k-l,x)$ is the number of ways that $x-(k-l)$ links may be selected from the remaining $k-(k-l)$ available.[1] The ratio of $C(k,x)$ to $D(k-l,x)$ thus represents the conditional probability that if x links in the first stage are busy, then the remaining links in the last stage are also busy, and Eq. (8.64) follows. Since $D(k-l,x)$ is given by

$$D(k-l,x) = \binom{l}{x-k+l} = \frac{l!}{(x-k+l)!(k-x)!} \tag{8.65}$$

the ratio simplifies to give

$$\frac{D(k-l,x)}{C(k,x)} = \frac{l!x!}{k!(x-k+l)!} \tag{8.66}$$

and one task that remains is to choose suitable distributions for $J(x)$ and $G(l)$, that is, the probabilities that the links in the first and final stages are busy.

As an example, let us assume that $J(x)$ is binomial and $G(l)$ is Erlang distributed. Then we have, by direct substitution into Eq. (8.64),

$$H(k-l) = \sum_{x=k-l}^{k} \frac{n!}{x!(n-x)!}p_i^{x}(1-p_i)^{n-x}\frac{l!x!}{k!(x-k+l)!} \tag{8.67}$$

which can be shown simplifies to give

$$H(k-l) = \frac{l!n!}{k!(n-k+l)!}p_i^{l} \tag{8.68}$$

---

[1] $C(k,x)$ is the standard "choose" function given by $C(k,x) = k!/x!(k-x)!$.

Thus

$$p_L = \sum_{l=0}^{k} \frac{l!\,n!}{k!(n-k+l)!} p_i^l E_l(\rho) \qquad (8.69)$$

which can be shown to give

$$p_L = \frac{E_k(\rho)}{E_n(\rho/p_i)} \qquad (8.70)$$

In order to compare the loss probabilities predicted by the two models presented, Eqs. (8.62) and (8.70) are plotted as functions of traffic for the two cases n and k both equal to 4 and 10 in Figure 8.19. In both situations the loss probability given by Eq. (8.62), that is, assuming that the line probabilities are independent, result in the upper curve and predict the worst case as expected. It should be noted that the results obtained using the two methods, though similar in trend, are quite different. In fact, they quickly separate as n and k increase. Great care is therefore necessary in choosing the correct input distributions required. Models using alternative distributions for $J(x)$ and $G(l)$ are relevant in teletraffic analysis. Moreover, it is possible to extend this method of analysis to switches with more stages, and the interested reader is referred to Bear's text [7].

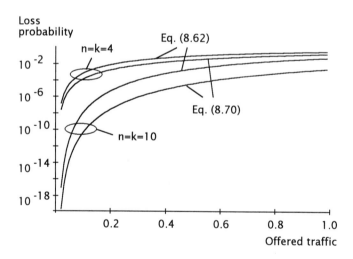

Figure 8.19 Blocking probability; comparison of models.

8.4.2 Queued Call Systems

Telecommunications exchanges may be produced with facilities enabling blocked calls to be placed in a queue and these are known waiting, or queued switching systems. The following simple model for a queued call system represents a single-stage switch with an infinite number of Poisson sources, an infinite size queue, and N trunks at the output. Note that this is similar to the $M/M/m/k$ queue of Section 3.4.1. In fact, it is the same if we let $m = N$ and $k \to \infty$. In this case, the birth and death rates are given by

$$\lambda_n = \lambda \quad \text{for } n = 0,1,2,\ldots \tag{8.71}$$

and

$$\mu_n = \begin{cases} n\mu & \text{for } 0 < n < N \\ N\mu & \text{for } N \le n \end{cases} \tag{8.72}$$

Following the standard procedure, utilizing Eq. (3.84), the solution for the state probabilities must be separated into the two parts for which $n < N$ and $n \ge N$. After simplification the solution may be written

$$p_n = \begin{cases} \dfrac{\lambda^n}{\mu^n} \dfrac{1}{n!} p_0 & \text{for } n < N \\ \dfrac{\lambda^n}{\mu^n} \dfrac{1}{N!\,N^{n-N}} p_0 & \text{for } n \ge N \end{cases} \tag{8.73}$$

As usual, the p_ns must sum to one, according to Eq. (3.90), and we can write

$$p_0 = \dfrac{1}{1 + \displaystyle\sum_{n=1}^{N-1} \dfrac{\lambda^n}{\mu^n} \dfrac{1}{n!} + \sum_{n=N}^{\infty} \dfrac{\lambda^n}{\mu^n} \dfrac{1}{N!\,N^{n-N}}} \tag{8.74}$$

Finally the probability that a new call must join the queue because all the trunks are busy, p_Q, may be obtained using

$$p_Q = \sum_{n=N}^{\infty} p_n \tag{8.75}$$

and after some algebra this may be written as

$$p_Q = \dfrac{\dfrac{\lambda^N}{\mu^N} \dfrac{1}{N!} \dfrac{N}{(N - \lambda/\mu)}}{\displaystyle\sum_{n=0}^{N-1} \dfrac{\lambda^n}{\mu^n} \dfrac{1}{n!} + \dfrac{\lambda^N}{\mu^N} \dfrac{1}{N!} \dfrac{N}{(N - \lambda/\mu)}} \tag{8.76}$$

This expression is known as Erlang's C formula. The notation $E_{2,N}(\lambda/\mu)$ is one of a number that have been used to represent the function. The appearance of the formula is often improved by replacing the fraction λ/μ with the symbol A, representing the traffic in Erlangs.

A more realistic model when the number of inputs is relatively small is perhaps given by the finite source $M/M/m/k/s$ queueing system. The solution in this case is provided in Section 3.4.2 and corresponds to a switch with s traffic sources, m output trunks, and room for a total of k calls, both queueing and in progress. Now the probability that a call must join the queue is

$$P_Q = \sum_{n=m}^{k} p_n \tag{8.77}$$

with the state probabilities, p_n, given by Eq. (3.132). Note that the $M/M/m/k/s$ queueing system permits both queued and lost calls. The latter occurs with a probability given by Eq. (3.131) with $n = k$, which is equivalent to the probability that the system is full.

As an example, the probability that a new call must join the queue is plotted as a function of the traffic intensity for infinite and finite queueing models with $N = 8$ and 16 in Figure 8.20. In each case the infinite source and waiting room model predicts the poorest performance, with the queueing probability being greater than that obtained using the finite model. Moreover, as expected, the probability that a call must queue is also greater when the number of trunks is reduced. Of course, alternative criteria for measuring the system performance will reveal a number of trade-offs. Throughput will be better in the infinite case, for example.

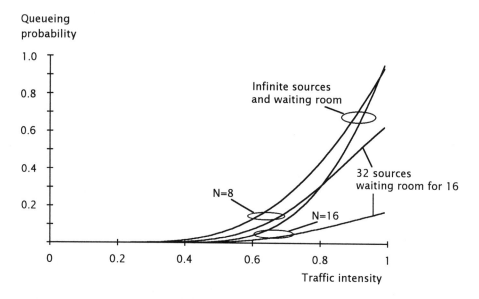

Figure 8.20 Queueing probabilities for switches with waiting facilities.

The average waiting time for a call may be calculated using Little's result in the usual manner. For example, the mean number of calls waiting in the infinite system is

$$\overline{Q} = \sum_{n=N+1}^{\infty}(n-N)p_n \tag{8.78}$$

and the waiting time is calculated using

$$\overline{w} = \frac{\overline{Q}}{\lambda} \tag{8.79}$$

The queueing statistics for multiple-stage switching is also of interest in teletraffic engineering. When a call has found a free outlet at the first stage it may have to join a queue in the next or subsequent stages. If it is assumed that the incoming calls are independent, then it is also true that the probabilities of delay in each stage are independent. The average delay may therefore be calculated as the sum of the delays in each stage. The delay distribution may be obtained as the convolution of the distribution at each stage in a similar manner as described for the two-node network in Section 8.2.

8.4.3 Circuit Switching

Calls on a telecommunication network are facilitated by means of circuit and packet switching mechanisms. A simple model for a switched two-node network is depicted in Figure 8.21. Any communication between the users connected to each node, originating from one of the users connected to node A, join a queue if one of N trunks are not available.

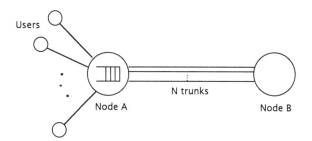

Figure 8.21 A two-node switched network.

The circuit switching control signals, which include the connect and release requests, are assumed here to be transmitted in-band. The total time for a call setup, T, is the sum of a number of variables and these include the transmission time for the send request from a user to node A (t_r), the queueing time in node A (w), the transmission time for the connect message from A to B (t_c), the transmission time for the answer message from B to A (t_a), and finally the transmission time for the start-to-send message from node A to the user (t_s). Thus

$$T = t_r + w + t_c + t_a + t_s \tag{8.80}$$

The contributions of the processing delays in A and B are assumed to remain constant for the purposes of this simple model, while the other terms on the right-hand side of Eq. (8.80) depend on the parameters that have an immediate impact on the traffic performance. These parameters include the data transmission rate on local lines, d_L, that is, between the users and the primary switching node, and the transmission rate, d_t, on the trunks that connect the switches. The numbers of users and trunks and the waiting capacity in the switch are also important.

The transmission times of the control signals are easily calculated using the data transmission rate and the number of bits in the signal. The waiting time in the queue is perhaps the most awkward variable with which to deal. As we have already seen that the waiting time depends on most of the system parameters. If the switch is a purely blocking system, then of course the waiting time is zero and the probability that a call is lost may become an important performance indicator. On the other hand, if the switch has queueing facilities, then the waiting time may be calculated using the methods described in the previous section. The probability that a call set-up request must queue, for example, in the case where the number of users and the system capacity are assumed to be infinite, is given by $E_{2,N}(\lambda/\mu)$, or Erlang's C formula. The function is plotted for different numbers of trunks in Figure 8.22 to illustrate the point that the performance improves as the number of trunks increases.

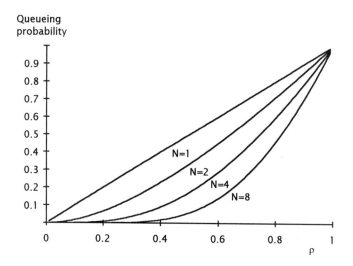

Figure 8.22 Probability that a call set-up request must queue.

The actual waiting time then, from Eqs. (8.78) and (8.79), has a mean value given by

$$\overline{w} = \frac{1}{\lambda} \sum_{n=N+1}^{\infty} (n-N) \frac{\lambda^n}{\mu^n} \frac{1}{N! N^{n-N}} p_0 \tag{8.81}$$

where the p_n have been substituted by the expression for which $n > N$ in Eq. (8.73). After simplification this equation may be expressed in terms of Erlang's C formula as

$$\overline{w} = \frac{1/\mu}{(N - \lambda/\mu)} E_{2,N}(\lambda/\mu) \tag{8.82}$$

To illustrate the use of waiting time calculations Eq. (8.82) was used to complete Table 8.2. The expected waiting time in seconds when an average call lasts 30 sec, that is, $1/\mu = 30$, is tabulated for different loads and numbers of trunks. The telephone bill in our home shows that a 30-sec call duration is probably a fair average. When a call is requested every 32 sec this requires, on average, at least three trunks to reduce the waiting time to less than 1 sec. Thankfully the demand in our home does not quite reach this level! It is probably fair to expect such frequent requests in a relatively small office however.

Table 8.2
Waiting times (sec) for average call durations of 30 sec

$1/\lambda$	$N = 1$	$N = 2$	$N = 3$	$N = 4$	$N = 5$
32	450	6.453	0.881	0.131	0.018
36	150	4.964	0.644	0.087	0.011
44	64	3.250	0.375	0.043	0.004
60	30	1.739	0.161	0.014	0.001
120	10	0.445	0.023	0.001	-

We return now to the calculation of T in Eq. (8.80) and assume that w, the waiting time in the queue, may be calculated using Eq. (8.82), with $1/\mu$ set to be the holding time for the duration of the connection. The holding time includes the connection request, answer, and start transmission times (t_r, t_a, and t_s), plus the time to transmit the signaling messages required to take down the circuit as well as the time taken to actually transact the call.

In order to illustrate the use of Eq. (8.80) let us assume that all signaling and control messages are of equal length t and the actual message is of length t_m. In Figure 8.23(a) we plotted the mean value of T, normalized with respect to t_m, as a function of traffic assuming that for the two cases when $t = 0.1t_m$ and $t = 0.01t_m$. As expected the useful capacity of the link is greater when the control signals are relatively small. In Figure 8.23(b) we take the two cases when the connection request from A to B is the same as the other signaling messages, that is, $t_r = t$, and also when $t_r = 0.1t$. Here the condition $t = 0.1t_m$ is assumed and, as was the case in (a), $N = 10$. Again the capacity is significantly greater when just one of the signaling message types is reduced in length. Such comparisons may become important when particular signals are required to carry a significant amount of overhead information. Connect request signals, for example, are often used to transmit lists of addresses for the purposes of routing.

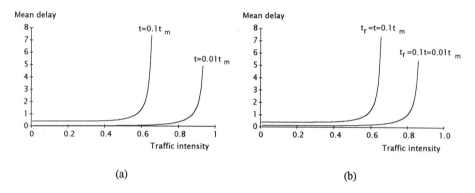

(a)   (b)

Figure 8.23 Mean delay for circuit switching.

8.4.4 Packet Switching

The alternative strategy for establishing end-to-end connections in a telecommunication network is to send the data in chunks. The chunks, or packets, may travel along different routes in a multiple-hop communication. The unpredictability associated with packet switching, such as may be caused by packets arriving out of sequence, or even not at all, means that the use of acknowledgments is almost mandatory.

Let us carry out the analysis of the simple two-node network in Figure 8.21 with packet switching in order to facilitate a comparison of the two methods. A communication session begins with the user sending its message, or a portion thereof, in a fixed-size packet to node A. This packet must wait in the switching node until the output trunk is available. It is assumed that $N = 1$ for the packet switching model. When the packet is received at the destination, following its receipt and transmission at B, an acknowledgment packet is transmitted in exactly the same way following the path back to the user from which the message originated.

The packet switching equivalent for the call set-up time may be written as

$$T = t_m + t_h + w_m + w_a + t_a \qquad (8.83)$$

Again, only the major components have been accounted for, the processing time in the switches is neglected, and as before t_m is the transmission time for the message. In addition, we account for the transmission time of the header, t_h, which must be included to accommodate control information in the same way that the signaling and control messages are included in the circuit switching analysis. The components w_m and w_a represent the waiting times for the message and the acknowledgment, respectively. Finally the transmission time of the acknowledgment is denoted by t_a.

Since the output trunk is only taken up for a period of time equal to that of the transmission time for the packet, it is assumed that only one trunk is required. In order to preserve the fairness for comparison the data transmission time of the single trunk will be taken to be N times that for one of the circuit-switched trunks. Adopting the same assumptions as for traffic arrivals, the waiting times for both messages and acknowledgments may be modeled as $M/M/1$ queues. Thus, using the fact that $E_{2,1}(\lambda/\mu) = \lambda/\mu$ in Eq. (8.82), we can write

$$\overline{w}_{m,a} = \frac{\lambda/\mu_{m,a}^2}{(1 - \lambda/\mu_{m,a})} \tag{8.84}$$

where $\mu_{m,a}$ are the mean departure rates for messages and acknowledgments, such that $1/\mu_{m,a}$ are the mean service times. The arrival rates for messages and acknowledgments are the same because an acknowledgment is generated for every message.

The message delays for the simple packet switching model are plotted as functions of traffic intensity in Figure 8.24. For each packet size of 1000 and 10,000 bits, acknowledgments of length 160 and 16 bits were used. The length of the message packet header was assumed to be the same as the acknowledgment, corresponding to the requirement for similar addressing space. A data transmission rate of 2 Mbit/s, which is the speed of a typical WAN data link, was taken; and it should be noted that the propagation distance has been ignored. It may be observed that the effect of changing the acknowledgment packet size can have just as dramatic an effect on the performance of the link as changing the message packet size.

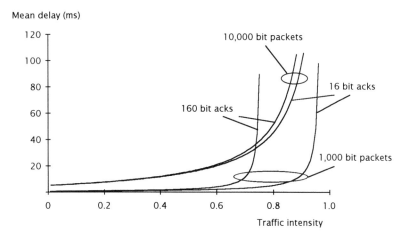

Figure 8.24 Mean delay for packet switching.

Of course, the preceding model assumes that the capacity of nodes A and B are infinite. Finite buffers will be present in real systems. Thus, it is increasingly likely, in both circuit and packet switching, that as the traffic intensifies useful information may be lost. It is possible to introduce alternative queueing models, such as those described elsewhere in the book, to include this factor in a more thorough analysis of performance. It should also be noted that the possibility of losing information introduces the requirement for retranmisssion, and there are mechanisms for achieving this. The reader may recall the introductory material on retransmission protocols in Chapter 2.

A comparison of the performance of circuit and packet switching is informative. Schwatrz [8] provides an excellent discussion in his book that may be summarized as follows. The flexibility of utilizing telecommunication networks in either way presents a choice, and certain applications may be better suited to one or the other in different circumstances. In Figure 8.25 we plotted the mean delay for comparable systems of circuit- and packet-switched links. The data transmission rates in the trunk lines were taken to be 9600 bits/s, and the number of trunks in the circuit switching model was chosen to be 50. The aggregate of $50 \times 9600 = 480$ kbit/s was therefore taken to be the transmission rate of the single trunk in the packet-switched system. The message length was used as the variable for the horizontal axis. Two curves, with traffic intensities of $\rho = 0.4$ and 0.5, for each method are included in the figure.

The results illustrate a particular point that is often discussed in such analyses. When the message lengths are large, the efficiency of circuit switching is better than that of packet switching because the overhead signaling becomes less significant. This may be observed on the right-hand side of the graph where the delay for circuit switching has become steady at around 20 ms or so, that is, the time required to transmit the signaling and control messages. The delay for packet switching on the other hand increases without bound due to the requirement for acknowledgments, the transmission of which cannot occur before the message packet is received. On the other hand, the delay for packet switching can be lower than that of circuit switching when the message packets are small enough. In this case the delay due to the transmission of signaling packets in a circuit switch system provides the most significant contribution to the overall figure.

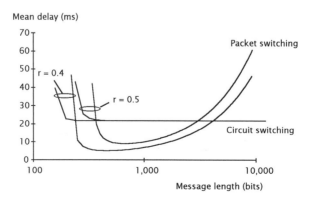

Figure 8.25 Comparing mean delays for circuit switching and packet switching.

8.5 INTEGRATED SERVICES

Telecommunication networks are required to deal with a variety of transport mechanisms that service a number of traffic types. These are often referred to as integrated service networks and that which is perhaps cited the most often is known as the *integrated service digital network* (ISDN), which is described in detail in Chapter 2. Essentially, for the purposes of traffic analysis, ISDN provides the specification of a standard format for the length and duration of the time slots on a telecommunications link. As with a number of other specifications that are in use, different services are permitted to use different slots. Hence the aggregate traffic is supported by a single link and the associated traffic statistics will in general be different than those that are, for example, either purely data communications or voice calls.

Slotted systems were analyzed using the discrete-time Markov technique in Chapter 6. Indeed that type of analysis could be readily extended to deal with multiple traffic types, and one method was dealt with in the final section of that chapter. Here we will describe the alternative continuous-time analytic method, in similar fashion to Schwartz [8], utilizing z-transforms. This is the method used to solve many of the queueing systems described in Chapter 3. The model analyzed and depicted in Figure 8.26 is a simple two-service system that is integrated on to a single, multiple-channel trunk. Equivalently, the output may be viewed as consisting of multiple output lines, as in the Schwartz case. The incoming traffic consists of circuit-switched calls, arriving at an average rate λ_1, and packet-switched data, with arrival rate λ_2.

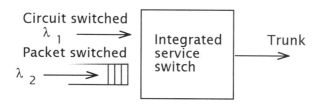

Figure 8.26 Simple model for integrated service switching.

Assume that all arrivals are Poisson so that the system state probabilities may be treated as a Markov chain. Also assume that the output is a single channel and the circuit-switched traffic is blocked if it arrives to find that there are any data packets in the buffer or the switch. The data packets, on the other hand, which constitute the packet-switched traffic, may queue in a buffer with infinite space. Let the service rates corresponding to each traffic type be denoted by μ_1 and μ_2. The model is most easily represented by the two-dimensional state space (n,c), with $n = 0,1,2,...$ representing the number of packets both in the queue and in service and $c = 0,1$ indicating the activity of the circuit-switched source. The state transition diagram for the system is depicted in Figure 8.27.

The state probability distribution, $p_{n,c}$, is most conveniently found by considering

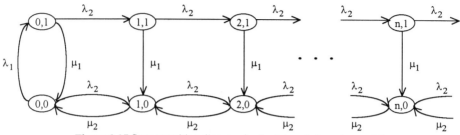

Figure 8.27 State transition diagram for the integrated service model.

the states for which $c = 0$ when there is no circuit-switched traffic and $c = 1$ when the trunk is occupied by a call. The balance equation about $(0,0)$ may be written by inspecting the state transition diagram as

$$(\lambda_1 + \lambda_2)P_{0,0} = \mu_1 P_{0,1} + \mu_2 P_{1,0} \tag{8.85}$$

and about $(n,0)$ as

$$(\lambda_1 + \lambda_2)P_{n,0} = \lambda_2 P_{n-1,0} + \mu_2 P_{n+1,0} + \mu_1 P_{n,1} \tag{8.86}$$

Similarly, the balance equations about $(0,1)$ and $(n,1)$ may be written as

$$(\mu_1 + \lambda_2)P_{0,1} = \lambda_1 P_{0,0} \tag{8.87}$$

and

$$(\mu_1 + \lambda_2)P_{n,1} = \lambda_2 P_{n-1,1} \tag{8.88}$$

As usual, the objective is to express the active state probabilities, $p_{n,c}$, with $n \geq 0$ when $c = 1$ or $n > 0$ when $c = 1$, in terms of the empty system probability $p_{0,0}$. The case $n = 0$, $c = 1$ is easily obtained using Eq. (8.87) as

$$P_{0,1} = \frac{\lambda_1}{(\mu_1 + \lambda_2)} P_{0,0} \tag{8.89}$$

Further, the case $n = 1$, $c = 0$ is obtained using Eq. (8.89) in Eq. (8.85) and rearranging to give

$$P_{1,0} = \frac{\lambda_2}{\lambda_1} \left\{ 1 + \frac{\lambda_1}{(\mu_1 + \lambda_2)} \right\} P_{0,0} \tag{8.90}$$

It is more convenient to express this equation in the form

$$P_{1,0} = \rho_2 \left\{ 1 + \frac{\rho_1}{(1+\alpha\rho_2)} \right\} P_{0,0} \qquad (8.91)$$

where we used the relationships $\rho_{1,2} = \lambda_{1,2}/\mu_{1,2}$ and $\alpha = \mu_2/\mu_1$.

The cases for which $n \geq 0$ and $c = 1$ are also obtained in a straightforward manner. From Eq. (8.88) we obtain the following recursive relationship for $p_{n,1}$ in terms of $p_{0,1}$:

$$P_{n,1} = \left(\frac{\alpha\rho_2}{1+\alpha\rho_2} \right)^n P_{0,1} \qquad (8.92)$$

Thus, using Eq. (8.89), in terms of $p_{0,0}$ we have

$$P_{n,1} = \frac{\alpha^n \rho_1 \rho_2^n}{(1+\alpha\rho_2)^{n+1}} P_{0,0} \qquad (8.93)$$

Finally the cases for which $n > 0$ and $c = 0$ are required and the z-transform method may be used. Let the moment-generating function for $p_{n,0}$ be defined by the transform

$$G(z) = \sum_{n=0}^{\infty} P_{n,0} z^n \qquad (8.94)$$

Following the technique used in Chapter 2, $G(z)$ is obtained by multiplying the terms in the appropriate balance equation by z^n and summing over the states encompassed by that equation. Using Eq. (8.86) we find that

$$(\lambda_1 + \mu_2) \sum_{n=1}^{\infty} P_{n,0} z^n = \lambda_2 \sum_{n=1}^{\infty} P_{n-1,0} z^n + \mu_2 \sum_{n=1}^{\infty} P_{n+1,0} z^n + \mu_1 \sum_{n=1}^{\infty} P_{n,1} z^n \qquad (8.95)$$

Before gathering terms the last summation on the right-hand side may be replaced with a simplified expression obtained using Eq. (8.93). If we let

$$A(z) = \frac{\mu_1}{\mu_2} \frac{\lambda_1 \lambda_2 z}{(\mu_1 + \lambda_2)(\mu_1 + \lambda_2 - \lambda_2 z)} \qquad (8.96)$$

then it may be shown that

$$(\lambda_2 + \mu_2)(G(z) - P_{0,0}) = \lambda_2 z G(z) + \frac{\mu_2}{z}(G(z) - P_{0,0} - z P_{1,0}) + \mu_2 A(z) P_{0,0} \qquad (8.97)$$

Rearranging this equation and simplifying, the expression for $G(z)$ is easily found to be given by

$$G(z) = \left\{ 1 + \frac{\rho_1 \rho_2 z}{1 + \alpha \rho_2 (1-z)} \right\} \frac{1}{(1 - \rho_2 z)} p_{0,0} \tag{8.98}$$

The empty system probability $p_{0,0}$ is, as usual, evaluated using the fact that the sum of the probabilities over all states is one. Thus

$$\sum_{n=0}^{\infty} p_{n,0} + \sum_{n=0}^{\infty} p_{n,1} = 1 \tag{8.99}$$

Now, the first summation on the left-hand side is the same as the right-hand side of Eq. (8.94) with $z = 1$. Hence, putting $z = 1$ in Eq. (8.98), we obtain

$$\sum_{n=0}^{\infty} p_{n,0} = \frac{1 + \rho_1 \rho_2}{1 - \rho_2} p_{0,0} \tag{8.100}$$

The second summation is found using the expression for $p_{n,1}$ in Eq. (8.93). The resulting summation may be simplified to give the result

$$\sum_{n=0}^{\infty} p_{n,1} = \rho_1 p_{0,0} \tag{8.101}$$

Equations (8.99), (8.100), and (8.101) therefore permit the empty system probability to be calculated using

$$p_{0,0} = \frac{1 - \rho_2}{1 + \rho_1} \tag{8.102}$$

The relevant steady-state performance statistics are now easily obtained. For the circuit-switched traffic the blocking probability, p_b, is simply the probability that the system is found not to be empty, or $1 - p_{0,0}$, thus

$$p_b = \frac{\rho_1 + \rho_2}{1 + \rho_1} \tag{8.103}$$

The mean waiting time for packet-switched traffic, $\overline{w}$, is given by Little's result as

$$\overline{w} = \frac{\overline{n}}{\lambda_2} \tag{8.104}$$

where $\overline{n}$ is the mean number of packets in the system. The value of $\overline{n}$ is given by

$$\bar{n} = \sum_{n=0}^{\infty} np_{n,0} + \sum_{n=0}^{\infty} np_{n,1} \tag{8.105}$$

The first summation here is, by definition, $G'(1)$, and the second summation may again be obtained using the expression for $p_{n,1}$ in Eq. (8.93). After some straightforward manipulation the mean waiting time for packets in the system is found to be given by

$$\bar{w} = \frac{1}{\mu_2} \left\{ \frac{1}{1-\rho_2} + \frac{\alpha\rho_1}{1+\rho_1} \right\} \tag{8.106}$$

Reassuringly, if we put $\rho_1 = 0$, then the model is that of a pure packet switching system equivalent to the $M/M/1$ queue, and the result is identical.
    Some results are presented in Figure 8.28, to illustrate the use of the simple model for integrated service switching. The mean service time for a circuit-switched call was taken to be 30 sec, and the mean packet transmission time was taken to be 1 ms.

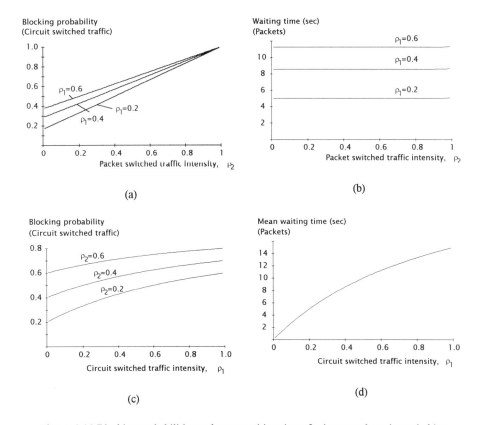

Figure 8.28 Blocking probabilities and mean waiting times for integrated service switching.

These values correspond to that which might be considered reasonable for voice and data communications. In (a) we plotted the blocking probability for the circuit-switched traffic as a function of the packet-switched traffic intensity, ρ_2 when the total circuit switched traffic intensity, ρ_1, is 0.2, 0.4, and 0.6. If $\rho_2 \to 1$, then most of the transmission time on the trunk will be taken up by packet transmissions, and the blocking probability will also approach one. At the lower end, when $\rho_2 \to 0$ and there is very little packet switching, the blocking probability will be roughly the same as the probability that a circuit switch is already established or, equivalently, that a call is in progress, that is, $p_b \approx \rho_1$. In the middle region the relationship is linear because there is no waiting allowed for the ρ_1 traffic, and all three factors are clearly illustrated in each of the characteristics.

In (b) the mean waiting time for the packet-switched traffic is plotted under the same conditions. Here the dominant effect is caused by the second term in Eq. (8.106), which represents the delay caused by the duration of a circuit-switched call. For example, at $\rho_1 = 0.2$, the mean waiting time for a packet when $\rho_2 = 0.5$ is 5 sec. This contrasts with the value of 2 ms obtained when there is no circuit-switched traffic.

In (c) and (d) the blocking probabilities and waiting times are plotted again, but this time as functions of circuit-switched traffic intensity, ρ_1, with $\rho_2 = 0.2$, 0.4, and 0.6. The same arguments presented for (a) and (b) also apply here. There is, however, a number of distinguishing features. In (d) the curves for $\rho_2 = 0.2$, 0.4, and 0.6 are identical. Again this is caused by the dominance of the waiting time due to the circuit-switched traffic. Furthermore, in both (c) and (d) the relationships are more obviously nonlinear. This is because increases in the circuit-switched traffic offered does not result in a directly proportional increase in that actually transmitted.

In this simple model, which considers only one single output trunk, it would appear that there are no advantages to be gained through the integration of services. Only one service— the transmission of packets or the provision of a circuit— may be catered for at the same time. Increasing the number of trunks and introducing variable-length service times, however, could be facilitated by means of dynamic frame structures. Such systems present a range of opportunities for further study.

8.6 CONCLUDING REMARKS

The analysis of WANs is more complex than for LANs. In the latter case it is often possible to develop a single method of analysis that can be used as the tool for performance evaluation. The former case involves communications over greater distances and between larger populations. Hence additional mechanisms are required, such as switching and routing, and these should be accounted for. The result is that a large number of system variables may be realized, and one has to either make general assumptions or consider the constituent parts of the whole system. In the analysis of inter-connected LANs, for example, it was assumed that the switching mechanism was perfect. Thus each of the segments could be assumed to be statistically similar. The switching process, which is a part of the majority of large span communications systems, was thoroughly dealt with in its own section.

The performance impacts of the routing algorithm have not been addressed in great detail. However, the routing mechanism can have a dramatic effect. The inherent complexity of establishing dynamic links means that the mathematical analysis of all but the most basic systems, such as that described in Section 8.2, is quite involved. Beyond basic calculations of the capacity, in terms of the proportion of useful bandwidth occupied, most works on the subject are presented as qualitative discussions and simulations. Given a number of basic properties for specific designs and a knowledge of the wide variety of algorithms, it is usually possible to provide an informed opinion. Flood routing, for example, will not be suitable for networks with a high density of links and intense traffic volumes. In this case a routing algorithm with a low duplication factor and multiple path choices will be best.

This chapter is a collection of diverse techniques that may be singly or collectively applied to the performance evaluation of the most complex networks. The overall performance of inter-connected CSMA/CD segments may be evaluated using the analysis in the first section. If design constraints for the routing algorithm are important or if high-speed switching is required, then the additional methods described in the second and third sections may be employed. The fourth section concentrates on the general subject of teletraffic engineering, which is the established approach in modeling telecommunication networks. The techniques used are also generally applicable to modern data communications, however, since the distinction between the types of network, with respect performance analysis, are becoming less well defined. The connection-oriented and connectionless protocols, which are more traditionally associated with X.25 networks, are also relevant in ATM technologies, for example. In the final section an analysis for a simple integrated service system is presented.

Exercises

8.1 Consider a network of inter-connected 1-persistent CSMA/CD segments. Assume that each segment has N nodes and that they are connected using a perfect switch. Let the probability that any of the nodes generate and transmit a packet and the corresponding probability for the switch connection be σ and σ_s. Similarly, let the retransmission probabilities be v and v_s. Write down expressions for the following probabilities when the number of active connections, i, is less than $N-1$.

(i) The probability that a single first transmission attempt from a node occurs while there are no retransmission attempts from other nodes.
(ii) The probability that a single retransmission is attempted while the remaining nodes defer or remain inactive.
(iii) The probability that a transmission attempt on the switch connection occurs.

Thus derive Eq. (8.2).

8.2 Numerically solve the system described in Question 8.1 for the mean delay at any given traffic generation probability using suitable network parameters. Compare the results with those obtained using alternative transmission algorithms. Investigate the effect of changing the retransmission probability.

8.3

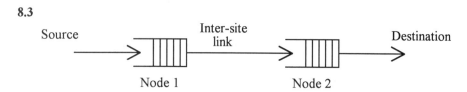

In this two-node system data units arrive at node 1 according to the exponential distribution, with parameter λ. The service times in each node are also exponentially distributed, with parameters μ_1 and μ_2. Derive the Laplace transform for the delay distribution stating any assumptions that may be required. Thus derive an expression for the overall mean delay.

8.4 Formally derive the product form solution for an open queueing network assuming that each of the queues are exponential and independent.

8.5 Write a program to calculate the solution of the three-node system in Section 2. Allow for a variable number of assumed buffer sizes. Compare the results obtained when the buffer size is increased.

8.6 Write down at least one reason why a network of finite queues may not be assumed to perform exactly as independent exponential queues.

8.7 What is the saving, in terms of the number of crosspoints required for a nonblocking, three-stage switch with 64 inputs and the same number of outputs, compared with a single-stage switch?

8.8 What is the maximum time that a byte must wait to be switched in a time-slot interchanger if there are 10 input channels and an equal number of output channels? The input rate is 64 kbit/s, and the output rate is 2 Mbyte/s.

8.9 Calculate the mean switching delay for packets arriving at a shared memory switch with an aggregate rate of 5000 packet/s. Assume a 10×10 switch with an infinite memory capacity capable of switching at a speed of 10,000 packet/s. Repeat the calculation for an arrival rate of 9000 packet/s. Obtain the corresponding values of delay for an output buffered switch and account for any discrepancies.

8.10 Use Erlang's B formula to calculate the blocking probability for a switch with 100 outputs at traffic intensities of 0.5, 0.6, 0.7, 0.8, and 0.9. What has been assumed about the system, in general, and the arrival and service times, in particular, in order to facilitate these predictions?

8.11 Repeat the calculations for a system that may be modeled assuming the number of busy outputs and inputs follows the Engset distribution.

8.12 Verify Eq. (8.64) beginning with the general form for a probability distribution function.

8.13 Calculate the number of lines required to service a medium-sized office in order to ensure that the waiting time for access to an outside line should be less than 1 sec. Assume that the average call duration is two minutes and that six lines are required per minute. State any assumptions that are imposed.

8.14 How might a significant switch processing time affect the delay of packet and circuit-switched traffic ?

8.15 Draw the state transition diagram for an integrated circuit- and packet-switched system with a capacity for up to three circuits and buffer space for up to two packets. Write down the 12 balance equations that may be used to model the system.

References

[1]   Takine, T., Y. Takahashi, and T. Hasegawa, "Performance Analysis of a Polling System with Single Buffers and Its Application to Interconnected Networks," *IEEE Journal on Selected Areas In Communications*, Vol. 1 SAC-4, No. 6, pp. 802–812, Sept. 1986.
[2]   Kleinrock, L., *Queueing Systems, Volume 1: Theory*, New York: John Wiley & Sons, 1975.
[3]   Kershenbaum, A., *Telecommunications Network Design Algorithms*, New York: McGraw-Hill, 1993.
[4]   Clos, C., "A Study of Nonblocking Switching Networks," *Bell Systems Technology Journal*, Vol. 32, No. 2, pp. 406–424, March 1953.
[5]   Karol, M. J., M. G. Hluchyj, and S. P. Morgan, "Input Versus Output Queueing on a Space-Division Packet Switch," *IEEE Transactions on Communications*, Vol. COM-35, No. 12, pp. 1347–1356, Dec. 1987.
[6]   Hluchyj, M. G., and M. J. Karol, "Queueing in High Performance Packet Switching," *IEEE Journal on Selected Areas in Communications*, Vol. 6, No. 9, pp. 1587–1597, Dec. 1988.
[7]   Bear, D., *Principles of Telecommunications Traffic Engineering*, third edition, IEE Telecommunications Series, Vol. 2, London, UK: Peter Peregrinus Ltd., 1988.
[8]   Schwartz, M., *Telecommunication Networks; Protocols, Modeling and Analysis*, Reading, MA: Addison-Wesley, 1987.

Appendix A

Probability, Stochastic Processes, and Transforms

This appendix is included as a refresher of the theory of probability, probability distributions, stochastic processes, and the use of transforms. The reader should be familiar with this material before any attempt is made to proceed beyond Chapter 2. The treatment is not rigorous. It is presented to a depth that is appropriate to gauge the level of understanding required for the majority of the analyses in the main text.

A.1 PROBABILITY

Probability theory is the basis of all mathematical analyses that deal with attempting to predict the occurrence of some event. In the usual terminology an event is the outcome of one or more trials, and the set of all possible events is known as the sample space. If the event that is the outcome of a trial is uncertain to occur yet the possibility that it will occur is finite, then the event is a random one. A joint event is said to occur when two different events are the result of the same trial.

Probability is a measure of the possibility that an event occurs. The probability of an event that is a certainty is 1, and the probability of an impossible event is 0. The probability that event A occurs is written $P[A]$, and for any event X, $0 \le P[X] \le 1$. A result of this basic property is that the sum of the probabilities of all possible outcomes of a trial is 1.

Conditional probability, denoted by $P[X/Y]$, is the probability that event X occurs given that event B occurs. It is defined by

$$P[X/Y] = \frac{P[XY]}{P[Y]} \tag{A.1}$$

Effectively this expression is the result of restricting the sample space to be the event Y. A definition that is closely associated with this result is known as independence. Two events X and Y are independent if

$$P[X/Y] = P[X] \tag{A.2}$$

Hence the occurrence of X does not depend on the occurrence of Y. The remaining laws of probability may be summarized as follows

$$P[X \text{ or } Y] = P[X] + P[Y] - P[XY] \tag{A.3}$$

$$P[X \text{ and } Y] = P[X/Y] \cdot P[Y] \tag{A.4}$$

Equation (A.3) is known as the addition law, and it gives an expression for the probability that either event X or Y will occur. If the events are mutually exclusive, or in other words the probability that both may result from the same trial is zero, then the term $P[XY]$ disappears. Equation (A.4), which is Eq. (A.1) rearranged, is known as the multiplication law, and it gives the probability that both events X and Y will occur.

Imagine that the outcome of a trial may be represented as a number. In other words, each event has a numerical value. If the events occur at random the outcome of a trial is called a random variable. Normally a random variable is represented by an upper case letter. The relationship between the probabilities for random variables often form patterns, or distributions, and these may be conveniently written as equations.

A.2 PROBABILITY DISTRIBUTIONS

Let X be a random variable. The probability distribution function, $F(x)$, is defined as the probability that X is less than the threshold value x. Hence the distribution function, often referred to as the cumulative distribution, may be written as

$$F(x) = P[X \le x] \tag{A.5}$$

For example, imagine that X represents the number of data units in a buffer. Assume that the buffer may store a maximum of five units. There are six possible states in which a buffer may exist; and the sample space consists of the integers 0, 1, 2,...,5. If the integers are represented by the term x_i, for $i = 0, 1, 2,...,5$, then

$$F(x) = \sum_{i=0}^{5} p_i \delta(x - x_i) \tag{A.6}$$

where p_i is the probability that the buffer is found with i data units and $\delta()$ is the unit step function defined by

$$\delta(t) = \begin{cases} 1 & \text{for } t \ge 0 \\ 0 & \text{for } t < 0 \end{cases} \tag{A.7}$$

If there is an equal probability of finding the buffer in any of the states, then $p_i = 1/6$ for all of the i and that distribution looks like that plotted in Figure A.1.

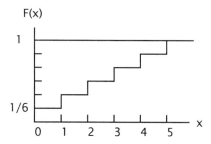

Figure A.1 Distribution function for the buffer.

There is a number of special properties associated with the distribution function, and these are summarized in the following expressions:

$$F(-\infty) = P[X \le -\infty] = 0$$

$$F(\infty) = P[X \le \infty] = 1$$

$$F(b) \ge F(a) \quad \text{if } b > a$$

$$F(x) \ge 0 \quad \text{for all } -\infty < x < \infty$$

$$F(b) - F(a) = P[a < X \le b] \tag{A.8}$$

The first four expressions should be intuitive. In words, the final one states that the probability of finding the variable in the given range is obtained by the difference in the values of the distribution function at the extremes of that range. Thus our buffer has a probability $F(1) - F(0) = 2/6 - 1/6 = 1/6$ of being found empty.

The random variables described previously are discrete. Take the time that the buffer waits for the arrival of a data unit, t, as an example of a continuous variable. Assume that the distribution function for t is given by

$$F(t) = \begin{cases} 1 - e^{-\lambda t} & \text{for } t \ge 0 \\ 0 & \text{for } t < 0 \end{cases} \tag{A.9}$$

In fact, this is the celebrated exponential distribution function. This is just one of a number of special distributions that are discussed in Chapter 4. The parameter λ is a scaling factor that determines the growth rate of the function, as can be seen in Figure A.2. The value of λ is the mean duration of the interval $(0,t)$. If $\lambda = 2$ unit/s, for example, then the probability that an arrival occurs in the first second is $F(1) - F(0) = -e^{-2} + e^{-0} \approx 0.865$.

The probability density function, denoted by $f(x)$, is an alternative and often more convenient method for describing the probability distribution. It is defined in terms

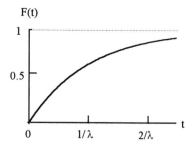

Figure A.2 Distribution function for the time that the buffer is empty.

of the distribution function as

$$f(x) = \frac{dF(x)}{dx} \qquad (A.10)$$

So for the exponential distribution the density function is easily found to be given by

$$f(t) = \begin{cases} \lambda e^{-\lambda t} & \text{for } t \geq 0 \\ 0 & \text{for } t < 0 \end{cases} \qquad (A.11)$$

Now the probability that the continuous random variable t is found to be in the region $a < t \leq b$ is given in terms of the density function by the equation

$$P[a < t \leq b] = \int_a^b f(x)dx \qquad (A.12)$$

So the probability that a data unit arrives in the first second when $\lambda = 2$ unit/s is $\left[-e^{-2t}\right]_0^1 \approx 0.865$, as before.

Distributions of more than one variable may be expressed similarly. So the distribution function for two variables X and Y, which is the probability that both variables do not exceed the thresholds x and y at the same time, may be written as

$$F(x,y) = P[X \leq x, Y \leq y] \qquad (A.13)$$

and the corresponding joint probability density function is obtained as

$$f(x,y) = \frac{d^2 F(x,y)}{dxdy} \qquad (A.14)$$

Finally, when two random variables are independent, the joint density function factorizes exactly into the product of the individual density functions

$$f(x,y) = f(x)f(y) \tag{A.15}$$

When a trial is repeated over a period of time, a sequence of values for the outcomes is obtained as a list of variables. Often there are patterns associated with these sequences that permit the calculation of meaningful parameters. These parameters relate to the physical properties of the system and may be used to predict the evolution of similar stochastic processes.

A.3 STOCHASTIC PROCESSES

A stochastic process is a collection of random variables that have some dependence on time. For example, imagine that the state of a buffer is observed every so often. The sequence of integers that represent the number of data units present at each instant of observation form a stochastic process. Hence a random variable that is part of a stochastic process has a time-varying parameter, and it may be denoted by the function $X(t)$. The complete set of values that $X(t)$ may assume are known as the state space.

Stochastic random variables may be continuous or discrete. The notation X_n, where n is a positive integer, is often used to represent discrete-time stochastic variables. The normal rules of probability are relevant, and again the relationship between these variables may be expressed in terms of probability distributions. The joint probability distribution function of a stochastic process may be expressed as

$$F(x,t) = P[X(t_1) \le x_1, X(t_2) \le x_2, \dots, X(t_n) \le x_n] \tag{A.16}$$

since there are n possible values for t. The corresponding joint probability density function is obtained as

$$f(x,t) = \frac{d^n F(x,t)}{dx_1 dx_2 \cdots dx_n} \tag{A.17}$$

This is sufficient notation to enable the definition of a number of special kinds of stochastic process. As an example consider the number of data units in a buffer, of length L, as observed every so often. Then the sample space may be taken to be the integers $0, 1, 2, \dots, L$.

The most simple stochastic process is the one for which the sequence of random variables are independent. In this case the joint probability density function factors into the product

$$f(x,t) = f(x_1, t_1)f(x_2, t_2) \cdots f(x_n, t_n) \tag{A.18}$$

This is not an interesting case because there is no structure or dependence on time, and the sequence might as well be treated as a set of regular random variables.

Stationary processes are those for which the probability distribution is not dependent on shifts in time. That is, $F(x,t) = F(x,t+\tau)$. For the buffer this means that the probability that there are so many arrivals or departures is the same at every observation.

A memoryless, or Markov process, is a special type of stationary process. The memoryless property simply states that the value of the next sample depends only on the current sample and not on the values of any previous samples. Hence, for the sequence X_n, the value of $P[X_{n+1}]$ depends only on $P[X_n]$. This may be expressed analytically as

$$P[X(t_{n+1}) = x_{n+1} \,/\, X(t_n) = x_n, X(t_{n-1}) = x_{n-1}, \dots, X(t_1) = x_1]$$
$$= P[X(t_{n+1}) = x_{n+1} \,/\, X(t_n) = x_n] \tag{A.19}$$

A birth-death process is a special type of Markov process for which a change in state to the nearest neighbor only may occur. Hence, if the sample space is represented by the set of integers and if $X_n = i$, then $X_{n+1} = i, i+1$, or $i-1$ only. If the buffer were being modeled as a birth-death process, then only one arrival or departure may occur between observations. The fact that an arrival may have occurred at some time before an arbitrary observation does not affect the possibility that an arrival has occurred since, and the same may be said of departures. The process for which data units arrive at fixed time intervals, for example, is not memoryless.

A sequence of X_n that has the memoryless property is said to form a Markov chain, regardless of the number of states that can be traversed between each observation, or transition. Markov chains that possess one or two special properties are systems that present themselves as ideal candidates for modeling the evolution of time-dependent physical processes. Communication networks provide a suitable application of the methods.

A.4 TRANSFORMS

The characteristics of any random variable are captured in the probability distribution of that variable. For example, the mean, or expected value $E[X]$, of a discrete variable is given by

$$E[X] = \sum_{i=0}^{\infty} i \cdot P[X = i] \tag{A.20}$$

The expected value is the first-order moment of the distribution. The variance is another characteristic that is of the second order. It is given by the difference between the expected value squared and the square of the expected value or, alternatively,

$$\mathrm{Var}(X) = E[X^2] - (E[X])^2 \tag{A.21}$$

Often it is favorable to consider an alternative form of the probability distribution, which has properties that make it easier to determine the values of these characteristics. One such alternative form is known as the probability-generating function, which in the discrete case is defined as

$$E[Z^X] = \sum_{i=0}^{\infty} Z^i P[X = i] \tag{A.22}$$

This function, denoted as $X(Z)$, has the property that first, second, and successively higher order moments may be obtained by differentiation. For example, the first and second moments are given by

$$E[X] = \frac{dX(Z)}{dZ}\bigg|_{z=1} \tag{A.23}$$

and

$$E[X^2] = \frac{d^2 X(Z)}{dZ^2}\bigg|_{z=1} + \frac{dX(Z)}{dZ}\bigg|_{z=1} \tag{A.24}$$

Thus transforming the probability distribution into the probability-generating function provides a method for calculating the moments.

One of the most useful techniques utilizing transforms in this text is the z-transform method for solving linear difference equations. Models that result in a system of discrete time-dependent equations, or linear difference equations, may be manipulated in such a way as to obtain the z-transform of the discrete probability distribution for the system. Hence the inverse transform of the function may be used to obtain the probability distribution itself. The z-transform of a probability distribution is another name for the moment-generating function. Some of its properties are listed in Table A.1, and a selection of transform pairs is listed in Table A.2.

Another useful property of transforms often simplifies the investigation of systems that depend on more than one variable. The convolution of independent probability distributions is equivalent to the product of the transforms of each. In the text we make use of the Laplace transforms of continuous variables in this respect.

Table A.1
Properties of z-transforms

Sequence	Transform
X_n	$X(z) = E[z^n] = \sum_n X_n z^n$
$aX_n + bY_n$	$aX(z) + bY(z)$
$a^n X_n$	$X(az)$
X_{n+k}	$\dfrac{X(z)}{z^k} - \sum_{i=1}^{k} z^{i-k-1} X_{i-1}$
X_{n-k}	$z^k X(z)$

Table A.2
Some z-transform pairs

Sequence	Transform
$u_n = \begin{cases} 1 & \text{for } n = 0 \\ 0 & \text{otherwise} \end{cases}$	1
u_{n-k}	z^k
$\delta_n = 1, n = 0, 1, 2, \ldots$	$\dfrac{1}{1-z}$
$A\alpha^n$	$\dfrac{A}{1-\alpha z}$
$n\alpha^n$	$\dfrac{\alpha z}{(1-\alpha z)^2}$

Appendix B

Code Listings

In this appendix code listings are provided for two of the simulation programs described in Chapter 4. A complete program for the simple token passing simulation may be obtained by amalgamating the procedures listed in Section 4.2 with the code listed below in Section B.1. A complete listing for the multiple segment token passing system is given in Section B.2.

The programs should compile successfully with most PASCAL compilers. It may however be necessary to modify the random number function. The syntax for the random number function provided by different manufacturers can vary. The code provided assumes a function *random* which returns a uniformly distributed random number x in the region $(0 < x < 1)$.

B.1 SIMPLE TOKEN PASSING

```
procedure report_results;
var
    total_delay, mean_delay, off_load, total_packets,
    throughput, total_rejected_packets, rejection_probability : real;
begin
    total_delay := 0;
    total_packets := 0;
    total_rejected_packets := 0;
    for count := 0 to node_population - 1 do
    begin
        total_delay := total_delay + node_array[count]^.av_que_time;
        total_packets := total_packets + node_array[count]^.packet_count;
        total_rejected_packets := total_rejected_packets + node_array[count]^.rejected_packets;
    end;
    mean_delay := total_delay * btu / node_population;
    off_load := total_packets / (clock_time * btu);
    throughput := transmitted_packets / (clock_time * btu);
    rejection_probability := total_rejected_packets / total_packets;
    writeln;
    writeln('Mean delay                              = ',mean_delay * 1000, ' ms');
```

```
   writeln('Throughput                              = ',throughput, ' packet/sec');
   writeln('Offered load                            = ',off_load, ' packet/sec');
   writeln('Packet rejection probability = ', rejection_probability);
   writeln;
   writeln('*** Simulation completed ***');
end;

procedure tidy_up;
begin
   for count := 0 to node_population - 1 do
      dispose(node_array[count]);
   while event_que_front^.event_time < 1.0e38 do
   begin
      event_que_front := event_que_front^.que_front;
      dispose(event_que_front^.que_back);
   end;
   dispose(event_que_front);
end;

{ Main code section. }
begin
   new_node_array;
   new_event_list;
   run_sim;
   report_results;
   tidy_up;
end.
```

B.1 Multiple Segment Token Passing

```
program token_wan_simulation;

{ Global declarations. }
const
   datarate = 10000000;
   btu = 1/datarate;
   propagation_delay = 1000/(btu*2e8);
   max_lan_population = 20;
   max_buffer_size = 20;
   segment_population = 3;
   load_fraction = 1.0;
   buffer_size = 10;
   hub_buffer_size = 15;
   packet_length = 1000;
   token_length = 20;
   token_pass_time = token_length + propagation_delay;
   max_packets = 2000 * max_lan_population * segment_population;

type
   event_type = (pass_token, tx_packet, tx_switch_packet, rx_packet,
                      rx_switch_packet, switch_packet, gen_packet);
```

```pascal
address = record
    lan_id, node_id: integer;
end;

event_ptr = ^event;
event = record
    event_time: real;
    que_back, que_front: event_ptr;
    control_procedure: event_type;
    source, destination: address;
end;

packet = record
    arrival_time: real;
    source, destination: address;
end;

buffer = record
    que_length: integer;
    contents: array[1..max_buffer_size] of packet;
end;

node_ptr = ^node;
node = record
    index, packet_count, tx_packet_count, rejected_packets, lost_packets: longint;
    tx_que: buffer;
    lambda: real;
    av_que_time: real;
end;

switch = record
    packet_count, rejected packets: longint;
    tx_que: array[0..segment_population] of buffer;
end;

lan_ptr = ^lan;
lan = record
    lan_population: longint;
    node_array: array[0..max_lan_population - 1] of node_ptr;
    token_id: integer;
end;

{ Global variables. }
var
    clock_time: real;                        { The system clock }
    transmitted_packets: longint; { Total number of transmitted packets}
    count1, count2: integer;          { Used locally }
    event_que_front: event_ptr;      { Pointer to front of event queue }
    an_event: event;                       { Used locally }
    a_node: node_ptr;                     { Used locally }
    a_lan: lan_ptr;                          { Used locally }
    event_count, token_count: longint;
    network: array[0..segment_population - 1] of lan_ptr;
```

```
    hub: switch;
    output: text;
```

{ Insert an event into the linked list - events are inserted in
chronological order with new events inserted before existing
events with the same time. }

```
procedure insert_event(an_event: event);
var
    search_ptr, temp_ptr: event_ptr;
    search_time: real;
begin
    new(temp_ptr);
    temp_ptr^ := an_event;
    search_time := temp_ptr^.event_time;
    if event_que_front^.event_time >= search_time then
    begin
        temp_ptr^.que_back := nil;
        temp_ptr^.que_front := event_que_front;
        event_que_front^.que_back := temp_ptr;
        event_que_front := temp_ptr;
    end
    else begin
        search_ptr := event_que_front;
        while search_time > search_ptr^.event_time do
            search_ptr := search_ptr^.que_front;
        with temp_ptr^ do
        begin
            que_front := search_ptr;
            que_back := search_ptr^.que_back;
            que_back^.que_front := temp_ptr;
            que_front^.que_back := temp_ptr;
        end;
    end;
end;
```

{ Inspect the queue length at the node which possesses the
token; if greater than zero transmit a packet otherwise
pass the token on. }

```
procedure allocate_token(the_source, the_destination: address);
var
    active_node_found, event_found: boolean;
    next_event_time: real;
begin
    with network[the_source.lan_id]^ do
        begin
            active_node_found := false;
            event_found := false;
            next_event_time := event_que_front^.que_front^.event_time;
            repeat
                inc(token_count);
                if token_id = lan_population then
                begin
                    if hub.tx_que[the_source.lan_id].que_length > 0 then
```

```
            begin
               active_node_found := true;
               with an_event do
               begin
                  control_procedure := tx_switch_packet;
                  source.lan_id := the_source.lan_id;
               end;
            end;
         end
         else
         begin
            a_node := node_array[token_id];
            if a_node^.tx_que.que_length > 0 then
            begin
               active_node_found := true;
               with an_event do
               begin
                  control_procedure := tx_packet;
                  source.node_id := token_id;
                  source.lan_id := the_source.lan_id;
               end;
            end;
         end;
         if active_node_found then
         begin
            an_event.event_time := clock_time + packet_length;
            insert_event(an_event);
         end
         else
         begin
            if (clock_time + token_pass_time) < next_event_time then
            begin
               inc(token_count);
               clock_time := clock_time + token_pass_time;
            end
            else
            begin
               event_found := true;
               with an_event do
               begin
                  control_procedure := pass_token;
                  event_time := clock_time + token_pass_time;
                  source.lan_id := the_source.lan_id;
               end;
               insert_event(an_event);
            end;
            token_id := (token_id + 1) mod (lan_population + 1);
         end;
      until active_node_found or event_found;
   end;
end;

{ Decrement the que length at the node which possesses
```

the token, insert a receive packet event and pass the
token on. }
procedure transmit_packet(the_source, the_destination: address);
begin
    a_lan := network[the_source.lan_id];
    a_node := a_lan^.node_array[the_source.node_id];
    with an_event **do**
    begin
      if the_source.lan_id = a_node^.tx_que.contents[1].destination.lan_id **then**
        control_procedure := rx_packet
      else
      begin
        control_procedure := switch_packet;
        destination.lan_id := a_node^.tx_que.contents[1].destination.lan_id;
      end;
      source.lan_id := the_source.lan_id;
      source.node_id := the_source.node_id;
      event_time := clock_time + propagation_delay;
    end;
    insert_event(an_event);
    with an_event **do**
    begin
      control_procedure := pass_token;
      event_time := clock_time + propagation_delay + token_length;
      source.lan_id := the_source.lan_id;
    end;
    insert_event(an_event);
    with a_lan^ **do**
      token_id := (token_id + 1) mod (lan_population + 1);
end;

{ Decrement the que length at the hub,
insert a receive switch packet event and pass the
token on. }
procedure transmit_switch_packet(the_source, the_destination: address);
begin
    a_lan := network[the_source.lan_id];
    with an_event **do**
    begin
      control_procedure := rx_switch_packet;
      event_time := clock_time + propagation_delay;
      source.lan_id := the_source.lan_id;
    end;
    insert_event(an_event);
    with an_event **do**
    begin
      control_procedure := pass_token;
      event_time := clock_time + propagation_delay + token_length;
      source.lan_id := the_source.lan_id;
    end;
    insert_event(an_event);
    with a_lan^ **do**
      token_id := (token_id + 1) mod (lan_population + 1);

end;

{ Remove the packet from the network and update node
statistics. }
procedure remove_packet(the_source, the_destination: address);
var
   que_time: **real**;
begin
   a_lan := network[the_source.lan_id];
   a_node := a_lan^.node_array[the_source.node_id];
   with a_node^ **do**
   begin
      inc(tx_packet_count);
      que_time := clock_time - tx_que.contents[1].arrival_time;
      av_que_time := ((tx_packet_count * av_que_time) + que_time)/(tx_packet_count + 1);
      dec(tx_que.que_length);
      if tx_que.que_length > 0 **then**
      for count1 := 1 to tx_que.que_length **do**
         tx_que.contents[count1] := tx_que.contents[count1+1];
   end;
   inc(transmitted_packets);
end;

{ Remove the packet from the network and update node
statistics. }
procedure remove_switch_packet(the_source, the_destination: address);
var
   que_time: **real**;
begin
   a_lan := network[hub.tx_que[the_source.lan_id].contents[1].source.lan_id];
   a_node := a_lan^.node_array[hub.tx_que[the_source.lan_id].contents[1].source.node_id];
   with a_node^ **do**
   begin
      inc(tx_packet_count);
      que_time := clock_time - hub.tx_que[the_destination.lan_id].contents[1].arrival_time;
      av_que_time := ((tx_packet_count * av_que_time) + que_time)/(tx_packet_count + 1);
   end;
   with hub.tx_que[the_source.lan_id] **do**
   begin
      dec(que_length);
      if que_length > 0 **then**
      for count1 := 1 to que_length **do**
         contents[count1] := contents[count1+1];
   end;
   inc(transmitted_packets);
end;

{ An internet packet has been transmitted -
insert into the destination LAN buffer of the switch. }
procedure arrival_at_switch(the_source, the_destination: address);
var
   buffer_overflow: boolean;
begin

```
      buffer_overflow := false;
      inc(hub.packet_count);
      with hub.tx_que[the_destination.lan_id] do
      begin
         if que_length = hub_buffer_size then
         begin
            buffer_overflow := true;
            inc(hub.rejected_packets);
         end
         else
         begin
            inc(que_length);
            contents[que_length] :=
            network[the_source.lan_id]^.node_array[the_source.node_id]^.tx_que.contents[1];
         end;
      end;
      a_lan := network[the_source.lan_id];
      a_node := a_lan^.node_array[the_source.node_id];
      with a_node^ do
      begin
         if buffer_overflow then
         begin
            inc(lost_packets);
{
Include these statments to allow lost packets to contribute to average que time
            que_time := clock_time - tx_que.contents[1].arrival_time;
            av_que_time := ((packet_count * av_que_time) + que_time)/(packet_count + 1);
}
         end;
         dec(tx_que.que_length);
         if tx_que.que_length > 0 then
            for count1 := 1 to tx_que.que_length do
               tx_que.contents[count1] := tx_que.contents[count1+1];
      end;
end;

{ Generate a packet. }
procedure generate_packet(the_source, the_destination: address);
begin
   an_event := event_que_front^;
   a_lan := network[the_source.lan_id];
   a_node := a_lan^.node_array[the_source.node_id];
   with a_node^ do
   begin
      inc(packet_count);
      if tx_que.que_length = buffer_size then
      begin
         inc(rejected_packets);
      end
      else
      begin
         with tx_que do
         begin
```

```
              inc(que_length);
              with contents[que_length] do
              begin
                  arrival_time := clock_time;
                  source.lan_id := the_source.lan_id;
                  source.node_id := the_source.node_id;
                  destination.lan_id := round((segment_population * random) + 0.5) - 1;
              end;
          end;
      end;
      an_event.event_time := clock_time + ((-1*ln(random))/(lambda / (a_lan^.lan_population *
          packet_length)));
      insert_event(an_event);
  end;
end;

{ Execute the simulation by inspecting each event type
in the linked list. }
procedure run_sim;
begin
  writeln('*** Executing simulation ***');
  writeln(output, '*** Executing simulation ***');
  transmitted_packets := 0;
  event_count := 0;
  token_count := 0;
  clock_time := 0;
  for count1 := 0 to segment_population - 1 do
  begin
      network[count1]^.token_id := 0;
      with an_event do
      begin
          control_procedure := pass_token;
          event_time := clock_time + token_pass_time;
          source.lan_id := count1;
      end;
      insert_event(an_event);
  end;
  repeat
      with event_que_front^ do
      begin
          inc(event_count);
          clock_time := event_time;
          case control_procedure of
              pass_token            : allocate_token(source, destination);
              tx_packet             : transmit_packet(source, destination);
              tx_switch_packet : transmit_switch_packet(source, destination);
              rx_packet             : remove_packet(source, destination);
              rx_switch_packet : remove_switch_packet(source, destination);
              switch_packet        : arrival_at_switch(source, destination);
              gen_packet           : generate_packet(source, destination);
          end;
      end;
      event_que_front := event_que_front^.que_front;
```

```
      dispose(event_que_front^.que_back);
   until transmitted_packets = max_packets;
end;


{ Output results. }
procedure report_results;
var
   lan_delay, mean_delay, off_load, lan_packets, lan_tx_packets,
   throughput, lan_rejected_packets, lan_lost_packets,
   rejection_probability, loss_probability,
   lan_que_length, mean_que_length, utilisation,
   wan_delay, wan_packets, wan_tx_packets, wan_rejected_packets,
   wan_lost_packets, wan_que_length, wan_population: real;
begin
   wan_delay := 0;
   wan_packets := 0;
   wan_tx_packets := 0;
   wan_rejected_packets := 0;
   wan_lost_packets := 0;
   wan_que_length := 0;
   wan_population := 0;
   for count1 := 0 to segment_population - 1 do
   begin
      lan_delay := 0;
      lan_packets := 0;
      lan_tx_packets := 0;
      lan_rejected_packets := 0;
      lan_lost_packets := 0;
      lan_que_length := 0;
      with network[count1]^ do
      begin
         for count2 := 0 to lan_population - 1 do
         begin
            lan_delay := lan_delay + node_array[count2]^.av_que_time;
            lan_packets := lan_packets + node_array[count2]^.packet_count;
            lan_tx_packets := lan_tx_packets + node_array[count2]^.tx_packet_count;
            lan_rejected_packets := lan_rejected_packets + node_array[count2]^.rejected_packets;
            lan_lost_packets := lan_lost_packets + node_array[count2]^.lost_packets;
            lan_que_length := lan_que_length + node_array[count2]^.tx_que.que_length;
         end;
         wan_delay := wan_delay + lan_delay;
         wan_packets := wan_packets + lan_packets;
         wan_tx_packets := wan_tx_packets + lan_tx_packets;
         wan_rejected_packets := wan_rejected_packets + lan_rejected_packets;
         wan_lost_packets := wan_lost_packets + lan_lost_packets;
         wan_que_length := wan_que_length + lan_que_length;
         wan_population := wan_population + lan_population;
         mean_delay := lan_delay * btu / lan_population;
         off_load := lan_packets / (clock_time * btu);
         throughput := lan_tx_packets / (clock_time * btu);
         rejection_probability := lan_rejected_packets / lan_packets;
         loss_probability := lan_lost_packets / lan_packets;
         mean_que_length := lan_que_length / lan_population;
```

```
        utilisation := throughput * btu * packet_length;
    end;
    writeln;
    writeln('Results summary for LAN number ', count1:1);
    writeln('------- ------- --- --- ------ -');
    writeln('Mean delay                        = ',mean_delay * 1000, ' ms');
    writeln('Throughput                        = ',throughput, ' packet/sec');
    writeln('Offered load                    = ',off_load, ' packet/sec');
    writeln('Packet rejection probability = ', rejection_probability);
    writeln('Packet loss probability      = ', loss_probability);
    writeln('Mean queue length            = ', mean_que_length:5:2);
    writeln('Utilisation                  = ', utilisation:5:2);
    writeln;
    writeln(output, 'Results summary for LAN number ', count1:1);
    writeln(output, '-----------------------------------------------');
    writeln(output, 'Mean delay                        = ',mean_delay * 1000, ' ms');
    writeln(output, 'Throughput                        = ',throughput, ' packet/sec');
    writeln(output, 'Offered load                    = ',off_load, ' packet/sec');
    writeln(output, 'Packet rejection probability = ', rejection_probability);
    writeln(output, 'Packet loss probability      = ', loss_probability);
    writeln(output, 'Mean queue length            = ', mean_que_length:5:2);
    writeln(output, 'Utilisation                  = ', utilisation:5:2);
    writeln(output);
    if count1 < segment_population then
    begin
        write('Press a key to continue..');
        readkey;
        writeln;
    end;
end;
mean_delay := wan_delay * btu / wan_population;
off_load := wan_packets / (clock_time * btu);
throughput := wan_tx_packets / (clock_time * btu);
rejection_probability := wan_rejected_packets / wan_packets;
loss_probability := wan_lost_packets / wan_packets;
mean_que_length := wan_que_length / wan_population;
utilisation := throughput * btu * packet_length / segment_population;
writeln;
writeln('Results summary for WAN');
writeln('------- ------- --- ---');
writeln('Mean delay                        = ',mean_delay * 1000, ' ms');
writeln('Throughput                        = ',throughput, ' packet/sec');
writeln('Offered load                    = ',off_load, ' packet/sec');
writeln('Packet rejection probability = ', rejection_probability);
writeln('Packet loss probability      = ', loss_probability);
writeln('Mean queue length            = ', mean_que_length:5:2);
writeln('Utilisation                  = ', utilisation:5:2);
writeln;
writeln('*** Simulation completed ***');
writeln(output, 'Results summary for WAN');
writeln(output, '----------------------------------');
writeln(output, 'Mean delay                        = ',mean_delay * 1000, ' ms');
```

```pascal
         writeln(output, 'Throughput                          = ',throughput, ' packet/sec');
         writeln(output, 'Offered load                        = ',off_load, ' packet/sec');
         writeln(output, 'Packet rejection probability = ', rejection_probability);
         writeln(output, 'Packet loss probability         = ', loss_probability);
         writeln(output, 'Mean queue length            = ', mean_que_length:5:2);
         writeln(output, 'Utilisation                           = ', utilisation:5:2);
         writeln(output);
         writeln(output, '*** Simulation completed ***');
      end;

   { Create a list of generate message events. }
·  procedure new_event_list;
   begin
      new(event_que_front);
      event_que_front^.event_time := 1.0e38;
      for count1 := 0 to segment_population - 1 do
      begin
         with network[count1]^ do
         begin
            for count2 := 0 to lan_population - 1 do
            begin
               with an_event do
               begin
                  control_procedure := gen_packet;
                  event_time := ((-1*ln(random))/(node_array[count2]^.lambda / (lan_population *
         packet_length)));
                     source.node_id := count2;
                     source.lan_id := count1;
                  end;
                  insert_event(an_event);
               end;
            end;
         end;
      end;
   end;

   { Create a network. }
   procedure new_network;
   begin
      for count1 := 0 to segment_population - 1 do
      begin
         with hub do
         begin
            packet_count := 0;
            rejected_packets := 0;
            tx_que[count1].que_length := 0;
         end;
         new(network[count1]);
         with network[count1]^ do
         begin
            lan_population := max_lan_population;
            for count2 := 0 to lan_population - 1 do
            begin
               new(node_array[count2]);
```

```
         with node_array[count2]^ do
         begin
            lambda := load_fraction;
            tx_que.que_length := 0;
            av_que_time := 0;
            packet_count := 0;
            tx_packet_count := 0;
            rejected_packets := 0;
            lost_packets := 0;
         end;
      end;
   end;
   end;
end;

{ Dispose all the pointers. }
procedure tidy_up;
begin
   for count1 := 0 to segment_population - 1 do
   begin
      for count2 := 0 to network[count1]^.lan_population - 1 do
         dispose(network[count1]^.node_array[count2]);
      dispose(network[count1]);
   end;
   while event_que_front^.event_time < 1.0e38 do
   begin
      event_que_front := event_que_front^.que_front;
      dispose(event_que_front^.que_back);
   end;
   dispose(event_que_front);
end;

{ Main code section. }
begin
   new_network;
   new_event_list;
   assign(output, 'wantok.dat');
   rewrite(output);
   run_sim;
   report_results;
   close(output);
   tidy_up;
end.
```

Author Biography

Gary N. Higginbottom was born in Stockport, England, in August 1964. In 1985 he graduated from the University of Central Lancashire, then Preston Polytechnic, with an honors degree in mathematics and physics. In the following year he obtained Master of Science in optoelectronics at the University of Northumbria in Newcastle-Upon-Tyne. During the period from October 1986 to November 1989 he carried out research in optical fiber networks, and published a number of articles on the subject. Since then he has been employed as a lecturer in computing, and as a communications network technical support engineer.

He obtained the degree of Doctor of Philosophy in 1994 after completing his thesis entitled "Optical Fiber Local Area Networks for the Industrial Environment." He then returned to the department of Electrical and Electronic Engineering at Manchester Metropolitan University, where he carried out his initial research, to continue as a post-doctoral research assistant. At present he is a telecommunications software engineer with Apion Ltd. of Belfast, Ireland.

Index

The Artech House Telecommunications Library

Vinton G. Cerf, Series Editor

Videoconferencing and Videotelephony: Technology and Standards, Richard Schaphorst

Voice Recognition, Richard L. Klevans and Robert D. Rodman

Wireless Access and the Local Telephone Network, George Calhoun

Wireless Communications in Developing Countries: Cellular and Satellite Systems, Rachael E. Schwartz

Wireless Communications for Intelligent Transportation Systems, Scott D. Elliot and Daniel J. Dailey

Wireless Data Networking, Nathan J. Muller

Wireless LAN Systems, A. Santamaría and F. J. López-Hernández

Wireless: The Revolution in Personal Telecommunications, Ira Brodsky

Writing Disaster Recovery Plans for Telecommunications Networks and LANs, Leo A. Wrobel

X Window System User's Guide, Uday O. Pabrai

For further information on these and other Artech House titles, including previously considered out-of-print books now available through our In-Print-Forever™ (IPF™) program, contact:

Artech House
685 Canton Street
Norwood, MA 02062
781-769-9750
Fax: 781-769-6334
Telex: 951-659
email: artech@artech-house.com

Artech House
Portland House, Stag Place
London SW1E 5XA England
+44 (0) 171-973-8077
Fax: +44 (0) 171-630-0166
Telex: 951-659
email: artech-uk@artech-house.com

Find us on the World Wide Web at:
www.artech-house.com